In the Jaws
of the Dragon

Also by Eamonn Fingleton

Making the Most of Your Money (1977)

The Penguin Money Book (with Tom Tickell, 1981)

*Blindside: Why Japan Is Still on Track to
Overtake the U.S. by the Year 2000* (1995)

*In Praise of Hard Industries: Why Manufacturing,
Not the Information Economy,
Is the Key to Future Prosperity* (1999)

*Unsustainable: How Economic Dogma
Is Destroying American Prosperity* (2003)

In the Jaws
of the Dragon

AMERICA'S FATE IN THE COMING ERA
OF CHINESE DOMINANCE

Eamonn Fingleton

Thomas Dunne Books
St. Martin's Griffin ♏ New York

THOMAS DUNNE BOOKS.
An imprint of St. Martin's Press.

www.thomasdunnebooks.com
www.stmartins.com

The Library of Congress has catalogued the hardcover edition as follows:

Fingleton, Eamonn.
    In the jaws of the dragon : America's fate in the coming era of Chinese hegemony / Eamonn Fingleton.—1st ed.
        p.   cm.
    Includes bibliographical references and index.
    ISBN-13: 978-0-312-36232-4
    ISBN-10: 0-312-36232-3
    1. United States—Relations—China.   2. China—Relations—United States.
3. Economic forecasting—China.   4. Economic forecasting—United States.   I. Title.

    JZ1480.A57C645   2008
    303.48'273051—dc22   2007045754

ISBN-13: 978-0-312-56162-8 (pbk.)
ISBN-10: 0-312-56162-8 (pbk.)

First St. Martin's Griffin Edition: August 2009

10 9 8 7 6 5 4 3 2 1

In memory of my parents, Simon (1903–1974) and Marian (1914–2006), and in gratitude for the values they passed on to the succeeding generation

Contents

In the Jaws
of the Dragon

ONE

A Dragon on Steroids

Two bets are on the table. One has been placed by the Washington policy-making establishment; the other, by the leadership of the Chinese Communist Party.

Analyzing China's prospects in terms of the currently fashionable globalist ideology, the Washington establishment is betting that a rich China will be a free one.

The theory is that the only way China can continue to grow is by embracing Western democracy and capitalism. Moreover, the very process of China's enrichment is supposedly serving to undermine the Beijing government's authoritarianism. Thus a feedback effect is said to be at work: more wealth means more freedom means more wealth. . . .

This view has been championed by many American political figures in the last fifteen years. Here, for instance, is how President George W. Bush put it in 2005: "As China reforms its economy, its leaders are finding that once the door to freedom is opened even a crack, it cannot be closed. As the people of China grow in prosperity, their demands for political freedom will grow as well. . . . By meeting the legitimate demands of its citizens for freedom and openness, China's leaders can help their country grow into a modern, prosperous and confident nation."

Similar optimism is poured forth daily by the American press, not least by the *Wall Street Journal*. Here is a typical *Journal* comment from 2006: "Sooner or later China's economic progress will create the internal conditions for a more democratic regime that will be more stable, and less of a potential global rival. . . . China's burgeoning middle class, created and buoyed by economic growth, will drive internal change."

Abroad too the Washington view is increasingly prevalent. In Britain, for instance, it has now been embraced not only by the media but by many top politicians. After visiting Chinese premier Wen Jiabao in 2005, then British Prime Minister Tony Blair, for instance, cited the rise of a huge Chinese middle class and the spread of the Internet as factors that had produced "an unstoppable momentum . . . towards greater political freedom [and] progress on human rights."

The Washington view's prevalence probably owes something to its implicitly flattering regard for Western culture. After all, it is founded on the premise that Western philosophy constitutes universal truth.

Those who espouse it, moreover, often loudly claim to occupy the moral high ground. Skeptics are made to feel either that they do not fully comprehend the perfection and universal salience of Western values or that they are denying the Chinese people's essential humanity.

Claims to the moral high ground apart, however, the Washington view has also been propelled by something more reliably persuasive: money. The fact is that various powerful interests, most obviously countless multinational corporations, see profit in promoting the Washington view. Thus vast amounts of money have been pumped into a propaganda program to win over key opinion makers, not least elected officials, top editors, press pundits, government bureaucrats, and think-tank scholars.

As more and more money has been applied to the task, the Washington view has come to be accepted by more and more erstwhile skeptics. In particular many hawkish Sinologists from the cold war era have now reversed themselves. Up to the late 1990s they had generally held that China's economy diverged too sharply from Western capitalism ever to amount to much. China's continuing export surge in the new century has forced a total rethink—and corporate America's lobbying money has sweetened this bitter ideological pill.

So widely accepted has the Washington view become that until recently almost no one had noticed there was another bet on the table. This second bet—that of the Chinese leadership—is on a disturbingly different proposition: that a future China can be both rich *and* authoritarian.

If the Washington view is right, the future is unclouded, and a fast-rising, fast-Westernizing China can readily be accommodated within the existing Western-defined world order. But what if it is wrong? What if—surprise!—China's top leaders turn out to understand the Chinese character better than anyone in Washington? What if in, say, 2025 or 2030 the United States finds itself facing off against a China so rich that it has surpassed all other nations in military technology, yet a China that remains resolutely opposed to Western values? The implications are hard to exaggerate. Yet so far they have received remarkably little consideration. It is past time that this oversight was rectified.

New China: Rich *Because* It Is Authoritarian

In the great debate over China's future, Chinese leaders have more at stake than most. After all, their jobs, if not their heads, are on the line. It is reasonable to conclude that they have considered their options carefully.

Moreover, they enjoy the priceless advantage of local knowledge. They read and speak the language. They have studied their nation's history and know its mind.

By contrast, those on the other side, with virtually no exceptions, are pathetically uninformed. As they have never lived in China—or in any other part of the Confucian world for that matter—they have had no practice in the mental gymnastics often needed to make sense of the distinctly Confucian way modern China explains itself. Even worse, the fundamental ideological framework within which newcomers to the Confucian region try to understand China is completely wrong.

For a start, contrary to all conventional wisdom, the Chinese economic system is *not* capitalism, nor is it converging toward capitalism. Thus any deterministic Washington analysis based on the history of Western capitalism is doomed from the start.

The truth is that China is operating an adaptation of the so-called East Asian economic system. Launched in the then Japanese colony of Manchuria in the 1930s, this system was perfected in Japan proper in the 1950s and 1960s and has now been widely copied throughout East Asia.

As James Fallows has pointed out, the Chinese version differs from the Japanese original in being more atomized; hitherto at least, the role of government in micromanaging outcomes is far less in evidence than in the mature version of the model seen in Japan. Nonetheless in its key elements it is the same system. As itemized by the authors Richard Bernstein and Ross Munro in their 1997 book *The Coming Conflict with China,* these are just some of the more obvious features of the Chinese version of the East Asian economic model:

- A labyrinthine system of trade barriers
- An artificially undervalued currency
- An industrial policy that focuses on developing so-called pillar industries and uses export subsidies and other unfair tactics to give them a competitive advantage in world markets
- Systematic pressure on foreign companies to transfer their most advanced production technologies to China

While the East Asian approach to economic development resembles capitalism in some ways (it makes extensive use of markets, for instance, particularly at the level of small business), its fundamental logic is quite different. A key difference is that whereas authoritarian political controls constitute a hindrance to the full efficacy of capitalism, such controls are really essential to the functioning of the East Asian system.

The ability of top officials to keep tabs on everything is greatly enhanced by the fact that, as James Fallows has pointed out, Confucian econo-political culture diverges fundamentally from the West in its approach to power. In his 1994 book *Looking at the Sun: The Rise of the New East Asian Economic and Political System,* Fallows wrote: "Anglo-American ideology views concentrated power as an evil ('Power corrupts, and absolute power...'). Therefore it has developed elaborate schemes for dividing and breaking up power when it becomes concentrated. The Asian-style model views concentrated power as a fact of life. It has developed elaborate systems for ensuring that the power is used for the long-term national good."

One critical way in which power is deployed to economic advantage in China—as in other East Asian economies—is in savings policy. However counterintuitive this may seem to Westerners, China's famously high savings rate is imposed on the nation from above. By dint of various authoritarian policies, vast savings surpluses have been generated. These have provided the principal driver of China's rise, making possible a superfast rate of growth in investment not only in industry but in the sort of advanced infrastructure needed to maximize the nation's exports.

Top Chinese leaders have been inspired by the now voluminous evidence that, in modernized form, authoritarian Confucianism almost effortlessly outperforms Western capitalism. The impact of the East Asian system on the world economy has already been massive. Based on figures cited by the Berkeley-based political scientist T. J. Pempel, between 1960 and the early 1990s alone, East Asia's share of the world economy multiplied sixfold—rocketing from less than 5 percent of total world output to about 30 percent. For several decades to come we can expect East Asia's share to continue to rise as China rapidly catches up with earlier Confucian industrializers in deploying the most advanced production technologies.

Understanding Why We Misunderstand . . .

As we will see in detail in chapter 2, the West faces special difficulties in understanding the Confucian world.

Part of the problem is ideological. Almost without exception, American opinion leaders hold as a matter of high ideology that Western logic is universal and thus is destined to sweep the world.

It is an assumption that repeatedly down the centuries has led to disastrous miscalculations. In our own time only the most obvious instance has been the tragic quagmire in Iraq. It is a striking fact that many of the top neoconservative commentators who so insistently sold the Iraq war to the American people have been similarly insistent in promoting the Washington view of China. They include the New York Times's chief foreign affairs commentator, Thomas Friedman; the Economist magazine's erstwhile editor in chief Bill Emmott; and both Paul Gigot and the late Robert Bartley of the Wall Street Journal. Perhaps the most remarkable instance of the "invade Iraq/appease China" syndrome was Francis Fukuyama. In his famous essay "The End of History" in 1989, he was one of the earliest proponents of the view that China was converging with American values. In late September 2001—just days after the September 11 attacks—he called for the United States to invade Iraq even if no evidence existed to link Saddam Hussein "directly" to the atrocities. It is also striking that the main architects of the Iraq disaster, George W. Bush and Tony Blair, are, as we have noted, leading proponents of the Washington view.

(Conversely, many prescient opponents of the war have been outspokenly critical also of the Bush administration's China strategy. They include James Fallows, Pat Choate, Patrick Buchanan, Paul Craig Roberts, Chalmers Johnson, and Ralph Nader. They also for that matter include me. In the *International Herald Tribune* two days before the war started, I wrote: "Whatever the merits of America's case for going to war, one aspect of its Iraq strategy seems badly misconstrued: the assumption that the reform of post-Saddam Iraq will run as smoothly as the U.S. Army's occupation of Japan after World War II.... Even in the unlikely event that Iraqis forbear from settling old scores among themselves, their mutual jealousies will make it tough to work together in restoring order to a devastated nation.")

History will record that the major problem with the Bush administration's Iraq strategy has been that ideology was allowed to overrule common sense. The same is true, if for the moment less obviously, of its China strategy.

Another key problem is that few interpreters of today's China have had any experience in analyzing the rise of the earlier East Asian "miracle" economies. Anyone familiar with the Japanese economy in particular has a major advantage because Beijing is now so clearly copying policies pioneered decades ago by the Japanese. For the most part, however, today's China watchers have paid little attention to Japan. The result is an American approach in China that, to long-term observers of the Confucian world, seems distinctly Sisyphean. This point has been made in particular by Ivan Hall, author of *Bamboozled! How America Loses the Intellectual Game with Japan and Its Implications for Our Future in Asia*. A Harvard-educated cultural diplomat and Japan historian who lived most of his professional life in Tokyo, Hall comments: "We seem to go on repeating with China all the mistakes we made with Japan, having learned nothing from them."

That said, the West's comprehension problems do not spring primarily from ignorance or feeblemindedness. Rather, they reflect a remarkable policy of obfuscation—and sometimes outright deception—by East Asian leaders, and even more so by their many stooges in the Western expatriate communities of the Confucian world.

Some of these stooges have clearly succumbed to illegitimate blandishments or pressures. Others have been confused by the Confucian world's aptitude for Potemkin village–style dramatics. Not only have East Asian leaders not explained how their economic model works but they have often gone to extraordinary lengths to keep Western policymakers and commentators misinformed about it. For good reason. If this model were more widely understood, it would long ago have been comprehensively opposed in the West. The point is that, like the Soviet system before it, the East Asian model is incompatible with Western capitalism. In fact, precisely because the East Asian model is so much more successful than Soviet Communism, it entails an even greater problem of political and economic incompatibility for the West.

Seen from a Western point of view, the most immediately obvious problem with the East Asian economic system is its mercantilist approach to trade. To that subject we now turn.

Closed Markets and Tall Stories

The fact that East Asian markets are largely closed is, of course, hardly news to American labor activists, let alone to American industrial exporters. Nonetheless, the elites who set American foreign policy have long chosen to pretend otherwise. Every step of the way as the United States has unilaterally opened its markets to East Asia's concept of "one-way free trade," these elites have argued that continuing East Asian protectionism does not represent a failure of intent by East Asian policymakers, let alone a fundamental philosophical divergence. Rather, it supposedly reflects temporary political glitches that East Asian policymakers have been sincerely trying to rectify. The principal problem has allegedly been that petty vested interests in East Asia—"backwoodsmen" in the jargon—have been obstructing their more enlightened fellow citizens' efforts to embrace Western economic ideals. In the long run there is no doubt that enlightened leadership will prevail. Thus the right thing for the West to do is simply to be patient, considerate, and statesmanlike while the East Asians work to remove remaining obstacles to free trade.

In reality, as this book will show, this train of logic is disastrously wrong. Opposition to Western-style free trade in East Asia is hardly confined to a few self-serving "backwoodsmen." On the contrary, it is all-pervasive and is quietly led by the very top officials who are assumed to be the West's greatest allies in bringing Western economic ideas to the region.

Faced with evidence that top leaders in Beijing are backsliding on their commitments to open the Chinese market, advocates of the Washington view tend to urge yet more patience. The evidence from America's previous experience with other mercantilist East Asian nations, however, is not encouraging. Take, for instance, Japan. As the first Confucian nation to become rich, Japan was also the first to profess a commitment to Western-style open markets. That was more than forty years ago. Yet all the evidence is that even today Japan continues, in so-called targeted industries at least, to pursue a comprehensively protectionist trade policy. True, in some product categories, foreigners in recent years have been permitted a share—usually a small share—of the Japanese market. But in many others foreigners find the door slammed in their face.

The Japanese car market, as we will see in chapter 7, provides a particularly chastening insight into Japan's true trade policies. Thirty-five years after Japan's trade lobbyists first proclaimed the Japanese market "one of the world's most open," carmakers on three continents agree that it is still one of the world's most tightly closed. Even Paris-based Renault has never been able to sell in Japan though it ostensibly controls, through a major stake in Nissan, Japan's second largest car distribution network.

It may be that China will prove more sincere in its commitment to free trade than Japan—but a close look at the logic of China's economic strategy suggests otherwise.

In any case, from the point of view of the Western-defined world economic order, there is, as we will now see, another crucial problem—the system's parasitical approach to technology.

Technology: Heads We Win, Tails You Lose

Throughout the East Asian region, governments pursue remarkably similar technology policies. On the one hand, they avidly suck in advanced technologies from all over the world. On the other hand, they allow few homegrown advanced technologies to leak abroad.

Again Japan, as by far the region's richest economy, has hitherto been the most important exemplar. The Japanese economy has been built largely on foreign technologies, particularly American ones. Yet Japan strictly prohibits its own companies from transferring their most advanced technologies abroad. In the electronics industry, for instance, Japan now monopolizes the manufacture of many of the sophisticated materials and production machinery that have made possible the unparalleled miniaturization of today's electronic gadgets.

The techniques for making such products are regarded as national secrets that must not be allowed to leave the country.

For now China has few technological secrets to guard. But it is already benefiting handsomely from the other side of East Asian technological policy in that, even more than nations like Japan and Korea before it, it has been expertly winkling key technologies out of the United States and Europe.

How Big Might China Become?

One thing that is indisputable is that the East Asian economic system is palpably far more effective in building wealth—and, by extension, national power—than the American system. As we will see, the experiences of South Korea and Taiwan offer strong hints of China's future trajectory. Both nations adopted versions of the East Asian system in the early 1960s, at a time when they ranked roughly as low as China does today in the world per capita income league. They proceeded in subsequent decades to enjoy some of the fastest sustained growth in world history.

As the scholar Robert Wade has documented, in both cases per capita income measured in current U.S. dollars (that is, before adjustment for dollar inflation) increased by more than 20 times between 1962 and 1986. This compares with a rise of a mere 5.6 times in the United States in the period. Moreover, except for a brief interruption during the East Asian financial crisis of 1997–1998, both South Korea and Taiwan have continued to outperform dramatically. Thus as of 2006 South Korea's per capita income at market exchange rates was $18,400—making it a fully accredited member of the First World. By comparison in 1962, with a per capita income of a mere $110 a year, it ranked below Sudan in ninety-ninth place in the world income league.

That said, if South Korea's performance seems impressive, it pales by comparison with that of Japan, which by 2006 had reached a per capita income of $38,500, up from just $610 in 1962.

The ultimate geopolitical point here is that if the Chinese economy were merely to match South Korea's current income level, it would already be by far the world's largest economy with roughly twice America's total output. Were it to match Japan's, it would boast four times America's output.

Even with merely a Korea-level per capita income, the Beijing regime would have little difficulty outspending all other nations in military technology, and thus displacing the United States as the world's premier military power. To say the least we in the West are not prepared for the scale of the geopolitical adjustments entailed by such an eventuality.

Chinese Savings: Inexhaustible Wellspring

Asked to identify the secret of China's supergrowth, the best Western economists can do is reflexively point to China's high savings rate. But this is hardly more helpful than positing cloudy skies as the reason why it rains in London. We have to ask why the Chinese save; more important, why do they save so much more now than they did in the past?

These are momentous questions, yet they have gone almost entirely unaddressed in previous studies of the Chinese economy. Indeed the word "saving" is notable for its absence in the most widely read accounts of East Asia's rise. It does not appear in the index of Thomas Friedman's best-selling *The World Is Flat*, for instance. Nor does it even in Nicholas Lardy's much more scholarly *Integrating China into the Global Economy*.

That said, China's savings rate is hard to ignore. Described by the *Economist* as "the world's highest by far," it is certainly one of the most geopolitically significant phenomena of our time.

Western economic commentators such as London-based Will Hutton argue that the key to modern China's high savings rate is that the Chinese social security safety net is inadequate to look after people in their old age. But this explains little. After all, most nations lack an adequate social security safety net, yet their savings rates remain dismally low.

In trying to explain the Chinese savings phenomenon, Westerners suffer a crucial blind spot in that they assume that a nation's savings rate is determined merely as the aggregate of millions of freely made decisions by individual savers. This, of course, is how things work in the West. In the case of China, however, in typical groupist East Asian fashion, the key factor is government policy.

As this book will show, in their utterly un-Western approach to savings and consumption, Chinese leaders boast a devastating secret weapon. Following in the footsteps of other high-growth Confucian nations, they have established a highly ingenious, almost invisible, administrative ability to force society to save. The adoption by one East Asian nation after another of a policy of forced saving ranks as one of the great turning points in world history. It is a fair bet that in its long-term geopolitical implications it will prove the most consequential geopolitical change agent since Henry the Navigator launched the Age of Discovery in the fifteenth century.

Why has it received so little attention? Part of the reason is that—at least in the more important economies of the East Asian region—officials have assiduously hidden their true agenda. Instead they have suggested that the region's high savings rates stem from rather quaint, even deplorably backward, cultural eccentricities (such as the inadequacy of China's social security net). These eccentricities, moreover, are ones over which East Asian leaders disclaim all control.

That this "cultural" explanation is suspect is immediately evident from a consideration of East Asian history. The fact is that in earlier times, the region's savings rates were generally modest. In each nation, the savings rate took off at precisely the moment that government adopted other, more visible aspects of the East Asian economic system. In the case of China, this point came in the late 1970s. Within four years of China's embrace of an export-led approach to economic growth, Chinese savings deposits had rocketed.

One of the least understood aspects of modern economics is that government officials can control a nation's savings rate. The tool of choice is *not* the Western one of tax incentives. Such incentives have proved almost entirely ineffective wherever they have been tried. Nowhere has this been more obvious than in the United States. As Christopher Swann of the *Financial Times* has pointed out, though American lawmakers have created at least twenty separate breaks for savers in the three decades after 1974, the American savings rate has fallen from around 10 percent to little more than zero.

The reason East Asians save is simple: they are not allowed to consume. Various policies, many of them quite indirect, create artificial barriers to consumption.

As the late J. K. Galbraith has explained, this approach is hardly new. Nor is it exclusively East Asian. Indeed one of its most important early manifestations was not in East Asia at all but in the United States. By acting directly to curtail consumption during World War II, the Franklin D. Roosevelt administration raised the American savings rate from, on Galbraith's numbers, 5 percent to 25 percent in the space of three years. The resulting torrential capital flows underwrote a massive expansion in production of everything from tanks to fighter planes.

The lesson was not lost on postwar East Asia. First in Japan and later in

South Korea and Taiwan, extensive measures were taken to suppress consumption. One of the earliest Western observers to understand the enormous geopolitical ramifications was the noted Japan-born scholar Edwin Reischauer. In *Wanted: An Asian Policy,* a book published in 1955, he predicted that suppressed consumption would soon be widely used to boost savings rates throughout East Asia. In retrospect we can see that this was a historic insight. Yet the news traveled remarkably slowly. Indeed there is no record that Reischauer, who went on to become John F. Kennedy's ambassador to Japan in 1961, ever raised the matter again. It may yet come to be regarded as one of the most significant silences in history.

As we have noted, there are several quite different ways consumption can be suppressed. Sometimes the increased saving arises in the household sector, sometimes in the business sector. In the latter case often this occurs when artificially induced shortages of luxury goods generate huge profits for oligopolistic local suppliers. Provided such profits are reinvested, they count as part of the national savings rate. This helps explain the paradox that while the macroeconomic data indicate that East Asians underconsume, Western news media often run stories about big-spending East Asian shoppers who think nothing of paying exorbitant prices—far higher than in the West—for Louis Vuitton handbags or Rolex watches. The key point is that while it is easy in East Asia to spend (because prices of luxuries are so high), it is difficult to consume (because big spenders get so little for their money). The larger economic point is that suppressed consumption creates savings *somewhere*. Exactly where is secondary. As China's former supreme leader Deng Xiaoping reportedly said in another context, it doesn't matter if a cat is black or white, so long as it catches mice.

To understand the Chinese suppressed-consumption policy, think of a drain that is blocked by leaves. No one leaf can stop the flow of water, but fifty leaves are a different matter. The suppressed-consumption policy depends on a panoply of constrictions on consumption. While most of these seem relatively insignificant, in the aggregate they constitute a tight tourniquet. In chapter 4, we will look in detail at China's version of the East Asian suppressed-consumption regimen. For the moment let's itemize some of its key aspects:

Trade barriers. The logic is simple: if China does not import things, it can't consume them.

Credit controls. Consumer credit hardly exists in China, and for the most part even mortgages for home purchases are unavailable. In practice those who aspire to buy a home have to save a large proportion of their income for many years beforehand. Despite much talk in recent years of financial liberalization, credit for smaller purchases such as home appliances and cars is also strictly rationed.

Anticonsumer land policies. China's land-zoning policies greatly restrict not only the size of people's homes but the amount of space available for retailing. Home prices and rents are extraordinarily high relative to incomes. China's demand for everything from home heating fuel to Swedish furniture is greatly curtailed.

Corporate price gouging. Price-fixing cartels dominate many industries, with the result that living costs are much higher than in other nations at a similar level of development. High prices reduce consumption directly, and the cartels' profits add to the national savings rate. As in other East Asian economies, cartels in China are under regulatory pressure to plow their profits into investing in ever more productive manufacturing processes. Commenting in 2006, the management professor Luke Froeb described China as "the last major economy without antitrust laws." (He could have added that although elsewhere in East Asia antitrust laws do exist, they are enforced only highly selectively, and, as in China, government officials turn a blind eye to massive rigging of consumer prices.)

Travel restrictions. The Chinese travel industry is tightly regulated to make it difficult and expensive to take vacations abroad.

Of course it has to be pointed out that a high savings rate is not a sufficient condition for a nation to grow. It is essential that the savings are not only invested but invested productively. To Western economists, this would appear to be the Achilles' heel of the forced-savings system. After all, Western theory predicts that artificially boosting the flow of capital to industry will result in disastrous gluts in production capacity. In reality there is no problem. East Asian officials organize cartels and other devices to curb overcapacity and ensure that corporations' investment returns are adequate.

All in all, a high savings rate more than compensates for a host of imperfec-
tions in other aspects of a nation's economic functioning. This fact was once
well understood in the West, not least in the United States. In days gone by,
huge savings flows were widely and correctly credited as the main factor behind
America's then commanding lead in manufacturing productivity. The point was
well made by the famous Austrian economist Ludwig von Mises. In a speech in
Milwaukee in 1952, he commented: "The average standard of living in this
country is higher than in any other country not because American statesmen
and politicians are superior to foreign statesmen and politicians but because
the per-head quota of capital invested in America is higher than in other countries."

In our own time, the economic thinker Ralph Gomory has provided a memorable illustration of the point. America's economic superiority in the mid-
twentieth century, he argues, was exemplified in the fact that American workers
were already using backhoes to dig trenches at a time when workers in Europe
and Japan were still using shovels. The American workers were not better educated than their counterparts elsewhere—just better equipped. Capital investment was the key to their much higher wages.

It is a fair bet that few Chinese policymakers have heard of Ludwig von
Mises or Ralph Gomory. But the salience of saving and investment in building
a nation's prosperity is more fully understood in contemporary Beijing than almost anywhere else.

China's Apologists Beg the Question

We have seen that China's phenomenal savings performance is rooted in a policy of harshly suppressing consumption. This is the centerpiece of the huge
program of authoritarian regulation that has been driving China's rise.

Because ordinary Chinese citizens are condemned to a much lower standard
of living than they would otherwise enjoy, the key question in assessing the system's future is how long they will put up with such deprivation. Conventional
wisdom in the West says not very long. Supposedly as living standards improve,
political conditions will become more liberal and newly assertive Chinese citizens will insist on more consumer-friendly economic policies.

In reality, as anyone who has studied the history of East Asian industrialization can testify, the idea that rising living standards will necessarily lead to

political liberalization is a myth. The point has now been convincingly doc-umented by the New York University political scientists Bruce Bueno de Mesquita and George W. Downs. Basing their conclusion on a study of 150 na-tions, they have found that many authoritarian regimes around the world have developed ways to deliver fast growth while maintaining a tight political grip.

Presenting what they described as their "ominous" findings in *Foreign Affairs* in 2005 and citing China as a prime illustration of their thesis, they com-mented: "Authoritarian regimes around the world are showing that they can reap the benefits of economic development while evading any pressure to relax their political control.... Economic growth, rather than being a force for democratic change in tyrannical states, can sometimes be used to strengthen oppressive regimes.... Authoritarian regimes are getting better and better at avoiding the political fallout of economic growth."

If this is so, why is it that so many political scientists have hitherto assumed that a rich China will be a free one? It is a fair guess that they have been merely "mirror imaging"—making assumptions about China based on what they know about the United States. They simply cannot imagine the extent to which in a Confucian society top leaders control the agenda.

The problem is that precisely because the Chinese system is so authoritar-ian, no trend of any significance can develop without at least the tacit approval of those at the top. Thus we can assume that any potential challenge to their leadership will be suppressed in its earliest stirrings. Remember that for any political challenge to get under way individuals have to have some way of com-ing together and rallying their forces. In particular they need to have the right to set up associations, and to communicate with sympathizers via newspapers and Web sites. But independent Chinese associations, newspapers, and Web sites are a contradiction in terms. Those who assume that a political challenge can arise by osmosis are making one of the most elementary mistakes in logic: they are assuming what is to be proved. The fact is that Chinese society is ex-plicitly structured to preclude the sort of bottom-up, liberalization-by-osmosis tendencies assumed by those who predict that political freedom is in China's future.

Certainly it should be clear that China's leaders are unlikely to cooperate in their own downfall. Given that the Chinese Communist Party controls the People's Liberation Army, this would appear to settle the matter. Certainly it did at Tiananmen Square in 1989.

In any case the key point is that digital-era authoritarianism rarely has to resort to massive shows of force to get its way. The tools of modern surveillance and communication greatly facilitate a preferred strategy of "soft authoritarianism." People who pose a potential threat to the establishment can be identified far earlier and either taken out of circulation entirely (via incarceration or worse) or at least rendered ineffectual through denunciation and sabotage. To the extent that they succeed in creating any independent institutional structures, these can readily be disrupted by infiltrating agents into their hierarchies and driving wedges between leaders.

Ultimately, of course, the sort of gradual societal metamorphosis the apologists are positing can be led only by individuals. The problem is that in China, as in the rest of East Asia, individuals are tightly controlled ciphers. They always have been. It is time to consider the intellectual origins of Chinese authoritarianism.

Eastern Values: The Group Rules, OK

In China as throughout most of the rest of East Asia, the political ethos has been greatly shaped by Confucius, or at least by ideas attributed to him. Born in what is now the Shandong province of northeastern China, Confucius (or Kong Fuzi, as he is known to the Chinese) was a philosopher who lived about five centuries before Christ. While he seems to have emphasized the importance of benevolence in rulers, the reality is that most of the governments that ostensibly espouse his ideas today are strongly authoritarian.

While scholars may argue that such governments are not truly Confucian, for the sake of convenience (and with due apologies to Confucius) we will use the term Confucianism here to refer to modern East Asian authoritarianism. We feel sanctioned to do so in part because Confucius's ideas unquestionably play a crucial enabling role in modern East Asia's political structuring. While the modern philosophical edifice built on Confucian foundations may differ in important respects from what Confucius might have prescribed, the structure could not exist in the first place without these foundations. In truth, as interpreted in modern East Asia, Confucianism's principal political significance is that it enjoins the populace to obedience, loyalty, and self-sacrifice. Hence it clearly plays an important role in legitimizing the undemocratic, unaccountable forms of government we see throughout East Asia. Its most important effect is precisely to perpetuate the governmental status quo, and it does so in large measure by enlisting millions of ordinary citizens as collaborators.

We draw support for our usage, moreover, from the fact that all the major East Asian societies attribute their political cultures principally to Confucius. This goes these days even for China, which, as we will see in chapter 5, officially rehabilitated Confucius in the 1990s.

Confucius had previously been an intellectual whipping boy, particularly in Mao Zedong's heyday. As recounted by Willy Wo-Lap Lam, author of *The Era of Jiang Zemin,* the move back to Confucianism received a strong push from former Chinese president Jiang Zemin. Quoting an unnamed source, Lam reported that Jiang, who became president of China in 1993, was "impressed by how traditional virtues have been a stabilizing factor in Asian countries influenced by Confucius such as Japan, South Korea, and in particular, Singapore."

Confucianism has generally been held in high regard in the West since it was first described by the Italian Jesuit Matteo Ricci four hundred years ago (it was Ricci who Westernized Kong's name as "Confucius"). But, as the New Zealand–based China scholar Xiaoming Huang has pointed out, it is not all benevolence. In a recent book in which he traced the Confucian origins of the East Asian economic system, he wrote: "Over time the Confucian model of moral conformity increasingly requires a level of suppression of private interests, mainly through state coercion and social discipline."

The ultimate question here is the seemingly merely mystical one of the relationship between the group and the individual. In China, as in other Confucian societies, the rights of the group are strongly emphasized. Sympathetic Westerners often present this as merely meaning that a Confucian individual is expected to be "considerate" in taking account of the impact of his actions on the community. Stated this way, group ideology may seem little different from the Christian principle of "Do unto others as you would have them do unto you." Unfortunately Confucianism—at least the version of Confucian ideology espoused by top officials in modern East Asia—goes far beyond this. Too often its concern for group solidarity tends to crowd out all other ethical considerations. This opens the door to quasi-fascist policies utterly at odds with Western ideas of freedom.

A key reason Westerners are not more alert to the implications is they fail to understand the East Asian idea of a group. Whereas in the West we think of groups as amorphous, generally leaderless, hordes (exemplified perhaps by the baying mobs of the French Revolution or the throngs of wildeyed speculators on Wall Street in 1929), the assumption in the East is that a group is a disciplined, hierarchical entity. Not only are its leaders well defined, but their right to lead is carefully reinforced by various institutional structures and conventions. Not only are subordinates expected to follow loyally, but robust methods are available to pressure anyone who wavers. Moreover, the whole of society is seen as composed of hierarchical arrays of groups. Thus, superior groups are entitled to lord it over inferior groups.

As a matter of the highest priority, the top group—in the case of modern China that means the Chinese Communist Party—makes it its business to maintain powerful levers of control over every other group. Any group not under control presents a potential threat to the established order and must quickly be brought to heel.

It should be noted that, contrary to its presentation of itself as a paragon of radical egalitarianism, the modern Chinese Communist Party is a highly elitist organization and membership is by invitation only.

A key tool of control in Confucian societies is group punishment. If one individual steps out of line, his entire group can expect to be punished by some higher entity. In premodern China one manifestation of this was the practice of a whole family being punished for the offenses of a single member. This powerfully concentrated the minds of, in particular, political dissidents. Anyone who challenged the established order risked an excruciating death not only for himself but for his entire family—wife, parents, children, even in-laws. Punishing a family for the offenses of a single individual was revived in the Maoist era, and even today in diluted form it is widely used throughout the Confucian world. An important variant on the concept is the punishing of an entire work group for the lapses of an individual member. (We should note that though group punishment is a characteristic of the Confucian world, its origins are attributed not to Confucianism but to a more authoritarian early Chinese political philosophy known as Legalism.)

Because modern Confucian societies are structured as hierarchies of groups, administration is far more top-down and authoritarian than in the West. Leaders not only practice a highly manipulative managerial style but preside over societal structures that for untold generations have been honed specifically to cow or at least brainwash the individual.

The result is a degree of intellectual claustrophobia that no one who has not lived long term in a Confucian society can fully credit. Few writers have captured the Orwellian implications of group logic in present-day East Asia more graphically than Steven Mosher. In his book *A Mother's Ordeal,* he provides a devastating account of how the Chinese establishment whips up societal wrath against couples who would flout China's one-child policy. Among other things, the government threatens pay cuts for all workers in an enterprise or division if any of them has a second child. The effect often is to coopt dozens if not hundreds of workers in pressuring a woman to have an abortion.

In recent years, this side of Chinese reality has had less attention than it deserves because for the most part foreign correspondents tend to cast developments in China as being grounded less in Confucian authoritarianism than in its polar opposite, Western globalism. Any aspect of Chinese reality that jars with the media's globalist background music tends to be downplayed or misrepresented.

In any case, historically greater wealth has tended to hide from Westerners the less acceptable aspects of Confucian reality. Western residents of the Confucian world have traditionally lived in wealthy ghettos far removed from ordinary life. To the extent that such residents have ever experienced the more negative aspects of Confucian group logic, they have tended to dismiss the problems as merely transitional ones that will soon be swept away by the supposedly inevitable triumph of Western individualism. Yet, as is now becoming clear, the richer the region becomes, the more difficult it is to accommodate within the traditional Western-defined world order.

All this said, it is only fair to note that top Chinese leaders have been working in recent years to shake off their reputation as a brutal dictatorship. Luckily for them, it is possible for an East Asian government to have its cake and eat it—it can aspire to an increasingly liberal image abroad while maintaining an authoritarian grip at home. It is time to look at state-of-the-art Confucianism.

Blackmail: Age-old Tool of Chinese Power

The key to modern Confucian power is a characteristically Machiavellian concept called selective enforcement.

In China these days, as in most of the rest of the Confucian world, the standard regulatory pattern is a paradoxical combination of strict laws and lax enforcement. Enforcement is indeed often so lax that the more naive sort of Westerner assumes the inmates are running the asylum. For anyone who understands the Confucian bureaucratic mind, however, the coercive implications are obvious: the point is that enforcement is not *always* lax. On the contrary, officials retain the right to crack down hard on anyone who displeases them.

This is the definitive version of selective enforcement as used not only in China but throughout East Asia. In China officials also often use a less sophisticated variant involving not strict rules but rather the reverse, vague and ambiguous ones. These are interpreted selectively to the disadvantage of those the state feels the need to punish.

Irrespective of which form is used, selective enforcement is a subtle—and sometimes not so subtle—form of blackmail. Although little publicized in the West, it is a greatly feared tool of authoritarianism throughout the Confucian world and does much to explain why, though nations like Japan, South Korea, and Taiwan are presented in the West as democracies, virtually all real power resides in the hands of an unaccountable and virtually invisible class of elite bureaucrats. (It should be noted that selective enforcement is hardly entirely unknown in the West. It is occasionally invoked by Western officials, particularly against whistleblowers, but is generally viewed as an act of desperation. A notorious recent case in point in the United States concerned Major General Thomas Fiscus of the U.S. Air Force. After he opposed the use of harsh interrogation techniques at Guantanamo, his superiors demoted him two ranks on the pretext that, in having affairs with female members of the armed forces, he had broken obsolescent—and often flouted—military fraternization rules.)

To Western observers the most flagrant example of how selective enforcement works in modern East Asia is South Korea's notorious technique for protecting its car market: the government simply lets it be known that anyone who buys a foreign car risks a rigorous tax audit. Given that the South Korean tax authorities normally turn a blind eye to a considerable amount of "acceptable" tax evasion, this is a widely feared gambit. It has remained so even though in recent years officials have begun denying they stoop to such tactics. It is largely responsible for the fact that the combined share of all foreign markets in the South Korean car market as of 2005 had been kept to just 3 percent. (Thus American makers sold only about 4,000 vehicles in Korea that year, whereas Korean makers sold about 800,000 in the United States.)

As for China, selective enforcement is nothing new. It was a tool of unaccountable bureaucratic power in premodern times, but in the chaos of twentieth-century China it was replaced by more vicious forms of authoritarianism. Now it is undergoing a renaissance as Chinese leaders seek discreet ways to maintain their grip. Increasingly since the Tiananmen Square massacre they have worked to introduce at least a semblance of Western-style human rights in the treatment of suspects and prisoners. There have even been efforts to introduce some token democracy at the local government level. Behind the scenes, however, this ostensible liberalization has been balanced by increasing resort to various tools of soft authoritarian power such as selective enforcement.

I first noticed selective enforcement in Japan in the early 1990s and my account in my 1995 book *Blindside: Why Japan Is Still on Track to Overtake the U.S. By the Year 2000* seems to have been the first extended reference to it in the English language. But the idea was evidently in the air and had been commented upon the previous year by both James Fallows of the *Atlantic* and Richard Hornik of *Time*. Suggesting in the May-June 1994 issue of *Foreign Affairs* that Chinese officials used the technique to marginalize private enterprise, Hornik wrote: "Private businesses are ... subject to arbitrary enforcement of regulations, many of which are unpublished. China's periodic anticorruption campaigns, for example, invariably target even legitimate private entrepreneurs." More recently the University of California law professor Laura W. Young spotlighted the phenomenon in an Internet article in 1998. "China's laws are strict but are sporadically enforced," she wrote.

As the scholars C. Simon Fan and Herschel I. Grossman have pointed out, China's anticorruption laws have offered a particularly fruitful pretext for selective enforcement. On the one hand, corruption is rife in China (in a league table of corruption compiled by the Berlin-based organization Transparency International in 1996, China ranked near the top, outclassed by only Bangladesh, Kenya, Pakistan, and Nigeria). On the other hand, China's penalties for corruption are among the world's most draconian.

In a commentary published in 2001, Fan, of Hong Kong's Lingnan University, and Grossman, of Brown University, noted that because of the pandemic nature of corruption in China, Chinese Communist Party leaders always "have something" on those below them. Echoing an earlier analysis by the San Diego–based Sinologist Susan Shirk, they added: "Because high officials could charge lower officials with corruption at any time, low level bureaucrats offer steadfast political support to those above them. In this way, corruption serves the party's goal of maintaining cohesiveness and absolute power. Indeed, until recently, few corrupt officials were ever punished. The threat of punishment, together with selective enforcement of this threat, was enough to maintain control."

One way of looking at selective enforcement is that it creates a culture of self-regulation—at least self-regulation on issues of transcendental importance to the powers that be. Each actor in the body politic is required to calculate for himself how far he can stick his neck out without risking his head being chopped off.

The implications have not been lost on China's most successful business-people (who by definition have more occasion than most to buy the cooperation of New China's notoriously venal bureaucrats). As Charles Lee, author of *Cowboys and Dragons,* has pointed out, Chinese businesspeople have little to fear so long as they do nothing to challenge the established political order. But it would be a brave Chinese tycoon who dared to fund, say, a sincere effort to introduce democracy in China. He would not remain rich for long—and arguably might not remain alive for long. After all, the death penalty, typically administered by a bullet in the back of the head, is not unknown for corruption offenses. Selective enforcement of anticorruption laws amounts to a formidable catch-22.

For our purposes a key point is that, like several other aspects of New China's workings, selective enforcement flies under the West's radar. For a start, as pointed out by Michael Dutton, a Melbourne, Australia–based expert on the Chinese legal system, it is virtually impossible to document. Worse, it utterly defies efforts by international lawyers to create a level playing field in global business.

Yet selective enforcement can readily be adapted to draw foreign companies and individuals in to the net of Chinese power. To say the least, a society deliberately designed to entrap people will prove hard to integrate into any American-led world order. In truth it constitutes a deal breaker for the entire globalism project.

Last Days of the American Order?

If the rise of Chinese power were the only thing to worry about, America's geopolitical quandary would be serious enough. But there is another concern here that is at least as significant: American political and economic decline. It is fair to say that the United States is undergoing probably the fastest power implosion of any major nation in history.

The economic side of America's predicament alone is far worse than almost anyone in Washington realizes. As I have been outspokenly critical of America's economic strategy since the late 1980s, I may be perceived as biased. But it is not necessary to take my word for it. In recent years several of America's most perceptive business leaders have, if anything, been even more outspoken.

Few witnesses to American decline are better placed to testify than Andrew Grove, chairman of Intel Corporation. As quoted by *Newsweek* in 2006, he said: "America ... [is going] down the tubes and the worst part is nobody knows it. They're all in denial, patting themselves on the back, as the *Titanic* heads for the iceberg full speed ahead."

Then there is the world's most successful investor, Omaha-based Warren Buffett. He has said: "The U.S. trade deficit is a bigger threat to the domestic economy than either the federal budget deficit or consumer debt and could lead to political turmoil."

Even Jeffrey Immelt, chief executive of General Electric, has joined in the clamor. A trenchant critic of the American education system, he has said: "More people will graduate in the United States in 2006 with sports-exercise degrees than electrical engineering degrees. So if we want to be the massage capital of the world, we are well on the way."

Nowhere is American weakness more apparent than in advanced manufacturing. Leadership in this category has long been a sine qua non for a superpower. Indeed America's effortlessly assured dominance of the mid-twentieth-century world order was based on little else. That leadership has now been thrown away as smart-aleck pundits in Washington, many of them funded directly or indirectly by the foreign trade lobby, have embraced an ephemeral intellectual fashion to scorn manufacturing. As we will see in chapter 2, this fashion flies in the face of fundamental economic logic. The truth is not everyone can be a software engineer at Microsoft or an investment banker at Goldman Sachs. *For the broad mass of ordinary workers,* advanced manufacturing (that is, the sort of manufacturing that is conducted in expensively equipped factories that are well endowed with ultrasophisticated, generally secret production know-how) is a far better source of highly productive, well-paid jobs than the service industries that Washington has come to consider America's salvation. It was on the world-beating productivity of this broad mass of ordinary workers that America's erstwhile economic dominance was based.

Unfortunately, so many of America's advanced manufacturing industries have already been eviscerated by foreign—principally Japanese—competition that a U.S. Department of Defense report in 2005 pronounced America's security at risk.

"There is no longer a diverse base of U.S. integrated circuit fabricators capable of meeting trusted and classified chip needs," the report said. "From a U.S. national security view, the potential effects of this restructuring are so perverse and far reaching and have such opportunities for mischief that, had the United States not significantly contributed to this migration, it would have been considered a major triumph of an adversary nation's strategy to undermine U.S. military capabilities."

To anyone who takes it for granted that corporate America is destined to dominate the world economy in perpetuity, the reality on the ground abroad these days is chastening. Quite simply, apart from a few token American brand names such as Coca-Cola, America's economic influence has long since disappeared.

Other nations have been quick to fill the void, and among them China is increasingly to the fore. Here is a sampling of how fast China has been turning the tables on the United States:

1. China's foreign currency reserves are now not only the world's largest (China passed Japan in this respect in 2006) but the largest in world economic history. Totaling $1.2 trillion as of May 2007, they had multiplied more than sixfold just since the end of 2001.
2. In partnership with other major East Asian central banks, the People's Bank of China effectively controls both the level of American interest rates and the value of the American dollar. This follows from the fact that in an effort to finance America's trade deficits it has become a huge purchaser of American treasury bonds. Absent this buying, the dollar would collapse and American interest rates would rocket. While China is unlikely to force the issue, it holds the upper hand in a vast game of chicken in which weak-willed, easily divided American government officials consistently come off second best. No nation has enjoyed this much power over the world's currency system since America's greatest days of economic influence in the early decades after World War II.
3. Chinese interests have now established effective control of the formerly American-owned Panama Canal. In particular the key ports at

either end of the canal have been quietly bought by Li Ka-shing, a Hong Kong–based tycoon widely regarded as a Beijing surrogate. Li also controls ports on Mexico's Pacific coast that are playing a rapidly increasing role in shipping Chinese goods to the American market. For those who know their history (and Chinese leaders certainly do), America's loss of control of key ports is strikingly reminiscent of what happened to China in the mid-nineteenth century, when the Western imperial powers seized control over major Chinese ports such as Hong Kong, Shanghai, and Amoy.

4. Chinese and other East Asian interests now largely control the vast network of communications satellites and undersea cables that make up the world's international telecommunications system. Up to the early 1990s, the system had been under American control. Indeed it was considered a cornerstone of American power (among other things it provided American intelligence services with a unique ability to listen in on the world's telephone conversations). All that changed as a result of America's high-technology stock crash of 2000 and 2001, when dozens of key telecommunications companies teetered on the verge of bankruptcy and were bought out by East Asian interests. (War on terror note: American intelligence officials still listen to telephone calls but for the most part these days they are limited to calls to and from the United States. For calls from the Arab world to, say, Europe or East Asia they increasingly depend on the grace and favor of other governments.)

5. Considerably more of the next Boeing plane, the superadvanced 787, will be built in East Asia than in the United States. This will constitute the big-league debut for China's ambitious and fast-rising aerospace industry. Of the 787's components, only the vertical fin will be made in Boeing's erstwhile manufacturing base in Washington State. Even the wings, considered to be the most technically difficult manufacturing challenge, will be made in East Asia. Up to the late 1990s Boeing officials had said that wing making was such an important function that it would never be outsourced. Full disclosure: for now the Chinese continue to play second fiddle to the Japanese in the East Asian aerospace challenge (the 787's wings will be made in Japan). But it is a fair bet that China is already planning for the day when it will match or surpass Japan's high-precision engineering skills.

Of course, many commentators insist that the United States is finally turn-ing the corner. In particular they often argue that American corporations are holding their own or even gaining in the most advanced areas of manufactur-ing. Such claims are rarely backed up with convincing figures but are, instead, based on anecdotes, often flimsy or highly misleading ones. Many of the "Amer-ican manufacturing revival" stories cite, for instance, the Caterpillar bulldozer company. What is rarely mentioned is that much of the most serious added value in its products these days is created by Japanese workers employed by its Japanese-managed joint venture with Mitsubishi Heavy Industries.

The test of all optimistic manufacturing talk is the international trade fig-ures. Unfortunately these tell a particularly bleak story.

In former times the United States was by far the world's strongest trading nation. On virtually every yardstick it was number one—from the volume of its exports to the strength of its trade surpluses. It also generally ranked as the largest source of other nations' imports. No longer. With its trade surpluses now a distant memory (the last recorded American trade surplus was in 1991), the United States ranks number one in a very different category—as the world's largest deficit nation.

As of 2007, the United States had been passed by China in the total value of its exports. By contrast as recently as 1996 the United States outexported China by four to one.

As for the United States' former status as the largest source of other nations' imports, in many cases China has now taken its place. The trend has been par-ticularly marked in East Asia, where only Malaysia buys more from the United States than from China.

The turnaround has been particularly momentous in Japan, which as re-cently as 1991 bought nine times as much from the United States as from China (spending fully $92 billion on American goods versus just over $10 billion on Chinese). As of 2006 it bought more than 50 percent more from China than from the United States.

Measuring both imports and exports, China has now displaced the United States as Japan's largest overall trading partner. As recently as 1992, Japan did more than five times as much business with the United States as it did with China.

America's loss of position has been even more shocking in South Korea, Tai-wan, and Thailand (all of whom now buy far more from both Japan and China than from the United States). Moreover, the United States no longer even ranks as China's largest source of imports. That role has been taken by Japan, whose exports to China are now twice America's. This despite the fact that the Chinese are supposed to hate the Japanese. As we will see in chapter 7, Sino-Japanese relations are much closer than is generally understood in the United States, and one aspect of the Sino-Japanese rapprochement in recent decades has been a fast-burgeoning trade relationship—a relationship in which the United States has increasingly been treated as a spare wheel.

Perhaps the most devastating point about America's loss of position is that it is not reflected in any similar trend among other advanced nations. Indeed for the developed nations of East Asia, China's rise has on balance been a boon, as evidenced by the fact that not only Japan but South Korea and even Taiwan enjoy broadly balanced two-way trade with China. China actually runs a *deficit* with Japan, despite the fact that factory wages in Japan are now higher than in the United States. Even ultra-high-wage Germany exports almost as much to China as it imports. The fact is that unlike the United States, Japan and Germany have fought hard to maintain and indeed enhance their position in advanced manufacturing.

America's trade position has worsened catastrophically not only with China but with virtually every other major nation. As of 2006, America's current account deficit—the widest and most meaningful measure of the trade position—represented 6.5 percent of gross domestic product. This was not only a record for the United States but represented a more than threefold rise on the 1.9 percent ratio recorded in 1989. Indeed the latest figure was the second-worst recorded percentage trade deficit ever incurred by any major nation in peacetime. The one worse performance was a figure of 7.7 percent incurred by Italy in 1924, the year before Benito Mussolini seized dictatorial power.

For our purposes let's simply note that a nation that cannot balance its trade must rely on other nations to keep its economy afloat. As Paul Craig Roberts, a former top Treasury Department official who was chief architect of the Reagan administration's economic reforms, has pointed out, all that saves the dollar from total collapse is its role—for a few years longer—as the world's reserve currency. "When the dollar loses its reserve currency role, America will not be able to pay for the imports on which it has become dependent," he has written. "Shopping in Wal-Mart will be like shopping at Neiman Marcus."

No other major nation in modern times has become remotely so dependent on foreign creditors. Indeed the closest parallel to America's predicament today is that of the Ottoman Empire a century ago. American presidents these days, like the Ottoman sultans of old, are surrounded by flatterers uttering soothing words. Such assurances are no more reliable today than they were in the Ottoman Empire's twilight years.

March of the Chocolate Soldiers

The updated Confucian values by which China is ruled are not only fundamentally incompatible with those of the West but, in head-to-head competition, prove strikingly more robust. At first sight this statement may seem surprising, but it requires no more than a moment's reflection to see that more and more Westerners who do business in China are already modifying their behavior—often quite troublingly—under Beijing's influence.

This is part of a larger pattern in which for decades Americans have increasingly compromised themselves throughout the Confucian region. Westerners arrive confident not only of the superiority of their values but of the region's receptivity to those values. Their expectations undergo rapid adjustment. As a general rule, Westerners either find an early exit, or they end up espousing the very Confucian values they once scorned.

The pattern is so marked and consistent that it can be aptly compared to a phalanx of chocolate soldiers marching into a blowtorch.

Several Confucian societies have now had generations of experience in breaking the resolve of even the most apparently strong-willed Westerners. Though China has been slower than Japan and Korea to learn the subtleties of this art, it is catching up. For a start, the Beijing authorities provide plenty of carrots for those who compromise themselves. The carrots range from the merely delicately corrupting to the blatantly so. In a society where everyone is just a bit compromised, it is hard for a Westerner to hold the line—but once he succumbs, he is perpetually thereafter in the authorities' thrall.

The most common way Westerners compromise themselves is simply by doing business "the Chinese way." Peter S. Goodman of the *Washington Post* has pointedly illuminated the problem. Writing from Shanghai in 2005, he commented: "American business leaders often describe their China operations idealistically, suggesting that their presence here will compel Chinese competitors to adopt more ethical business practices. But in one key regard, the dynamic operates in reverse, with U.S. companies adopting Chinese-style tactics to secure sales, as they compete in a market in which Communist Party officials routinely control businesses, and purchasing agents consider kickbacks part of their salary." In an effort to escape criminal liability, many American corporations use Chinese "consultants" to deliver bribes but such intermediaries are never completely reliable and, subjected to suitable pressures (or offered suitable blandishments), might well be induced to incriminate an American client.

When Chinese leaders feel the need to get tough, moreover, there is little in the Confucian ethical code to hold them back. As the former *Wall Street Journal* Beijing bureau chief James McGregor has pointed out, they believe the end justifies the means—and not just sometimes, as in the West, but all the time. This view can be invoked to legitimize the use of a multitude of highly manipulative, even Orwellian, techniques for ensuring the citizenry's support in pursuit of national goals. Many such techniques involve entrapment or blackmail or both. Such techniques can readily be extended to the Western community in China—and the evidence is that increasingly they are. Certainly many Western residents assume their phones are tapped. The evidence is that they are not imagining things.

What is beyond question is that the carrot alone has already worked wonders in inducing one American corporation after another in China to embrace the Confucian way. As we will see in chapter 6, in their eagerness to make money in China, American corporations have consented to conduct—let's put this delicately—mendacious public relations on Beijing's behalf. They have even acted as enforcers of Beijing's one-child policy, and in that endeavor have coerced women employees into having abortions.

In the words of Carolyn Bartholomew, chairman of the United States–China Economic and Security Review Commission, many American companies have struck "Faustian bargains" with Beijing. She has cited such respected American corporations as Yahoo!, Google, and Microsoft. As we will see in chapter 6, these companies have agreed to abide by China's censorship rules in serving Chinese Internet users. Moreover, Yahoo! voluntarily handed over evidence that led to one Chinese Internet user being sentenced to ten years in prison. Bartholomew commented: "Far from capitalism changing the Chinese government, it is the Chinese government changing capitalists. Rather than the birth of freedom with telecommunications and the Internet serving as the handmaiden of democracy, we have the Internet entrepreneurs selling rope to the hangmen."

If our concern were merely that Americans *in China* were being induced to forfeit their values, it would be serious enough. But, as we will now see, Beijing is increasingly changing the way Americans behave *in America.*

Introducing Reverse Convergence

What does the future hold for Chinese foreign policy? It is useful to consider first the historical context. China's instincts, in common with those of other Confucian nations, are strongly isolationist. For centuries before the arrival of Westerners, all the Confucian nations kept to themselves. This policy was broken only with the coming of Western gunboats in the mid-nineteenth century. First China opened up under pressure from the British in 1842, and a few years later Japan succumbed to pressure from the United States.

It is a fair bet that if it were possible, both China and Japan would be happy to return to the isolationism they insisted upon before the rise of the West. With the best will in the world, however, traditional Confucian isolationism is no longer an option. The world is just too small and too dangerous. Most if not all of the world's principal nations, after all, possess the power to launch nuclear war at a moment's notice.

The position is further destabilized by the mutual incompatibility of Confucianism and Western individualism. In a world that has been drastically shrunk by fast travel and cheap telecommunications (not to mention intercontinental missiles), it is hard to see how the two ideologies can continue to coexist as equals. One will increasingly dominate the other—and if the authorities in Beijing have anything to do with it, Western individualism will not emerge the winner.

One thing is certain: assuming no change in present policies, Beijing and Washington are headed for confrontation. Seen from Beijing's point of view, Washington's instinct to "change China" implies, of course, the eclipse, if not the demise, of the existing Chinese Communist Party leadership. Moreover, by insisting that Beijing abandon its own institutions and values in favor of American ones, Washington stands accused of interfering in China's internal affairs. This, of course, in the eyes of Chinese leaders, legitimizes a response in kind by Beijing.

Chinese leaders hardly need to be reminded of Clausewitz's maxim that attack is the best form of defense. Indeed an ancient Chinese proverb, *Yi gong wei shou,* makes the same point: "Use attack as a defense."

Certainly, by proclaiming American institutions and values not only more desirable than those of any other nation but inherently more robust, Washington has virtually guaranteed that Beijing's rejoinder will be a sotto voce "We'll see." Faced with an overreaching Washington, Beijing is provided with a pretext to do what it probably aches to do anyway: change America. If the world is to be run on Confucian principles, after all, outcomes everywhere will have to be fixed in advance, vested interests will have to be squared, the media will have to be muzzled, dissidents will have to be suppressed, and the public will have to be bamboozled—in perpetuity.

To put this in pugilistic terms, it is as if an American boxing champion challenged a Chinese kung fu master. Confident that the world is converging to Western values, the American assumes his Chinese adversary will fight by Queensberry rules. The kung fu master, however, sees nothing wrong with kung fu rules. Particularly as they give him an unbeatable advantage.

Given the troubling nature of these matters, it is important at this stage to enter some qualifications. For a start, it should be noted that while this book will pull no punches in exposing the Chinese leadership's duplicity and authoritarianism, no hostility is, of course, intended toward the Chinese people. Quite the reverse. It would be ungracious to say the least for the West to begrudge the Chinese people their increasing prosperity or their wish to play a larger role on the world stage.

It should also be made clear that however Machiavellian their intentions, Chinese leaders are not looking for war, at least not against the world's major nuclear powers. That said, they are greatly influenced by the ancient Chinese military theoretician Sun Tzu, one of whose aphorisms seems particularly relevant: "To subdue the enemy without fighting is the acme of skill."

The betting is that China will penetrate American society by stealth in ways that will slowly but surely undermine American values and institutions. In other words instead of China becoming more like the United States, the United States will become more like China. It is a process that is best called reverse convergence. Building on the extensive if unobtrusive groundwork laid by earlier East Asian industrializers, China can, for instance, be expected in the fullness of time to become a major factor behind the scenes in shaping outcomes in Washington. Indeed this can be expected to happen willy-nilly, given the extent to which American elites have already embraced the doctrine of globalism. The effect of globalism has been to create a political vacuum in Washington, where an alert eye to the American national interest was once present.

Of particular concern is how well Western intellectual organizations will stand up under the strain. Take the Western media. The idea that they might be vulnerable to pressure from Beijing may seem preposterous, but there is plenty of evidence that things are already going the wrong way. Certainly other East Asian nations have long been known to influence Western media coverage. This explains why key media organizations in the United States have rarely investigated protectionist practices in nations like Japan and South Korea in recent years. When was the last time a major American newspaper took a searching look at the car markets of Japan or South Korea, for instance? When, for that matter, did CNN's otherwise refreshingly frank Lou Dobbs produce such a report? In truth, any attempt by the American media to focus serious attention on Japanese or Korean protectionism would raise the specter of a boycott by key advertisers, probably acting in concert under covert government leadership (the fact that government-guided cartels dominate both the Japanese and Korean economies makes coordinated action easy).

In the fullness of time—give them fifteen to twenty years—the Beijing authorities will enjoy similar clout in the American advertising market. It is a fair bet that the American media will prove similarly selective in their coverage of the underside of Chinese economic policies. The key thing here is that Confucian nations enjoy an ability to forge a degree of group solidarity in pursuit of national goals that is rarely if ever matched by Western nations.

We are still in the early stages, but it is clear that the United States is highly vulnerable to illegitimate Chinese influences. So much so that key elements of American society are already Confucianizing themselves.

Allegations of reverse convergence have been around for a while. As far back as 1998, the right-wing policy commentators Robert Kagan and William Kristol thought they detected such a pattern in the actions of the Clinton administration. Writing in the *New York Times*, they commented: "The [Clinton] administration has always argued that its policy of engagement will make China more like us. In fact it is making us more like them."

Harsh words indeed—but actually all the evidence is that the administration of George W. Bush has shown even less fortitude in the face of Confucian pressures.

Then there is the ever malleable American business community. Already, as we have seen, top American Internet companies have reneged on Western values in pursuit of lucrative business in their Chinese subsidiaries. How long will it be before they prove similarly malleable in their American operations?

Meanwhile, as Tina Rosenberg has pointed out, the wider American business community also seems dangerously unreliable. Writing for the *New York Times* on a conference in Shanghai in 2005, she recounted how top American business leaders openly fawned on Chinese Communist Party officials. She added: "Let's not pretend that foreign investment will make China a democracy. That argument was born out of desperation and self-interest. Because China is too lucrative a market to resist, American and European businessmen have ended up endorsing the party line through their silence—or worse. They are not molding China; China is molding them."

Any American who understands the power dynamics by which the Chinese empire has been held together over the last three thousand years will not be sanguine about the outcome. It is time Uncle Sam looked over his shoulder: his coattails are caught in the jaws of a dragon.

TWO

"Don't Worry, Be Happy"

As a weakened United States faces off against a rising China, it is important to understand why Washington has been so slow to sense the magnitude of the challenge. American policymaking not only on China but on the entire East Asian region is plagued with treacherous information blocks and intellectual pitfalls.

It is hardly as if China's rise should have come as a complete surprise. After all, already by the late 1970s several Confucian nations had demonstrated an extraordinary capacity for fast, sustained economic growth. The implication surely was that if China adopted similar methods, it would achieve similar results. And sure enough, in the five years to 1984, it almost doubled its exports, as measured in U.S. dollars—a growth rate of almost 18 percent a year. Even so, it was to be another fifteen years before Washington began to take the Chinese economy seriously. In the interim, China's exports had grown more than ninefold to hit nearly $250 billion as of 2000.

As we will see, many Western observers remain in denial to this day and, even after China's exports grew by an annual average rate of more than 20 percent in the first five years of the new century, continue to invoke a plethora of reasons to underestimate the Chinese challenge. Their arguments are often mutually contradictory but nonetheless by some process of twisted logic always seem to lead to the same "Don't worry, be happy" conclusions.

One analytical controversy concerns first principles: whether or not there is really such a thing as the East Asian economic system. While, as this book shows, the facts have never left much room for doubt, many American commentators have long argued that no such system exists.

One of the more prominent naysayers has been the economist Paul Krugman, who in 1994 published an influential article in *Foreign Affairs* entitled "The Myth of Asia's Miracle." He argued that the East Asian region's economic system was not very different from that of the West and that its performance had generally been what Western theory would have predicted. While conceding that the region's growth rate was higher than the world average, he argued that this "merely" reflected the fact that the region saves a lot. But why does it save so much? Not only did Krugman not address this question but he did not seem to realize it was significant.

Another matter of first principles is whether the new economic system that the Chinese adopted in the late 1970s really is modeled on those used elsewhere in the region, or is instead, as is often suggested, "Western capitalism with Chinese characteristics." All through the 1980s, when corporate Japan's success in besting American competition was at its most conspicuous, Beijing's trade lobbyists argued that "China is no Japan." Alluding to China's continuing ostensible commitment to Communism as well as to a host of practical problems allegedly slowing Chinese economic development, they thereby fostered general complacency in Washington at a time when American policymakers should already have identified China as the greatest miracle economy of them all.

Many of these analysts went on in the 1990s to compound their disservice to American understanding by belatedly reversing themselves. Their reversal came as the American press was suddenly filled with reports of ostensibly devastating economic dysfunction in Japan. Yes, these analysts now concluded, China was in fact copying the Japanese model—and precisely for this reason it could confidently be eliminated from contention as a challenger to American power. After all, the result of decades of economic interventionism in Japan had been to turn the country into an economic "basket case"—or at least so it seemed at the time. This analysis played directly to one of Washington's most cherished preconceptions: the idea that any effort to flout the laws of the market will end in tears. The extraordinary truth, which we will consider in detail later in this chapter, is that in the ways that mattered to American policymakers, Japan kept on forging ahead—with the result that, far from collapsing as many "experts" predicted in the early 1990s, Japan's trade surpluses went on to triple in the next fifteen years.

American policymakers have also been hampered by a notable—and clearly culture-based—tendency to gullibility. Quite simply, they have been far too credulous in believing what they are told not only in Beijing but in several other capitals (where officials have often had a vested interest in promoting Beijing's agenda). Though Americans rarely discuss their national tendency to credulousness, it is a fact of life that is well understood by tricksters and con men around the world. Even in nations like Britain, Ireland, and Australia, where the truth ethic works much as it does in the United States, the naïveté of American tourists is a perennial butt of local humor.

More than probably anywhere else in the world, East Asia is culturally equipped to make good use of American gullibility. For anyone who wants to understand how the East Asian system is changing the world, the beginning of knowledge is to understand the Confucian truth ethic. To that controversial subject we now turn.

Never the Twain Shall Meet

For reasons of misplaced political correctness, the Confucian truth ethic is rarely discussed these days. Certainly things have changed since the 1970s, when Henry Kissinger considered it politic to describe Japan's top bureaucrats as "mean and treacherous."

In Washington these days, it is considered a sign of general enlightenment to assume that the whole world is converging to the American truth ethic. Thus, although people abroad may not always tell the truth (any more than they do at home), at least when they lie they are assumed to do so in an American way.

In reality the truth ethic differs widely around the world; and, for an American observer, nowhere are the differences more startling or consequential than in East Asia.

Let's be clear: Just as anywhere else, most people in East Asia tell the truth most of the time (no society gets very far without a serviceable truth ethic). By the same token, they don't *always* tell the truth.

The key to the East Asian truth ethic is *context*. The management writer Peter Drucker provided a useful insight in an article in *Forbes* magazine in 1981. Emphasizing that Confucian ethics are highly dependent on the relationship between the parties involved (whether father-son, employer-employee, or whatever), he added: "Right behavior—which in the English translation of Confucian ethics is usually called sincerity—is that individual ethic which is truly appropriate to the specific relationship of mutual dependence because it optimizes benefits for both sides."

In some contexts, East Asians tend to be more truthful than Westerners. At the workplace, for instance, juniors are strongly obligated to answer superiors' questions truthfully. Likewise, sales assistants in reputable East Asian stores tend to be more reliable than their counterparts in the West (in deference to the Confucian view of the customer as a quasi boss).

In many other contexts, however, telling the literal truth is considered highly inappropriate. Why? Because to do so would violate another ethic, the ethic of loyalty. A person's debt of loyalty to his or her parents, work unit, boss, company, and nation counts as a superior ethic, and where it might be compromised by telling the truth, it takes precedence.

The East Asian businessman Dawson Kwauk has pointed out that the Chinese are helped in this by their notoriously ambiguous linguistic conventions. Echoing a crack that President Bill Clinton once made about the Japanese, Kwauk notes out that when the Chinese say "Yes," what they mean may be no more than "Yes, we heard you say something."

Part of the problem is simply that East Asians are far more discreet than Westerners. Countless topics that would be regarded as open to frank discussion in the West are considered no-go areas in the East. The problem is particularly acute in China. Fox Butterfield, a top Sinologist and former *New York Times* correspondent, says that the maxim "Information is power" is better understood in China than almost anywhere else. Chinese institutions and organizations make a policy of withholding even the most innocuous information, the better to keep potential critics and challengers at bay. In a country where blanket secrecy is the norm, anyone who oversteps the mark risks being accused of endangering national security, a charge often punishable with imprisonment, if not death.

As a practical matter, much of what is said for public consumption is in any case not only nonsense but obvious nonsense. Having been brought up in such an intellectual climate from birth, the Chinese see little wrong with it. They automatically discount everything they hear and assume that anything they say will be similarly discounted. It seems merely common sense to recognize that much publicly promulgated information is not only not to be taken literally but is at best allegory. Take, for instance, the famous story of Mao Zedong's swim in the Yangtze River in 1966. Although the portly, chain-smoking Mao was already seventy-two years old, the Chinese press suffered no embarrassment in reporting that he had supposedly swum nine miles in sixty-five minutes. Not only that, he had somehow found time along the way to teach other swimmers new strokes.

Unfortunately, not all Confucian fibbing is so laughably obvious. In fact, as the American China watcher W. A. P. Martin recorded more than a century ago, the ability to lie convincingly is regarded in China almost as a hallmark of superior character. "Truth is not a point of honor with Chinese," he wrote, "and adroit lying is with them admitted to be one of the prime qualifications of a mandarin."

As James McGregor has warned in his 2005 book *One Billion Customers: Lessons from the Front Lines of Doing Business in China,* the Chinese elite's tradition of skillful deceit is still going strong in the twenty-first century. McGregor comments: "Many foreign business people who negotiate in China bring along too much goodwill and trust. Chinese negotiators have no qualms about exploiting that by outright lying. That ability is a tremendous advantage for them. For the Chinese outcomes are more important than the truth."

One of the more controversial aspects of the Confucian truth ethic is that it legitimates what is best described as institutional mendacity—a pattern in which several sources collude in presenting a tissue of lies to the uninitiated. This phenomenon, which is facilitated by the notably theatrical nature of Confucian public life, is exemplified in a common routine described by McGregor. Chinese companies often cite imaginary government regulations—conjured up from the ether—to deceive a foreign joint-venture partner into modifying its expectations and strategies. The deception works because local lawyers, government officials, and interpreters are invariably prepared to play along in pulling the wool over the foreigner's eyes. It is fair to say that this routine is much used not only in China but throughout the Confucian world.

Institutional mendacity is also notably exemplified in the existence of a special caste of ostensibly Westernized facilitators who specialize in deceiving foreigners. Many such people are highly astute observers of human psychology who have spent years studying Western blind spots and preconceptions. Almost by definition they are consummate, in many cases highly charming, liars. They often seek to win the confidence of their foreign clientele by posing as trenchant critics of their home country's faults. Their criticisms tend to be of the hackneyed sort that gives little away—in the case of China, for instance, such facilitators may loudly lament (with clichés and platitudes) their country's corruption or income inequality.

Ivan Hall, author of *Bamboozled!: How America Loses the Intellectual Game with Japan and Its Implications for Our Future in Asia*, points out, a special hazard for the more gullible sort of American is a caste of "suavely mannered, Western-educated Japanese of high rank" who mediate between the United States and Japan. Adept at varying their pitch to suit each foreigner's level of knowledge, such "handlers" come in many guises, most notably as government officials, professors, corporate executives, management consultants, stock analysts, economists, bankers, and journalists. Similar handlers exist throughout East Asia, and virtually every East Asian government department, university faculty, media organization, and corporation that has regular contact with foreigners boasts at least one member of the profession.

Many of the more skilled write often for publication in English. It is fair to say that almost every Chinese, Japanese, or Korean commentator who is published in, say, *Foreign Affairs* or the editorial pages of the *New York Times* is a member of this profession.

An especially influential exemplar of the art was Zhou Enlai, China's foreign minister in the Maoist era. A polished and witty cosmopolitan who had had an elite education in Tokyo, Zhou was often almost magically effective in misleading Western diplomats and press correspondents. His style was memorably summed up by Laszlo Ladany, a Hong Kong–based Catholic priest who was a key China watcher in the Maoist era: "Zhou Enlai was one of those men who never tell the truth and never tell a lie. For them there is no distinction between the two. The speaker says what is appropriate in the circumstances."

In recent decades the problem of institutional mendacity has been exacerbated by the fact that many American and European residents of East Asia have been recruited to the task. Whether in Japan, South Korea, Taiwan, Hong Kong, or Singapore, the more established and prominent a Western resident is, the more likely he or she is to be a conscious—if often well-disguised—facilitator for his or her adopted country. Such people tend to be heavily overrepresented in running chambers of commerce, foreign correspondents' clubs, and similar foreigner-oriented organizations throughout the region. Meanwhile there are many other Western residents who, desperately clinging to what is left of their Western truth ethic, remain silent—and thereby far too often are complicit in letting their more mendacious peers set the agenda. The few Western residents who are cussed enough or brave enough to speak frankly are subjected to highly orchestrated whisper campaigns. It is often suggested, for instance, that they somehow "hate" their country of residence or that their mind has become unbalanced from living too long abroad.

Until recently, Western residents in China were an exception to the general pattern in East Asia in that, consonant with the general wariness of Sino-Western relations, they maintained a firewall against the local truth ethic. Unfortunately this is now changing. Certainly many American members of the long-term foreign communities in Beijing and Shanghai have to varying degrees been coopted by the Chinese authorities. As recorded by the former *Los Angeles Times* correspondent James Mann, even those who refuse to be coopted are often so intimidated that they avoid frank discussion of sensitive issues. All this closely resembles the self-censorship the Chinese people themselves have always shown in discussing political issues.

The Confucian truth ethic greatly discombobulates American policymaking, particularly on trade. Not to put too fine a point on it, Beijing has systematically lied to the United States in promising early opening of its markets.

A trade deal concluded with China in 1992 provides a prime example. President George H. W. Bush hailed the agreement as a "breakthrough." Yet, as the trade economist Jeff Faux has pointed out, the Chinese almost immediately reneged on their commitments. The United States fell for the same trick again when in a blaze of publicity in 1995 major tariff reductions on four thousand categories of imports were announced by President Jiang Zemin. Although the reductions were duly implemented, new trade barriers were immediately introduced to achieve broadly the same protectionist effect. Even United States trade representative Charlene Barshefsky, an official otherwise noted for a strong China-friendly attitude, was provoked to rebuke Beijing. With a bluntness rarely heard in trade diplomacy, she said: "To make progress, China must stop erecting new trade barriers to replace those previously removed."

Beijing has also repeatedly lied about its policies on export subsidies. Although such subsidies were supposedly abolished as far back as 1991, they were still being extensively used as this book went to press sixteen years later. In a complaint to the World Trade Organization in 2007, the United States government documented nine categories of subsidies that had boosted China's exports of everything from steel to computers.

Then there is the story of Beijing's repeated promises to crack down on the theft of Western intellectual property. The story began as long ago as 1980 when Beijing agreed to join the World Intellectual Property Organization. Various laws were duly promulgated that ostensibly provided Western owners of trademarks, patents, and copyrights with extensive protection against theft.

After American corporations complained that these laws were mere window dressing, Beijing assured first Washington and then the World Trade Organization that it would tighten enforcement. Yet all the evidence is that the problem has just kept getting worse—so much so that China was recently reckoned to account for fully two-thirds of all the world's output of pirated and counterfeit products. Moreover, China's counterfeiting style has in recent years developed in a way that poses a qualitatively different, much more devastating, threat than previously. Whereas in the 1990s China confined itself largely to producing rather obvious knockoffs of luxury items such as Rolex watches and Louis Vuitton handbags, these days it is heavily involved in producing fake versions of everything from General Motors spare parts to Otis elevators. China also exports vast quantities of counterfeit pharmaceuticals, most notably drugs like Prozac and Viagra, which sell particularly well on the Internet. Not only does such counterfeiting damage American corporate interests but it raises major questions of consumer safety. In recent years there have been many reports of deaths caused by Chinese counterfeiting activities. In Panama in 2006, more than 100 people died after taking cough medicine laced with a toxic Chinese-made ingredient.

As documented by the author Tim Phillips in 2005, whole cities in China are devoted to various counterfeiting specialities. The city of Yiwu in eastern China even functions as a sort of "Wall Street" for the industry, providing a vast marketplace where, Phillips states, 100,000 counterfeit products are openly traded and 2,000 metric tons of fakes change hands daily. Meanwhile, as Edmund Andrews of the New York Times has reported, in big cities like Shanghai, vendors still openly sell pirated goods even along major thoroughfares.

Not only has the Chinese government turned a blind eye to all this, but large sections of the Chinese establishment, not least many sons and daughters of top leaders (known to China watchers as "princelings"), are heavily implicated in the racket.

As Pat Choate, author of a book on the theft of intellectual property, has commented, "Chinese promises on intellectual property are at best meaning-less."

The record shows that the major Confucian societies sincerely do not wish to be understood. On the contrary, they have often in recent decades mounted highly elaborate programs to mislead or otherwise manipulate the West. The politest thing that can be said is that they stand on the other side of a yawning East-West culture gap.

Watching the China Watchers

Given the problematic nature of the Confucian truth ethic, it is incumbent on China scholars to approach their responsibilities with special care. Unfortu-nately, few do.

Perhaps we should not be too hard on them. With rare exceptions, they are evidently out of their depth. This seems preordained, as they typically start from a background in political science; a first degree in economics or even his-tory would be more useful. Economics seems particularly relevant because, of course, a pivotal concern for Western policymakers should be China's growing economic clout.

What is beyond dispute is that key economic questions are largely over-looked by leading China scholars. Here are some examples:

· Why is China so protectionist?
· Why is its savings rate so high?
· How does Chinese corporate governance work and what part do state-owned banks play in it?
· If the banking system has been teetering on the brink of collapse for so long (at least since 1991, if one prominent observer is to be believed), why hasn't it collapsed yet?

Economics apart, even on their home ground of politics, the West's China-watching political scientists often seem to be waffling. None of them seems ever to have studied selective enforcement, for instance, and for the most part they seem ignorant of its existence.

It does not help that, with few exceptions, they have never lived in China or indeed in any other part of the Confucian world. They visit only occasionally and then typically only for a few weeks. Such visits evidently rarely get much beyond "After you, Alphonse" pleasantries and banquet toasts. Yet, as Ivan Hall has pointed out, even in the much more open Confucian societies of Japan and South Korea, it typically takes a Western resident at least five years *to begin* to understand his or her surroundings.

Things are not made any easier by the Beijing authorities' comprehensive program of controlling Western scholars. In an article headed "Have China Scholars All Been Bought?," which was posted at the *Far Eastern Economic Review* Web site in 2007, the Hong Kong–based economic scholar Carsten Holz commented: "Our incentives are to conform, and we do so in numerous ways: through the research questions we ask or don't ask; through the facts we report or ignore; through our use of language; and through what and how we teach." While accusing some Western economic observers of openly accepting favors from the Chinese Communist Party, Holz conceded that scholars who do not conform face almost insuperable obstacles. For a start they will be blackballed by Chinese colleagues, whose cooperation as research partners is often essential in doing original work in China. Such colleagues make sure that research programs are conducted in a way that does not offend the Chinese Communist Party and that only politically acceptable questions are asked.

More direct disincentives may also play a part. Holz suggested that some scholars have to worry about possible blowback for relatives in China. Others who own apartments in China have to wonder about retaliatory actions that might damage their properties' value.

In general, however, Beijing relies more on the carrot than on the stick. In a moment of commendable frankness, the California-based China watcher Orville Schell described the process. As he explained it, Beijing lets it be known that certain favored China watchers are officially acknowledged as "friends of China." It is a designation that Western scholars work hard to acquire. Understandably so. It guarantees privileged treatment at every turn. Not only are "friends of China" given preferential access to information, but they are also often housed in official guesthouses reserved for top cadres. Indeed, many of them quickly come to expect a level of "chop-chop" service on their visits to China that in other parts of the world is reserved for film stars or royalty.

Simple "face time" with senior officials is in itself a crucial privilege and is generally reserved for just a few of the most prominent pro-Beijing scholars.

It is hardly surprising therefore that the "friends" syndrome is highly insidious in undermining Western observers' objectivity. Reminiscing years after the fact about a visit he made to China in the 1970s, Schell wrote: "A 'friend of China' felt constrained from disappointing his host by writing anything critical or unflattering. . . . All the special treatment and effort extended on one's behalf seemed to require repayment. . . . The 'friends' felt some fear of seeming impolite or ungrateful, or of endangering Chinese acquaintances. But one fear above all predominated: the fear that if one uttered or wrote 'incorrect' thoughts one would never again be allowed back. And in one degree or another I think most of us who have written about China did capitulate to this fear."

China watchers have been capitulating in this way for a long time. Even at the height of the Maoist mania of the 1950s and 1960s, when Chinese propaganda was a lot cruder and more readily seen through than it has been more recently, the West's China scholars affected a sort of militant naïveté in refusing to confront the evident mendacity of official sources.

The definitive account of how China scholars misled the West in the Maoist era is Steven Mosher's 1989 book *China Misperceived.* Time and again, as Mosher has documented, Western scholars whitewashed Mao Zedong's record of mayhem and mass murder.

They embarrassed themselves particularly in their apologist interpretations of the food shortages created by the so-called Great Leap Forward, the disastrous economic experiment launched by Mao in the late 1950s. Instead of listening to the graphic testimony of the many famine refugees who had reached Hong Kong, China scholars preferred to base their assessments on Potemkin village–style tours provided by the Beijing authorities. Thanks to Jasper Becker's moving book *Hungry Ghosts,* not to mention increasingly frank admissions by Chinese leaders in recent years, we now know that the famine was one of the worst in world history.

Few of the West's supposed experts came out of the Maoist era more discredited than the faculty at the Harvard Center for East Asian Research. The center's founder, John Fairbank, led his colleagues in strongly denying the famine reports. Harvard also provided a platform for Maoist stooges to provide ostensibly authoritative rebuttals of the famine rumors. The most notable case was the famous author Edgar Snow, who by virtue of his unique access to Mao wielded exceptional influence over American scholarly opinion.

Mao's propaganda was also ably disseminated by the banker David Rockefeller. Now in his nineties, Rockefeller is a noted philanthropist whose indefatigable support for such institutions as the Council on Foreign Relations, the Trilateral Commission, and the Bilderberg Group has been a key factor in

American China scholarship for generations. His message—and that of the institutions he supports—has long been that China is rapidly converging to Western values. (It should be noted that China is not the only nation whose propaganda he has promoted. Like many of the most important propagandists in the field, he has also served the agendas of Japan and South Korea.)

He seems unabashed by his record in the Maoist era. Not to put too fine a point on it, he was one of Mao's principal American apologists. In the immediate wake of the disastrous Cultural Revolution, for instance, this is how he chose to characterize late-era Maoism: "Whatever the price of the Chinese revolution, it has obviously succeeded not only in producing more efficient and dedicated administration but also in fostering high morale and community of purpose. . . . The social experiment in China under Chairman Mao's leadership is one of the most important and successful in human history." This was published in 1973, just six years before Mao's successors took a torch to the Maoist legacy.

If Americans have good reason to wonder about Rockefeller and the institutions he funds, they should be at least as wary of another major influence on Western perceptions: the corporate China lobby. As American corporations have ridden the outsourcing boom to ever larger profits, they have become more and more generous in lining the pockets of suitably minded China scholars. The most obvious way the money changes hands is via speaking fees. Between $5,000 and $10,000 seems to be the norm for run-of-the-mill China watchers speaking to small seminars. Much more is possible for speakers who have authored well-received books or have served as government officials. And, of course, for the real highfliers, there are consulting opportunities at upwards—often way upwards—of $20,000 a month.

One scholar who seems to have done particularly well is the University of Michigan professor Kenneth Lieberthal. A former Clinton administration adviser on China, he unembarrassedly combines his professorial duties with a job as senior director of Washington-based Stonebridge International, a major China consulting firm.

Money apart, favored scholars can hope to have their careers boosted in myriad ways. Thus when a major American media organization needs an "acknowledged expert" to interpret the news from China or to comment on a new book, certain people—for the most part conscious stooges—are constantly recommended by the lobby. Well disguised as "independent" academics, think-tank analysts, lawyers, or even journalists, such stooges form an intellectual

cartel and systematically bolster one another's reputations and back one another up in asserting untruths. And as with all cartels, their prime concern is to
keep "interlopers" out.

One of the most notable examples of this phenomenon is Nicholas Lardy, a
dominant figure in Washington China-watching circles whose "rise without
trace" we will consider in chapter 8.

As for interlopers, their fate is distinctly Orwellian. By "interloper" is
meant, of course, any expert who refuses to toe Beijing's propaganda line. Here
again Steven Mosher offers crucial guidance: "Beijing keeps score, rewards its
friends, punishes its enemies, and has a tenacious memory."

The most obvious way enemies are punished is that they are refused admission to the country. Tougher remedies are also available. Li Shaomin, a Hong
Kong–based marketing professor and a U.S. citizen, spent five months in a
Chinese prison in 2001 for "endangering state security." Li's employer, the City
University of Hong Kong, played an implicitly collaborationist role by pointedly refusing to support him. He returned to the United States and, as recounted by Carsten Holz, has been effectively silenced.

Many more subtle techniques are also employed. Ivan Hall has pointed out
that the classic Confucian approach to dealing with independent thinkers is
neither to try to defeat them in argument nor to burn them at the stake. Rather,
it is to dispatch them "into isolation and silence through conspiratorial power
plays aimed at cutting them off from their sources of political patronage and
public esteem." Those who go "too far" in uttering unwelcome truths are frozen
out by their more pliable peers. Hall used a German word to capture the nu-
ance: Those who stand apart from the cartel are rendered *salonunfähig,* meaning
"unfit for the front parlor."

He added: "Their literary product in some cases has been subjected to coordinated broadsides; in other cases it is systematically ignored. Quiet campaigns
of defamation have been conducted. . . . The velvet glove moves softly and subtly for the most part, but it proves brutally effective in the end."

Hall was speaking mainly of Japan watchers, but the Japan lobby's techniques have now been extensively replicated in other areas of East Asian studies. The result is pervasive self-censorship, a factor that was particularly
important in the run-up to China's accession to the World Trade Organization.
This was a time when China scholars should have been the first to point out how
unready China was for Western-style free trade. For the most part, however,
they held their tongues. The few exceptions were mainly scholars associated

with the Taiwan lobby. Yet even they fell short. Although their willingness to talk back to Beijing was refreshing, they often seemed more concerned to defend Taiwan's interests than America's.

Pro-Taiwan scholars apart, most China watchers have felt compelled to compete in the intellectual equivalent of a slow bicycle race, in which they try to outdo one another in their obtuseness in failing to see through Beijing's mendacity.

As described by Steven Mosher, most China watchers have embraced the "scholarship of benevolence"—the idea that because China is assumed to be inevitably converging toward Western values, the West should cut it some slack. Mosher, who boasts powerful credentials as someone who not only reads Chinese but lived several years in the Chinese countryside, has named the Harvard China watcher Ezra Vogel as a leading appeaser.

Referring to Vogel in his book *China Misperceived,* Mosher summed up the China-watching community's failures in these terms: "The central weakness of the scholarship of benevolence is its failure to attend to politics. Vogel and others are guided, perhaps unconsciously, by the Marxist premises of their paradigm. They believe that economic interactions are fundamental, with political and legal relations mere end products of such interactions. In this view, if economic reform is carried out long enough, and with sufficient intensity, it must inevitably result in a more pluralistic political system. In reality it is the political system, through the conscious exercise of political will, that largely determines the course of the economic."

For our purposes the biggest problem with Sinology is that it has done next to nothing to challenge the torrent of self-serving "don't worry, be happy" propaganda pumped into the American media by the China lobby. Such propaganda, orchestrated by people who know no higher value than their own wallet, has not only legitimated a massive outsourcing rush but increasingly facilitated a pattern of reverse convergence, particularly in ethical standards.

Slivers of Truth, Layers of Misinformation

If we can't trust the scholars on China, how do we find out what is going on? The best we can do is read the press. But here again there are problems. For the most part, top editorial executives in the American press know less than nothing about the country. Worse, their views are badly distorted by Western ideology.

One practical consequence is that the highly influential editorial pages of America's major newspapers are functionally mendacious in their presentation of most China-related issues.

As for correspondents in the field, it has to be conceded that they are much more knowledgeable and less ideological than their colleagues at home. But this is hardly saying much, and even they are rarely qualified to take on the special intellectual challenge posed by a rising China. Ideally China correspondents should tick a long list of boxes: besides meeting the normal demanding requirements for any foreign reporting assignment, they should be fluent in both spoken and written Chinese; have an exceptional head for finance, economics, and accounting; boast sterling strength of character (they will need it in resisting the pressures of a highly manipulative state); have had long experience in decoding the Confucian truth ethic; and be thoroughly grounded in the history not only of modern China but of the rest of East Asia. It is fair to say that this counsel of perfection is rarely matched in practice. Indeed most China correspondents readily acknowledge—privately, if not publicly—their inadequacy to the task.

But here's the rub: even for that rare correspondent who can tick all the boxes, the task of reading the tea leaves day-to-day in China is little short of impossible. Why? Because the first thing every correspondent needs is sources. And sources of any kind, let alone reliable ones, are thinner on the ground in China than just about anywhere else in the world. Moreover, the few people who are prepared to talk on a regular basis are almost invariably controlled by the establishment.

The remarkable difficulties faced by the Western press have been documented in a survey by the Foreign Correspondents' Club of China. In the first half of 2007 alone the club's members recorded fifty-seven cases of sources being harassed after talking to the foreign press. In seven of these cases the victims suffered physical violence. Moreover foreign correspondents were subjected to violence on three occasions and Chinese staff on four. Some high-profile sources who have defied the authorities have been imprisoned or subjected to house arrest.

As recounted by Jonathan Watts, Beijing correspondent for the *Guardian* of London, there have been increasing problems with thugs acting for local governments and real estate developers. In one of the most notorious cases, Fu Xiancai, a vocal critic of the vast Three Gorges Dam electrification project, was interrogated by the police in 2006 and then, on his way home, set upon by unidentified thugs. He was so badly beaten that he is now paralyzed from the neck down. Fu's "offense" had been to talk to a German television crew. Even when sources are available, correspondents face another problem: how far to credit what they are told. The dilemma has been described by Seth Faison, a former *New York Times* correspondent in China. In an article in *Foreign Affairs* in 1999, he commented:

> The political gossip that seeps from the network of political cognoscenti in Beijing is so scarce that observers must inevitably rely on second-, third-, and fourth-hand accounts. By its very nature, such information is highly unreliable, containing perhaps a sliver of truth wrapped in layers of misinformation and misunderstanding.
>
> Historians, political scientists, and journalists hungry for reliable information about Chinese politics have to rely on official publications, and on the semi-official and non-official accounts that bubble up in Hong Kong. These are the same methods of tracking and analyzing China's political movements that outsiders have used for decades.

Just how marginalized foreign observers are is illustrated by a memorable anecdote in *Tiger on the Brink,* a biography of Jiang Zemin by the Hong Kong–based China watcher Bruce Gilley. Although Gilley spent several years writing the book, he ruefully admitted that the nearest he ever got to Jiang was in the men's room at the Great Hall of the People. Needless to say the moment passed without the awestruck Gilley ever hazarding a greeting, let alone framing a question.

All this would not be so bad if China had a free press, but of course it does not. Not only is the Chinese press entirely government-owned and comprehensively censored, but it glories in functioning as the Beijing regime's propaganda arm. Underlying all this is what is best described as a Confucian concept of journalistic ethics. In common with officials of the Chinese Communist Party, Chinese journalists believe that the public interest is best served by strictly censoring the news. As a commentary published in the *People's Daily* in 1985 put it, "The mass media . . . see themselves as 'the eyes, ears and mouthpieces' of the Communist Party."

The mind-set of the Chinese press also bears significantly on the quality of local support a Western correspondent can hope to enlist. There is, for instance, a clear limit to how useful Chinese research assistants can be. With few if any exceptions, their loyalty is to their own country. In any case, whatever their loyalties, locally recruited research assistants know that unlike their Western bosses, they do not have an "exit strategy." They cannot simply catch the first plane out when things get hot. They will, whether they like it or not, be fated to live in China for the rest of their lives. Given China's past pattern of shifting ideologies and ferocious political inquisitions, any Chinese citizen working in a Western media organization must always keep in mind how his or her present service might be interpreted by the thought police of a future regime.

Certainly Chinese research assistants are likely to be far more aware than their Western bosses of the unhappy fate that awaited some of their predecessors. In the immediate aftermath of the Chinese Communist Party's victory in 1949, for instance, many Chinese citizens who had worked for the foreign press were victimized by the new government. At least one of them, the Associated Press journalist J. C. Lao, was found guilty of counterrevolutionary crimes and executed.

A further problem is that most China correspondents are relative newcomers who do not stay long. Certainly the Orwellian nature of the Chinese state does not encourage people to linger. This is how Elaine Kurtenbach of the Associated Press put it in 1998: "Foreign journalists working in China live with constant government surveillance and the possibility of having homes and offices searched or of being detained while conducting news coverage that would be considered routine elsewhere."

Of course, even in the face of these difficulties, some Western correspondents stay for the long haul. But in their case a different constraint is apparent. They live in constant fear that their visas will not be renewed or at least that what meager sources they have cultivated will dry up. The longer they stay, the more they have at stake. After an interval of perhaps five or ten years, it would be difficult to say the least to pick up the threads back at the home office. (Only the most obvious re-entry problem is that their Rolodex will be out of date.)

The problem was highlighted some years ago by Edward Luttwak: "It is only the rare newspaperman who makes his own prior decision that he will seek no second visa who can be counted on to serve us, and not the Chinese." Although Luttwak's comment was made in 1976 and thus preceded the era of Dengist reform, the threat of expulsion still hangs like a sword of Damocles over every China correspondent.

Expulsion is the standard penalty for any foreigner found guilty of violating China's state-secrets laws. Writing from Hong Kong in 2005, Wang Xiangwei noted that in China anything that has not been reported in the mainland's state media is, in theory at least, a state secret.

As a general rule it is the most accomplished and capable correspondents who have to worry most about expulsion. Precisely because they are more effective, they are more feared by the authorities. It does not help that Beijing's expulsion policy is subject to unpredictable ups and downs. At least four Western correspondents were expelled in the immediate wake of the Tiananmen massacre, for instance. Among them were Alan Pessin, Beijing bureau chief of the Voice of America, and John Pomfret of the Associated Press. Others who have been expelled in recent decades have included five correspondents representing organizations from Hong Kong and Taiwan (in 1996), three BBC journalists (in 1997), and a German correspondent (in 1998). In 2005 an ethnic Chinese journalist from Singapore was arrested on spying charges.

Another important influence on how China is perceived is books. Unfortunately that influence is often highly unhelpful. Many people write books as a sideline to a day job as a consultant, banker, securities analyst, or lawyer. In other fields this might not be a problem, but in Sinology it immediately raises questions of conflict of interest. After all, to be effective in their day jobs in China, such authors need to maintain good relations with the Chinese authorities. As the Hong Kong–based economics scholar Carsten Holz has pointed out, the Chinese Communist Party's grip on analysts at Western investment banks seems particularly tight. Many of the books that result—written by people who to the ordinary American reader seem to boast superb credentials—are subtle or not so subtle exercises in propaganda.

Authors are constrained by the fact that the processes by which books are promoted are hardly politically neutral. Authors who need book tours, for instance, must pander to gatekeepers at the various forums where American China policy is discussed. Virtually without exception such gatekeepers are establishmentarian, and many are conscious agents for transnational corporations (such corporations provide much of the funding for major international-relations forums such as the Council on Foreign Relations in New York). Furthermore, any author who aspires to maximize his income from speaking fees knows that self-censorship is the royal road to success in China watching.

While it is rarely possible to prove that such factors have influenced any particular author, there is no question that in the aggregate they make a difference—and a large one. By default the field becomes silted up with authors with a weak commitment to the Western truth ethic.

Thus, the evidence is that though the press has generally done better than the scholarly community over the years, it has nonetheless failed the American public at crucial points. In particular it played the role of "the dog that did not bark" at the time of China's negotiations to join the World Trade Organization. The general tone of press coverage was supportive of China's bid. At a time when the American reading public needed the facts, these were generally swept under the carpet.

Most foreign correspondents in Beijing were guilty merely of sins of omission—they simply did not write the story. But at home top editors went further, in that their management of editorial-page commentaries strongly favored China's bid. Worse, many of the editorial-page contributions were written by lobbyists or others with a strong vested interest. Not only were such contributors highly selective in presenting the facts, but not infrequently they were seriously inaccurate.

Take, for instance, an opinion article by the New York–based banker Stephen Robert published by the *New York Times* on April 24, 1994. This seems to have been the first commentary in the *Times* to advocate the then unpopular view that the United States should "delink" its trade and human rights policies. Robert's only qualification to adjudicate seems to have been that he had visited Beijing some weeks previously. In painting a picture of a China fast converging to Western values, he made much of the supposed fact that Beijing had permitted ordinary Chinese television viewers to use satellite dishes and therefore to access uncensored television news from beyond China's boundaries.

He wrote: "At one reception I asked a provincial official how he had become so well informed about what is happening in Europe and the United States. 'I watch CNN, the same as you,' he explained. Some 100 million Chinese, many there say, now have access to TV programs transmitted by satellite. 'Ten years ago,' the official added, 'I could have been arrested for owning a satellite dish.'"

Robert added: "The vast middle class now forming in China almost assures the triumph of democracy and its freedoms. . . . Capitalism is nothing more than democracy of the marketplace—the right of people to make their own decisions about economic matters. Once a free market system is established it is but a short step to political democracy."

Encouraging stuff. Unfortunately, the article's entire premise was wrong: satellite dishes had not been legalized. In fact, they remain banned to this day. Authorized users are limited to a few special institutions such as government departments and foreigners' hotels. Unauthorized use is punishable with a fine of up to $6,000—a fortune in a nation where the per capita gross domestic product at market exchange rates as of 2006 was still less than $2,000 a year.

It should be added that the only Chinese-language programs available by satellite are little more informative than those pumped out by China's state-owned broadcasters. The point is that most of the external Chinese-language broadcasters are Hong Kong–based companies that explicitly comply with Beijing's censorship agenda (a prime example is a subsidiary of Rupert Murdoch's News Corporation).

A couple of observations are in order on the Stephen Robert article. First, it seems clear that the *Times*'s top editors did not get the article reality-checked by any of the paper's China correspondents. Indeed, it seems that such correspondents have never had any influence over the *Times*'s opinion articles. Moreover, even after the fact, none of the *Times*'s correspondents seems to have asked for a correction.

A further addendum is in order. When in March 2007 I first became aware of Robert's article (via a footnote in a book I read), I tried to find it in the Nexis news clipping database. It was not there. It had either been deleted or had never been loaded in the first place. In the end I had to dig out the hard-copy version at a major library. All this brings to mind Jasper Becker's observation that not only do China's present and future keep changing, but so does its past. Although we cannot be sure what happened to the Robert article, there is a pattern in China watching for commentaries whose propagandistic nature subsequently becomes embarrassingly obvious to disappear down the memory hole.

Much more could be added, but already it should be clear that the American nation has not been well served by the American press's China coverage. But then, as Senator Byron Dorgan of Nebraska has pointed out, no newspaper editor has ever lost his job to outsourcing. Nor for that matter has any Pulitzer Prize–winning columnist. It is time to consider one of the most influential sources of misinformation on China: the *New York Times*'s chief foreign affairs columnist, Thomas Friedman.

Tom Thumb and the Taming of the Dragon

Few Americans have done more to further China's economic and political agenda in recent years than Thomas L. Friedman, renowned columnist and nonstop globalist. Although he has backed away from an earlier, wildly utopian optimism about Sino-American relations, he remains probably the American media's single most insistent advocate of a "Don't worry, be happy" approach to the dragon.

His key message is his fanatical support for the convergence theory: China, he argues, is more or less inevitably going to Americanize itself and cannot become a great power otherwise.

China's Americanization will be driven by an ever more emboldened Chinese press, which by challenging the Chinese Communist Party will open the door to greater freedom and eventually democracy. In his 1999 book *The Lexus and the Olive Tree,* he comments: "China is going to have a free press. . . . Oh, China's leaders don't know it yet but they are being pushed straight in that direction."

A historic insight—assuming, that is, that Friedman is better informed than China's leaders. Unfortunately, Friedman's knowledge of the Confucian world is limited entirely to what he has gleaned on short trips (and his sources, as far as can be seen, are drawn exclusively from the "usual suspects"—establishment surrogates, albeit often well-disguised ones, who specialize in misleading American observers). Anyway, he has a record of wrong calls even on more familiar ground. A graduate in Mediterranean studies from Brandeis University, he badly blindsided the American public on, for instance, the benefits of going to war in Iraq. He was also famously proved wrong by the war in the former Yugoslavia, a war his once vaunted "McDonald's Theory of Warfare" implied would never happen.

Friedman's pattern is that the more controversial or implausible his conclusion, the less substantiation he feels is needed. Although he provides detailed documentation for some of his points, these are typically uncontroversial ones (such as the fact that cheap communications have fostered a foreign outsourcing rush by American corporations). Furthermore, his more valid insights tend to be ones that sharper observers reached years earlier. Thus the main theme of his 2005 book *The World Is Flat* was anticipated by Frances Cairncross in *The Death of Distance* in 1997 (and indeed also by me in less extensive form in *Blindside* in 1995).

As for the idea that the Chinese press is going to become increasingly free, he devotes less than 2 of *The World Is Flat*'s 378 pages to an attempt to substantiate this point. His logic is that as China's financial markets develop, investors will clamor for more financial information. The Beijing government will—for some reason—feel compelled to oblige and in so doing will open up a Pandora's box of problems for itself. Friedman explains: "Once the Chinese government tells the press they are free to write about business, newspapers [will] use that opening to cram in all sorts of quasi-political abuses by officials on the business pages. That is how a free press will get born in China."

Implicit in this is the view that in the absence of more financial information, China's financial system would more or less grind to a halt. This reckons without the real world. The fact is that all along, financial disclosure has been farcically skimpy in China. This indeed reflects a pattern throughout the Confucian region—yet there has been no discernible negative impact in slowing the region's overall performance (certainly where trade is concerned). The larger point—on which Friedman is evidently completely in the dark—is that the entire Chinese financial system is so different from the West's that outside shareholders are almost totally irrelevant, and certainly they have no influence over how companies are run. Almost without exception, key financial decisions are made by corporate executives in negotiation with government bureaucrats and bankers. By contrast, outside investors are treated like proverbial mushrooms.

Even if we concede Friedman's point that Chinese newspaper editors will be permitted more space for business news, it hardly follows that this will pull the rug from under the established order. After all, as we will see in detail in chapter 5, top leaders have formidable ways of maintaining control. As a practical matter, self-censorship is the order of the day among journalists in China, as it is throughout the Confucian world. Short of the government authorities' explicitly permitting more openness, there won't be any. The kindest thing to say about Friedman's position is that it assumes what is to be proved.

Friedman's fact-free account of China is typical of his general approach: if the facts do not accord with his theories, he believes the theories and discards the facts. Certainly this is what he implied at a public meeting in the American industrial heartland some years ago. Asked by a hostile questioner whether there was any free trade agreement he would oppose, Friedman responded: "No, absolutely not. . . . You know what, sir? I wrote a column supporting the CAFTA, the Caribbean Free Trade initiative. I didn't even know what was in it. I just knew two words: 'free trade.'"

This statement is remarkable first for the fact that he misstated what the CAFTA agreement was about. The region was not the Caribbean but rather

Central America—the agreement's full title was the Central American Free Trade Agreement. The episode drew a ripe riposte from David Sirota at the Huffington Post Web site: "Tom Friedman, the person who the media most relies on to interpret trade policy, now publicly runs around admitting he actually knows nothing at all about the trade pacts he pushes."

As Sirota said, so-called free trade agreements are not subject to truth-in-labeling laws. The devil is in the details, and such agreements all too often set the United States up for "one-way free trade." In other words, while the foreign side's exporters secure full access to the American market (guaranteed under American law), such agreements rarely provide similarly copper-bottomed assurances of reciprocal treatment for American exporters. In addition, as the CAFTA case demonstrated, such agreements generally come up short on a host of key issues such as human rights, environmental protection, and labor safeguards.

For our purposes the most important aspect of Friedman's work is its advocacy of an "India strategy" for the United States. His message is that Americans should emulate India's success in software. Indeed he has publicly credited the Indian software tycoon Nandan Nilekani as the inspiration for *The World Is Flat.* As I pointed out in 1999 in *In Praise of Hard Industries,* however, precisely because software works for a low-wage nation like India, it cannot provide continuing high-wage jobs for Americans. A high-wage economy needs to concentrate on capital-intensive, not labor-intensive, industries, and software these days is one of the world's most labor-intensive industries. The salience of capital intensity as the fundamental support of the advanced world's prosperity is mentioned nowhere in Friedman's books and is evidently lost on him.

Elsewhere Friedman's analysis is overtly self-contradictory. In *The World Is Flat,* for instance, he suffers no embarrassment in suggesting that authoritarianism has worked for China. "No doubt China is benefiting to some degree from the fact that it has an authoritarian system that can steamroll vested interests and archaic practices," he writes. "Beijing's leadership can order many reforms from the top down, whether it is a new road or accession to the World Trade Organization."

In this observation he is undoubtedly correct, but how does he square it with his constant assurances that a commitment to democracy and openness will enable the United States effortlessly to outperform all comers in the years ahead? And why—more important—does he think top Chinese leaders might initiate any liberalization that might lead to democracy?

Let's be fair to Friedman. He is a relative innocent compared to the many consciously mendacious propagandists who have now colonized the upper reaches of China watching. Although his views are dangerous nonsense, his sincerity in expressing them seems clear. Nonetheless his "rise without trace" to the top ranks of American journalism adds to a sense of despair that intelligent Americans have long felt about the course of intellectual debate in recent years. The point has been well put by former vice president Al Gore: "The persistent and sustained reliance on falsehoods as the basis of policy, even in the face of massive and well-understood evidence to the contrary, seems to many Americans to have reached levels that were previously unimaginable."

Kowtowing to Political Correctness

A key problem for the West in trying to understand China is that political correctness often gets in the way. Scholars and journalists are particularly badly afflicted. Indeed a pattern of extreme political correctness pervades the entire East Asia studies field.

Many Western scholars are evidently consumed with guilt about previous Western contacts with East Asia. Japan in particular seems to evoke such guilt. As the only nation ever to have been subjected to the atomic bomb, it has long received special consideration, particularly from politically correct Westerners. Other East Asian nations seem to have benefited by association, particularly as they share Japan's sense of victimhood about such grievances as nineteenth-century Western gunboat diplomacy and America's so-called Asian Exclusion Act of 1924.

One of the most important effects of political correctness has been to discourage China watchers from seeing Beijing's strategy in the larger regional context. Instead of frankly acknowledging the Chinese system's antecedents in the earlier East Asian miracles, China watchers have tended to view China in isolation. Of course, they have some excuse for doing so. After all, China is ostensibly to this day a communist country and, of course, it remains far poorer than South Korea and Taiwan, let alone Japan. But many scholars have also clearly given way to a weak-minded concern to avoid saying anything that might possibly—however unfairly—be construed by hostile interlocutors as political incorrect. Cognizant of the deplorable way that Yellow Peril rhetoric undermined the world diplomatic order in an earlier era, they have tended to take a better-safe-than-sorry attitude in shrinking from identifying the common policies driving growth throughout East Asia. Unfortunately this has shut the West off from a vast reservoir of institutional memory that could have helped policymakers anticipate China's future progress, particularly in trade matters.

Political correctness seems also to have obscured from Americans the degree to which East Asian nations are actively cooperating with one another. (We will take a close look at Sino-Japanese cooperation in chapter 7.) Thus scholars and journalists who criticize China, for instance, feel compelled to "balance up" by endorsing Japan's disavowals of the same mercantilist policies that China copied in the first place. For the same reason, observers who are critical of Japan often feel obligated to embrace China. It all seems to work a bit like inoculation: to criticize one East Asian nation, you must first inoculate yourself against "Yellow Peril" charges by espousing the propaganda positions of another. It does not seem to occur to anyone that the issue here is not race but philosophy. The Confucian/Legalist principles on which East Asian societies are run are fundamentally incompatible with Western individualism.

Political correctness aside, many interpreters of the Chinese phenomenon suffer from a deeply condescending attitude toward the Chinese people. This may seem to be in tension with their political correctness, but the reverse is the case. It is because they take such a condescending view that they feel obligated to lay on political correctness with a trowel.

Unfortunately their attitude invites industrial-strength deception on the part of their Chinese hosts. Certainly, like an unpopular schoolmaster who has had a "Kick me" sign affixed to his back, many Western observers are seen in China as preachy fools who deserve everything they get. It does not help that many of these China watchers seem deeply self-absorbed and thus are easy marks for the insincere compliments that Chinese handlers heap on anyone who writes the approved version.

Chinese Mercantilism: Worse Than Japan's

A key way in which Beijing's apologists have misled the West is in suggesting that China is less mercantilist than earlier Confucian miracle economies.

Here, for instance, is how the *Washington Post* put it in an editorial in 2004: "Unlike Japan or South Korea, . . . China is modernizing in a much more open way." Meanwhile in the *National Interest* in 2002, the policy analysts George

Gilboy and Eric Heginbotham argued that the Chinese economy was so open that it should be held up as an example to Japan.

In a similar vein, writing from Beijing in 2006, the *Wall Street Journal*'s Andrew Batson suggested that China had never been more open and added: "China's economy is in many ways more open than Japan's was during its rise in the 1980s and India's is today."

Such statements invariably come unaccompanied by any macroeconomic data. For good reason—because the data suggest a diametrically opposite conclusion. After all, China's current account surplus, at $249.9 billion in 2006, represented fully 9.5 percent of its gross domestic product. This was a truly phenomenal performance—indeed, as far as I can tell, the highest ratio of any major economy in history. For the record, Japan's current account surpluses in the 1980s, at an average of 2.9 percent of gross domestic product, represented less than half of China's 2006 performance. The largest percentage surplus Japan ever achieved was 4.0 percent, in 1986. As for India, it has not been running surpluses in recent years but rather *deficits*, not least a deficit in 2006 of 3.3 percent!

Of course, proponents of the "open China" story point out that China's imports are relatively high compared to its gross domestic product. But this does not reflect true openness but merely China's status as a vast export-processing center. Exporters are given special permission to import all sorts of components and materials that China cannot yet make domestically.

The authors Richard Bernstein and Ross Munro have argued that the scale of its overall trade surpluses indicates that China is pursuing one of the most mercantilist trade policies in history. It is by definition a beggar-my-neighbor policy, and few if any nations have suffered more than the United States. Already by the mid-1990s, China exported four times more to the United States than it imported, and in recent years the ratio has often exceeded five to one. Again, the contrast with Japan, which before China came along was of course by far the most notorious bogeyman for American trade policy, is startling. Japan's exports to the United States have almost never totaled more than three times its imports, and the ratio has generally been more like two to one.

In truth, those who argue that China's economy is "open" start out with definitions of openness that, to say the least, are intended to conceal rather than reveal.

Some commentators seem to base their assessment on nothing more than the fact that certain American brand names are now much in evidence in

China. Unfortunately, many American brand names are visible for entirely the wrong reason. China after all leads the world in counterfeiting famous brands, not least such American brands as Levi Strauss, Kate Spade, and New Balance.

It is true that a few American companies do serious business in China. Coca-Cola, KFC, and McDonald's are the examples most often cited. But here again there is less than meets the eye because these companies' Chinese operations import remarkably little from the United States (or anywhere else). Thus for Chinese economic planners anxious to maintain a general policy of mercantilist trade, the cost in lost foreign exchange revenues has been negligible. After all, most of the added value in serving a glass of Coke, for instance, is generated locally using Chinese labor and ingredients. Ditto for a Big Mac or a portion of KFC's BBQ wings. Typically only a thin sliver of profit is remitted back to the United States. Meanwhile the propaganda value is enormous, as many American observers take the presence of such brand names as synonymous with general openness to American exports.

Such token openness has long been a characteristic of the entire East Asian region. It is noteworthy, for instance, that McDonald's set up in Japan as far back as 1971, half a decade before it reached Britain. Meanwhile KFC has been a familiar name in Japan since 1970 and Coca-Cola since the late 1940s. Japan opened its doors to them for the same public relations reasons as China; and reports of their Japanese successes have proved equally effective in lessening the political impact in the United States of wider complaints of mercantilism.

To be fair to the apologists, there is more to the American presence in China than a few famous brand names. Gilboy, a China-based research analyst for the Center for International Studies at the Massachusetts Institute of Technology, has been the most outspoken proponent of the "open China" story, so let's consider his argument in more detail.

Here, for instance, is how he put it in an article in *Foreign Affairs* in 2004: "China cannot maintain its domestic market as a protected bastion for domestic firms, something both Japan and South Korea did during their periods of rapid growth. Instead, it has allowed U.S. and other foreign firms to develop new markets for their goods and services, especially high value-added products such as aircraft, software, industrial design, advanced machinery, and components such as semiconductors and integrated circuits. Thanks to this appetite for imports, powerful domestic coalitions, particularly China's growing ranks of urban consumers and its most competitive firms, will continue to favor trade openness."

What Gilboy is referring to is China's so-called open-door policy (since 1978) of accepting factory investments by top American industrial corporations. While such investments have certainly been welcomed by China, Gilboy glosses over a key point: on balance, they do less than nothing for the long-term health of the American economy. To be sure, to the extent that such investments are successful, they generate profits for American corporations. Unfortunately this benefit is more than offset by the rather serious implications for American labor. The point is that as a condition for investing in China, American corporations are generally expected to transfer their most advanced production technologies to their Chinese factories. As such technologies were previously the cornerstone of American labor's lead in world competition, once they are transferred, American workers are vulnerable to layoffs. This applies in spades when American corporations, in compliance with Beijing's "mercantilism über-alles" trade policy, start supplying the American market from their new Chinese factories.

The cost to the American national interest is not just soaring layoffs in the industrial heartland but ever mounting trade deficits that have left the United States more and more dependent on foreign creditors.

Given how beneficial American corporate investment has proved for China, the only question is why earlier miracle economies such as Japan and South Korea pursued a policy of avoiding such investments. The answer is a poignant reminder of how far the balance of power has shifted in the world order. In the 1960s and 1970s, Japan and South Korea feared—with good reason—that once established on their soil, American business would quickly want to remake the entire local economies on American lines. Specifically American corporations would not—as they meekly do today in China—submit to sourcing many components and materials from local suppliers. Nor would they consent—as they have done in many cases in China—to export essentially all their output. Rather, they would have insisted on the right to sell locally, thus presenting formidable competition to still backward local counterparts. Outraged by economic policies that diverged so sharply from American norms, expatriate American executives would have complained to Washington—and their complaints would have been heard.

In other words, the Japanese and the Koreans reasoned that they would generate less ill will if they eschewed American corporate investment entirely than if they let the American Gulliver in and then sought, Lilliput-style, to shackle him with myriad mercantilist restrictions.

These days, by contrast, there are no similar fears in Beijing. On the contrary, Chinese regulators have found that corporate America has become so fully house-trained in East Asia that it hardly even puts up a token fight against Beijing's mercantilist agenda.

According to the Washington-based China watcher James Mann, some American corporations have gone even further by consenting to pay several times the local going rate for Chinese labor—with the difference being pocketed by Chinese joint-venture partners. Many such partners go on to become direct competitors, usually after stripping their American partners of crucial production technologies.

Gordon Fairclough of the *Wall Street Journal* suggested in 2007 that this has happened even to General Motors. Shanghai Automotive Industry Corporation, GM's partner in making Buicks in China for a decade, went on to develop and make its own models using know-how and capital it had acquired from selling joint-venture cars.

Perhaps the most telling sign of how cowed America business has become is that, as we will see in chapter 6, American corporations rarely complain to Washington when they encounter problems with Chinese regulations or practices. *The reason is that they fear retaliation by Chinese officials.*

It hardly needs to be said that this contrasts stunningly with how things used to be. In the old days, of course, American executives were infinitely more concerned about how their actions were viewed in Washington than in Beijing. To say the least, nobody in those days pushed Uncle Sam around.

Had American corporations in Japan in the 1950s been subjected to the sort of regulatory treatment that they so meekly accept today in China, there would have been hell to pay.

In the early decades of the East Asian miracle, American corporations automatically operated abroad in ways that tended on balance to further the American national interest. China's openness to American investment bespeaks not China's acceptance of American values but the complete reverse. By disavowing their roots in the United States and doing business the Chinese way, American corporations have become an important instrument of Chinese mercantilism. There is a difference between Chinese mercantilism and earlier East Asian versions: the Chinese variant is even stronger and, from the viewpoint of the American national interest, even more damaging.

The Truth About Laissez-Faire

As we have noted, thanks to their faith in American economic dogma, many American policymakers have been lulled into a false sense of security about recent economic trends. They have been assured that America's trade deficits will automatically prove self-correcting, if only policymakers would leave everything to free markets. Equally, they have been persuaded that Beijing's current highly interventionist economic strategy will prove self-defeating. Chastened Chinese leaders, it is argued, will embrace laissez-faire quickly enough once they discover the error of their ways.

The assurances about American trade deficits can be disposed of in a few sentences. The idea that the deficits will prove self-correcting has been a standard shibboleth of Washington discourse since the 1970s. While reasonable people might have been persuaded to give this view the benefit of the doubt thirty years ago, they can hardly be expected to continue to do so today.

Of course, in recent years many defenders of the Washington view have shifted ground to argue that even if the deficits do not prove self-correcting, we need not worry. The deficits-don't-matter view has been prominently championed by Vice President Dick Cheney as well as by many other influential neoconservative thinkers. (In Ron Suskind's *The Price of Loyalty* [2004], former U.S. Treasury Secretary Paul O'Neill quotes Cheney saying at a cabinet meeting in 2002, "Reagan proved deficits don't matter.") Yet those who argue that deficits don't matter no longer have a leg to stand on. The reality is that every dollar America spends in projecting power abroad—indeed every dollar it spends on defense—has to be borrowed abroad. Not only that, much of the money comes from its main power rival, China. To say the least, America's attempts to pursue an independent foreign policy will be subject increasingly to a veto in Beijing. In any case, it is the sheerest of wishful thinking to imagine that the United States can long remain a world power if all it has to sell to the world, besides wheat and oranges, is treasury bonds.

More generally, it should be noted that laissez-faire has proved a disappointment almost everywhere it has been tried. The fact is that in the last four decades those advanced nations that have been most faithful to laissez-faire—the United States and Britain—have been notable for economic mediocrity, if not downright dysfunction. Their currencies have on balance fallen precipitately, their trade positions have spun out of control, and they have lost the advanced manufacturing industries that provided a bedrock of well-paid secure jobs to support broad-based prosperity.

The problems with Western economic dogma have long been particularly clear in the automobile industry. The nations that have believed in open markets have largely lost their car industries; the United States and Britain are the two obvious examples.

On the other hand those nations that have most avidly protected their car markets have seen their car industries boom. The principal examples are Japan, which has boosted its world market share four-fold since 1970, and South Korea, which has achieved a phenomenal twenty-fold increase. It is worth noting that, as of 2007, South Korea was described by DaimlerChrysler as "the most closed market in the industrialized world."

All the empirical evidence suggests that a laissez-faire-faire approach to trade no longer works, at least not for large nations like the United States and Britain, not to mention Japan and South Korea. (Full disclosure: open markets have worked a lot better in leveling up small, previously poor economies like Ireland and Finland—but that is another matter.)

After decades of denying any problems, American economic scholars are now finally beginning to ask what is wrong with laissez-faire. Thus, the Nobel Prize–winning economist Paul Samuelson has made some "heretical" public comments questioning the standard case for free trade. Meanwhile, in their book *Global Trade and Conflicting National Interests* (2000), Ralph Gomory and William Baumol have shown—with the sort of rigorous mathematical modeling that doctrinaire economists insist on—that in certain circumstances outsourcing can be a net negative.

Among other top economic thinkers who have recently publicly questioned the orthodoxy are Alan Blinder, a Princeton professor and former vice-chairman of the Federal Reserve; Lawrence Summers, a Harvard professor who served as Treasury Secretary in the Clinton administration; and the Berkeley-based Nobel Prize winner George Akerlof.

The basic problem is that laissez-faire is an old dogma born in the very different economic conditions of Europe two centuries ago. Although the theory's early enunciators, Adam Smith and David Ricardo, stated their case as timelessly applicable, and this is how it continues to be interpreted today (at least in the English-speaking world), they failed to anticipate the dramatic economic changes we have seen in the last fifty years.

A fundamental flaw in the Smith-Ricardo model is that it is static, whereas the real world is dynamic. The model concerns itself merely with the allocation of resources *at just one moment in time*. It considers the capital and labor available to society at that moment and predicts that these resources are likely to serve most efficiently in satisfying consumers' needs if all economic actors—investors, managers, workers, and consumers—are allowed full freedom to maximize their individual positions.

While this theory was helpful in times gone by (and it is still useful in analyzing countless narrowly focused economic problems today), it has become more and more misleading as a guide to the workings of today's highly complex modern global economy. A key point never considered by Smith and Ricardo is that, as we have already pointed out, a nation like China can use authoritarian controls to achieve a preternaturally high savings rate. Suitably channeled into fast-growth industries, the resulting capital can power a fast rate of growth in real wages. Thus the promise to consumers is that their involuntary early sacrifices will result in a much more prosperous old age. It is a promise that has been honored in one East Asian nation after another.

Part of the reason the strategy works is that poor nations start with many easy opportunities for "technology catch-up." That is, by investing in standard production technologies already widely used in richer countries, they can generate massive increases in productivity. Such investment therefore is the nearest thing in economics to a racing certainty. But here is the crucial point: because the lion's share of the returns accrues to workers (in the form of rapidly rising wages) rather than to corporate shareholders, the incentive for conventionally profit-seeking Western corporations to invest in the necessary productivity-enhancing machinery is weak. This constitutes a case of what economists call "market failure," and all American dogma to the contrary notwithstanding, it provides an opportunity for government intervention to improve on laissez-faire outcomes.

Laissez-faire theory is crucially flawed in a different sense in that it makes no allowance for the possibility that nations can manipulate technological progress to benefit themselves at the expense of others. Laissez-faire theory is based on an assumption that breakthroughs in production technology, if they occur at all, will accrue to all producers equally. Although this assumption was broadly realistic two centuries ago (when most of the know-how to compete at the leading edge either was already in the public domain or could readily be acquired by dint of rudimentary industrial espionage), it is completely mistaken today. After all, leading-edge corporations these days spend ever larger sums each year to achieve proprietary improvements in their production technologies and thus establish a decisive lead over their competitors.

For a nation like China that wants to boost its technological position at the expense of its rivals, the course is obvious:

1. **Extort technologies from rival nations.** In this regard Beijing's control of access to the Chinese market is a huge bargaining chip: foreign corporations are simply told that if they want a fair shot at the Chinese market they must transfer more and more technology to China. Key American corporations such as Intel, Microsoft, and General Motors have meekly complied. One of the more spectacular beneficiaries of this strategy has been China's fast-rising aerospace industry. By adroit bargaining, Beijing has pressured both Boeing and Airbus to transfer key production technologies. Thanks in large measure to such transfers, Beijing is planning to launch a full-size commercial airliner by 2020.

2. **Fund research and development.** This strategy has played little part so far in China's rise, but it will become increasingly important as Chinese industry becomes more technologically advanced. Here again Japan has set an important example. Thanks to considerable help from their national government, Japanese corporations spend nearly $100 billion a year on research and development. Most such research is devoted to improving production processes with the aim of making Japanese factories ever more competitive.

3. **Prevent Chinese industry's key technologies from leaking abroad.** For now Chinese industry does not have many technologies to guard, but this strategy will become increasingly relevant in future years. What is clear is that the governments of the more advanced nations of East Asia have long carefully guarded their key technologies from leaking abroad. Japan and South Korea have been the two prime examples.

As China climbs the technology ladder the impact on other nations' economies will become ever greater. This is because at the leading edge of technological progress, global competition is increasingly characterized by a winner-take-all syndrome. A nation that achieves a narrow competitive edge in making, for example, a new type of advanced microchip can at a stroke wipe out its competitors worldwide. The rewards therefore will increasingly accrue to nations like China that take a highly focused national approach to technological competition.

Part of the problem, argues the Washington-based trade expert Patrick Mulloy, is that the interests of American corporations are increasingly at odds with those of the American nation. In a personal addendum to the 2006 report of the United States–China Economic and Security Review Commission, Mulloy, who served as a top Commerce Department official in the Clinton administration, commented:

> The interests of the U.S.-based multinational corporations, which have done so much to influence our current policies toward China, are often not aligned with the broader interests of our nation. This is not because they have malevolent intent. It is a systemic problem for which we must develop a public policy response. These corporations, as they are charged to do in our economic system, are focused on "shareholder value."
>
> They are not charged to consider the larger impact of their decisions on the American economy and workers, and the impetus they give to China's growing international, political, and military strength.

While we do not have space for a full discussion of the problems with laissez-faire in modern conditions, let's simply note that economic planning chiefs in Beijing do not necessarily "shoot themselves in the foot" when they assume a strongly assertive role in steering China's economic development. While laissez-faire advocates are right in arguing that government intervention has often proved counterproductive in, for instance, Latin America, the lesson of East Asia is that, in the hands of intelligent, patriotic, and well-organized officials, government intervention has proved on balance a strongly positive force. As we will now see, few instances of market intervention have been more rationally based than the strongly promanufacturing bias of Chinese industrial policy.

In China, Too, Manufacturing Matters

As we have noted, heavy investment in manufacturing is a central feature of the Beijing regime's economic strategy. For many in the West, and particularly in the United States, this is an easy policy to underestimate. For a start, of course, it offends against the conventional wisdom that attempts by governments to shape economic outcomes are generally counterproductive. In any case, manufacturing is widely seen in the West as an inherently unpromising sector for an advanced nation to invest in. In the view of American economic commentators and Washington think-tank analysts in particular, manufacturing is supposedly fast becoming a "commodity business" suitable only for low-wage nations with large reserves of unskilled labor. By contrast, for an advanced nation like the United States, wage rates and growth prospects are supposedly far more promising in advanced services such as finance, Internet development, and computer software.

Chinese policymakers are of course fully aware of such "postindustrial" arguments—and reject them out of hand. Like their counterparts in richer manufacturing-based nations such as Germany, Switzerland, Japan, and South Korea, they know that those in the United States who argue the merits of postindustrialism—let's call them postindustrialists—simply do not know what modern manufacturing is.

The postindustrialists set up a straw man by implying that state-of-the-art manufacturing these days consists merely of assembly plants churning out consumer products using "commodity" components. There is no question that *final assembly* tends to be highly labor-intensive and therefore is not very sophisticated or economically significant. But the manufacture of the *components* used in such assembly is often an extremely sophisticated challenge that only a few of the world's most advanced nations can address. Moreover, the manufacture of the often highly purified *materials* used to make such components is generally even more sophisticated.

While much manufacturing in China today consists merely of final assembly, the Chinese have no intention of staying in assembly forever. On the contrary, they look forward to the day when they will make the advanced components and materials without which China's assembly plants would grind to a halt. At the moment, most of these inputs are imported from abroad, mainly from ultra-high-wage Japan.

To get to the bottom of America's failure to grasp the paramount importance of advanced manufacturing, it is useful to be aware that economic discourse is notoriously prey to fallacies, particularly so-called fallacies of composition. A fallacy of composition arises when an erroneous conclusion is drawn about a whole from an examination of its parts. To cite a simple example, it is a fallacy to believe that because both sodium and chlorine are toxic, all combinations of the two are equally toxic. One such compound, of course, is salt, which in moderation not only is *not* toxic but is essential to life. A more relevant fallacy concerns spectators watching a sports event: although any one spectator can get a better view by standing up, it is wrong to conclude that all spectators will improve their view if they all stand up.

The postindustrialists are confused by not one but multiple fallacies of composition. The most obvious concerns wages. As the postindustrialists point out, an individual can probably earn more as, say, a software engineer at Microsoft than as a factory hand at General Motors. But they are utterly wrong in believing that an attempt by a nation's entire workforce to move into software or similarly well-paid postindustrial activities will result in a general improvement in wage levels. For a start, there is the problem that only a small proportion of workers have the necessary capabilities to do serious software work. Moreover—and this is crucial though less obvious—the postindustrialists commit a fundamental error in implying that high postindustrial wages reflect something uniquely productive about postindustrial work. In reality, the reason wages are generally high in postindustrial businesses is merely because most of that work demands exceptional intelligence. In other words, postindustrial businesses employ disproportionately talented people who could expect good pay in any field (not least in manufacturing, where they could aspire to top jobs in engineering, research, marketing, or general management).

In my book *In Praise of Hard Industries* (1999), I exposed the fallacies of America's then passionate affair with the New Economy and went on to show that manufacturing was a far better bet for a farsighted nation. Although we do not have space here for the full argument, the case for manufacturing can be summed up in three points:

1. **A better job mix.** Manufacturing generally creates a broad range of jobs that closely match a nation's job-creation needs. Although it creates plenty of jobs for highly capable people, it provides many more jobs for people of ordinary ability (who, of course, constitute a healthy majority in any nation's population). It thus offers a nation the chance to make full use of everyone's capabilities, not just those of a talented minority.

2. **Higher productivity.** In the more advanced areas of modern manufacturing, workers can often be massively more productive than in services. This is because modern advanced manufacturing tends to be

highly capital-intensive, meaning that each worker's output is leveraged by a large amount of sophisticated manufacturing equipment. The capital intensity in modern manufacturing can be truly stunning—in advanced factories each worker may be backed by as much as $500,000 worth of equipment or even more. The more sophisticated the machinery, the greater each worker's output is likely to be. Productivity is further enhanced by advanced production know-how, often in the form of secret processes that can be withheld from competitors for decades to come. (By contrast, most services, not least postindustrial services, are highly labor-intensive and typically do not involve much secret production know-how. Other things being equal, therefore, they are more appropriately carried out in poor countries where capital is scarce and wages are low. Indeed, as I predicted as far back as 1995, such services are now rapidly migrating to low-wage nations like India and Russia.)

3. **Increased exports.** In *In Praise of Hard Industries* I calculated that, per unit of output, American manufacturers export on average more than ten times as much as American service businesses. Advanced manufacturing industries are particularly big exporters.

So much for the case for a nation to hone its manufacturing prowess. Now let's see how a fully mature manufacturing-based economy works. It is time to take a look at the economy that China would like to be—Japan's.

Sisyphus Revisited: Japan's "Lost Decade"

Optimists about America's China strategy like to recall Washington's Japan-ophobia phase of the late 1980s. They argue that just as fears then about "juggernaut Japan" were quickly dispelled, so too will fears today about the "unstoppable dragon." This is how the Hoover Institution economist Russell Roberts has put it: "The next time you find yourself losing sleep over China, remember that you were worried about Japan and . . . everything turned out OK."

In an editorial-page article in the *Wall Street Journal* in 2007, he explained: "Remember when Japan was a big threat to the American economy? You have to go back to the late 1980s. Back then, every politician in the mood for pandering to economic ignorance could scare a bunch of folks with worries about how the

Japanese were stealing our jobs. How our trade deficit with Japan was going to destroy the American economy . . . But then the Japanese economy hiccupped and played Rip Van Winkle for a decade, while America kept growing."

The Columbia-based economist Jagdish Bhagwati has put it even more pointedly. Commenting in 2007 on the rise of the Chinese economy, he argued that American concerns about the Japanese economy in the 1980s "appear astonishing now." Writing in the *New York Times,* he added: "For well over a decade Japan has been deeply mired in macroeconomic failure, its feared dominance has been dissolved into dreary ordinariness."

Comments like these sound like a convincing case for complacency. In reality, however, although a lot of people want you to believe otherwise, the idea that a suddenly "resurgent" United States turned the tables on Japan in the 1990s is nonsense.

In promoting grossly exaggerated accounts of Japanese economic difficulties, American observers lost sight of the one thing that mattered: trade. This, of course, had long been the key issue in U.S.-Japanese economic competition, and it was after all the reason why Japanese economic policies had become an issue in Washington in the first place. Japan's trade surpluses had soared in the 1980s while the U.S. incurred worsening deficits. By the late 1980s Americans had correctly come to see that aggressively expansionist Japanese exporters were eating corporate America's lunch. Add in the fact that the Japanese market was perceived—again correctly—to be closed, at least as far as key American exports were concerned, and it was understandable that by 1989 an "all-conquering" Japan was being widely blamed for America's deindustrialization.

Before considering the stunning truth about Japan's trade performance in the 1990s, I ought to declare an interest. I have been writing about the Japanese economy since the late 1980s, when I was alone among Tokyo-based financial observers in publicly predicting Japan's financial implosion (which I did in three articles in *Euromoney* magazine). I went on in 1995 to publish *Blindside,* a book that argued that Japan would come out of the crash stronger than ever. The book's subtitle was *Why Japan Is Still on Track to Overtake the U.S. by the Year 2000.* That was wrong, but not in the way you might think. My error was not in misreading Japan but rather in misreading the United States—or, more precisely, Washington. Aware that America's continuing vast trade deficits bespoke disastrous manufacturing competitiveness problems, I was convinced that the dollar would have to undergo another massive devaluation, similar to the 50 percent devaluation instigated by the Reagan administration in 1985–1987. Had such a devaluation been implemented, American industry would have been positioned to make a real comeback—and, with American economic output suddenly valued at a much lower exchange rate, Japan would have, at least temporarily, drawn ahead. Thus the subtitle of my book would have been fulfilled!

The subtitle aside, virtually every other aspect of the *Blindside* analysis has been unquestionably vindicated. Thus, far from going into "reverse" (to use Jagdish Bhagwati's term), Japan's export economy continued triumphantly to surge ahead in the 1990s. It did so, moreover, even though exporters elsewhere in East Asia were hardly standing still. Quite the contrary: the South Koreans, the Taiwanese, the Singaporeans, and, of course, the Chinese were aggressively increasing their share of world markets (which they did at the expense of the United States and Europe, not Japan).

Thanks to a strong performance in boosting both quality and productivity, Japan stayed well ahead of the competition, boosting its exports by 73 percent in dollar terms in the decade. Thus by 1999 the Japanese current account surplus had hit $107 billion, representing a gain of nearly 90 percent over 1989. And as of 2006 it had reached $174 billion, or fully three times the 1989 figure that Washington had once considered so unacceptably high.

As for the United States, its trade went from the merely disastrous to the totally catastrophic. Although its exports *seemed* to rise strongly, this was only because it had resorted more and more to assembly and distribution activities that depended on ever greater imports of components and indeed entire products. By 2006, fueled by soaring imports, the American current account deficit had hit $862 billion, a world record for any nation and *more than eight times* the deficit in 1989!

Why has Japan's trade performance been so remarkably different from America's? One key issue has been investment: all through the 1990s and into the new century, Japanese industry quietly invested ever more heavily in productivity-enhancing new manufacturing technologies. One result has been that, as recorded by the Central Intelligence Agency, Japan, with just 2 percent of the world's population, was at last count home to fully 57 percent of all the world's industrial robots.

As I recounted as one of my main themes in 1995, Japan's performance was also powered by a policy of establishing monopolistic positions—"chokepoints" in the jargon—in more and more advanced manufacturing fields, particularly in producers' goods such as materials, components, and machine tools.

Perhaps Japan's single most surprising—and significant—success has been aerospace. After decades of quietly capturing key chokepoints in avionics, carbon fiber, titanium, and advanced ceramics, Japan has now passed a fast-declining United States in all but name to become the world's premier aerospace power. Not only Boeing and Airbus, but also jet engine makers like Pratt & Whitney, Rolls-Royce, and GE depend on Japanese suppliers for their most advanced components and materials.

One indicator is that Japanese contractors are building 35 percent of the new superadvanced Boeing 787, up from a mere 21 percent share of the Boeing 777. These are Boeing's own published figures, and they probably greatly understate the true Japanese contribution (because Boeing counts only what it buys direct from Japan, thus leaving out of account Japanese-made inputs supplied to Boeing's American contractors). Although Boeing maintains that broadly as much of the new plane will be made in the United States as in Japan, in the view of David J. Pritchard, coauthor of a major study on the hollowing-out of Boeing, the 787 will be more a Japanese plane than an American one. What is officially known is that the only part of the plane Boeing will fabricate itself is the vertical tail fin. For the rest it will snap together large sections made by contractors in the United States, Japan, and elsewhere.

Let's now consider some of those 1990s reports about how the United States had supposedly "turned the tables" on Japan.

Take, for instance, the television set industry. It seems hard to credit now but in the early 1990s it was widely reported that a resurgent America had made a brilliant comeback in the industry. Supposedly the Japanese had been outmaneuvered by such American corporations as Zenith and General Instrument in developing high-definition television (HDTV). Although the Japanese had spent two decades developing a so-called analog version of HDTV, the Americans had come from nowhere with a much more advanced digital version. The *Nikkei Weekly,* the main Tokyo-based English-language business newspaper, hailed the "rebirth" of the American consumer electronics industry. The *Economist* talked of a "startling triumph." *Newsday* headlined its report, "Build 'Em Here; U.S. Has High Definition Lead." Even the *New York Times* joined in the inanity, suggesting that Japan's technology development system had proved a "liability." Not to be outdone, *Business Week* talked of a Japanese "fiasco." In reality Zenith and General Instrument were never heard from again. All they had done was help American regulators define a new broadcast standard. Contrary to all the press hype, this did not give them any inside track in manufacturing products to the new standard. The advantage remained with the Japanese who had merely to make minor changes to their home version of high-definition television to serve the American market. Long skilled in fashioning their products to meet countless standards around the world, they quickly made the necessary adjustments. The result today is that they continue utterly to dominate not only the American HDTV market but every other HDTV market around the world. Even non-Japanese makers like Philips and Samsung depend on Japan for advanced components and materials. Thus although a few American patent-holders receive a trickle of royalties from Japanese HDTV makers, most of the most valuable manufacturing jobs have been captured by Japan.

Another widely publicized "turning the tables" story was supposedly in semiconductors. True enough, such American corporations as Intel and AMD consistently increased the speed of their microprocessors during the decade. But, overlooked by American commentators, the Japanese were hardly resting on their laurels. Far from it. The Japanese continued to dominate most other advanced areas of the semiconductor industry. In any case, the Americans depended crucially on the Japanese for highly sophisticated inputs that the United States no longer made. Just the most obvious of the Japanese chokepoints is semiconductor-grade silicon, which has to be refined to ever more fantastically pure levels for each new generation of chip. For more than fifteen years Japanese corporations such as Shin-Etsu and SUMCO have completely monopolized the purest semiconductor grades.

Besides, the idea—widely publicized in the United States in the 1990s— that the Americans had recovered the lead in microprocessor speed was nonsense. The Americans led merely in *personal computer* microprocessors, whereas the Japanese led in games-machine microprocessors. These latter are far more advanced—and more difficult to make. (While Japan's leadership in the games category may seem underwhelming to the non-technical, the skills the Japanese have acquired position them to dominate the market in all sorts of superfast chips used in missiles and other defense systems.)

A host of other examples could be cited. Take the car industry. In 1994 two Pulitzer Prize–winning business journalists, Paul Ingrassia and Joseph White, published *Comeback: The Fall and Rise of the American Automobile Industry*. Describing Japanese carmakers as in "retreat," they presented Chrysler as "the envy of the auto industry around the world." All in all the Americans were now "formidable global competitors."

Such wishful thinking was soon to be dispelled and by 2007, Japan, with half of America's population, had passed the United States in total car production.

Toyota boosted its sales revenues by 61 percent in the 1990s, whereas General Motors managed an increase of only 34 percent. Toyota continued to charge ahead in the new century, with the result that by 2007 it had passed General Motors to become the world's largest automaker. Back in Japan's "juggernaut" days of 1989, by contrast, its sales were a mere 45 percent of General Motors'.

By now it should be sufficiently clear that, at least where direct U.S.-Japanese economic rivalry was concerned, the "Japan hits the wall" notion was farcically at odds with reality. Let's now consider Japan's domestic economy. Although we do not have space for an extensive discussion, here are a few indicators of how well the Japanese did in advancing their living standards in the "lost decade":

Car-navigation systems. Launched in the latter half of the 1990s, these supersmart gadgets (which pinpoint a car's position, suggest routes, and provide alerts on traffic jams) caught on far faster in Japan than anywhere else. By 2000, Japanese drivers accounted for more than half of all such devices in use anywhere in the world.

The Internet. Recovering from a hesitant start, Japan raced ahead of the United States in the speed of its Internet connections in the latter half of the 1990s. Japan now leads the world in so-called FTTH (fiber to the home)—a reflection in part of the fact that Japanese companies dominate the manufacture of optical fibers.

Mobile phones. Japan made a slow start in this category also, but by the late 1990s it had jumped two product generations ahead of the United States (with cameras already standard features). By 2003 nearly 29 percent of the Japanese population enjoyed Internet service on their mobile phones. From the start, incidentally, Japan has dominated the manufacture of the enabling components in mobile phones. A survey by Deutsche Bank found that as of 2000, twenty-nine of the world's thirty-six suppliers of the nine key components in mobile phones were Japanese.

Health care. Between 1990 and 2005, Japan's universal health-care system cut infant mortality by more than one-quarter, to just 3.28 per 1,000 live births—roughly half the American rate. Despite a marked increase in the Japanese people's consumption of Western-style fatty foods, they now live about four years longer on average than Americans (and almost a decade longer than the Chinese).

As should be clear from testimony like this, there was no "lost decade." Yes, the Tokyo stock market crashed. So did the real estate market. And the consequences for the Japanese banking system were painful. But the problems were kept well contained within the financial system. It is a fact, for instance, that not a single bank customer was inconvenienced (because not a single bank shut its doors, let alone reneged on its obligations). And most areas of the nonfinancial economy did fine.

Why did the American press correspondents get the story so wrong? The truth is they were encouraged by their Tokyo sources to exaggerate Japan's problems. This reflected a hidden agenda by the Japanese establishment, which had noticed that reports of the Tokyo stock market crash had greatly softened anti-Japanese sentiment in the United States. With their unerring eye for the main chance, Japanese officials began emphasizing Japan's economic negatives while hiding the positives. Not the least of their tactics was to understate Japan's economic growth rate.

Stephen D. Cohen of the American University in Washington argues that the psychological effect of the Tokyo crash was particularly strong in Washington. Writing at the height of American concern about the Japanese economy in 1998, he commented: "The implication of this negative view of Japan's economic future is that its trading partners should stifle their criticism; temper their demands; and not try to take advantage of a weakened, unstable Japanese economy."

The gambit worked because Western economists desperately wanted to believe that, after decades of scorning Western economic rules, Tokyo had finally had its comeuppance. Meanwhile, in an unholy alliance with the Tokyo Finance Ministry, top Western securities firms made huge profits in the so-called carry trade. The term refers to a complicated foreign exchange maneuver in which favored Westerners have consistently benefited from a low Japanese yen. As a matter of firmwide policy (and one clearly insisted upon by the Finance Ministry), Western investment banks not only consistently talked down the Japanese yen but gave widespread credence to the most extreme rumors of a coming Japanese economic Armageddon.

One of the most revealing aspects of the "lost decade" story was the behavior of Japan's top industrialists. In April 1998, Sony Corporation chairman Norio Ohga, for instance, made world headlines when he commented: "The Japanese economy is on the verge of collapsing." A few months later, Toyota president Hiroshi Okuda opined that Japan's problems could trigger a "worldwide financial crash." When corporate chiefs talk like this, we might assume their own businesses were suffering. In fact, both corporations did just fine that year, at home as well abroad; indeed, Toyota's 1998 profits were up 56 percent over 1989 (the last year of the Tokyo stock market boom), while Sony's were up fully 131 percent.

The contradictions in the "lost decade" story have probably been most pointedly critiqued by Robert Locke, a New York–based contributor to the *American Conservative*. In an essay in *Real World Economics* (London: Anthem Press, 2007), Locke suggests that Westerners have been victims of an elaborate hoax, perpetrated by officials and corporate chieftains in Japan on the one hand, and globalists and free trade ideologues in the West on the other. He comments: "That is a formidable set of potential liars, equipped with money, technical experts, transnational reach, and state power." Referring to the Japanese government's authoritarian control over society, he added: "Journalists and academics who in America or Europe would have challenged its [the government's] version of the economy by now, are loyal collaborators of the system, not its critics. So from a Japanese point of view, there is nothing immoral, unusual, or terribly difficult about misrepresenting Japan's economic performance. In fact because it is in the national interest, it would be unpatriotic not to do so."

Locke is right, of course, to suggest that Japanese officials have cooked the numbers. But even in Japan some statistics are less easily cooked than others. One statistical series in particular is worth considering: electricity output. In an energy-deficient nation like Japan whose electric utilities' imports of oil, uranium, coal, etcetera, are not only easily cross-checked against other nations' exports but are closely monitored by various Western experts, electricity statistics cannot be significantly faked. Thus, as Lester Thurow has pointed out, when the veracity of a nation's economic growth statistics is in question, electricity output, which is now closely tracked to true economic growth, provides a highly revealing cross check.

It is interesting therefore to note that Japan's electricity output statistics flatly contradict the "lost decade" story. According to the International Energy Agency, Japan's electricity output grew by 30.0 percent in the 1990s—a startlingly stronger performance than America's 23.9 percent, yet the American economy was supposed to have boomed. Japan's performance moreover put many other advanced nations in the shade, most notably Germany, Sweden, and Switzerland. With strong capital goods industries, these nations moreover boast economic profiles very similar to Japan's. It is true that their electricity growth was tempered by conservation efforts. But then so was Japan's. As a rich and extremely densely populated nation, Japan has long been curbing electric power growth by, for instance, strongly promoting recycling and phasing out such electricity-intensive industries as smelting and "metal-bashing." All this is the more significant for the fact that in the 1980s Japan and the United States saw broadly similar growth in electricity output—an increase of 35.7 percent in Japan versus 33.3 percent in the United States.

Perhaps the most revealing aspect of this story is how Japanese officials treated the electricity evidence: they swept it under the carpet. Whereas in any other country this remarkable contrary indicator would have been widely discussed by officials, elected representatives, and press commentators, in Japan in the 1990s there was dead silence. Not only that, there was the interesting matter of how the series was treated in *Japan: An International Comparison,* a handy semi-official statistical booklet relied on by virtually every Western journalistic and diplomatic observer. This publication had long provided a detailed historical series showing the rising trend in electricity output in the immediately preceding several years. This practice was stopped with the 1995 edition (whose series ended with the 1992 figure). In subsequent editions the most recently available figure was published but only in isolation so there was no hint of how fast output had been growing. The electricity numbers were eventually dropped entirely and now the booklet itself has ceased publication.

I will sum up by noting that I have extended a standing invitation to debate the "lost decade" story either in Tokyo or in Washington. My offer was first made in 1999 to the then two most prominent Tokyo-based sources of the "Japan hits the wall" story, the stock analysts Peter Tasker and Alexander Kinmont. I later extended it to their peers Kenneth Courtis, Robert Feldman, and Jesper Koll. All these people knew Japan in the 1980s—and none has been prepared to enter into a debate.

Let's get back to our main theme. As we have seen in this chapter, Westerners have great difficulty in assessing the full significance of China's rise. Not only do many observers have a vested interest in conveying a "Don't worry, be happy!" message, but the true facts of the Chinese economy are inherently difficult for outsiders to understand. In the following chapter we'll make a start on understanding them, beginning with an examination of how the East Asian economic model emerged in the first place.

THREE

Genesis of a New System

In chapter 1 we emphasized the extent to which American policymakers have been blind to the rise of the East Asian economic system. They have been laboring under an epochal misunderstanding—one whose origins can be traced to the early years after World War II, when jubilant American policymakers began claiming an unlikely success in transplanting Western values to East Asia.

Although previously the Confucian world had seemed particularly unreceptive to Western values, somehow in the second half of the 1940s something had changed—or so it seemed. A trend for Confucian nations to embrace Western ideas had begun. It started in a defeated Japan in 1945, then jumped to Taiwan and South Korea, and, by the 1980s, even to China. It was a story that seemed too good to be true. And, of course, it was.

In reality, as we will see in this chapter, those who credit this story are prime victims of the sorts of intellectual pitfalls and blind spots we described in chapter 2. It is worth reconsidering the history of modern East Asia. Let's start in Japan, which has long played a decisive role in shaping American attitudes about not only the East Asian miracle but the entire Confucian world.

"New Tokyo": Uncle Sam in Wonderland

Few aspects of modern American history are more fondly recalled by American political commentators than the story of the American occupation of postwar Japan. As conventionally told, the Americans performed nothing less than a prodigy of political engineering.

Initially vengeful, the American occupation's leader, General Douglas MacArthur, arrived in Tokyo in late August 1945 vowing that the Japanese would "have a hard enough time eating." Within days, however, his heart had been melted by the respectful reception he was accorded, and he and his troops went on to lead by example in Americanizing the Japanese nation. At least that is how the story is generally told. Thus an ancient, non-Western people went on wholeheartedly to embrace Western capitalism and democracy—and did so almost overnight. As the speed of the conversion is supposed to have stemmed largely from the favorable impression created by the GIs, the story has not surprisingly come to be regarded as a defining part of America's national mythology.

The reality, however, was quite different. Although MacArthur seems not to have understood this at the time (and many American Japan watchers have never admitted it to this day), the idea that a few months' contact with American GIs would bring about such a cultural miracle was absurd. As it turned out, not only did the Japanese not sincerely embrace American values, but in deflecting MacArthur's attempts to impose those values they evolved highly sophisticated techniques of deception—techniques that were quickly imitated in neighboring countries and have continued to play havoc with American policy ever since.

One of the most important consequences has been that American policymakers have been induced to open the American market ever wider to East Asian exports. They have hoped that in "showing leadership," they would inspire reciprocation from East Asia. It has proved a vain hope. Constantly convinced that the final triumph of free-market ideology was just around the corner, Washington has acquiesced for more than half a century in a policy of "one-way free trade" with the Confucian world.

Despite the now massive evidence of the policy's failure, even today Washington persists not only in believing the original myth but in using it as Exhibit A in advancing the so-called convergence theory of world progress—the highly influential if dangerously erroneous idea that non-Western nations are predestined to converge to American values. One consequence is that Washington has increasingly been inspired to take an evangelistic, and all too often counterproductive, approach in spreading democracy around the world. (The most tragic consequence of this self-flattering delusion in recent years has been the catastrophe in post-Saddam Iraq.)

The occupation of Japan changed American thinking not only about the world beyond American borders but even about the American nation itself. As postwar Japan's apparent transformation came to fill the front pages in the late 1940s, the United States fell in love with a new vision of itself as a geopolitical Lady Bountiful with an ostensibly unlimited capacity to solve the world's problems.

As far as the argument of this book is concerned, the occupation had an even more important consequence, in that the Americans were persuaded to play midwife to the birth of the East Asian economic system. They did so quite unwittingly by accommodating the Japanese bureaucracy's hidden agenda to minimize private ownership of the Japanese economy and thus to move to a highly ingenious postcapitalist system for maximizing economic growth. We will look at this in detail in a moment, but first let's consider the wider context.

Although the story of Japan's "miraculous conversion" to American values has long since become unquestioned conventional wisdom in the United States, the fact is that it was originally greeted with considerable skepticism. Although many of the most outspoken skeptics were British or Australian, several knowledgeable American correspondents also questioned the story. Notable among them were correspondents for the *Christian Science Monitor,* the *San Francisco Chronicle,* the *Nation,* CBS, and McGraw-Hill. For the most part, though, American correspondents chose to go along with the story. Even if they privately entertained doubts, they knew that to voice them would shut them off from the news flow from a vengeful MacArthur.

In any case, their home-office editors loved the story. Thus began a pattern of American correspondents in Tokyo seizing on any alleged evidence, however ambiguous, of the Japanese people's Westernization as a basis for sweeping generalizations about a highly unlikely cultural transformation. Certainly for any ambitious correspondent who wanted to make a name for himself in Japan, the "miraculous conversion" story was from the start a passport to constant appearances on page 1. It has remained so ever since.

Nobody did more to promote the hoax than General MacArthur himself. Soon after he arrived as supreme commander for the Allied powers, he professed himself convinced that the Japanese people, on the strength of a few days' contact with the GIs, had become firm admirers of "the free man's way in actual action." Within a year, he was claiming credit for the most amazing cultural transformation in history. In an address on the first anniversary of his arrival, he described the Americans' impact on Japan thus: "A spiritual revolution ensued almost overnight, tore asunder a theory and practice of life built upon two thousand years of history and tradition and legend. . . . This revolution of the spirit among the Japanese people represents no thin veneer to serve the purposes of the present. It represents an unparalleled convulsion in the social history of the world."

Any attempt to reconstruct what *really* happened in occupied Japan must start where the Japanese started, with a consideration of MacArthur's character. Recognizing that MacArthur was notoriously vain and self-absorbed, Japanese leaders determined—right from the moment of his arrival—to treat him as a quasi emperor. A massive ceremonial guard of honor was therefore laid on to line the fifteen-mile route to his hotel from the Atsugi military airport. Significantly, the troops presented their backs to him. Although some of the American party considered this an insult, MacArthur knew better: this stance was a gesture of respect that hitherto had been reserved only for Emperor Hirohito. As biographer William Manchester would put it in the title of a famous book, MacArthur had become an "American Caesar."

One of MacArthur's more troubling weaknesses was that he surrounded himself with yes-men. Concerned to rid his entourage of anyone who might, by dint of superior knowledge, contradict him, he sent most of the American military's most accomplished Japan experts to Korea. His problematic character was well understood by contemporary observers. Here is how the British-born mid-twentieth-century Japan watcher Richard Storry put it: "A tendency towards complacent self-dramatization was encouraged by the adulation of a devoted wartime staff that he took with him to Japan. Some of these sycophants were given appointments at the top of the Occupation machinery, and they took almost ludicrous care that only the rosiest reports of the progress of the occupation should reach the outside world. In their debased opinion the slightest criticism of [MacArthur] amounted to something approaching sacrilege."

The occupation's problems were compounded by the fact that other top American officials were "bamboozled by deceit or corrupted by flattery." Storry, who had taught in Japan for several years in the 1930s and returned there in the late 1940s as an Australian diplomat, continued: "It is easy to derive amusement from the thought of a few hundred enthusiasts . . . interfering at almost every level with the traditional practices of a much older civilization and race, of whose language, culture, and psychology they were often remarkably ignorant."

MacArthur's psychology, moreover, was heavily influenced by the fact that he aspired to be the Republican candidate for the presidency of the United States in the 1948 election. What mattered therefore was not so much to create a true success in Japan but merely an *impression of success*—and the earlier the better. This inspired a pattern in which Japanese officials made an elaborate effort to *appear* to conform to MacArthur's agenda, and MacArthur reciprocated by pretending not to see through the charade. In a word, this was a geopolitical version of "Don't ask, don't tell." The Japanese were acting a part—something that would be inconceivable in a Western society but actually comes naturally in Japan's very different culture.

Though it suited neither side to draw attention to this fact, the Americans had to work almost entirely through Japanese officials in trying to induce reform. In effect Japanese leaders had a veto on the reforms. Though they rarely said no, they were adept at finding ways to deflect or eviscerate any American initiative considered to constitute a threat to the more important aspects of Japan's "essence." As the leading American East Asia expert Chalmers Johnson has pointed out, Japanese officials have a special term for such behavior, *menju fukuhai*, which means roughly to cooperate with the face but disobey in the belly.

The important point is that, in sharp contrast with, for instance, Iraq in our own time, Japan in the late 1940s never suffered a dearth of indigenous leadership. Of course, with defeat, Japan's erstwhile military leaders were discredited. In accordance with Japanese tradition they willingly resigned. (Indeed, conveniently for those who followed, several leading militarists committed suicide in the first hours after Japan's surrender, and many more were soon arraigned by the Americans on war-crimes charges.) In a prearranged transition, the military leaders handed over the reins of power to top civilian agencies. Of these, by far the most important was the ministry of finance, a secretive and Machiavellian institution run by the brightest and most ambitious graduates of Japan's best universities. As it controlled not only the tax system but the banks and the national budget (among many other levers of power), it enjoyed unobtrusive but highly effective oversight over virtually everything the Americans did.

Japanese leaders sensed that the more publicly cooperative Japan appeared to be, the sooner the occupiers would leave. Thus the first order of business was to make sure that personal relations with the Americans went as smoothly and pleasantly as possible.

In the interval between the surrender and the arrival of the first American occupiers, the Japanese government prepared the way by calling on the Japanese people to be patient. Official posters were put up all over the country advising on the right attitude. As recorded by the author Willard Price, these read: "Never has great Nippon known defeat. The present difficulty is but a stepping stone to the future. Rally around the imperial throne and fight on, for this is a one-hundred-year war."

Japanese leaders made sure that the occupiers were afforded maximum cooperation on innumerable unimportant issues—thus building a bountiful store of goodwill to help smooth relations on a few key issues where they needed to dig their heels in. Whatever private resentments the Japanese people might have, they were to put on a friendly, welcoming face. In truth, of course, many Japanese citizens concealed deep bitterness. Many military veterans had been physically or psychologically traumatized by the war. The women had lost husbands; the children, fathers; the elderly faced a bleak future without the support of precious sons. Given the scale of the war and the fact that the United States had resorted to atom bombs to end it, it is fair to say that the Japanese secretly felt an even greater sense of grievance than the formerly dominant Sunnis of Iraq in our own time.

Although the official story has always been that the occupiers' unique sensitivity and decency saved the day, not everyone behaved particularly nobly. It is a fact, for instance—though one that has always been swept under the carpet in both Washington and Tokyo—that the Americans were somewhat complicit in the sexual exploitation of the so-called comfort women. The term refers to hundreds of women who had been forcibly recruited in Japanese colonies and elsewhere to provide sexual services to the Japanese Imperial Army. As the author George Hicks has recorded, many of them found themselves just months after Japan's surrender providing similar services to the Americans in occupied Japan.

Although most GIs did their best to act as fitting ambassadors for American society, a significant minority fell short. Indeed there were enough bad eggs that, had there not been constant efforts by Japanese officials to maintain control and project an impression of harmony, the occupation might have descended into something approaching the sort of Hobbesian chaos of post-Saddam Iraq.

As in Iraq in recent years, some GIs, for instance, took to conducting unnecessary searches and road checks just to show who was boss. Although such behavior is hardly a hanging offense, it dangerously inflames the already tortured sensitivities of a defeated people.

Some of the provocations were far from trivial. In *Failure in Japan,* a devastating account of the underside of the occupation, Robert Textor recounts how one Kyoto-based American general developed a bizarrely expressed concern for his troops' health. Textor, who had himself served the occupation as military officer in Kyoto, wrote: "It was common knowledge among local occupation employees for a period of some months that this general's military police were entering private homes in Kyoto at night without warrant—ostensibly to keep the troop venereal disease rate down. In 1947 and 1948 hundreds of ordinary female pedestrians were picked up off Kyoto streets at random, and completely without cause, by Japanese police under U.S. Army orders and sometimes under U.S. military police supervision. To determine whether they were carriers of venereal disease, these women were then forced to submit to embarrassing inspections of their genitalia."

The real significance of this episode was what happened next—or rather what didn't. In any other country one would have expected the outraged victims or their even more outraged menfolk to have raised Cain. There would have been letters to elected representatives and banner headlines in the newspapers. Yet although Japan by then was supposedly a model Western democracy with a free press, the whole affair was swept under the carpet.

It is all such a contrast with the worldwide scandal that was created by the sordid goings-on at the Abu Ghraib prison in the early days of "Operation Iraqi Freedom." Yet the troops at Abu Ghraib had at least the excuse that their victims were suspected of grave offenses. There was no similar excuse in Kyoto.

To anyone who understands Japan, the episode was entirely in character. Because Japanese leaders had already determined the story line, they rarely allowed any contrary evidence to create confusion. Moreover, they impressed on their people the absolute necessity of maintaining total restraint in the face of any American provocation.

Let's sum up on the psychology of the occupation. The Americans, thinking short-term and pursuing individual agendas, faced off against a Japanese nation that consistently kept its eye on the long term and maintained complete group solidarity. The lasting effect of the occupation was that it provided the Japanese—and by extension their neighbors throughout East Asia—with an invaluable lesson in how to manipulate the Americans. The lesson was well learned and in subsequent decades would prove crucial in persuading Washington to acquiesce in the rise not only of Japan's version of the East Asian economic system but all the subsequent copies.

The Americans Push on an Open Door

None of this is to suggest that the reforms implemented in occupied Japan were entirely a sham. Certainly some of the changes were genuine. But for the most part these were ones that Japanese officials would have embraced anyway.

Take, for instance, Japan's postwar pacifist stance. As popularly presented, this was entirely the Americans' doing. The reality is quite different. To the extent that MacArthur instigated the pacifist clause in Japan's postwar constitution, he was pushing on an open door. By the time Japan surrendered in August 1945, few nations could ever have longed more passionately for peace. Certainly, having had two of their biggest cities wiped out by atomic bombs, the Japanese hardly needed MacArthur to tell them their foreign policy needed rethinking.

Besides, all Hollywood stereotyping to the contrary, the Japanese national character is hardly particularly militaristic. Indeed, for most of its history, Japan has enjoyed exceptionally peaceful relations with the outside world. Things began to change in the late nineteenth century when Japanese leaders determined to set up a Western-style overseas empire. For the most part, particularly early on, Japan's colonial incursions remained little more controversial than those of the Western powers. Imperial Japan's phase of egregiously brutal repression began as late as 1937 and thus accounted for less than eight years of a two-thousand-year history.

It should be remembered too that Japanese leaders regarded empire not as an end in itself but merely as a means. Their ultimate objective was to eject the Western powers from East Asia. In the meantime they wanted to find markets for their burgeoning exports. As the Western powers had already demonstrated, the best way to boost exports was to colonize weaker nations and turn them into captive markets. (It should be noted that Western markets were largely closed to Japanese exports at this time. So too were many markets on Japan's doorstep that had been colonized by the West, most notably Malaya and the Dutch East Indies.)

Also, in renouncing war in the late 1940s, Japanese leaders had a strong incentive in that they hoped that "New Japan" would soon be granted specially privileged access to the American market. As the American market was several times larger than the combined markets of all of Asia, this was a prize worth winning. In the end Japan's strategy paid off: by playing the model prisoner, it was rewarded with astoundingly valuable trade privileges.

What of Japan's much celebrated conversion to democracy—surely this at least represented a great victory for the Americans? Hardly. First publicized at the height of the cold war, the story of this conversion was greatly "enhanced" for propaganda purposes. Not the least significant aspect of the story was that it entirely overlooked Japan's extensive pre–World War II experiments with pseudo-democratic institutions. As far back as the late nineteenth century Japanese leaders had espoused a superficially impressive, if carefully circumscribed, facsimile of Western democracy. Even as Japan geared for war in the early 1930s it remained a formal democracy and indeed had a quasi-democratic general election as late as 1937.

Japan's late-nineteenth-century leaders had embraced democratic forms for a characteristic reason: they hoped that by currying favor with the West they would improve Japanese exporters' access to Western markets. In the newly friendly atmosphere of the late 1940s, it was a foregone conclusion that as Japan worked to mend its fences with the West it would revive the impressive, if largely cosmetic, democratic persona it had assumed more than fifty years earlier.

The reality, however, is that Japan has, if anything, been less democratic in the post–World War II period than it had been in the 1920s or even the 1930s. The untold story of the occupation is that, right under MacArthur's nose, Japan's elite bureaucrats quietly arrogated to themselves sweeping powers to set the rules for Japan's electoral system. Then, as the British political scientist Peter Campbell pointed out, they resurrected the same electoral system that had governed Japanese "democracy" from 1900 until World War II. The clear intention was to create a Potemkin village—a pseudo democracy that could be presented to outsiders as the real thing, yet one in which the voice of the electorate was systematically muffled. Suffice it to say that the architects of Japan's electoral system aimed for two key results:

1. To create a one-party state
2. To make sure that the "permanent party of government" was fatally divided against itself in ways that made it utterly ineffectual as a counterweight to the unelected, virtually invisible bureaucrats who, in all but name, are modern Japan's true rulers

We do not have space here to go into the considerable, quite Machiavellian, intricacies of Japan's electoral history. As always with ersatz democracies, the devil is in the details. Japan's electoral rules are riddled with catch-22s. Just the most obvious is that it is almost impossible for politicians to win election without breaking overly strict rules on electoral funding. Essentially almost every successful candidate is on the wrong side of the funding rules and thus can at any time be selectively targeted for enforcement of the law. It just so happens that it is the elite bureaucracy that is entrusted with this task. Thus, elected representatives in Japan live in constant fear of offending the bureaucracy.

The main party, the so-called Liberal Democratic Party (LDP), is controlled by Japan's state-guided corporate sector acting as agent for the ultimate power holders in the elite bureaucracy (this epitomizes a pattern widely apparent throughout the more advanced societies of the Confucian world). At best, elected representatives in Japan are no more than glorified ombudsmen whose principal role is to raise petty complaints on behalf of individual constituents with bureaucratic agencies. (The bureaucracy's powers and prerogatives in lording it over society are beyond anything that Westerners unfamiliar with East Asia can imagine. Even Ezra Vogel, a noted apologist for Confucian approaches to governance, has made this point. As he has delicately put it, Confucian society has traditionally been "less concerned than Western theory with how to structure restraints on the power of leaders.")

It is obvious that Japan is a one-party state. With the exception of an interruption of less than one year after a general election in 1993, the Liberal Democratic Party has been the majority party since the 1950s. Moreover, the interruption was highly contrived and was quite clearly engineered merely to try to shake off Japan's embarrassing image as a one-party state. What is undeniable is that the interruption arose not because the LDP was voted out of office. Almost all sitting LDP members were reelected in 1993. The only difference was that for the purposes of just this one election they chose to renounce their LDP affiliation and run instead as candidates for a plethora of new and, for the most part, highly transitory parties. Thus, although the story was covered in the West as if the Japanese people had voted to "throw the bums out," nothing of the sort had happened. After a few months most of the defectors quietly returned to the LDP, which has proceeded to form every cabinet since.

The point to note is that Japan's postwar one-party state contrasts remarkably with the considerably more pluralistic look of Japan's prewar system. A feature of the prewar system was a genuine rivalry between two almost equally strong main parties, the Seiyukai and the Minseito. These parties were hardly paragons of Western democracy, but the system was considerably more open than the LDP's postwar hegemony.

Further puncturing the myth of Japanese democracy is the highly attenuated nature of Japanese-style "free speech." Top Japanese journalists reject the Western concept of a free press. Not only are they not antiestablishment, they are the establishment. Guided by Confucian ethics, they glory in a role as the Japanese system's propaganda department. Thus the main organs of the Japanese press constitute a cartel of Newspeak-like institutions that function quite overtly and cheerfully as mouthpieces of the elite bureaucrats. In particular they often function as attack dogs in destroying the bureaucrats' designated adversaries. Moreover, the whole business of news gathering is dominated by a system of pooled reporting in which virtually identical reports run in every major newspaper. The only equivalent of this system in the West is the way news is reported in wartime. And the motive in each case is to allow the authorities to control what is known.

Much more could be said about how contrived is Japan's version of democracy. Although we do not have space for a full discussion, we can readily show that the conventional American view is naive. The fact is that the Japanese "democratic" system consistently fails to deliver democratic outcomes. Hence the fact that women—who outnumber men by about 8 percent on the electoral rolls—have never been able to make their voice heard.

Japanese consumers have been similarly marginalized. Indeed the "consumer movement" in Japan is a sham consisting almost entirely of front organizations controlled by the elite bureaucracy. So Japanese "consumer advocates" loudly campaign *against* imports of, for instance, American rice.

Why does all this matter? Contrary to all conventional wisdom in the West, the reality of postwar Japan has been of an authoritarian society with a strongly nationalist agenda. Japan's nationalism and its authoritarianism were both essential preconditions for what followed: the emergence of Japan's pioneering version of the East Asian economic system.

The Doormat Strikes Back

We have gone to some lengths to show that the Americans were out of their depth in occupied Japan. Not only did they fail in many of the things they set out to do, but they inadvertently did many things they never intended to.

For our purposes in tracing the ultimate intellectual roots of China's supergrowth, the key point is that the Americans unwittingly played a pivotal role in the rise of the East Asian economic system.

The system had been in gestation long before the Americans ever got to Tokyo. Indeed, one important aspect of the system, its relentless focus on exporting, had already been embraced by the Japanese as early as the 1870s. But the boldest, most politically controversial changes came only later.

These changes were first tried out not in Japan proper but in the former Japanese colony of Manchuria. Nominally independent and known at the time as Manchukuo, Manchuria was dominated by Japan's Kwantung Army during the 1930s. Already by the middle of the decade, the Manchurian economy had been radically transformed into a postcapitalist engine of growth not unlike the China we know today.

In *MITI and the Japanese Miracle,* Chalmers Johnson has identified the Manchurian experience as the principal influence on Japan's post–World War II economic planners. In a hell-for-leather dash to build up Manchurian industrial output in the run-up to World War II, the colony's Japanese military government decided that Western capitalism was too slow and uncertain a tool. Inspired in part by the industrial successes of Joseph Stalin's Soviet Union and Adolf Hitler's Germany, they therefore took direct control of the region's industrial development.

The Manchurian economic experiment soon came to be accepted as a signal success. Certainly, as the historian Marius Jansen has recorded, Manchuria in the late 1930s was noted for its "orderly ports, sleek trains, and luxurious hotels." It was an amazing advance compared to just thirty years previously, when the region was still a godforsaken, largely uninhabited wasteland. According to the geographer Norton Ginsburg, land under cultivation increased from 33 million acres to 44 million acres between 1930 and 1940 alone. The Japanese invested massively in railroads, and their legacy was still evident as recently as 1970, when it was estimated that Manchuria accounted for 42 percent of all the rail mileage in Communist China.

Not the least impressive aspect of the region's progress was its electrical infrastructure, which was Asia's most advanced outside Japan. Anticipating by seventy years Beijing's vast investment in the Three Gorges Dam, Japan's Manchurian planners completed an epic spree of hydroelectric projects that were to bring electricity to virtually every resident of urban Manchuria. The Harvard-educated British historian F. C. Jones, in his 1949 book *Manchuria Since 1931,* described how one Japanese-built dam rivaled America's Grand Coulee as the world's tallest dam. Completed in 1941, the Shuifeng Dam rose 525 feet, whereas the Grand Coulee Dam, completed the following year, was to rise

550 feet. According to Ginsburg, electricity generating capacity in Manchuria by 1944 exceeded that *in the whole of China proper* by more than 30 percent. All in all, Manchuria was by far the richest part of Greater China by the end of World War II.

One indication of the high regard in which the Manchurian experiment was held was that many of the ideas behind it were soon applied in the home islands of Japan. Indeed in 1940, as the militarists frantically prepared to attack the United States, they tried as far as possible to organize the entire Japanese economy on Manchurian lines.

In a further acknowledgment of the Manchurian success, a clique of key decision makers from occupied Manchuria was rapidly promoted to the highest levels of the military government in Tokyo. This clique, consisting of four public servants plus the founder of the Nissan group (then heavily state-guided and known as Manchurian Heavy Industries), became so widely known that it was dubbed the *ni-ki san-suke* clique (the term translates as two *kis* and three *sukes*—a reference to Chinese characters in the protagonists' given names).

The clique was headed by Hideki Tojo, who served as army chief of staff in Manchuria in the late 1930s. After a spell as war minister in Tokyo, he became Japan's prime minister in 1941 and in that capacity led Japan into war with the United States. He was hanged by the Americans as a war criminal in 1948.

Another member was the finance ministry bureaucrat Naoki Hoshino, who seems to have been the Manchurian economic system's principal conceptualist. He went on to become Emperor Hirohito's chief cabinet secretary in 1941. Sentenced to life imprisonment after the war, he emerged from prison in 1955 to head a top Japanese publishing house.

Then there was Yosuke Matsuoka, who headed the semigovernmental South Manchurian Railway, which provided most of Manchuria's infrastructural backbone. He went on to become Japan's foreign minister in 1940. Soon after the war he died a natural death in prison awaiting trial for war crimes.

Most significant of all was Nobusuke Kishi, who was to become prime minister in the 1950s. A left-leaning advocate of a Japanese version of national socialism, he served as a top official in the Manchurian industrial development department in the late 1930s. His performance so pleased the top leadership that he was appointed minister for commerce and industry in the imperial cabinet. It was during his term as prime minister that Japan made the final adjustments that established the Japanese economic system in more or less its present form.

As we look back from the vantage point of the early twenty-first century, it is clear that Manchuria provided ideal conditions for road-testing the key ideas on which the East Asian economic system is based. First, Manchuria was decidedly not a democracy. With no voters to worry about, Japanese officials enjoyed a free hand in introducing a harsh regimen of forced economic growth.

In *Manchuria Since 1931,* F. C. Jones recounted how the region's military planners systematically boosted capital flows to industry. They instituted a system of compulsory savings in which a large proportion of each worker's income went into a state-run fund. (This anticipated by more than two decades a similar system of compulsory savings established in Singapore. The Singaporean system raised the city-state's savings rate from about 7 percent in the early 1960s to nearly 20 percent in the late 1970s.)

More portentously, Manchuria's military planners also pioneered the concept of suppressed consumption. They started by erecting a high wall of tariffs against imports of consumer goods and went on to institute a comprehensive system of price controls that kept prices of many locally produced consumer goods artificially high. Producers were obligated to plow back the resulting huge profits into building their efficiency via investment in ever more advanced production machinery.

All this was made easier and more effective by the fact that Manchuria was, of course, blessedly bereft of capitalist vested interests. There were no private fortunes to speak of—at least no Japanese ones—and therefore no disgruntled plutocrats who might use back channels in Tokyo to undermine the Manchurian officials' authority.

A key point is that almost nothing of what was going on in Manchuria was understood in the United States at the time or even later. Thus, when the Americans arrived in Japan in 1945 intent on massive reforms, they had no idea that the Japanese bureaucracy secretly aspired to turn postwar Japan into Manchukuo writ large.

One way MacArthur helped pave the way for the new system was that he failed to institute true democracy. In a truly democratic postwar Japan, a free press would surely have rallied both voters and their elected representatives against the draconian anticonsumption measures that powered the nation's superfast recovery from the war. Candidates for public office would have been free to undercut the policy by promising higher living standards in the form of more-spacious housing, better and more convenient stores, lower prices, higher incomes, and easier consumer finance.

If MacArthur's failure to institute true democracy proved helpful, something else he did proved vital: he facilitated a breathtakingly brazen program by the Japanese bureaucracy to expropriate Japan's hereditary capitalist class and thus establish public control over the higher reaches of corporate Japan. It is hardly an exaggeration to say that MacArthur effectively abolished Western-style capitalism in Japan—although, of course, he did so entirely unwittingly.

This is a complicated story that is worth considering in some detail because it provides vital evidence that the East Asian system is essentially postcapitalist (and as such would have had obvious appeal to an old-line Chinese communist like Deng Xiaoping, the principal architect of the Chinese version of the East Asian system).

Japan's prewar elite had been authentically capitalist in outlook and methods. Indeed a cabal of a few plutocratically wealthy families—descendants of the founders of such major industrial groups as Mitsui, Mitsubishi, Yasuda, and Sumitomo—controlled the commanding heights of the Japanese economy. The industrial groups, known in those days as *zaibatsu* (a compound word made from *zai* meaning "wealth," and *batsu* meaning "group"), typically included major banks and insurance companies as well as many manufacturing and mining offshoots operating almost right across the industrial waterfront. The so-called old zaibatsu (as distinct from several new zaibatsus built up by the Japanese military in the 1930s as compliant instruments of militarism) were largely family owned, and their managers took a conventionally capitalist approach to maximizing profits.

With a tradition of commercial leadership going back generations (in the Mitsui group's case, going back to the seventeenth century), the zaibatsu families were deeply entrenched in Japanese society. Constituting a large segment of Japan's then considerable titled aristocracy, they funded countless elected representatives and preempted the skills of some of Japan's wiliest lawyers and financial advisers. Moreover, many of them were English-speaking internationalists who mixed on equal terms with the Rockefellers and Rothschilds and could, if necessary, mobilize well-placed contacts around the world to pressure the Tokyo government. To say the least they often stood up to government officials. Indeed in the run-up to war in the 1930s at least one top zaibatsu official—a Mitsui director—so angered the militarists that they had him assassinated. Had their fortunes survived in the postwar era, the zaibatsu families would have proved a formidable stumbling block to the bureaucrats' plans to institute a strongly state-driven Manchukuo-style economic system in postwar Japan.

The bureaucrats therefore got in the first blow by persuading MacArthur that the zaibatsus had been the principal instigators of imperial Japan's militarism. Like so much else that he was told, this was actually a gross misrepresentation: in reality the zaibatsus were implicated only in the same general sense that almost everyone in Japan was—they had collaborated with the militarists only because it was dangerous to do otherwise.

The Finance Ministry expertly arranged for the effective expropriation of the zaibatsu families. To understand how this was done it is important to note a distinction between, on the one hand, the zaibatsus as organizational entities and, on the other hand, the plutocratically wealthy families who controlled them. Concerned merely to cut the organizational entities down to size (following American antitrust policy), MacArthur harbored no agenda to destroy the zaibatsu owners' personal fortunes. On the contrary, he undoubtedly would have wanted to preserve large family fortunes in Japan as a bulwark against the spread of international communism.

The Finance Ministry saw things differently. Entering into the full spirit of the Manchurian miracle, it saw the elimination of large concentrations of private wealth as a vital first step in building a state-guided postwar Japanese economic system. (It is a fair bet that the Finance Ministry shared the Manchurian faction's view that the zaibatsu fortunes were a major stumbling block to state-driven growth. According to F. C. Jones, the former top Finance Ministry official Naoki Hoshino had been bitterly opposed by the zaibatsus in his efforts to remake the Manchurian economy on statist lines.)

The ministry set about shaping the breakup in such a way that the zaibatsu families were effectively expropriated. Although on paper they were compensated, the compensation proved to be negligible because it came in the form of special long-term government bonds that were quickly rendered virtually worthless after a short but devastating burst of hyperinflation. As I showed in *Blindside,* the inflation was deliberately stoked by the Finance Ministry. Because the ministry had craftily stipulated that the bonds were "nonnegotiable"—they could not be sold—the zaibatsu fortunes were wiped out. At a stroke the dream of the Manchurian military planners had been realized and Japan became one of the most egalitarian societies on earth. It has remained so ever since, and egalitarianism, enforced through a progressive tax system as well as through government control of banking, is clearly a key objective of Japan's fully seasoned version of the East Asian economic system.

Once the American occupation ended in 1952, Japanese officials began in earnest to transform the nation's entire industrial system on postcapitalist lines. One of their first moves was to revive the zaibatsus in a new postcapital-ist guise known as *keiretsu*.

Organizationally a keiretsu functions quite similarly to a zaibatsu in that each consists of a group of affiliated companies that operate in dozens of di-verse industries and are committed to keeping business within the group. Thus, in the Mitsubishi keiretsu, the shipbuilding works of Mitsubishi Heavy Indus-tries buys steel from Mitsubishi Steel and chemicals from Mitsubishi Chemical and does its banking with Tokyo-Mitsubishi bank. Moreover, it sells many of its ships to the Mitsubishi shipping company, NYK. It is probably a fair bet that when NYK launches a ship, the celebration afterward features the products of the Mitsubishi brewing affiliate Kirin. This pattern of preferential trading serves an important economic purpose in that it helps achieve a higher level of capacity utilization than in a laissez-faire system.

The keiretsus differ from the zaibatsus in one crucial respect: the stockhold-ing structure on which their finances are based. Under the keiretsu system, each group's constituent companies are bound together by an essentially "horizon-tal" structure of elaborate cross-shareholdings. This contrasts sharply with the "vertical" ownership structure featured in the zaibatsu system (in which one top company controlled a pyramidlike hierarchy of subsidiaries and sub-subsidiaries). In the keiretsu system there is no one top company and therefore no one company through which wealthy private individuals might exercise con-trol over the entire group. Instead, each of a dozen or so major companies in each keiretsu owns substantial shareholdings in each of the others. This format has effectively shut out private shareholder control in perpetuity. Not the least of the consequences is that it has made it almost impossible for foreign corpo-rations to mount hostile takeover bids in Japan.

The most important feature of the new system is that, in sharp contrast with the old zaibatsu banks, the main banks in the keiretsu system are no longer under the private control of rich families. On the contrary, they are controlled by the Ministry of Finance (by dint of, among other things, the ministry's highly intricate system of regulation). The banks in turn control the flow of loans to each keiretsu member. In all but name therefore the banks are state-controlled and function as the Ministry of Finance's principal levers in implementing the nation's industrial policy. This result represents, of course, even more of an af-front to American ideas about dispersed economic power than the old zaibatsu system. Yet it was firmly established even before the occupation ended. As early as 1950 the British government's official representative in occupied Japan drew attention to the issue, complaining that just eight banks controlled 80 percent of Japanese industry.

Working through the banks, the Ministry of Finance went on to preside over an elaborate system of suppressed consumption that produced vast savings surpluses. Via the intermediation of the ministry-controlled banks, the money was then used to equip Japanese industry with ever more efficient production machinery. The resulting increases in industrial capacity had to be managed carefully. Hence arrangements were instituted to fix prices at high levels (often this was done through the creation of government-guided industrial cartels). High prices provided companies with the wherewithal not only to service their debts but to invest in building major export businesses.

All this could not have been possible had the government authorities been constrained by Western ideas of democracy. The authoritarian nature of the Japanese economic miracle was obvious from an early stage in Tokyo's environmental policy—or rather, the lack thereof. Particularly in the first decades of the miracle, pollution was a massive problem as Japanese corporations, with the deep complicity of government officials, furiously pursued growth.

Just how large were the consequences was illustrated by the outbreak of so-called Minamata disease, a terrible mercury-poisoning case in the town of Minamata in western Japan. The story became widely known through the happenstance that the famous American World War II photographer Eugene Smith lived nearby. First noticed in the mid-1950s, Minamata disease cost the lives of more than 1,700 victims and damaged the health of tens of thousands of others. Although the source of the poisonings—a factory owned by the Chisso Corporation—had been identified as far back as 1959, it was to be another nine years before Chisso's toxic effluent was shut down. With the collusion of both the Japanese press and the legal profession as well as, of course, government, the scandal remained almost completely unpublicized until 1972, when Eugene Smith turned it into a global cause célèbre. (This was the same year that the future U.S. national security adviser and now top Washington trade lobbyist Zbigniew Brzezinski published a book testifying to how "profoundly" attracted he was the culture of New Japan. His title said it all: *The Fragile Blossom*.)

It was not an easy fight. Smith sustained permanent injury to an eye after he was attacked by thugs acting in Chisso's name. When he took an iconic photograph of one of the victims in her bath, her parents were subjected to systematic harassment and character assassination. The photograph has since been withdrawn from circulation, purportedly reflecting the family's wishes. All the evidence, however, suggests that the family's attitude stems from establishment pressure.

So widely noticed was Smith's work that the Japanese establishment was shamed into initiating compensation negotiations with the victims. Even so, countless lawsuits remained unsettled as of 2007.

As the Minamata disease story exemplified, in virtually every aspect of economic policy, Japanese officials ruthlessly upheld the interests of producers over society. A full explication of the rationale for Japan's post–World War II economic model would require more space than we have here. The key point though is simply the obvious one: within a decade of the end of the American occupation, this authoritarian new system was already demonstrably powering a higher rate of sustained growth than any nation had ever achieved before. As we will now see, this growth did not go unnoticed.

A Tiger in Taiwan's Tank

By the late 1950s top officials and business leaders in Japan's former colonies had become mesmerized by the speed of the erstwhile mother country's postwar recovery. Sensing they were witnessing the first stages of a global economic revolution, they were quick to understand and emulate Japan's spectacularly successful new economic model.

None of Japan's neighbors moved faster than Taiwan. This was probably predictable. Unlike other former Japanese colonies, Taiwan had had a generally happy relationship with the mother country. Many Taiwanese citizens spoke fluent Japanese and retained extensive networks of friends and business associates in Japan.

While free markets play a greater role in present-day Taiwan than in either Japan or South Korea, the Taiwanese economic system is nonetheless based on a strongly state-guided, export-driven approach to wealth creation. And Taiwan's greater commitment to free markets reflects no sincere ideological conviction but rather political expedience. As a diplomatically isolated nation, Taiwan has seen special political advantage in attracting corporate investment from the United States and Europe. By contrast, both Japan and South Korea have traditionally shunned such investment out of a purist concern to exorcise all Western influence from their internal economic workings.

All this said, the Taiwanese system is recognizably a major departure from

Western laissez-faire, and probably nowhere has this point been better understood than in Beijing.

The economic rivalry between Taipei—the Taiwanese capital—and Beijing is palpable. Up to the late 1950s the Taiwanese people had been little better off than their perennially impoverished cousins on the mainland. In the subsequent two decades, however, the economic trajectories of the two Chinas could hardly have been more different. While Taiwan rocketed ahead, the mainland languished. This was not initially apparent to Western observers because Mao's statisticians greatly overstated the mainland's true performance, particularly during the Great Leap Forward and the Cultural Revolution (which were presented originally as signal successes, whereas in reality they were total catastrophes).

By the late 1970s it had become clear that Taiwan had achieved a per capita income fully seven times that of the mainland. Indeed, Taiwan ranked fourth in income in East Asia, exceeded only by Japan and the two rich entrepôt states of Singapore and Hong Kong (whose early success in each case was powerfully aided by links to Britain).

It is a fair inference that the Taiwanese experience was the single most important factor in the Beijing leadership's decision in the late 1970s to embrace the East Asian economic system. Certainly to policymakers in Beijing it was obvious that if little Taiwan could achieve such success, the mainland would have little difficulty following suit.

After all, Taiwan is closer culturally to mainland China than to any of East Asia's other miracle economies. Historically part of "Greater China," Taiwan came under Japanese rule in 1895. Then in the late 1940s, after Japan's defeat in World War II, the Taiwanese rediscovered their Chinese identity when they came under the sway of the Kuomintang, the Chinese nationalist party that for twenty years had fought Mao Zedong's Chinese Communist Party for control of the mainland. After the Kuomintang lost the mainland struggle to Mao in 1949, its supreme leader, Chiang Kai-shek, and more than 1 million of his followers fled to Taiwan, where they have constituted a highly authoritarian minority that has dominated the indigenous Taiwanese people ever since.

These days Taiwan is technically a democracy—but the operative word is "technically." Taiwan's electoral system is an almost exact replica of the system deployed in Japan for most of the period between 1900 and 1993. In other words, it is little more than a psephological Potemkin village. Certainly the Taiwanese system, like the Japanese original, is purpose-built to enable career bureaucrats to parry and generally suppress populist pressures.

The artifice in Taiwan's choice is apparent when it is realized that, apart from 1970s South Korea under the Japanese-educated dictator Park Chung Hee, Taiwan is the only country ever to have replicated Japan's "multimember single nontransferable vote system." The system features huge constituencies, each of which elects perhaps as many as a dozen representatives. The most obvious implication is that any major party must field several mutually opposed candidates in every constituency. Some European nations, most notably Ireland, boast systems that are superficially similar. But they differ in one crucial respect: votes in European versions are "transferable," meaning that if one's first choice is not elected, one's vote can go to a second choice (probably another candidate from the same party). The nontransferable stipulation in the Japanese/Taiwanese system is its key antidemocratic element. While we do not have space to fully illuminate the point here, it is the electoral (or, to be more precise, the *psephological*) equivalent of "pinioning" a bird. (Pinioning is a technique by which a bird's wings are surgically disabled to make sure it can never fly.) Like a pinioned bird, Taiwan's multimember single nontransferable vote system looks the part—but it is preordained never to achieve its natural purpose.

One of the few American scholars who has analyzed the Taiwanese electoral system is Larry Diamond of the Washington-based National Endowment for Democracy. As he has pointed out, the single nontransferable vote feature "is well known to foster factionalism, undermine party coherence, and inflate campaign costs." That is putting it mildly. The entire intent of the system is to favor candidates who are most brazen in breaking electoral funding laws. By definition such candidates are fundamentally compromised and are fated to live in perpetual fear of the bureaucracy's selective enforcement of funding laws.

The net effect is that "Taiwanese democracy" is a contradiction in terms. To this day Taiwan is run by a nearly omnipotent elite bureaucracy dominated by members of the mainland ethnic minority that seized power in the late 1940s.

In contrast with the indigenous people of Taiwan, whose ethnic roots are diverse and include a significant proportion of Malayan and Polynesian blood, the mainlanders share the same Han Chinese heritage as top leaders in Beijing. One of the more significant consequences is that the language of the Taiwanese elite is not the local Taiwanese dialect but Mandarin, the Beijing-region dialect that has always been the language of power in mainland China. Thus, although Taiwan and the mainland have constantly traded insults over the years, the two governments are much closer in both culture and psychology than is generally understood in the West. (The ethnic Taiwanese majority has made some progress in asserting itself recently, while the Han Chinese bureaucratic establishment has drawn back a bit from the Chiang Kai-shek legacy. But these are minor considerations in the larger picture of continuing Han Chinese hegemony.)

One reason the close intellectual ties between Taipei and Beijing need emphasis is that during the cold war, policymakers and policy analysts alike in the United States deliberately distorted the facts to make the Taiwanese economy appear as American as possible. The startling truth, however, is that the modern Taiwanese economy has always been highly statist. It thus represents the very antithesis of the economic ideals so fervently espoused by pro-Taiwan partisans in Washington.

Where economic policy is concerned, the intellectual roots of the Kuomintang have probably been almost as close to those of Stalin's Moscow as to present-day Washington. In the words of the prominent mid-twentieth-century Sinologist Conrad Brandt, "the Kuomintang owed its early successes largely to Soviet aid and advice and to close collaboration with the [Chinese] Communists."

How close was this collaboration? An interesting pointer lies in the identity of one of the Kuomintang's early officials: an obscure former librarian and schoolteacher named Mao Zedong. Mao held high office in the Kuomintang in the 1920s and in particular headed its propaganda department in 1925–1926. Nor was Mao unique. Other leading communists who held high office in the Kuomintang in those days included communist China's future foreign minister Zhou Enlai, who served as Chiang Kai-shek's political commissar.

When Chiang Kai-shek took over as Kuomintang leader in 1928, he was advised by Soviet experts. He had even been trained by the Soviets. Moreover, his son Chiang Ching-kuo, who succeeded to the Taiwanese premiership in 1972 and took over as president in 1978, spent twelve years in the Soviet Union. As a student in Moscow he was a classmate of Deng Xiaoping, the future leader of the mainland, and for a time he enthusiastically espoused Trotskyism. As this history suggests, the truth about the Kuomintang is that it can be considered right-wing only by comparison with the ultraleft Chinese Communist Party of the Mao era.

The important point is that from the earliest stages of the Taiwanese economic miracle, the Kuomintang rejected American economic ideology in favor of policies closely modeled on Japan's.

The first premonitions of the Taiwanese miracle can be traced back as far as the late 1950s, when, as Robert Wade has pointed out, the government began to assume a masterful role in shaping the economy. Wade cites in particular the story of how present-day Taiwan's reputedly wealthiest citizen, Wang Yung-ching, got his start. In 1957 the government chose him to lead the development of Taiwan's fledgling plastics industry. In one version of the story, officials spotted him by sifting through citizens' bank accounts and discovering that he had the savings and entrepreneurial ability to lead a major company. They then handed him—as it were, on a silver salver—control of an already running plastics plant they had just built with the help of public funds and American technology. That business, now known as Formosa Plastics, quickly grew to become one of world's biggest producers of polyvinyl chloride (PVC). As Wade points out, this is only one of many examples of state leadership of the "private" economy in Taiwan.

Taiwan's official embrace of the full East Asian system can be dated to 1960, when the regime unveiled a new industrial plan entitled the Nineteen Point Program for Economic and Financial Reform. The program's centerpiece was a strong system of incentives for exporters. The program also built on and extended a previously announced four-year economic plan.

Taiwanese economic policy was nominally under the control of the Kuomintang Central Standing Committee, but in reality, the committee delegated sweeping regulatory powers to technically trained bureaucrats. These latter had inherited a tradition of strong central government control from the Japanese militarists and in particular had started out with a Taiwanese economy that was largely state-owned. They took good care to retain state control as they launched the Taiwanese miracle and repeatedly resisted considerable American pressure to privatize the Taiwanese corporate sector. Crucially, virtually the entire Taiwanese banking industry remains to this day subject to detailed backseat driving from the Taipei Finance Ministry. State-owned enterprises were to form the backbone of the economy in Taiwan's years of fastest growth in the 1960s and 1970s. They included China Steel and the Chinese Petroleum Corporation.

State initiative has been the order of the day even in new industries. Take electronics. Taiwan's entry into this industry dates to 1973, when the government established the Industrial Technology Research Institute (ITRI). With a brief to establish high-growth modern industries, the ITRI quickly focused on electronics and set out to incubate a new breed of export-oriented high-technology company. An early example was United Microelectronics Corporation (UMC), which has since become a leading player in the so-called foundry subsector of the world semiconductor industry. In the jargon of the electronics industry, foundries are semiconductor fabrication plants that work on a contract basis for outside customers. Such customers are typically American and European semiconductor design companies that have no manufacturing facilities of their own. As of 2005 UMC employed twelve thousand people and boasted sales of $2.8 billion.

Encouraged by UMC's success, the ITRI went on in 1987 to establish an even more ambitious venture in the guise of the Taiwan Semiconductor Manufacturing Corporation. Similar to UMC in that its main business is contract manufacturing, it has proved even more successful. As of 2005, with sales of more than $8 billion and a workforce of more than twenty thousand, it claimed to be the world's largest foundry company.

All this helps explain why Taiwan, with a population of less than 23 million, ranks today as the world's fourth-largest producer of semiconductors.

Semiconductors apart, the ITRI has also been highly successful in developing a strong Taiwanese presence in optoelectronics. In particular it established the foundations for present-day Taiwan's leadership position in the manufacture of optical disk drives for the CD-DVD family of disks. In 1993, when the ITRI embarked on the CD-DVD project, Taiwan had no optical drive production. By 2001, it had captured 56 percent of the world market.

To achieve such growth, Taiwanese companies have had to invest massively in state-of-the-art plant and equipment. Where did they get the money? Like other fast-growth East Asian economies, Taiwan has long boasted a high savings rate. Particularly in the 1960s and 1970s, when government efforts to spur economic growth were at their most intense, Taiwan boasted one of the world's highest savings rates. The rate has drifted down since then but remains well above typical rates in free-market Western nations. As of 2005 Taiwan's fixed investment rate was estimated by the Central Intelligence Agency at nearly 21 percent of gross domestic product—a high rate by any standards and particularly so considering that Taiwan has also been funding huge capital exports (not only setting up factories in China but funding the American trade deficit).

Why do the Taiwanese save so much? As in most other parts of developed East Asia, the answer lies in a government policy of suppressing consumption.

One aspect of this policy should already be clear: Taiwan's neomercantilist emphasis on building export industries. Because so much of the economy has been laid out to serve export markets, this has by definition left less for home consumption. Meanwhile imports have been discouraged in a variety of ways. In the early days, tariffs were startlingly high: a study found that in 1969 the average tariff rate was 60 percent. Robert Wade reports in *Governing the Market* that the tariff rates varied sharply by type of product: low tariffs on producers' goods, high tariffs on consumer goods, and prohibitive tariffs on luxuries. This is the classic pattern favored by East Asian nations intent on suppressing consumption.

Of course, over the years Taipei came under pressure to open its markets. It duly responded with a round of tariff cuts. But this hardly meant that Taipei had been won over to American-style free trade. On the contrary, it remained fundamentally protectionist but, merely as a public relations gesture to Western sentiment, had chosen to switch more and more to nontariff barriers. One element of the new approach was numerical quotas on imports. The mercantilist effect was heightened by a highly discriminatory system of import permits. In some categories, only companies that were significant exporters were permitted import licenses. Given that such licenses were often quite valuable—licensed importers could often make enormous windfall profits selling scarce foreign goods in a closed domestic market—the effect was to provide hidden subsidies to export industries.

Well into the 1980s Taiwan remained largely closed to consumer imports. Here is how the Taiwanese market was described in a U.S. government report in 1983: "US exports to Taiwan face a number of significant trade barriers ranging from ... excessive customs duties to outright import bans. ... Many items, covering the spectrum from general household goods to kitchenware to processed and packaged foods and even to orange juice concentrate, have as much as 70 percent added to their cost before they reach the market."

Even as much of the rest of the world liberalized its trade in the 1990s, the Taiwanese government remained stubbornly protectionist—so much so that in 2000 the World Trade Organization noted major barriers to trade in key sectors. In the automobile sector, for instance, Taiwan levied tariffs averaging 17 percent on components and more than 60 percent on imported passenger vehicles. In the electronics industry, the tariff rates were ostensibly low, but the authorities used a legal loophole to impose high antidumping duties on certain semiconductors. The effect was equivalent to tariffs of 36 percent.

Another support for the Taiwanese savings rate has been the Taipei government's budget policy, which on a Western accounting basis has consistently produced a surplus of current revenues over current expenditures. According to Robert Wade, government saving accounted for 38 percent of Taiwan's net savings between 1970 and 1978. In contrast, by dint of running fiscal deficits, U.S. government policies resulted in a reduction in the American savings rate of about one-seventh in the same period.

Let's conclude by pointing out that Taiwan now ranks among the world's richest countries on many measures. Take life expectancy. As of 2005 the Taiwanese people boasted an overall life expectancy rate of 77.4 years—just a few months less than that of the United States. By comparison in 1960 life expectancy in Taiwan lagged that of the United States by six years.

Korea: Japan's Most Successful Pupil

While Taiwan's experience has probably proved especially influential in inspiring economic reform in Beijing, in many ways South Korea's record provides a better insight into the system's true potential. Although South Korea was slower to adopt the East Asian model than Taiwan, it has generally shown faster growth, particularly in the last decade. The result is that in 2006, as measured at market exchange rates, its per capita income exceeded Taiwan's by 19 percent. By contrast as recently as 1999 it had lagged by 34 percent.

Thus with the exception of Japan and the two special cases of Singapore and Hong Kong, South Korea is now the most prosperous nation in the region.

South Korea also happens to be the nation that has been most faithful to the Japanese original in its implementation of the East Asian economic model. The faithfulness has been noted by Nicholas Kristof of the *New York Times*, who in 1998 wrote that both Japan and South Korea relied on "a very similar system of industrial planning, huge inter-linked conglomerates, lifetime jobs in big companies, export assistance and protected domestic industries."

South Korea's cultural ties to Japan have played a vital role in the Korean miracle. As of the early 1950s, almost all educated Koreans could speak Japanese, and even as late as 1990 Koreans accounted for 70 percent of all foreign high-school students around the world then studying the Japanese language.

Commenting on the beginnings of the Korean miracle, one scholar wrote: "Korean leaders had a cultural background similar to that of the Japanese, and with a country that was also a poor late late developer without resources, they adopted organizations strikingly similar to Japan's."

Among key Korean institutions that have been closely modeled on Japanese counterparts are both the Finance Ministry and the Ministry of Trade and Industry. Other close copies of Japanese models include the Korean Development Bank and the Korea Trade-Investment Promotion Agency.

All that said, South Korea initially trailed Taiwan by several years in embracing the Japanese model. The delay was largely attributable to America's special influence in the first fifteen years after World War II. As a quid pro quo for receiving huge American military and economic support, Korean officials followed American economic prescriptions all through the 1950s. In particular they complied with an American request to privatize the Korean banking industry (which had previously been government-owned under Japanese rule).

In one major respect South Korea's American interlude proved importantly helpful for the later growth run: land policy. The Americans leaned on Korean officials to break up large landholdings. These had previously been owned either by wealthy indigenous landlords or by Japanese interests. The land was distributed to small farmers, who generally cultivated it much more efficiently than the previous owners.

Seoul's shift toward the Japanese model began after the American-educated president Syngman Rhee was toppled in a student uprising in 1960. An interregnum followed and then in 1961 Park Chung Hee seized power in a military coup. Park brought to his role as South Korea's president a uniquely deep familiarity with Japan. A near-native speaker of Japanese, he had been brought up in the then heavily Japanized southeastern corner of the Korean Peninsula. Having volunteered for the Japanese army in the late 1930s, he quickly so impressed his superiors that he was sent to the Japanese military academy in Manchuria. On graduating first in his class, he went on to study at the Japanese imperial military academy in Tokyo before serving in the imperial army until its defeat in 1945.

It is fair to say that he was a Japanese collaborator—a not unusual background among the political classes in early post–World War II Seoul (in the

words of the French journalist Philippe Pons, collaboration was a "vast problem" in colonial Korea). Park often preferred to speak Japanese in everyday
conversation and, more than most Koreans, he was aware of how fast Japan had
progressed in the 1950s. Even more important, he had been in at the birth of
the Manchurian prototype in the 1930s.

Moreover, it is probably significant that, as the noted Korea watcher Don
Oberdorfer has recorded, Park had been known from youth for left-wing
sympathies—sympathies evidently much in line with those of the Japanese
technocrats behind the Manchurian miracle. As a political leader, he drew his
earliest support in large measure from other Japanized Koreans, particularly
those who had served in the Japanese military in Manchuria.

Within a month of seizing power he established an economic planning organization as his first step in building a new type of "guided capitalism." As he
explained it, this concept entailed an enterprise system "in which the government will either directly participate in, or indirectly render guidance to the basic industries and other important fields." As Don Oberdorfer has noted, this
was a close copy of Japan's strategy. Park went on to initiate a series of five-year
plans modeled on Japan's wartime planning. In a critical preparatory move that
paved the way for the coming economic revolution, he renationalized the Korean banking system, thus establishing at a stroke the sort of fingertip control
over the nation's savings flows that Japanese officials already enjoyed via a nominally private, but in reality tightly state-controlled, banking system.

Japan's influence on the Korean miracle became explicit after Park in 1965
normalized diplomatic relations with Tokyo. Although normalization proved
highly unpopular with the Korean public, it paved the way for massive infusions
of Japanese financial and technical aid. The most obvious result was the establishment of the massive Pohang mill. This was one of Park's pet projects, and he
pressed ahead with it in the late 1960s even after prospective lenders at the
World Bank, evidently viewing it as a giant boondoggle, refused it vital funding.
Sharing Park's confidence, however, the Japanese stepped into the breach and
not only provided most of the money but also bestowed on it vital state-of-the-
art steelmaking know-how. Known eventually as POSCO, the company quickly
grew to become by the 1990s the world's largest steel mill. What the Japanese
knew that the World Bank didn't was that South Korea had embraced a highly
effective new economic system that promised to produce sustainable economic
growth at rates two to three times those possible under Western capitalism.
Not only were the South Korean economy's general growth prospects far better

than the World Bank understood, but soon major new industries, planned by Park with Japanese assistance, would take all the steel the new mill could produce. These new industries were shipbuilding and carmaking, both of which took off in the 1970s. These industries plus steel, as well as electronics, chemicals, and machinery, were to be named in Park's development plan as six pillar industries on which much of the nation's future growth would be based.

In jump-starting the development of new industries, Park emphasized large-scale production. Thus began a policy of permitting only a select few companies to enter any particular "targeted" industry. The effect, of course, has been to help each competitor quickly reach critical mass within the protected Korean home market.

A key role has been played by Japanese engineering consultants, most of them either currently employed by top Japanese industrial companies, or recently retired from such companies. Either way, it is clear that in transferring Japanese technologies to Korea they were doing so with the explicit support of the Japanese economic system. According to Alice Amsden, author of *Asia's New Giant*, the standard history of the Korean economic miracle, such consultants were "a gold mine for Korean industry."

Why did the Japanese transfer so much technology? There were several reasons, including a sense of obligation arising out of an unhappy previous history. In concrete terms, however, the Japanese economy benefited on balance from Korean growth. A key benefit was that the Koreans undertook to buy their capital equipment and other key supplies from Japan. Amsden cites figures to show that even in the 1970s, when the American capital-equipment industry was still almost entirely intact and in many categories remained the world leader, the Koreans bought more than half their capital equipment from Japan, versus less than one-fifth from the United States.

Korea then followed the classic East Asian trajectory. Initially unsophisticated Korean companies made huge profits in a protected domestic market. By reinvesting those profits they rapidly improved their production efficiency and output per worker. They then targeted foreign markets and used their home-market profits to subsidize rapidly rising exports. Finally, having captured large market shares abroad, they invested heavily in brand building. The result today is that such Korean brands as Samsung, Hyundai, and LG, virtually unknown outside Korea twenty years ago, have come to enjoy global recognition.

Yet even today, despite several rounds of ostensible market opening in the last forty years, the Korean market remains one of the most protected in the developed world. In a recent study, the London-based Economist Intelligence Unit (EIU) has detailed some of Korea's trade barriers. First, Korea has long operated a complex system of "flexible" tariff barriers that allow government officials to vary tariff rates by as much as 40 percent above or below certain prescribed levels. This equips the Korean government to play a giant game of Whac-a-Mole at the expense of would-be foreign entrants into the Korean market. In industries where Korean companies face little foreign competition, the government can drop the tariff rates to negligible levels, thus keeping Korea's average tariff level reasonably low. But if a foreign supplier tries to sell into the Korean market, he will find his way suddenly barred with high "pop-up" tariffs.

Then there are Korea's notorious nontariff barriers. As the EIU indicated, a key problem for Western companies is that certain ostensibly independent Korean civic organizations wage virulent propaganda campaigns against imports. Meanwhile the Korean media are, in the EIU's words, "harshly critical" of imported consumer goods. Apart from anything else they sometimes take full advantage of the Confucian truth ethic to lie about the quality of imported goods. A classic instance in the 1980s concerned American grapefruits, which were widely—and utterly falsely—alleged to have been treated with a carcinogenic chemical. The media have also occasionally identified Korean travelers who return home with "too many" foreign-bought goods. (Such goods in any case have been subjected to airport-levied "expedient tariffs"—at a rate of up to 50 percent on skiing goods, up to 55 percent on golf clubs, and up to 65 percent on jewelry.)

Even the Korean educational system has at times been enlisted in the national effort to keep imports out. In one instance, a comic book distributed to schools throughout Korea asked children to act as spies in making sure their mothers bought only Korean-made products.

Given the context of East Asian conformism, Korea's anti-import sentiment can be highly intimidating. Significantly, the national hostility to imports is masterminded by top government agencies, not least Korea's much feared tax administration. During one of the most notorious anti-import campaigns, in 1989, government officials openly threatened that anyone who displayed "extravagance beyond his reported means" would be targeted for tax scrutiny. The directive, noted by James Fallows in *Looking at the Sun* (1994), was aimed in particular at buyers of American cars, which were then a popular status symbol in Korea.

Under Western pressure, Korea has somewhat liberalized its trade policy over the years. In 2001 the National Tax Service even issued an unusual statement saying that local buyers of imported cars had never been and never would be subjected to discriminatory tax examination. The United States and the European Union, however, remain deeply concerned by South Korea's invisible trade barriers against car imports.

Their confidence has not been boosted by the fact that—in a classic exercise in Confucian pantomime—Korean government agencies have taken to using foreign cars for certain official purposes, not least for transporting foreign dignitaries. This seems at best like blatant tokenism, given that other aspects of government policy are so obviously intended to discourage imports.

One problem is that imported cars are subjected to expensive testing requirements. As William Holstein reported in the *New York Times* in 2002, the authorities have also continued to manipulate emissions and safety standards to put foreign makers at a disadvantage. In the circumstances, it would take a brave foreign chief executive to undertake the heavy investment necessary to try to establish a real presence in the South Korean market. At the end of the day, Korean car purchasers remain afraid that buying a foreign car will trigger a tax audit. The government's denial in 2001 looks less than convincing given that as recently as 1999 the Ministry of Finance and the Economy proposed a new regulation requiring all buyers of large-engined cars—virtually synonymous in South Korea with imported cars—to register their purchases with the government. This predictably sparked a firestorm of criticism abroad and was eventually shot down. What mattered was how this episode was viewed by Korean car buyers: the government had reiterated in scarcely veiled terms that it disapproved of people buying foreign cars.

A remarkable feature of the Korean economy is the extent to which it is dominated by so-called *chaebols*. These are diversified conglomerates that closely resemble the zaibatsus of early-twentieth-century Japan. In fact the name *chaebol* is simply the Korean pronunciation of the same two Chinese characters—one meaning "finance," the other "group"—used to write "zaibatsu" in Japanese.

In most cases the chaebols got their start as single-business entities in the 1930s, 1940s, and 1950s. In the 1960s, a select few were chosen as the nuclei for major new industrial groups. As such they were the Park administration's designated partners in creating the Korean economic miracle. In return for their cooperation in a series of five-year development plans, the nascent chaebols received many favors, not least cheap government financing. When, under new pressure from the United States, Seoul again denationalized the Korean banking system in the early 1980s, it handed the banks over to control by the chaebols. The move may have satisfied appearances but it merely perpetuated in ostensibly private form a previous pattern of chaebol members enjoying privileged access to the nation's savings flows.

Some of the better-known chaebols that grew out of these partnerships are the LG group (formerly Lucky Goldstar), Hyundai, Daewoo, and SK. Then there is the largest of them all, the Samsung group. Founded in 1938 as a trading company, Samsung entered the sugar and insurance industries in the 1950s, and retailing and publishing in the 1960s. But its real growth started only when it entered the electronics industry in the late 1960s. By the late 1970s it had also entered petrochemicals, construction, heavy engineering, and shipbuilding. As of 2006 it boasted sales of more than $100 billion and employed more than two hundred thousand people (including more than one hundred thousand in electronics alone).

Unlike Japan's keiretsus of the post–World War II era, the chaebols are still dominated by descendants of the founders. This may, however, be changing. In recent years, the Seoul government has tried to weaken family control. Whereas the entrepreneurial genius of the founders was regarded as a major net benefit to Korean society, Korean officials evidently see little advantage in upholding the ownership rights of the founders' heirs. Quite the contrary, they regard the chaebol heirs as a stumbling block to progress. Their attitude mirrors the impatience of Japanese officials with the zaibatsu heirs in the first half of the twentieth century. Although Korean officials have not dared to contemplate such a drastic solution as Japan's effective expropriation of the zaibatsu heirs in the late 1940s, they have resorted to extensive use of selective enforcement of tax and industrial laws to embarrass the chaebol heirs and generally marginalize them.

Still, the South Korean economy has generally thrived in recent years, so much so that South Korea ranks second only to China in the pace of its economic growth over recent decades.

To sum up on the Korean miracle, South Korea's per capita income in 1961 ranked it as one of the poorest nations in the world—poorer even than North Korea. Since then per capita income has multiplied more than two hundred fold in current dollar terms. Even as early as 1978, per-capita income had already increased nearly twenty-fold—a performance that surely was not overlooked by Chinese leaders as they searched for ways to boost China's economic performance. Certainly, as we will now see, the economic model they chose was the East Asian one, not the Anglo-American free-market model that then as now was being heavily promoted by Western theorists.

The Middle Kingdom Makes Its Move

Few Westerners paid much attention at the time, but the tone of the news from China changed in 1978. In the previous two years, Chinese political developments had been inconclusive and confusing. The only thing that was clear was that after Mao Zedong's death in 1976 a major power struggle had broken out. As the various protagonists were virtually unknown abroad, the significance of the struggle was at first almost completely lost on the West.

As we now know, a group of reformers led by Deng Xiaoping proved victorious in 1978. They lost no time in transforming China's agenda. One of their top priorities was to improve diplomatic relations with the West. An early success in this effort was to establish full diplomatic relations with Washington. This reversed thirty years of farce as Washington had treated the Taiwanese regime as the legitimate government of all China.

Thereafter news of "New China" came thick and fast. First there were announcements of a flurry of opportunities for corporate America:

- The Coca-Cola company was permitted to market its drinks in China.
- Pan American World Airways was authorized to establish direct flights between the United States and China.
- Boeing secured a contract to supply three 747 jumbo jets to the Chinese national airline.

The fact that these announcements were not only made on the same day but came within a week of the diplomatic breakthrough suggests that the timing, which evidently was controlled by the Chinese side, was intended as a statement in itself. Beijing wanted it to be known that it was not just its foreign policy that had changed but its economic policy, too.

China's new leaders had decided to abandon Maoist economics and develop instead their own version of the East Asian economic system. Of course, they never explicitly acknowledged this, and it would be nearly two decades before most China watchers concluded that this was the case. For sloganeering purposes, Deng disguised the story by subsuming it within the slogan of the "Four

Modernizations." This slogan, coined in 1978 to describe ideas that had been first proposed by Zhou Enlai, referred to a major effort to speed progress in four key areas: agriculture, national defense, science and technology, and industry. Zhou Enlai had been Deng's longtime patron and protector, and the conceptualization of the Four Modernizations was to be Zhou's last significant contribution before he died of cancer in 1976.

In the case of industry, modernization meant not only a move to markets and decentralized decision making but a major effort to attract direct investment from foreign corporations. The first concrete step toward this goal came in 1979, when a law was promulgated permitting Chinese enterprises to establish joint ventures with foreign partners.

Then, in a related move, Deng persuaded the Chinese Communist Party to authorize the establishment of four "special zones for export." The name was soon changed to "special economic zones"—probably after someone realized that the original name gave Western governments too frank a hint of the mercantilist economic philosophy that would guide China's subsequent rise.

The export-zone concept had been pioneered in Ireland in the 1950s (an export zone at Shannon Airport had been the Irish government's first gambit in a famously successful economic development program). The concept spread to Taiwan in the 1970s and it was the Taiwanese experience that evidently inspired Deng Xiaoping. The concept is that factories in specially designated zones are given preferential regulatory treatment on condition that they export most if not all of their output. Preferential treatment typically means exemption from customs duties on imports of key materials, components, and machines. It also often includes fast-track approvals and general relief from bureaucratic red tape.

For Deng Xiaoping the main attraction of the enterprise-zone concept was that it allowed him to hedge his bets: he wanted at first to keep China's free-market experiments ring-fenced while they were tested for unintended consequences. In particular Deng was evidently searching for a structure that would allow China to maximize its receipts of both foreign investment and new production technologies while minimizing the risk that economic growth might undermine the Communist Party's monopoly of power. Deng summed up this approach in his often quoted aphorism "We must feel for rocks as we cross the river."

In the early 1980s economic reform gathered pace as the profit motive was allowed ever greater play in corporate decision making. One key development was that corporate structures changed in baroque ways. Whereas previously all enterprises were ultimately owned by the state (albeit the state in many guises), in the new environment private investors were to become increasingly important. In many cases an enterprise's previous top management was allowed to acquire quasi-ownership rights. Although initially full-scale management buyouts were rare, many managers benefited from complicated contractual arrangements that gave them a share in their companies' profits. In some cases, for example, managers were given a lease to run an enterprise for an agreed number of years. They would share in any profits they earned beyond a certain level, while the base profits would go to the original state entity that had previously owned the business outright.

At first private enterprises were forbidden by law from employing more than eight people, but this rule quickly fell into abeyance and was eventually abolished. Meanwhile stock markets were set up in both Shenzhen, a southern Chinese city just across the border from Hong Kong, and Shanghai. At first stock trading was technically illegal, but again the rule fell by the wayside and was eventually rescinded.

By the late 1980s China had become a significant outsourcing platform for Western and Japanese corporations. Then came the Tiananmen massacre. For several years thereafter the flow of Western investment funds slumped. But the flow from Japan, South Korea, and Taiwan continued to burgeon. Thus as the 1990s wore on, China's industrial output continued to grow rapidly and so did its exports.

The Beijing authorities continued to hone China's industrial structure in a stereotypically East Asian way. In particular they embraced the keiretsu concept of closely knit families of affiliated companies. Companies like Qilu in the chemical industry and Baosteel in steel have become the focus of entire groups of affiliated companies—known as *qiye jituan*—that resemble the Japanese keiretsus. British economic commentator Will Hutton says that the Beijing government ment has now identified more than fifty keiretsu-like "strategic groups" as pillars of the economy. In his book *The Writing on the Wall,* Hutton comments: "The party exerts direct control over the strategic groups. The less strategic the party considers a sector or enterprise, the more it is prepared to loosen its control, but the shareholder and accounting structure is such that at any time the party can regain control if it is necessary."

China also embraced another controversial element of the East Asian model, cartels. As we have already noted, cartels play an important role in China's suppressed-consumption policy. By fixing prices, they gouge the consumer and thereby generate high returns on capital. The resulting profits are then channeled into ever more advanced production processes, thus achieving ever higher levels of productivity. Cartels also serve another important function in that they help government officials streamline efforts to "guide" industry. Generally each cartel regulates its members and thus becomes the government's surrogate in implementing industrial policy.

Although Western press correspondents tend to overlook or downplay the extent to which Chinese big business has embraced Japanese-style corporate structures, China's keiretsus and cartels have become an increasingly effective force in world commerce in recent years. Chinese steel makers, for instance, now cooperate on an industry-wide basis in minimizing the cost of their iron ore imports. In the past the Chinese used to bid freely against one another in negotiating with major iron ore producers such as Rio Tinto of the United Kingdom, BHP Billiton of Australia, and CVRD of Brazil. Now they have formed a united front under the leadership of the top Chinese steelmaker Baosteel, which was deputed by the China Iron and Steel Association in 2006 to negotiate on behalf of the entire Chinese industry. Why do the Chinese need to negotiate as a cartel? The answer is clear enough in a chart published by the PricewaterhouseCoopers consulting firm. Whereas as recently as 2001 China accounted for a mere 22 percent of the world's iron ore imports, its share as of 2007 had exceeded 80 percent. As reported by John Wilke of the Associated Press, the prices Americans pay for a growing list of products are now influenced by Chinese producer cartels. The most notable case so far has been vitamin C, whose supply worldwide is now controlled by a Chinese cartel. When this cartel tripled prices a few years ago, the effects were widely felt by American manufacturers of everything from pharmaceuticals and diet supplements to soft drinks and animal feeds. The Chinese producers are the successors to a previous German-Japanese cartel that up to the mid-1990s had dominated the industry. This cartel had finally lost its grip only when the U.S. Justice Department, in a rare breakthrough in its efforts to crack down on foreign price fixing, secured enough evidence to prove a charge of price fixing.

Other Chinese cartels are alleged to control the worldwide supply of saccharin, rayon, the pain reliever acetaminophen, and magnesite (a key additive used in the world steel industry). It should be noted that as yet Chinese cartels are modest in worldwide influence compared to their Japanese counterparts, which unbeknownst to most Westerners dominate the supply of countless so-called producers' goods, running the gamut from the "stepper" machines that make liquid crystal displays to the most precisely machined and heat-resistant components needed in jet engines.

To Western economists, Beijing's efforts to impose the latticelike keiretsu/ cartel structure on Chinese industries seem highly perplexing. After all, if standard economic theory is any guide, the East Asian model's structuring efforts should actually depress, rather than boost, economic performance. We don't have space to debate the issue here, but a careful consideration of the evidence (much of which is not readily available to Westerners) suggests that Western theory is wrong and that on balance East Asian–style industrial structuring has made a strongly positive contribution to productivity. (I have given an account of the argument in my 1995 book *Blindside: Why Japan Is Still on Track to Overtake the U.S. by the Year 2000.*)

For our purposes here it is sufficient to note that industrial structuring is an integral part of the East Asian model. But that model's most powerful driver is something different: suppressed consumption. This is the subject of the next chapter.

FOUR

Let There Be Savings!

As we have noted, East Asia's forced-savings system is a geopolitical game changer. By the simple and, as far as ordinary citizens are concerned, virtually invisible expedient of suppressing consumption, East Asian officials can powerfully boost their nations' savings rates.

Nowhere has the policy been more effective than in China. The origins of China's version of suppressed consumption can be traced back much further than most of the other reforms now driving the nation's growth. As the Columbia University scholar Andrew Nathan has pointed out, the system was already in use in embryonic form even before Mao Zedong's death in 1976.

As Chinese production rocketed in subsequent years, the effort to suppress consumption became increasingly effective in locking the nation into a consumption pattern that has lagged several years behind Chinese workers' rapidly rising incomes. Thus, in the five years ended December 2005 (the period covered by China's tenth five-year plan), consumption fell to a mere 51 percent of national income. This was sharply lower than the already low rate of 62 percent recorded under the ninth five-year plan.

Of course, the forced-savings system represents a blatant breach of the rules of world trade. Thus, as China has become an ever greater factor in the world economy in recent years, Chinese officials have become ever more assertive in denying the system's existence.

They have also quietly encouraged the West's China watchers to promulgate more acceptable explanations of Chinese savings behavior. According to one such explanation, the Chinese people are spurred to put large amounts of income aside to compensate for China's lack of a modern, Western-style social safety net. In reality this explains little. After all, most nations lack a so-cial safety net and have done so since time immemorial. Yet, with the exception of some of China's neighbors in East Asia in the last fifty years, no nation has ever come remotely close to matching the sort of savings performance we see today in China.

A related explanation, which was originally advanced by Franco Modigliani and Shi Larry Cao and has recently been championed by the prominent British economic commentator Will Hutton, focuses on China's unusual demograph-ics. In his 2006 book *The Writing on the Wall,* Hutton writes: "The main cause . . . of China's high savings rate has been the one-child policy introduced in 1980 to slow down China's population growth and relieve pressure on the land. Urban and rural people have built up their savings because they can rely on no more than one child to look after them in old age."

While the one-child policy probably has had *some* effect, Hutton's con-tention that it is decisive is not supported by the evidence. For a start, as the *Fi-nancial Times's* chief economic commentator, Martin Wolf, has pointed out, much Chinese saving is done not by individuals but by corporations. Indeed the contribution of corporations alone to China's savings rate has long been higher than America's total savings rate.

In any case, the time line is against Hutton's thesis. After all, if the one-child policy were decisive, we would expect a quite gradual change in savings be-havior as the age structure of China's population gradually changed. In the policy's early stages the family-planning decisions of only a fraction of Chinese women—mainly young mothers in their early thirties—had been affected. Older women had already had as many children as they wanted, so neither they nor their husbands can have altered their savings behavior in response to the new policy. Yet already by the mid-1980s, China boasted one of the world's highest household savings rates.

Moreover, Hutton is mistaken in implying that China's age structure is uniquely unbalanced. The birth rate is actually higher in China than in many parts of Eastern Europe, with the result that China boosts a higher proportion of young people than many Eastern European societies. Take Russia. The proportion of its population younger than fifteen was recently just 14 percent, versus 21 percent for China. If Hutton's thesis held we would expect Russia's savings rate to be even higher than China's. In reality it is unexceptional. A similar population structure is apparent in Lithuania and Latvia,whose savings rates are also puny compared to China's.

The most serious problem with Hutton's thesis, however, is that it does little to explain the larger context of an entire region long noted for high savings rates. After all, China's one-child policy is a China-specific factor. Yet the pattern of markedly high savings rates among China's East Asian neighbors has been a major anomaly of world economics for decades.

Here again the Japanese precedent is particularly telling. Japan's savings rate rocketed from 16.5 percent of gross national product in 1952–1954 to 24.9 percent in 1958–1960. Yet the Japanese population structure was then *one of the world's youngest*, with fully 33 percent of the population aged younger than fifteen in 1955. The record in both South Korea and Taiwan also stands in mute contradiction of the Hutton thesis.

Hutton makes no reference to China's comprehensive policy of suppressing consumption, and it is a fair guess that, based as he is in London, he is no different from virtually every other long-distance Western observer who puzzles over the East Asian savings phenomenon. Suppressed consumption, it seems, is the region's best-kept secret. It is past time that that changed.

The Reischauer Insight: News Travels Slowly

As we have noted, Edwin Reischauer spotlighted the salience of suppressed consumption as far back as 1955. As director of the Harvard-Yenching Institute, a partnership between Harvard and Beijing's Yenching University, Reischauer enjoyed a particularly deep early insight into East Asian development policies. In *Wanted: An Asian Policy*, he argued that the laissez-faire approach to development that had propelled Japan's early industrial success in the nineteenth century would not be fast enough for the impatient governments of post–World War II East Asia.

He added: "If there is to be even a partial achievement of the industrialization that most Asian leaders expect, the various governments of Asia will undoubtedly have to play a large part in the process of accumulating the capital. While this point is worth emphasizing for Westerners, who are accustomed to the primary role of individual citizens in saving and investment, it is usually taken for granted in Asia. Almost all Asian leaders assume that the government must take the lead in industrialization and modernization, and most also seem to realize that to do this the government must impose rigid controls over consumption."

I happen to be one of the first foreign observers to have spotted the significance of Reischauer's remarkable insight. Along with James Fallows, author of *Looking at the Sun,* I began mapping East Asia's suppressed-consumption/forced-saving system in the 1980s and published an early account in the *Atlantic* in 1989.

Since then other commentators have added to the West's knowledge. In 1996 the economist Lester Thurow, for instance, identified the suppression of consumer credit services as a key factor in China's then already superhigh savings rate.

The Singapore-based investment banker Daniel Lian has put it even more clearly. "Asia has suppressed its consumption to subsidize buyers of its exports," he said in 2004. "It [the suppressed consumption policy] also comes at the expense of future generations [in the United States and other Western nations]. At some point present consumption in these countries will have to give way to savings in order to restore macro-imbalances."

A similarly frank statement has come from Thailand's former prime minister Thaksin Shinawatra. An ethnic Chinese who is one of Thailand's richest citizens, Thaksin has suggested that in view of the way the East Asian system is transforming the world economy, traditional Western capitalism may no longer be a sustainable model for any nation intent on maintaining its jobs base. As quoted by the Sydney-based *Asia Today* magazine in 2004, he explicitly acknowledged the key innovation inherent in the East Asian model: "Consumption in Asia has been suppressed to encourage more exports and more savings."

The point has even made occasional appearances in the mainstream American media. Here, for instance, is a comment from *Newsweek* in 2005: "The debate over Asian underconsumption has raged since the 1970s, when Japan emerged as a world-beating exporter but kept its own citizens walled off from the fruits of global commerce. Following Tokyo's lead, governments across the region implemented regulatory measures to boost savings rates (to fund strategic industries) and tamp down household spending. High property prices and hard-to-obtain mortgages necessitated what economists call 'forced savings' for those aspiring to homeownership. Credit cards were denied to preserve cash-based traditions, and steep duties rendered foreign luxury items too dear for all but the wealthiest households."

In the Chinese version of the East Asian savings model, like that of Singapore and Malaysia, a considerable part of the effort to boost the savings rate takes the explicit form of compulsory savings. Under the so-called *tanpai* policy introduced in the mid-1990s by then Chinese financial supremo Zhu Rongji, every government organization was given a quota of government bonds to purchase. According to the Beijing-based economic commentator Laurence Brahm, even individual government officials are required to devote a proportion of their income to government bond purchases.

The Chinese authorities also rely heavily on taxes to suppress consumption. Thus they levy a value-added tax almost across the board at 17 percent. This is a far higher rate than in Canada, Australia, or New Zealand, where similar taxes are levied, and is about twice to three times the sales tax rates levied in many parts of the United States. The economist Huang Yasheng writes in *Foreign Policy* that the new tax increased the Chinese government's revenues by more than 22 percent in its first year of operation.

The Chinese authorities moreover exact specially hefty extra imposts (in addition to value-added tax) on various putative luxuries, from cosmetics to car tires. In many cities even dog ownership is heavily taxed. In both Shanghai and Tianjin, for instance, dog licenses cost 2,000 yuan a year—the equivalent of two or three weeks' wages for a factory worker.

Cars have long been singled out for special levies. As calculated by Clay Chandler of *Fortune* magazine, taxes and tariffs added as much as 65 percent to the base price of imported cars as of 2004. The anticonsumption tax policy was further tightened in 2006, when an existing special levy on cars of 8 percent was raised, in the case of large-engine cars, to 20 percent. At the same time Beijing introduced special levies on several other designated luxuries, ranging from expensive watches to boats.

Such measures are merely the tip of a vast iceberg. Of far greater significance are less direct curbs, most of which are almost invisible to the uninitiated.

Perhaps the most effective, as we will now see, is China's mercantilist approach to land zoning.

Zoning Out the Consumer

Whereas urban planners in the West think their job is to serve the consumer, their Chinese counterparts beg to differ. Their zoning policies unabashedly subordinate the interests of consumers to those of producers. Widely considered dysfunctional by unacclimatized Westerners, such policies reflect a hidden national agenda of suppressing consumption and thereby boosting the savings rate.

The pattern is exemplified in a general shortage of modern retailing space throughout China. Although department stores and luxury boutiques do exist, they are generally concentrated in the centers of a few major cities and thus are far from the suburban residential districts where most people live. Moreover, the general space shortage results in high commercial rents and fat retailing margins, which heighten the effect in suppressing consumption.

The anticonsumer bias of China's zoning system is even more obvious in housing policy. To say that China suffers a housing shortage is the mother of all understatements. In the words of the Australia-based China scholar Carolyn Blackman, housing in China's urban areas is "incredibly cramped." Furthermore, the quality of Chinese housing leaves much to be desired. The problem is particularly acute in older buildings, where residents in many cases still must share not only toilet and bathroom facilities but even kitchen facilities with neighbors.

Such conditions act directly to choke off consumption. With little space to heat and air-condition, Chinese urban dwellers use only about one-tenth as much electricity as Americans. Moreover, purchases of furniture, carpets, curtains, and electrical appliances necessarily run at a fraction of what they might otherwise be.

As in commercial property, the zoning policies serve powerfully to boost prices. Again, as in commercial property, the resulting profits are skimmed off by various government-owned companies and agencies that ultimately own most of China's land. The money is recycled in various guises into industrial investment, thus ultimately boosting the national growth rate.

According to an article in 2006 in *Housing Finance International* magazine, Chinese city officials often aim deliberately at creating "a booming real estate market." They are concerned apparently not only to produce high profits for city hall but to garner political favor with superiors in the Communist Party's national hierarchy.

Meanwhile the national tax administation has added another twist to the tourniquet by announcing new capital-gains tax rules in 2006 that have encouraged speculators to hold rather than sell. By postponing selling until at least five years from the date of purchase, speculators can avoid the tax. The evidence is that thousands of speculators who might otherwise have "flipped" their holdings for an immediate gain—and thus released some welcome supply into a supertight market—have been encouraged instead to wait out the five-year holding period.

The effect of all this on prices is hard to exaggerate. China's official news agency Xinhua reported that as of 2006 apartment buyers in Beijing were paying on average nearly $80 a square foot. This was fully two-thirds of the American average of about $120 a square foot. Yet per capita income in the Beijing region, at around $3,900 a year in 2005, ran less than one-tenth that of the United States!

According to the *People's Daily*'s figures, Beijing residents typically pay about eleven times their income for a small apartment—and they can consider themselves fortunate compared to residents of Shanghai, where the ratio can run as high as twenty times. As the Economist Intelligence Unit has pointed out, the ratio of house prices to incomes in China is shockingly out of line with international norms. Citing a World Bank assessment, the EIU suggested that house prices should be considered too high if they run much more than four times buyers' incomes.

Judging by official announcements, Chinese leaders are doing everything possible to alleviate the problem. Thus in the tenth five-year plan (covering the years 2001 through 2005), they announced an attempt to raise housing space to an average of more than 230 square feet per capita. All the evidence is that the result in 2005 fell way short of the plan, however.

China's housing crisis is greatly compounded by demographics: the country is, after all, in the midst of a vast migration from the countryside to the cities. Between 2001 and 2005 alone, the population of China's urban areas shot from 481 million to 562 million—an increase of 81 million, or nearly 17 percent. The proportion of the nation's total population living in urban areas went from

37.7 percent to 43.0 percent. Moreover, as recently estimated by the United Nations, the urban percentage is likely to reach 50 percent by around 2015, up from just 20 percent in 1980.

China's rate of new building falls way short of what is needed to reduce China's exorbitant ratio of house prices to incomes. Although the authorities have permitted a rush of construction of luxury apartment buildings in major cities, the space created is nowhere near adequate to the task of housing the world's most populous nation. Figures supplied by CEIC Data, a Hong Kong–based research firm, indicate that the total area of all new residential property sold in China in 2005 came to just 5.3 billion square feet. This was just 35 percent more than in the United States, a nation with less than one-quarter of China's population. Per head of population, China, with one of the world's most acute housing shortages, added just 4 square feet of new housing space in 2005 whereas the United States added fully 13 square feet. Of course, the United States is a much richer country—but actually this makes much less difference than might appear. Absent a government policy of deliberately constricting supply, there is no reason why the Chinese should not have far more housing space than at present. (Because wages are still very low in China, construction costs are also low, and in the absence of the suppressed-consumption policy, house prices would be correspondingly affordable.)

To see how powerful is the savings effect of China's housing shortage consider the plight of a typical young Shanghai-based executive cited by *China Daily* in 2006. Though his yearly salary was nearly $7,500 (which put him almost in the nouveau riche class by Chinese standards), he estimated it would take him nearly fifteen years to save enough to buy a suitable apartment (which he defined as one measuring about 1,000 square feet).

As a practical matter many residents in Shanghai and Beijing these days reportedly devote as much as 50 percent of their income to housing costs.

Of course, this may not seem that different from how things are in Manhattan or central London these days. But super-high housing costs are a permanent feature of the landscape in China, whereas the recent surge in house prices in the United States and Britain is surely a temporary phenomenon—a boom that in all probability will lead, if not to a bust, at least to a long period of relative stagnation while incomes catch up with prices. In any case, the crucial factor here is a fundamental difference in the way mortgage markets are regulated. In the West, refinancing deals are widely permitted that allow long-time home owners to boost their consumption by taking out second mortgages on their homes. Thus high house prices in the West have tended in recent years to boost rather than suppress overall consumption. Because refinancing to fund consumption is generally forbidden in China, high housing costs there serve entirely to depress consumption and thus they act unremittingly to boost the savings rate. They may well be the single greatest factor underpinning the Chinese people's phenomenal savings performance.

Clipped Wings: China's Grounded Tourists

Most of the mercantilist economies of East Asia have a record of greatly restricting their citizens' foreign travel opportunities. Restrictions have been particularly tight in the early years of implementation of the East Asian economic model. Thus in Japan, for instance, citizens were subject to an absolute ban on foreign leisure travel all through the early post-World War II era up to 1964, the year of the Tokyo Olympics. A similar ban applied in South Korea up to 1988, the year of the Seoul Olympics. (Why relax the ban in the Olympic year? The logic evidently is that the respective national airlines made permanent additions to their carrying capacity to cater initially for a rush of inbound travelers.)

The Chinese people have been permitted in theory to vacation abroad since the early 1980s. In practice, however, such travel has remained heavily circumscribed. Indeed up to the late 1990s Chinese citizens were permitted to take foreign vacations only if they could show that their expenses were being underwritten by a friend or relative abroad. Although this rule has gradually fallen into disuse, several other factors continue to stunt the Chinese people's opportunities to travel abroad. The cumulative effect is to keep foreign travel to probably less than one-quarter of what we might otherwise expect.

In 2004 the total number of Chinese citizens who traveled outside the Chinese mainland in any capacity (whether for leisure, business, or study) was just 28.9 million—just 2 percent of the total population. Moreover, a large percentage of these (probably a majority, though the statistics are not sufficiently detailed to say for sure) did not travel beyond China's own special administrative regions of Hong Kong and Macao.

What is undeniable is that Chinese tourists are notable for their absence in major vacation destinations. In recent years they represented fewer than 1 percent of all foreign visitors to India, for instance. Yet India's proximity and its economical prices, not to mention its distinction as the birthplace of Buddhism, should give it a special appeal to Chinese travelers.

Here are just some of the factors that have artificially constrained the Chinese people's overseas travel opportunities:

Cartel pricing by travel agents. Only a handful of travel agents in China are permitted to sell international air tickets, and they operate cartel pricing to keep fares artificially high. Under Chinese regulations only travel agents who are already big players in China's inbound travel industry (catering to foreign tourists visiting China) have been permitted to serve Chinese citizens going abroad. The point of this linkage seems to be to get Chinese citizens to subsidize the cost of developing China's burgeoning inbound travel business, thus turning it into a major invisible export earner. A recent check showed that typical roundtrip economy class fares from Beijing to the New York were about 20 percent higher than for Tokyo to New York. Yet the distance travelled is virtually the same and, because of vastly higher Japanese wages, airline ground-handling costs are actually much higher in Japan than in China.

Passport problems. Chinese citizens often have to wait months for a passport and even then may have to pay a sizable under-the-counter bribe. Writing in 1994, Nicholas Kristof reported that the going rate was several months' salary for a typical worker. The rate seems to have come down in the interim but can still be as much as much as $50, the equivalent of a week's wages in many parts of China. Moreover, a standard Chinese passport is valid for only one year (versus a norm of ten years for passports issued in the United States, the United Kingdom, and many other Western nations).

Inadequate vacation time. Up to the late 1990s, Chinese workers rarely received more than a few days' vacation a year. Then, in a show of liberalization, the Beijing authorities increased the allowance to an ostensible two to three weeks. In practice, however, many workers receive far less than this. And even those who are allowed their full quota generally must take time off during three officially designated holiday weeks, when countless other workers are also off. Of course, airport bottlenecks are particularly acute at such times, and only the lucky—or more likely the wealthy—can get out of the country.

Inconvenient itineraries. Much of China's still tightly limited airline capacity is reserved for business travel and freight. Moreover, international flights are permitted from only a few major cities such as Shanghai and Beijing. Thus, most Chinese citizens have no direct access to international flights. Flying to an appropriate domestic hub adds considerably not only to costs but to travel times and helps explain why few residents in China's vast interior ever travel abroad. Even for residents of Shanghai and Beijing, regulation of airline landing rights artificially limits their travel options. With few exceptions, flights out of China serve only the West's largest cities. Thus there are no direct flights to Scotland, for instance—an important consideration in that golf is a key pursuit of wealthy Chinese businessmen, who might otherwise be interested in playing at St. Andrew's. There is also a regulated shortage of capacity to more affordable holiday destinations in nations like Thailand and Malaysia.

Foreign exchange problems. Chinese tourists suffer major inconvenience in making purchases abroad because the debit cards they carry are typically for domestic use only.

Perhaps the biggest loser is the United States. Although it ranks as a favorite destination for tourists from all over the world (in the number of tourists it receives, it stands third behind France and Spain), it has hitherto received virtually no benefit from Chinese tourism. As of 2004, just 173,000 American nonimmigrant visas were issued to Chinese visitors. This was half the number issued to visitors from Ireland, a nation with less than 0.4 percent of China's population.

Part of the problem is that top policymakers in Beijing have snubbed the United States in their regulation of the Chinese travel industry. Instead they have promoted travel to Europe, particularly to Italy, which in 2003 was the top long-haul destination for Chinese tourists with a market share of 33 percent. Russia came second and Germany third. The United States came an extremely poor fourth with a market share of less than 9 percent.

This has not stopped Chinese officials from continually talking up the prospects of a boom in Chinese travel to the United States. Indeed, in an agreement signed in 2004, the Chinese government committed itself to promoting such a boom. Meanwhile Li Jiaxing of the China National Aviation Corporation in 2006 talked of the "huge potential" of travel by Chinese tourists to reduce Sino-American trade imbalances.

In practice a key problem is so-called approved destination status. Although Hong Kong, Japan, and South Korea were given approved status several years ago, Chinese regulators as of 2007 still had not approved the United States. The root of the problem seems to be that Chinese regulators want to control Chinese tourists' movements abroad and therefore insist that only certain travel agencies abroad should be licensed to deal with Chinese visitors. Washington has argued that such an arrangement would breach U.S. antitrust law.

All this is not to deny that vacation travel has increased in recent years. The growth, however, has been from a tiny base. Of course, under international treaties, China is committed to further liberalization of its travel industry. But, like Japan before it, China will probably find ways— albeit increasingly indirect ones—to continue to curb leisure travel. Even today the Japanese, with some of the highest incomes in the world, are only about half as likely as the British to vacation abroad.

Consumer Finance: Save Now, Buy Later

Few aspects of Chinese economic policy have had a more powerful effect in boosting the Chinese savings rate than Beijing's systematic suppression of consumer finance.

Although the relationship between consumer finance and savings is not obvious, consumer lending serves dollar for dollar to reduce national savings. Think of it this way: if I borrow your savings to buy a Rolls-Royce, I am effectively doing your consumption for you. From the point of view of the national accounts, consumer credit counts as "negative savings."

This incidentally sheds useful light on the savings trend in the United States. Massive growth in consumer credit in recent years has probably been the single biggest factor in reducing the American savings rate to almost nothing. The growth has been facilitated by computerization, which has both reduced the costs and simplified the managerial functions involved in extending mass-market credit.

Although American policymakers feel ideologically obliged not to resist the trend, in East Asia by contrast, regulators have displayed no similar restraint. In a region where it is taken for granted that the rights of the individual should be subordinated to the national interest, these regulators have worked assiduously to block the rise of consumer finance.

Of course, Beijing disavows any such intent and has indeed been highly successful in encouraging the Western media to write upbeat reports about a supposed Chinese consumer boom that any day now will start reducing China's trade surpluses.

This is how in 2001 *Business Week*'s Shanghai-based correspondent Alysha Webb announced one such false dawn: "Twenty years ago, China's government routinely extolled the virtues of the model worker who performed heroic feats on the factory floor. Today, Beijing is more likely to laud the model borrower: someone willing to fearlessly pile on debt for a piece of the Chinese Dream."

But where were the facts to support such hyperbole? Although Webb talked up a coming boom in credit cards and in mortgages, her article was largely devoid of substantiation. True, she pointed out that Chinese interest rates had fallen substantially in previous years. But this was beside the point given that in the highly regulated Chinese economy, interest rates have little influence on consumption. In any case, with the benefit of hindsight we can see clearly that the supposed consumption revolution Webb thought she detected was a mirage.

After all, far from falling in subsequent years, China's savings rate steadily increased: in 2004, it stood at 44.2 percent of national output, up from 38.0 percent in 2001. Moreover, lending to individuals remained a derisory part of Chinese banking business—so derisory indeed that it does not merit disaggregated mention in the *China Statistical Yearbook*, a phonebook-sized volume that provides figures on everything from the width of roads in Urumqi to the availability of tap water in Ningxia. As for consumer finance, the best this 900-page doorstopper can do is provide a bundled figure for total Chinese bank lending to both individuals and privately owned enterprises. As of 2003 such lending by China's national financial institutions accounted for a mere $7 billion, or less than 0.4 percent of their total funds. Only a fraction of this, if anecdotal evidence is anything to go by probably a negligible fraction, represented consumer finance.

One key result has been to suppress the sales of cars. Although the Beijing authorities have announced various measures ostensibly intended to increase credit to car buyers, only 10 to 15 percent of car purchases in 2004 were financed with credit. It is probably not a coincidence that the total number of cars sold in China that year, a mere 3.3 million, was way below what market experts considered to be the market's true potential. Certainly it looked puny compared to an estimate by Mercedes-Benz in the early 1990s that, given a deregulated car market, car sales would almost immediately rise to 8 million to 10 million a year. (If finance for car purchases is so scarce, why have the Detroit Big Three invested in new plants in China? For one thing, they are hoping the market will expand rapidly in the years ahead. They also see China as a future outsourcing platform to serve the American market.)

Eager to present China as rapidly Americanizing its consumption habits, many Western reporters have long suggested that credit cards are becoming a major factor in Chinese life. In 1994, for instance, they accepted at face value a prediction that Chinese banks would issue 200 million credit cards by 2000. This analysis was even picked up by the best-selling author and famed management consultant Tom Peters, who recycled it unchecked in his 1995 book *The Pursuit of WOW!*

Similarly, in 2003 the *Washington Monthly* reported that the Chinese were using "plastic" to make $200 billion worth of transactions a year. The author Bob Froehlich has also argued that the Chinese are eagerly embracing an American-style credit-funded lifestyle. In a book in 2006, he asserted that, expressed as a proportion of borrowers' incomes, consumer credit was nearly 50 percent higher in Shanghai than in the United States. Referring to young Chinese consumers, he added: "While their parents drank tea, they drink Coca-Cola. Their parents wore sandals; they wear Nike running shoes. Their parents ate rice; they eat chicken fingers at Kentucky Fried Chicken. Their parents bought everything with cash; they will probably buy everything with a credit card as more and more Chinese merchants embrace the world of purchases with plastic."

Froehlich did not cite any sources—perhaps because none exist, at least not reliable ones.

In any case, the verifiable facts confound the upbeat reports of a Chinese consumer credit boom. The truth is that Beijing remains committed to a long-established policy of slowing the development of credit cards. Not only do Chinese banks face extensive regulatory restrictions on providing consumer credit, but credit cards are the target of special restrictions intended to limit their usefulness. As of 2007, it was still not possible for the Chinese to use credit cards to make many types of purchases over the phone. And if they wanted to buy airline tickets, for instance, they were required by regulation to pay a surcharge of three percentage points over the cash price.

The result, as Jane Macartney pointed out in the *Times* of London in 2006, is that consumer credit remains almost unknown in China and banks rarely give loans except to companies or government bureaucrats.

So why have other correspondents talked of a credit "boom"? In part the confusion can be traced to a technical misunderstanding. To the extent that Westerners talk about the proliferation of credit cards in China, they are generally referring to something quite different: debit cards. These look like credit cards—many of them even bear the Visa or MasterCard logo—but, in sharp contrast to credit cards, debit cards actually *boost* rather than reduce the savings rate. This is because users are required first to put cash on deposit before they can make purchases.

What is undeniable is that Chinese regulators have authorized a vast proliferation of debit cards in recent years. By contrast, they have continued to suppress the growth of credit cards. Indeed, until recently they maintained an absolute ban on credit cards. Under pressure from the international banking community, this ban has now been relaxed somewhat—but only in the case of a few favored banks.

Even if the authorities were to permit a general free-for-all in credit card issuance, other constraints would still ensure that the credit card industry remained stunted. This is because issuers in China are stymied by an acute lack of information on prospective borrowers' credit histories. As in many other East Asian nations, the development of credit-checking agencies has been obstructed. This opens the way for petty racketeers to take advantage of any bank that moves too fast in expanding its credit services. As a practical matter East Asian banks apply ultraconservative lending criteria, thus greatly slowing the growth of their consumer credit operations.

In China's case the absence of reliable credit-checking information has been compounded by the fact that Chinese law has made it difficult for lenders to establish reliable recourse to borrowers' assets.

The Chinese consumer credit industry has been stillborn, and what little credit is available has generally been supplied not by respectable banks but by loan sharks, who charge superhigh interest rates and resort to gangster tactics against slow payers.

How many true credit cards are in issue in China? No official figures are published and unofficial estimates vary wildly. As reported by Alysha Webb in 2001, one Chinese bank alone supposedly had already more than 4 million credit cards in issue. Yet in the same year the McKinsey management consulting firm estimated that the total credit cards issued *by all banks* in China came to a mere 300,000. This represented just 0.3 percent of all bank cards in issue (with most of the rest being those savings-generating debit cards). In 2003 the U.S. State Department put the total number of credit cards at just 1 million, fewer than one for every one thousand citizens. Of course the total has been rising rapidly and as of 2006 the total ranged between 8 million and 50 million, depending on whether you believed HSBC or the People's Bank of China. But even the high estimate represented less than 5 percent of all plastic cards in issue.

If all this is so obvious, why does the press keep getting it wrong? Why indeed. Part of the reason is, as usual in East Asia, that they are being manipulated by their sources. Much of the disinformation about Chinese consumer credit emanates from Beijing- or Shanghai-based Western "analysts" who speak in round numbers and ask that their comments be kept nonattributable.

Most Western reporters are not financially astute enough to see through the spin. That said, some media organizations that should know better have also contributed to American confusion on this subject. Take the *Wall Street Journal*. In 2007, its correspondents James Areddy and Eric Bellman, reporting from Shanghai and Mumbai respectively, wrote: "Asia's biggest nations are racing to build an American-style consumer economy, seeking to rev up consumer spending by promoting mortgages and other types of loans.... Washington likes the strategy because making Asia less dependent on exports might help reduce the huge U.S. trade deficit and could create new demand for U.S. goods."

The article went on to report that 61 percent of the Chinese population already had plastic payment cards. There was no mention, however, of the fact that virtually all Chinese payment cards were debit cards. Nor, of course, did the article say that debit cards actually boost the savings rate.

The tone suggested that the Chinese authorities were desperately trying to promote a consumer credit boom. Although the article acknowledged that progress was slow, it attributed this to Chinese bankers' inexperience. But if this is the real issue, what explains the Chinese government's policy of marginalizing American and European banks (which, of course, are experienced in consumer lending and have long been eager to apply their expertise in China)? This question was not considered, and China's exclusionist attitude to foreign banks was not even mentioned. In reality a major reason why China sidelines foreign banks is precisely because it fears they would press for liberalization of consumer lending controls.

Although it is of course growing in China, consumer credit is still a negligible force. As recorded by *Time* magazine, personal debt represented a mere 20 percent of annual disposable income in urban China in 2005. This was less than one-fifth the rate in the United States.

Trade Policy: No Imports, No Problem

Judged by standard Western economic theory, China's mercantilist trade policies mainly serve to render the Chinese economy less efficient than it otherwise might be. But this analysis overlooks a crucial countervailing point: China's mercantilist trade policy greatly curtails consumption and therefore represents an easy and powerful way to boost the nation's savings rate. As we have already pointed out, if a nation does not import things, it can't consume them.

It is not surprising therefore that in the early stages of its application of the East Asian economic model in the 1980s, Beijing erected a high tariff wall against imports. This replaced a previous quota system that had kept imports to a trickle in Maoist days. The new tariff system rendered the Chinese economy more flexible but did not significantly boost imports as a percentage of national income. Quite the contrary, the Chinese economy remained extraordinarily mercantilist. According to the testimony of a Commerce Department official to a U.S. Senate committee in 1991, China raised tariffs on about ninety items between 1988 and 1990, most of them consumer goods. The new tariff rates ranged as high as 120 percent.

Under foreign pressure, China has gradually reduced these tariffs over the last decade and a half; according to the economists Thomas Klitgaard and Karen Schiele, the average level of tariff had fallen to 23 percent as of 1997. It has fallen considerably further since—but, like Japan and South Korea before it, China has switched to nontariff barriers as the main tools of a continuing mercantilist trade policy. Nontariff barriers are generally difficult to challenge under World Trade Organization rules.

As elsewhere in East Asia, manipulative standard-setting and product-testing regulations are extensively used to discriminate against imports. In a book published in 2005, the political scientist Margaret Pearson explained: "Tools such as requiring testing to meet Chinese standards of health and safety have been used in increasing numbers. These are barriers not just because they provide justification for barring entry of foreign goods but because such tests must be conducted in China or by Chinese inspectors."

Chinese officials, moreover, are increasingly manipulating the rules of China's national consumption taxes to support the mercantilist trade policy. As reported by the Office of the United States Trade Representative in 2005, the impact has been particularly powerful in semiconductors. Similar tactics have been used to discourage imports of everything from cosmetics to Swiss watches. Meanwhile, as Keith Bradsher of the *New York Times* has pointed out, a new higher tax rate on large-engine cars announced in 2006 seemed to be aimed explicitly at discouraging imports of foreign cars.

John B. Stuttard, the former chairman of PricewaterhouseCoopers in China, notes another problem: distribution within China is extraordinarily difficult. Not only do provincial governments levy protectionist fees on "imports" from other Chinese provinces, but independent distributors hardly exist. Thus, in many industries new entrants to the Chinese market have no alternative but to build their own distribution system from scratch. Such an endeavor not only takes many years—up to a decade or more in many cases—but is extremely expensive. Given the regime's pronounced hostility to imports, foreign producers naturally wonder whether, even after investing in their own distribution networks, they would be permitted a fair shot at selling their products in China. Given the record, they have good reason to believe rather that new nontariff barriers would simply be erected to frustrate them.

Another problem is exorbitant advertising rates. In the words of Tom Doctoroff, a Shanghai-based advertising executive, television rates in particular are "sky-high." Government-owned television companies often charge rates as much as ten times what might apply in a free market. So the cost to build a brand in Shanghai and Beijing can be as high as in New York or Los Angeles. Yet the spending power of Chinese consumers is, of course, only a small fraction of American levels. The effect is greatly to hamper the building of new consumer brands in China. By definition this works particularly to the disadvantage of foreign corporations new to the market.

Foreign corporations are also often stymied by China's labyrinthine retailing system. Like Japan before it, China has allowed its big manufacturers to control large chains of retail stores in which they promote their own products to the exclusion of those of competitors. For example, several makers of domestic

appliances now control important distribution outlets, enabling them to marginalize competitive imports, if not to shut them out entirely. Certainly only
the strongest foreign corporations can afford to replicate this approach. One
company that has attempted to do so is Matsushita, which has already built
similarly effective control of distribution in its Japanese home market. Most
other foreign electrical manufacturers simply do not have the resources or
management expertise to emulate such an approach.

As reported by Stuttard, foreign companies that complain about China's
distribution system are blandly told that independent distributors of the sort
that handle so much distribution in the West are "not traditional." The problem is so acute that, as recorded in 2005 by former Dow Jones Beijing bureau
chief James McGregor, some Western consumer-goods companies have resorted to enlisting the help of professional smugglers to get goods into China.

The obverse side of China's efforts to limit imports is apparent in a remarkable dearth of genuine American-made goods in Chinese stores. Of course, as
James Areddy of the *Wall Street Journal* reported in 2006, there is no shortage of
American *brand names* in China. For the most part products sold under these
brand names are made locally, using local labor and materials. Even where such
production is done with the full approval and participation of the American
companies concerned, it contributes virtually nothing to America's export revenues. Areddy underlined the point by conducting an informal audit of the
consumption of one affluent family in Shanghai. Although the family's income
was nearly $50,000 a year—a small fortune by Chinese standards—he discov-
ered that virtually the only authentic Made-in-America products they bought
were Heinz steak sauce from Pittsburgh and wine from the Gallo winery in
California.

Meanwhile China adds to the mercantilist effect with policies that strongly
promote exports. Like goods that are not imported, goods that *are* exported are
unavailable for domestic consumption. James Fallows has pointed out that as a
general rule, the consumer goods China produces in such abundance for the
American market are not available in Chinese stores. The result is an economic
vacuum. While the Chinese workforce is engaged disproportionately in making
goods for export, Chinese consumers are largely blocked from buying imports.

Too often they are faced with a Hobson's choice between locally produced
goods of poor quality or overpriced imports (the overpricing reflects profiteer-
ing by designated import agents, many of which are state-owned companies).
Not surprisingly, many consumers simply keep their wallets closed or spend

their money instead in China's inflated urban real estate market. Either way, the national savings rate receives a powerful boost (in the latter case because government entities control most of China's real estate and they recycle their huge real estate profits into industrial or infrastructural projects that powerfully strengthen China's economic muscle).

For more than a decade now, many China watchers have predicted a gradual phasing out of Chinese mercantilism. One of the more notable such predictions has come from Gordon G. Chang, who in the 1990s worked in the Shanghai office of a top New York law firm. Commenting in an influential book in 2001, *The Coming Collapse of China,* he wrote: "The export drive . . . will soon run out of steam. That's already happening. China's surplus declined in both 1999 and 2000. The trend has become so apparent that even central government officials realize there is a problem, and World Trade Organization membership could ultimately result in deficits as Beijing loses the ability to closely manage trade flows."

Although the book was strongly recommended by top analysts at the American Enterprise Institute and the Cato Institute, Chang's analysis could hardly have proved more wrong. The fact is that just as the book was published the trade surplus not only stopped falling but started rocketing: by 2006 it had hit a record $177 billion, a near eightfold increase on 2001. In retrospect it seems that Chang was blown off-course by a highly contrived propaganda effort by Beijing. As the United States and other Western nations considered China's application to join the World Trade Organization in 1999 and 2000, Chinese officials manipulated the statistics to create the impression of a reversal in the trade trend. (Such an illusion can readily be sustained for a year or so by, among other things, making judicious changes in national accounting conventions.)

Chang's analysis was challenged at the time by key Western executives on the ground in China. Unfortunately most of them spoke only privately and thus were underrepresented in American press reports. (They feared retaliation by Chinese officials.)

One of the few Western executives who openly questioned the idea that China's trade trend was turning around was Terry Barrett, head of the Chinese operations of Novartis, the Swiss pharmaceuticals giant. As quoted by John B. Stuttard, Barrett has implied that it will be decades before the Chinese market really opens up. "We all welcome China as a member of the World Trade Organization," Barrett said. "But there is probably overconfidence about the impact of WTO on our ability to do business in China in a freer manner, because WTO membership does not automatically confer that freedom. It will take time."

Even that may be putting it optimistically. After all, if the precedent of Japan is anything to go by, mercantilist behavior can be continued indefinitely. Even today, four decades after American policymakers first began market-opening talks with Tokyo, the Japanese market remains closed in key categories. (This is most obvious in cars, where foreign brands have been kept to a steady 4 percent market share for decades. Even Renault, which—at least on paper—controls the Nissan group, has not been able to break into the Japanese market.)

Even *Imports* Boost China's Savings Rate

The Beijing regime's latest gambit in its mercantilist trade policy is to encourage what can only be described as "mercantilist imports." While Beijing strongly discourages the importing of most luxuries, it has encouraged wealthy citizens to spend heavily on certain goods, such as diamonds and art objects, that constitute a permanent store of value.

The most publicized aspect of this policy has been a major effort to buy back countless Chinese antiques that fell into the hands of foreign traders and looters during China's long centuries of economic weakness. The policy not only serves to reduce China's apparent trade surpluses—a useful geopolitical gambit—but provides the Chinese nation with a permanent store of value. That it also helps salve some old geopolitical wounds is a useful psychic bonus.

One key objective has been to buy back thousands of items sold abroad by the Communist regime during Mao Zedong's time. As his opening shot in the Cultural Revolution, Mao had dubbed China's art treasures "poisonous weeds." In a desperate effort to raise foreign currency, the commander of his praetorian guard sold many priceless objects abroad.

Officially the buying spree has been attributed to a need to find items to fill nearly a thousand museums that Beijing has ordered built. But this story undoubtedly puts the cart before horse: the museums are needed to house items purchased in pursuit of a mercantilist national agenda.

The buyback policy is being conducted in part by state-owned corporations. One that has been publicly identified is Poly Corporation, a Shanghai-listed armaments-trading company that is controlled by the People's Liberation Army. Meanwhile the State Administration of Cultural Heritage has established a fund to recover Chinese treasures from abroad.

The result has been to trigger a spectacular boom in top-grade Chinese antiques. Commenting in 2005, the Belgian art dealer Gisele Croes suggested that Poly's maneuvers had, in the space of ten years, driven up the price of one notable imperial bronze from $800,000 to $3 million. Speaking to Bloomberg news agency reporter Craig Copetas, she added: "The People's Liberation Army is very rich, very powerful, and all-knowing."

How rich? According to the art consultant Elizabeth Casale, the PLA as of 2006 was often paying prices "far above market value" and may already have spent hundreds of millions of dollars. Prices had already been driven so high that analysts cited by Bloomberg have speculated about the possibility that the Chinese may diversify by buying Western artworks.

In pursuit of "mercantilist imports," the Beijing authorities have also been encouraging Chinese consumers to buy diamonds and precious metals, particularly platinum. This is a stunning reversal of a previous policy of strictly curbing imports of such items.

The result is that jewelry recently was rated the third-most-important consumption item in China after housing and cars. Jewelers' shops are springing up all over urban China. As of 2006, one well-known Hong Kong–based diamond-trading company, Chow Tai Fook Jewellery, already operated 400 jewelry stores in China and had plans to open 120 more.

China's new interest in jewelry, particularly diamond jewelry, comes as no surprise. Japan adopted a similar strategy as far back as the 1960s. There is no mystery here: as the advertisements say, diamonds are forever. As an indestructible store of value, they add permanently to a nation's wealth. They are, in other words, every mercantilist's idea of a dream import, serving as they do to reduce a nation's apparent trade surpluses while at the same time furthering the policy of national enrichment. It should be noted that China's diamonds are imported in bulk at rock-bottom trade prices, so the subsequent large markup at retail accrues to Chinese importers and retailers.

The diamond-buying program got its start in the 1990s when De Beers, the South African company that controls the world's diamond market, received a go-ahead to launch an extensive marketing campaign in China. De Beers boldly initiated an effort to transform Chinese marriage customs. Up to that time, Chinese families often celebrated weddings with purchases of jade. In a skillful advertising campaign, De Beers persuaded Chinese brides that diamonds were more in keeping with modern marriage.

Diamond sales quadrupled in the space of a decade, and as the campaign has been extended to more Chinese television marketing regions, they have continued to rise ever since. Meanwhile in 2002 the Chinese tax authorities gave the trend their blessing by cutting taxes on diamonds. The tax rate on crude diamonds was cut from 34 percent to the standard value-added tax rate of 17 percent, and that for finished diamonds from 42 percent to 17 percent. As reported by the *People's Daily* in 2004, about four-fifths of marriages in major cities were already then celebrated with diamond rings.

The Chinese system goes to extraordinary lengths to boost the nation's savings rate. It is important to emphasize, however, that the policies by which consumption is suppressed are not static. Rather, they are constantly evolving, and indeed the trend generally is toward liberalization. Western observers often take this to mean that the Chinese authorities have belatedly adopted a Western approach to consumption policy. But such a conclusion is ill-advised. Experience elsewhere in East Asia suggests that China has no intention of abandoning the suppressed consumption system but is merely intent on boosting consumption in line with rising incomes.

Such liberalization can be expected to continue. But it will be phased in at a pace that will ensure that the savings rate remains high.

We have outlined how the forced-savings system equips the Beijing regime with a uniquely efficacious tool in building the new Chinese superpower. Although huge savings are, of course, essential to this effort, they are not sufficient. Somehow the money must be invested intelligently and effectively in pursuit of the national interest. It is time to look at how China is governed.

FIVE

Power Begets Power

The cornerstone of China's economic system is tight governmental control. Anyone concerned to evaluate China's rise must wonder therefore how secure is the Beijing regime's grip on power and how efficaciously China will be governed in the years ahead.

Westerners can be forgiven for being confused. Certainly, if the Western press is to be believed, China often seems to be teetering on the brink of ungovernability. On three occasions in recent decades there have been widespread fears abroad that China was headed for total political chaos. The first was in the immediate wake of Mao Zedong's death in 1976, when the so-called Gang of Four challenged Mao's chosen successor, Hua Guofeng. The resulting leadership crisis was resolved only with the rise to ultimate power of Deng Xiaoping in 1978. Then in the spring of 1989 massive student protests seemed so threatening that the leadership resorted to the Tiananmen massacre. Again in the mid-1990s China's political stability was widely questioned in the West as supreme leader Deng Xiaoping entered his last illness.

China's stability apart, the Western press has also often raised major questions about the general sustainability of China's highly expansionist economic strategy. One problem increasingly cited in recent years is the yawning gap between rich and poor. Another is corruption. Then there is the question of whether economic liberalization and rising wealth will soften Chinese authoritarianism, perhaps to the point of derailing China's entire superpower strategy. Citing issues like these, many observers suggest that Chinese growth is destined to decline dramatically in the years ahead. Indeed a group of outspoken gloommongers even suggests that China may lapse back into the lethargy and disunity that characterized it in the first half of the twentieth century.

What everyone can agree on is that governing a nation as large as China is not easy. What is equally unquestionable, if less obvious, is that the Beijing leadership in recent decades has adroitly moved to strengthen several aspects of its control. This has been achieved despite the fact that a considerable degree of decentralization has been implicit in the move towards freer markets.

On balance, the betting is that China will not only hold together but remain relatively stable. And if it does, top leaders can be expected to maintain their relentless emphasis on building China's influence in the world community.

Chinese Power: The Story So Far

Before considering the reality of how power works in modern China, let's first consider the historical context. For most of its history, China has been one of the world's strongest states. That said, the Chinese state has not always been strong. Indeed in the two hundred years before the Chinese Communist Party came to power, China went through a prolonged period of administrative decay and greatly weakened central authority. The problems seem to have stemmed largely from an inability to adapt to the forces of modernization then emanating from Europe. Certainly China's imperial bureaucracy seemed increasingly flummoxed by the West's rising power. Assailed on one side by Western colonialism and on the other by increasingly assertive anti-Western activists at home, the ruling Qing dynasty was caught between a rock and a hard place.

The final crisis came in the early decades of the twentieth century. First the dynasty abolished the national examination system by which elite bureaucrats had traditionally been chosen. This seems to have been intended as the first step toward converting the Qing dynasty into a Western constitutional monarchy much like that of Britain. Instead, however, it led to the dynasty's final implosion in 1911. In succeeding years power became increasingly fragmented as so-called warlords—provincial leaders backed by local armed forces—strove to fill the vacuum left by the collapse of central authority.

China descended in the late 1920s into a continental-scale civil war as the Communists, with Soviet support, challenged the Nationalists' efforts to unify the country. Its torment was further intensified in the mid 1930s when Japan, which had increasingly been inserting itself into Chinese affairs for decades, launched an all-out effort at colonization. For a time Mao and Chiang redirected their hostilities from each other to fight the common Japanese enemy. After Japan was defeated in 1945, however, Mao and Chiang again resumed the effort to destroy one another. Chiang's partisans have always alleged that Mao left most of the work of opposing the Japanese to the Nationalists, while the Communists conserved their resources.

In the end, Mao won, and in establishing Communist Party rule throughout China in 1949, he opened a new chapter in Chinese history. Although he famously complained to Henry Kissinger that it was impossible to change China, to a large extent he reversed a previous tendency for China's provinces to go their own way in defiance of central authority.

The result is that China once again began to function as an effective nation-state. It was to continue to do so after Mao's death. Yet the sustainability of China's post-1949 era of unity continues to be questioned even today by many Western scholars and policymakers. In the manner of generals fighting the last war, they seem to regard China's chaos and self-destructiveness of the early-twentieth-century warlord era as the norm and expect a return to it sooner or later.

As the Chinese-born political scientist Huang Yasheng has pointed out, this gets the story upside down. Writing in *Foreign Policy* magazine in 1995, Huang commented: "Using the warlord period as a reference point to forecast the future profoundly miscasts Chinese history. The warlord period was precipitated by a remarkable coincidence of historical events not likely to be repeated: two Opium Wars; defeats at the hands of the Japanese, Germans, Russians, and French; a large segment of the territory carved out for foreign rule; and, to top it all off, a dynasty ruled by the Manchus, whom the Han Chinese had resisted for centuries as alien invaders. Today, none of the threats to the Chinese central authorities even remotely match those adversities in degree or in kind. If history is any indication, China tilts toward unity rather than disintegration."

But why exactly does China "tilt" toward unity? In part the answer is unsurprising: ethnic and cultural homogeneity. More than 90 percent of the Chinese people are of Han stock, which is to say they are of the same ethnic group from which the first emperor, Qin Shi Huang, sprang. Distinct from Tibetans, Mongols, and other minority Chinese races, they share a heritage of culture and history going back thousands of years.

Their writing system alone is a powerful unifying force. One of the world's oldest and most complex, this system nonetheless allows people who speak mutually incomprehensible dialects to communicate easily via the written word. This enables China's national print media—organs such as the *Renmin Ribao* (better known in the West as the *People's Daily*)—to function as yet another unifying force.

The Chinese people are also united by Confucianism. To that subject we now turn.

Harnessing the Confucian Tradition

In seeking to maintain its grip on power, the Chinese Communist Party enjoys a tremendous advantage in China's Confucian tradition. Once established, a tradition of strong Confucian government tends to be self-perpetuating. Certainly absent a large external shock—such as the disruption caused by Western colonialism in the nineteenth century—Confucian regimes have historically proved exceptionally stable and durable.

Not to put too fine a point on it, Confucianism is every enlightened despot's perfect ideology. For a start it enjoins the populace to passivity if not subservience. Moreover, it legitimizes authoritarian leadership and encourages leaders to focus single-mindedly on power to the exclusion of all else. Thus Confucian regimes regard it as a key principle of good government to eliminate all potential challengers. Proceeding in end-justifies-means fashion, they therefore seek to establish control over all other organized entities or at least to subvert and generally weaken them.

Of course officially China is still supposed to be a Marxist state, not a Confucian one. Moreover, until relatively recently Confucianism was not only disavowed but roundly condemned by the Chinese Communist Party. Apart from anything else it was blamed by Mao and his contemporaries as a key cause of China's nineteenth-century weakness. This characterization, however, was always somewhat unfair. In attempting to unify the nation, Mao Zedong found it convenient to have an ideological scapegoat. While he was right to suggest that the archaic and ultrarigid form of Confucianism espoused by the Qing dynasty rendered China backward-looking, this was hardly the whole story.

Indeed, well before the Qing dynasty's final collapse, Japan had already demonstrated that, suitably reformed to fit modern conditions, Confucianism could provide the ideological underpinnings for an East Asian economic renaissance. Starting in the 1860s, a new, postfeudal generation of Japanese leaders jettisoned the more archaic aspects of the Confucian tradition. Thus the hereditary privileges of the samurais and the daimyos were abolished and a start was made on land reform. At the center of Japan's modernized version of Confucianism was a transformed view of business. Previously in Japan, as throughout the Confucian world, merchants had been considered merely wealthy parasites and as such were accorded a humiliatingly low rank. In Japan's new Confucian order their rank was dramatically raised. They were seen not just as promoters of the common good but as essential to the building of a modern, powerful nation-state.

Japan's success in adapting Confucianism to modern conditions was a major inspiration for the revolutionaries who overthrew the Qing dynasty in the early twentieth century. Indeed, many of these revolutionaries, including their leader, Sun Yat-sen, had been educated in Japan. It is probably not a coincidence that, as the scholar Joseph Richmond Levenson has recorded, the key word in China's traditional Confucianism was *harmony*. The same word—written with the same Chinese character—remains the ideological touchstone of Japanese society to this day.

In post-Mao China, Confucianism has undergone a remarkable rehabilitation. This development seems to have begun in 1994 when the *People's Daily* called for a Confucian renaissance to fill the moral vacuum caused by "money worship." The regime has gone on to restore the Confucian classics to the secondary-school teaching curriculum. Abroad, it has been promoting Confucianism via branches of its recently established Confucius Institute.

This revival has evoked scorn from many Western scholars. As the Miami-based China watcher June Teufel Dreyer points out, modern China's political culture would be unrecognisable to Confucius. "What's being presented as Confucianism would surely horrify Master Kung," she comments. "It's an effort to soften the edges of what much of the rest of the world sees as a rising and not necessarily benign People's Republic of China. Hence, Confucius Institutes dispense the master's teaching at a level not far above that found in fortune cookies, and packages or adapts concepts that the Beijing government finds useful."

The Beijing-based Canadian scholar Daniel A. Bell agrees that the Confucian revival is motivated in part by an attempt to reassure the West, noting that Confucianism certainly enjoys a better image in the West than Marxism. He argues further that the Confucian revival also helps reassure the Chinese people at a time of jolting domestic economic change.

In any case, as the China watcher Steven Aufrecht has written, Confucianism is ingrained in the Chinese in much the way that Judeo-Christian values are ingrained in Westerners, even in those who think of themselves as nonbelievers.

That said, it is clear that, Mao's disavowals notwithstanding, there is much in modern Confucianism that is congruent with Communist ideology. The point has been well made by the Sinologist and longtime China resident Vera Simone. Writing with Anne Thompson Feraru in their book, The Asian Pacific [1994], Simone commented: "Of all the ideas to engage the minds of Chinese in their long struggle to reunify the country, Marxism succeeded because of its remarkable similarities to traditional Chinese culture. If one tried to construct a modern counterpart to Confucianism one could hardly improve on Marxism–Leninism–Mao Zedong Thought, as it is officially called. Like Confucianism, Marxism is comprehensive, all encompassing, secular and historical. Both have a cosmic vision."

For leaders of the Chinese Communist Party, a particularly reassuring aspect of Confucianism is that, just as securely as Marxism, it provides a philosophical justification for nondemocratic rule. Another key congruence is a groupist view of the human condition in which everyone is exhorted to subordinate himself to the wishes of society. Moreover, both philosophies rail against the sort of individual conscience and stand-on-principle idealism fostered by the Judeo-Christian tradition.

The best example of the congruence between Communism and Confucianism lies in present-day Japan. Although during the cold war, America's propaganda needs required that the Japanese economic system be presented not only as authentically capitalist but as a veritable showcase of capitalism, the truth was always startlingly different. With its keiretsus, lifetime employment, and government-controlled banks, the post–World War II Japanese econo-political system has always been much closer to Communism than to capitalism. This point has insistently been made by the Wall Street Journal's technology correspondent Walter Mossberg, and it was considered at length by Douglas Moore Kenrick in a book whose title said it all: *Where Communism Works: The Success of Competitive-Communism in Japan.*

Kenrick, a longtime Japan resident and businessman, explained: "While the pursuit of profit is clearly evident, competition in Japan is mitigated by powerful communalistic forces—including state planning to achieve national goals, the fundamental controlling mechanism of Communism." Japan's keiretsu system in particular ensures that most businesses function more like government-directed living things than American-style profit-maximizing machines.

For idealistic Communists charting a course for the nation in the immediate aftermath of Mao's death, perhaps the ultimate attraction of the Japanese system was its income distribution, which has long been one of the world's most egalitarian. They would also have been impressed by the way the Japanese model placed the state at the center of the economic development effort. To say the least, the Japanese model offered Chinese reformers a far more ideologically acceptable vision than that of the United States.

Of course, as China has reformed its economy, the gap between rich and poor has widened dramatically, to the point where it now seems a world away from Japanese egalitarianism. But this hardly contradicts the inference that the Chinese are imitating the Japanese model. The fact is that today's Japanese model is a mature creation that has already gone through more than a century of quite extensive evolution. At an earlier stage, particularly in the 1910s and 1920s, Japanese leaders tolerated a great deal of freebooting, sometimes piratical, entrepreneurship. The result was for a time a gap between rich and poor that was as wide as that in China today. The betting is that in the fullness of time, as the Chinese version of the East Asian model matures, top Chinese leaders will steer the economy closer and closer to the egalitarianism of today's Japan.

All in all, as the Japanese model shows, modern Confucianism can deliver outcomes very similar to those promised by idealistic Communism. Yet Confucianism is sufficiently congruent with free markets to allow for considerable corporate competition. Thus, just as mid-nineteenth-century Japanese leaders upgraded the status of the merchant class, the Chinese Communist Party suffered no discernible embarrassment when in 1992 in a major ideological shift it raised the image of the private sector and reversed its previous policy of excluding entrepreneurs from its ranks. The result has been a quiet political revolution: as recorded by the *People's Daily* in 2007, as many as 23,000 entrepreneurs were recently participating in people's congresses at various levels throughout China.

Significantly, it has to be added that Confucianism provides a traditional legitimization for the sort of coercive techniques of government control that are essential to the success of the East Asian economic model.

The Price of Despotism: Eternal Vigilance

Chinese institutions are carefully structured to maximize the Beijing regime's control of Chinese society. This structuring starts with the media, which with virtually no exceptions are under the direct statutory control of the Communist Party (not the state). The party thus denies opponents and dissident groups the oxygen of publicity. And without publicity, the emergence of any rival independent national political organization is more or less impossible.

The British economic commentator Will Hutton characterizes the Chinese media as crippled. Writing in the *Guardian* in 2007, Hutton added: "China now has more than 2,000 newspapers, 2,000 television channels, 9,000 magazines and 450 radio stations, but they are all under the watchful eye of the party in Beijing or provincial propaganda departments. These authorities issue daily instructions on what may and may not be reported; journalists who digress will be suspended from working or even imprisoned. China is estimated to have 42 journalists in prison, the highest number in the world."

As reported by the *People's Daily*, during 2004 alone, censorship agencies permanently shut down 338 publications for printing "internal" information, closed 202 branch offices of newspapers, and punished 73 organizations for illegally "engaging in news activities."

The party's control of the media creates an intellectual climate in which its monopoly of power comes to appear as natural a fact of life as the law of gravity or the changing seasons. Certainly with the media under control, rulers can readily present an impressive show of unity. Faction fights and other evidence of party tensions are rarely if ever reported. As far as members of the public are concerned, party decisions are made unanimously in an atmosphere of harmony, as well as, of course, wisdom.

Even the few media organizations that are ostensibly independent of the party can readily be reined in when they go too far. The story of *That's Shanghai*, an English-language magazine, provides an object lesson. The founder and ostensible proprietor Mark Kitto, a former British army officer, was doing fine until he wrote a book review considered too sympathetic to Islamic separatists in China's far West. The authorities moved in and unceremoniously ripped the entire business from him.

The episode illustrated in miniature a fundamental problem with New China: ownership rights are not well defined—and that is to put it politely. In large measure the source of the problem is the fact that the Chinese legal system is little more than a tool of party power. The point was made explicit some years ago when a major Chinese Internet search engine company, Sohu.com, was launched on the NASDAQ market in the United States. As part of its legal disclosures, the company stated: "It is possible that the relevant People's Republic of China (PRC) authorities could, at any time, assert that any portion or all of our existing or future ownership structure and businesses, or this offering, violate existing or future PRC laws and regulations."

To say the least, the Chinese legal system is based on a Confucian worldview that is highly compatible with the needs of a Communist dictatorship. The point has been well summed up in *Modern China,* a book by the British Sinologist Graham Hutchings. Attributing post-1949 China's failure to create an independent legal system to Confucian tradition, he commented: "In imperial times, the state used law to control society; individuals or society rarely used law to control the state. . . . The Party's concern is to establish rule by law rather than the rule of law. In this scheme of things laws are mainly rules for administration. . . . They cannot be used to challenge Party rule, query socialism, or challenge Marxism."

In a word, the Chinese Communist Party is above the law. This indeed is written into the Chinese constitution. Even after a largely cosmetic constitutional amendment in 1999 that was aimed at emphasizing the rule of law, ordinary courts have been permitted no jurisdiction over the party's acts or policies. Few party members are ever brought before the courts, and generally those who are are first subjected to party discipline and stripped of party membership.

The Beijing regime's obsession with control explains much about the structure of modern China. Virtually no civic or voluntary organization is permitted to exist other than organizations under explicit party control. Even religious groups must be brought under party control. The party's concern is evidently not so much ideological purity as power. Individuals in modern China are generally allowed to believe what they want and even say what they want, provided only—and it is of course a big proviso—that they do so behind closed doors.

The party's concern to curb organized religion stems from a recognition that religious sects have the potential to become the focal point of powerful institutional resistance to the regime. Although preexisting religious groups such as Christian churches are hard to stamp out completely, the party works systematically to undermine them by, for instance, inveigling its agents into positions of leadership.

As a general rule, the more organized and extensive a religious group is, the more threatening it appears to the party. Thus, among Protestant denominations, the broad Anglican faith is eyed with greater hostility than the less-organized local groups that characterize Presbyterianism.

By the same token, the Chinese Communist Party particularly fears the Roman Catholic Church. Catholicism's carefully structured hierarchical organization and its concern for worldwide doctrinal unity make it one of the world's most formidable institutions—and no one is more acutely aware of this than China's top leaders. As Steven Mosher points out, they have carefully studied the rise of Solidarity in Poland, and have noted its reliance upon the organizational structure of the Polish Church. They are determined never to allow the Catholic Church in China to become the institutional basis of any organized opposition.

A jealous concern to forestall the rise of potential power rivals also explains the party's extraordinary animus toward the Falun Gong. Founded in 1992, the Falun Gong espouses doctrines not much different from those of traditional Buddhism. As such it was at first of little concern to the party. But the sect's rate of growth proved phenomenal—already by 1998 it had accumulated 70 million followers in mainland China alone (with many more abroad). An organization on this scale clearly enjoyed considerable power to talk back to the Communist Party. What particularly rattled the Beijing authorities was the sect's ability in the spring of 1999 to mount a huge protest close to the top party leaders' homes in the Zhongnanhai compound near the Forbidden City. Energized by earlier government attempts to curb the sect's publishing activities, an estimated ten thousand Falun Gong supporters contrived to appear from nowhere to mount a silent protest. The party responded not only by banning the organization but by launching a brutal roundup of the sect's most outspoken activists.

Yet the Falun Gong's only real offense was that it was not controlled by the Chinese Communist Party. As the authors Richard Bernstein and Ross Munro have pointed out, the Beijing regime "will stop at almost nothing when it feels its monopoly on power is at stake."

The Falun Gong apart, there are few independent organizations of any size in China. So long as Beijing remains vigilant in nipping in the bud all prospective power rivals, it is hard to see where any threat to its power might come from. Aiding Beijing in the effort to suppress potential challengers is precisely the fact that it already enjoys so much power. Let's now consider the main elements of that power.

Follow the Money 1: Public Spending

If all power comes from the barrel of a gun, someone has to pay for the bullets. And if an army marches on its stomach, someone has to put food in its rucksacks. The food and the bullets by and large are funded out of tax revenues. Hence the fact that tax collection plays a central role in modern nation-states. There is a mutually reinforcing linkage between power and tax that is fundamental to the development of the nation-state. A weak government cannot levy taxes; yet without taxes, it will remain weak.

Although tax gathering is often taken for granted in advanced Western nations, it should not be. To see why, one need merely look at the failed states of Africa. One of the most important things they lack is an honest and effective tax system.

The rise of East Asia is in significant measure a story of improved tax collection. Up to the mid-nineteenth century, the region's tax systems had been archaic and geographically fragmented. The trend for reform and centralization was pioneered in Japan when, having just abolished feudalism, the Meiji Restoration leaders in 1873 introduced a 3 percent national levy on land ownership. They went on to impose national taxes on alcoholic drinks and tobacco. In further pioneering moves, they introduced a national income tax in 1887 and a national corporate tax in 1899.

A major reason why China lagged so far behind Japan economically was that the Chinese tax system remained primitive into the twentieth century. In fact, as the historian Chaoying Fang has pointed out, a crucial, if largely overlooked, reason for the collapse of the imperial system in 1912 was that rampant corruption in the previous four decades had proved the last straw for an already dysfunctional Chinese tax system. As China entered the twentieth century, most of the tax gathering was done by provincial rather than national agencies. This arrangement made it easy for provincial warlords to divert tax revenues into funding regional armed forces that challenged the central government.

It was only after Mao Zedong and the Communist Party rose to ultimate power in 1949 that a start was made on building a solidly unified tax system—and by extension a solidly unified nation. Previously the Communists had funded their rise in substantial measure from Soviet sources. What little indigenous revenues they had seem to have come largely from their land policy, which consisted mainly of redistributing land from landlords to peasants.

One of Mao's priorities was to start centralizing the flow of China's public revenues. The project had still not been completed when he died, and then for a while the centralization effort took a backseat as Deng Xiaoping instigated broad economic reforms. Centralization was resumed in the 1990s after top officials resolved that the central government's share of total tax revenues should be raised from 40 percent to 60 percent. Thanks to major reforms initiated in the time of Premier Zhu Rongji, the central government has generally increased its share of taxes year by year. The story can be summed up in a single statistic: of all the tax revenues collected in China, nearly 55 percent accrued to the central government in 2004, versus less than 16 percent in 1978. With so much of the nation's taxes flowing to the center, Beijing's power to pull the strings in provincial capitals has been correspondingly boosted. Beijing has further reinforced its power by tightly controlling local governments' access to alternative funding sources. As reported by Andrew Browne of the *Wall Street Journal,* Beijing does not allow local governments to issue debt.

Another key lever of central control is Beijing's jealously guarded power to make top provincial appointments. Economist Jeffrey Sachs notes that Beijing regularly rotates officials among different provinces to make sure they are loyal to the central government, especially when local interests conflict with those of the central government. A similar system is used to keep regional leaders of the People's Liberation Army loyal to Beijing.

A large proportion of China's tax revenues flows back to the provinces to fund, for instance, infrastructural projects. All but the largest of these are managed at the provincial or local level. But because the money is allocated as part of the national budget, top planners in Beijing enjoy enormous leverage over provincial and local leaders.

How has Beijing contrived to establish such control over the tax system? A key development has been its introduction of a value-added tax as one of the major tools of economic reform. Invented in France in the 1950s and now widely levied throughout Europe and East Asia, value-added tax is intended not only to ensure ease of administration (from the point of view of government officials certainly, if not that of taxpayers) but to minimize evasion. Although in its effect on consumers, a value-added tax works much like the state sales taxes familiar to Americans, a key difference is that it is levied on *all* businesses at every stage in the production chain, not just businesses that sell to consumers. Businesses pay the tax in full on their sales but claim refunds on tax paid on their inputs. Receipts for such inputs provide the tax authorities with a cross-check on how well every business in the value-added chain is complying.

The value-added tax was rolled out in 1994, and it quickly became by far the Chinese government's largest source of revenue. In 2004, for instance, it generated more than twice as much as the second-largest revenue source, corporate income tax. The initiative to introduce the value-added tax came from the central government, and the tax is of course national in scope. But the central government operates a revenue-sharing arrangement in which, as of 2004, the provinces received just over one-quarter of the proceeds (with the rest going to Beijing). This arrangement seems to be another example of the care that the central leadership has taken to align the interests of provincial bureaucrats with its own. Certainly the latter have been provided with a strong incentive to make common cause with national officials in maximizing taxpayers' compliance.

While control of the tax system is a key tool of Beijing's power, it is not the only one. It is time to take a look at banking Chinese-style.

Follow the Money 2: Bank Lending

Capitalism's triumph in China has been proclaimed in countless books in recent years. There is, for instance, *Chinese Capitalism* by Satya Gabriel, *The Spirit of Chinese Capitalism* by Gordon Redding, and *Dragon in a Three-Piece Suit: The Emergence of Capitalism in China* by Doug Guthrie. But is China really capitalist? Hardly. Certainly the higher reaches of its economy remain comprehensively controlled in a way that is the antithesis of everything we associate with Western capitalism.

The key to this control is the Chinese banking system. Little noticed by those who proclaim the triumph of Western capitalism, the Chinese banking system is not only state-owned but, as in other East Asian miracle economics, functions overtly as a major tool of the central government's industrial policy. Not only are bank directors and top managers appointed by the Beijing regime but many are Communist Party cadres who typically have previously held high posts in provincial or national government.

The Beijing regime's control is further strengthened by the fact that Chinese banking is highly concentrated. A cartel of just four huge banks dominates the entire Chinese banking industry. These so-called pillar banks emerged in more or less their present form in the 1980s. Their deposit interest rates are controlled at cartel level, and so no doubt are the rates they charge on loans (though rate tables for loans do not seem to be in the public domain).

Stated in order of the size of their workforces, the big four are the Industrial and Commercial Bank of China, the Agricultural Bank of China, the China Construction Bank, and the Bank of China. Their combined workforce comes to more than 1.1 million, with the Industrial and Commercial Bank alone employing about one-third of the total. As recorded by the Economist Intelligence Unit, these four institutions accounted in aggregate for fully 53 percent of the Chinese banking system's entire assets as of 2006.

They are controlled by the Beijing Ministry of Finance, and much of their share capital is held by the Central Huijin Investment Company, a publicly owned entity that holds title to many of the Chinese state's most important financial assets.

Underneath the big four is a tier of secondary banking institutions, which are also publicly owned. These recently numbered nineteen, of which the Bank of Communications, CITIC (China International Trust and Investment Corporation), and the China Merchants Bank are probably the best known in the West. By comparison with the Big Four these banks are relative minnows whose combined assets are less than the smallest of the Big Four.

For many years Western press commentators have predicted that Chinese banks would rapidly converge toward an American free-market managerial style. This supposedly would follow as an inevitable consequence of growing competition amid an increasingly "globalized" Chinese financial system.

In reality, however, the Chinese banks have remained avowedly statist and cartelized. Moreover the major corporations to whom they lend most of their money are themselves heavily state-influenced. The statist reality of Chinese corporate governance emerged clearly in a study conducted for the World Bank in 2002 by Stoyan Tenev and Zhang Chunling. They found that fully 70 percent of the directors of domestically listed companies in China were appointed by the government or by the Communist Party. All this is not an accident, but rather a central feature of Chinese economic policy. In common with other governments throughout the Confucian region, the Beijing regime sees control of banking as an essential concomitant of its forced-savings policy. The vast flows of investment capital generated by the savings policy must be carefully managed to make sure that dangerous levels of overcapacity are not spawned in key industries. Otherwise major Chinese corporations would be rendered chronically unprofitable, thus destroying their ability to repay their loans.

Of course, it is widely suggested that the Chinese banking system is highly dysfunctional and must Westernize itself if its inadequacies are not to lead to an eventual financial cataclysm. One key problem is said to be "policy lending"— lending forced on the banks by government officials anxious to keep shaky employers out of bankruptcy. This amounts to throwing good money after bad, and the only solution, Western analysts suggest, is to establish Chinese business on a Western free-market basis, free from backseat driving by government.

While much policy lending undoubtedly is money down the drain, there is another side to this story that so far has been largely overlooked. From the point of view of China's top planners, the banks are important tools of a vast program for subsidizing the expansion of Chinese industry. The effect is particularly significant among promising but undercapitalized export companies, whose growth is funded with easy bank loans for years or even decades on end. Many such companies will eventually become fully viable but for the most part only after their debts are forgiven and converted into equity. By forgiving debts, Chinese banks therefore provide hidden subsidies to China's targeted industries.

In this sense Beijing has much the same "problem" with its banking policy that the retail tycoon John Wanamaker reportedly had with his advertising budget. "Half the money I spend on advertising is wasted," he is credited with saying. "The trouble is, I don't know which half." In both advertising and banking, the more widely you cast your seed, the more seedlings will eventually poke their heads above ground.

Banking's covert role in channeling subsidies to industry is, of course, a breach of China's World Trade Organization undertakings, and it has recently become a flash point in trade diplomacy. Debt forgiveness was cited in 2007, for instance, as a factor in a trade dispute over rising Chinese exports of high-quality glossy paper. As reported by Steven Weisman of the *New York Times,* the U.S. Commerce Department was considering bringing an action against the Chinese paper industry on this issue.

Another factor that, it is often suggested, will sound the death knell for the Chinese way of banking is foreign competition. As Western free-market ideologues see it, more-efficient American and European banks will undermine the Chinese banking cartel. Thus in the fullness of time the cartel's members will have no choice but to break loose and compete in a Western fashion.

At first sight this argument seems to have some merit. After all, the Beijing regime is officially committed to opening the Chinese banking market to foreign competition. This was one of the promises it made to the World Trade Organization.

What the ideologues have overlooked, however, is that economic rhetoric and economic reality rarely coincide in East Asia. Although the Beijing regime has often paid lip service to opening the Chinese market, in reality it has proved highly adept at inventing catch-22–style traps to slow the foreigners' progress. Thus in 2006—nearly a quarter of a century after they were permitted to open branches in China—foreign banks remained ghettoized in narrow niche activities such as foreign-currency loans and deposits.

True, consequent on a program laid down by the World Trade Organization, Beijing announced further banking reforms in December 2006. These were supposed to represent a full opening of the Chinese market to foreign competition; but a study of the regulatory details suggested otherwise. The good news was that foreign banks would be permitted to go beyond simply operating isolated, and heavily restricted, branches in China. Now they could establish fully fledged Chinese subsidiaries that would—in theory at least—be granted full "national treatment" (meaning they would enjoy broadly the same rights as Chinese banks). Unfortunately there was some bad news as well: in a clear effort to blunt the reforms, the Beijing regime imposed specially demanding capital requirements on banking corporations. To satisfy WTO appearances, the requirements apply to all banking companies operating in China, but it just so happens that whereas they are easy for the big domestic Chinese banks to meet, they are discouragingly expensive for the foreigners.

Certainly, few Western experts are convinced that much has changed. Alistair Scarff of Merrill Lynch, for instance, expects Chinese regulators merely to switch from explicit to implicit barriers in restraining foreign banks. "I can't believe for one second that the Chinese government will give the foreigners an easy ride," Scarff told *Business Week*. He predicted that foreign banks would encounter delays when applying to the regulators for new product licensing. Foreign banks may be allowed to offer sophisticated foreign-currency products, but if the foreigners have any good ideas for local-currency products, these would be leaked by the regulators to Chinese rivals before the foreigners were permitted to go ahead.

As a practical matter only eight foreign banks have so far applied to establish full operations, and of these only one—Citigroup—is American. Of the other seven, all are either based in East Asia or are European banks that are fully "acclimatized" there—that is, they have been operating in the region since colonial days and are not in the business of rocking the boat. Certainly it is clear that these banks—led by Japan's Mizuho and Britain's HSBC—are well used to cartel etiquette and, in the time-honored tradition of East Asian business, can be trusted to refrain from the sort of American-style freebooting competition that might threaten the Beijing authorities' larger economic agenda.

For any foreign bank not prepared to go to the expense of establishing a China-based subsidiary, the alternative of merely operating a few isolated branches is available. But banks that go this route are subject to crippling disabilities, most obviously limited access to yuan deposits. Under the December 2006 regulations, this disability has been partially lifted but only for deposits in excess of 1 million yuan (equal to nearly $130,000). As only a few of China's richest citizens have this sort of money, the effect in boosting the foreigners' deposit base will be negligible. In practice therefore there has been little real change, and most foreign banks remain heavily dependent on the state-controlled Chinese banking cartel for their funds.

The full extent of the foreign banks' disadvantage in China was aptly summed up in one statistic cited by Bloomberg News in 2006: of nearly 70,000 bank branches in China all but 214 were Chinese-owned.

There is one other way foreign banks might make an impact on China: by acquiring Chinese banks. This option, however, is likely to remain closed indefinitely. Even after the "full opening" of 2006, no foreign entity is allowed to own more than 20 percent of a Chinese bank. And the total holdings of all foreign entities in any one Chinese bank is not allowed to exceed 25 percent.

Although several foreign banks have already been allowed to buy stakes in Chinese banks, these stakes are far too small to afford any management control. Thus although HSBC owns one-fifth of the Shanghai-based Bank of Communications, for instance, it has reportedly been permitted to nominate just two of nineteen board members. By contrast the Chinese Ministry of Finance, with a similar stake of about 20 percent, has enough seats to control the bank. Other foreign banks with significant stakes in Chinese banks include Bank of America,

Merrill Lynch, and Royal Bank of Scotland, but in no instance do the foreigners have control.

All in all, it is clear that China's banking reforms of 2006 are intended by Beijing merely as a tokenist exercise in "coprosperity." Because a few of the West's most powerful banks have been given a chance—via minority shareholdings—to participate by proxy in the growth of the Chinese banking system, it is assumed that this will parry their wish to secure direct access to China's fast-growing banking deposit base. Thus, China's vast savings flows will remain indefinitely under the control of a handful of state-controlled Chinese banking institutions.

None of this should come as a surprise. Certainly the evidence from elsewhere in East Asia is that, all globalist talk notwithstanding, any nation that is seriously concerned to protect its banking market can readily do so. Banking is just too complicated and culture-specific a business for foreign banks to have any chance against well-entrenched local banks protected by a powerful government. The proof lies elsewhere in East Asia—in Japan. More than thirty years after top Tokyo bureaucrats began presenting the Japanese market as "one of the most open in the world," the combined share of all foreign banks in Japanese banking was a mere 7 percent.

One thing is clear: so long as the Chinese banking system remains government-controlled, every expansion-minded Chinese tycoon will remain little more than a pawn in a game controlled from Zhongnanhai.

Selective Enforcement as a Swiss Army Knife

Each of China's 1.3 billion people presents a unique challenge to China's system of social control. Moreover, all precedent suggests that human beings are pre-programmed by millions of years of evolution to resist, often highly ingeniously, the sort of regimentation wished upon them by the Beijing regime. So how, in an era of increasing economic liberalization and international openness, can a few hundred power holders in Beijing continue to control such a large collection of potentially centrifugal individuality?

Here China's rich tradition of authoritarian manipulation of the human psyche comes into its own. The Beijing regime is equipped with countless subtle and not-so-subtle ways to discourage individualism. Most of them are variations on the principle of *selective enforcement*.

As we have noted, the concept is that officials write the rules overly strictly and then enforce them selectively. Writing from Shanghai for the *Atlantic* in 2007, James Fallows pointed out that selective enforcement is a widely used control mechanism both in China and in the wider East Asian region. "In principle, a large share of what people [in China] do each day violates some rule in some way," he wrote. "In practice, most rules go unenforced, and most people conduct their business without constant hassle from the authorities. The trick is that, whenever they choose, the authorities can start enforcing laws they had previously winked away, and suddenly people are in big trouble for 'breaking' 16 different rules no one had cared about before."

If Wikipedia's entry for Legalism is to be credited (and although it does not seem to be confirmed by more reliable sources, it seems plausible), China's tradition of selective enforcement goes back to the time of the first emperor, Qin Shi Huang, whose agents deliberately set out to create an atmosphere of "legal paradox," in which many mutually contradictory laws were promulgated. The result was that no matter what you did, you found yourself on the wrong side of some law or other and could therefore be targeted for enforcement.

In modern China, selective enforcement is the Swiss army knife of Confucian power (although the principle behind the concept was one that Confucius himself would probably have disowned). A handy tool with practically unlimited applications, selective enforcement is particularly effective in China because almost every Chinese citizen spends much of his time on the wrong side of the law. The point has been made forcibly by the former *Wall Street Journal* Beijing bureau chief James McGregor. In his book *One Billion Customers* (2005), he has pointed out that most large fortunes in China have been made illegally and Chinese economic life is suffused with a "Don't ask, don't tell" ethos. He comments: "The overall system is almost incompatible with honesty."

As the British human rights campaigner Robin Munro has pointed out, Chinese political dissidents face constant harassment over technical breaches of petty regulations. In one case, a dissident was arraigned for breaking some minor ordinance requiring that fax machines be registered. Another dissident was arraigned for visiting a prostitute. This despite the fact that, as Ethan Gutmann has documented, sexual mores are more lax in China these days than almost anywhere else in the world. Just the most obvious indication of this is that Chinese cities boast huge red-light districts where prostitution is routinely plied in plain sight of the authorities.

In a similar spirit of petty harassment, the Beijing-based lawyer Gao Zhisheng was threatened with the shutdown of his office. His ostensible offense was merely that he had not completed the necessary paperwork in connection with a recent office move. His real offense was that he specialized in representing dissidents and other anti-establishment figures such as prominent Falun Gong members (who are considered subversives by the authorities).

In the never-ending task of harassing dissidents, China's laws on public discussion provide a cornucopia of opportunities for selective enforcement. As virtually everything in China is a state secret, those who write or speak publicly can readily be arraigned on technicalities. As a practical matter, if they keep their comments within "reasonable" limits they have little to fear. The law is, however, often harshly enforced against political dissidents.

The treatment of the democracy advocate Wei Jingsheng illustrates the point. Wei came to prominence in the latter half of the 1970s as a leader of the so-called Democracy Wall movement. The term refers to an outpouring of complaint that was aired in posters put up by individuals throughout China in 1978. Wei was promptly arrested on a charge of disclosing state secrets. As Wei was a largely uneducated man who worked as an electrician at the Beijing Zoo, he had little access to any seriously sensitive information. It turned out that the charge referred to the fact that he had talked to foreign reporters about military losses in China's brief war with Vietnam in 1979. Wei had no direct access to information about the losses and was merely repeating hearsay.

The rise of the Internet has provided China's mind-control czars with a plethora of new opportunities for selective enforcement. Virtually anything a Chinese citizen posts on the Internet, however noncontroversial, can be considered a technical breach of rules announced in 2000 by the Bureau for the Protection of State Secrets. In the words of one Shanghai-based American lawyer, the sweep of the rules is "breathtaking." If the rules were strictly enforced they would essentially shut down the Chinese Internet, he suggested, and official news would be reported only after weeks of delay. In a recent report reviewing China's human rights performance, Amnesty International found that in 2004 alone more than fifty people had been either arrested or imprisoned for Internet-related political activities. One man received a sentence of fifteen years' imprisonment after posting articles attacking official corruption and advocating a reassessment of the 1989 prodemocracy movement.

For Chinese business executives, the fear of selective enforcement centers mainly on China's industrial regulations. Written strictly, these are in practice, as the Shanghai-based *New York Times* reporter David Barboza has observed, rarely enforced. The trouble is that no one can be sure that he will not be the one singled out for special attention.

The threat of selective enforcement hangs over virtually everyone at every level in Chinese society. The problem is particularly obvious at lower levels. Take the 100 million poor migrants who now live outside their registered area of abode. Without their tireless labor China's booming coastal regions would grind to a halt. Because they are working illegally, they make an eminently docile workforce utterly unable to organize strikes or other forms of collective action. The minute a leader emerges among them, he or she can be unceremoniously targeted for selective enforcement of the work-permit laws.

By the same token, anyone who employs migrants is also breaking the law—and therefore must cower in fear of the selective-enforcement sword of Damocles hovering above his head.

A recent study of the Chinese toy industry provided some compelling insights into how far theory and practice diverge in Chinese labor relations. Of eleven factories investigated by China Labor Watch in 2005, only one was found to be broadly in compliance with Chinese employment law. As for the rest, almost invariably work schedules exceeded legal limits, and pay levels in some cases were more than 40 percent below the statutory minimum. Workers were housed in grossly overcrowded conditions with in one case twenty-two workers forced to share a single room.

Another classic gray area rife with opportunities for selective enforcement is industrial safety. As in much of the rest of East Asia, industrial-safety laws in China are regarded in large measure as mere window dressing. Industrial inspectors routinely make sure that factories are alerted ahead of an "unscheduled" inspection.

That way management is afforded plenty of time to clean up, create fake time sheets, and coach workers on what to say. . . . By the same token, if the authorities want to crack down on any particular factory owner, all they need to do is drop in unannounced.

For top Chinese power holders, like their counterparts elsewhere in the Confucian world, the tax system offers exceptionally efficacious opportunities for selective enforcement. The effect is particularly powerful in keeping the nation's wealthiest citizens in line.

Here experience in South Korea may have proved a particular inspiration for Chinese officials. Certainly tax scandals are particularly common there. In 1991, for instance, the founder of the giant Hyundai group was presented with a tax bill of $180 million. The bill was widely seen as punishment for failing to cooperate sufficiently closely with the nation's top industrial planners. Again in 2000 tax evasion was invoked to bring down Park Tae Joon, the then prime minister and former head of the giant POSCO steel company.

As seen by the *International Herald Tribune,* the scandal was merely business as usual Korean-style. Quoting a member of the Korean public as saying, "They all do the same thing," the newspaper explained: "South Koreans, inured to the spectacle of seeing previous leaders besmirched by charges of bribery and other misdeeds, tended to view the latest headline-grabbing scandal with a mixture of cynicism and boredom."

What the newspaper could have said but did not is that Korean tax law seems to have been deliberately designed to encourage certain sorts of evasion. The bizarre reality of the Korean tax system was highlighted some years ago in an investigation by the Newark-based shipping newspaper the *Journal of Commerce.* By law entrepreneurs are not allowed to take a salary out of their businesses but, officially at least, must rely on dividends for any income they draw. The problem is that dividends are subject to exceptionally high rates of tax. As a practical matter, therefore, entrepreneurs contrive to get around this by paying themselves off the books. Moreover, as if to encourage such a possibility, the tax authorities have decreed that up to one-tenth of corporate expenses can be kept confidential, with no receipts required.

This state of affairs has resulted in massive ambiguity as to how Korea's top entrepreneurs are compensated. In effect they are encouraged to cross an ethical line. But once they cross it, they can never sleep soundly again.

China is similar to South Korea in that large-scale tax evasion has always been the norm among businesspeople. As recorded by the Atlanta-based historian Lu Hanchao, Shanghai shopkeepers in the 1930s typically paid only one-sixth of their theoretically applicable taxes. Kenneth Lieberthal of the University of Michigan has noted that Chinese companies in the late 1940s kept two sets of books, declaring only half their profits for tax purposes.

The tradition seems to have continued down to the present. According to the Economist Intelligence Unit in a commentary in 2006, tax evasion among wealthy individuals seems to be a particular problem: "Tax morality in China is poor, especially in the high-income brackets. The State Administration of Taxation estimates that high earners holding 80 percent of the nation's bank deposits contribute less than 10 percent to total income tax revenue."

Modern Chinese corporations are also noted for paying little tax. Take

Lenovo, the Chinese computer company that in 2005 bought IBM's personal computer business. Its fiscal 2004 tax burden came to just $1 million on profits of $144 million.

Even the U.S. State Department, which rarely involves itself in the fine detail of other nations' tax arrangements, is unhappy with the way that Chinese tax laws are enforced. In a specially written article distributed to the international press in 2005, a State Department writer reported that the Chinese government generally does not enforce tax collection on Chinese corporations. He quoted an unnamed U.S. official in Beijing saying that the top problem in U.S.-China economic relations is "the abject failure of China to enforce its laws in a consistent and transparent manner." The writer suggested that the authorities wanted to provide a covert subsidy to Chinese-owned businesses, at the expense of foreign-owned ones, which are held to higher standards of compliance. A point he left unmentioned but one that was at least equally relevant was that China's selective approach to tax collection obviously serves as a widely feared lever of arbitrary governmental power.

This seems the appropriate interpretation of the fate of Sun Dawu, an entrepreneur who set up a quasi-banking service that outperformed the established banks. Sun's achievement might have seemed to naive Westerners as a badly needed service to society. But in a country where central control of banking is an essential part of a mercantilist savings regimen, a freelance effort to improve the lot of the nation's bank customers was not necessarily considered in the national interest. As reported by the *New York Times*'s Joseph Kahn in 2003, the authorities resorted to the simple expedient of billing Sun for unpaid taxes and thereby shut him down. Although the full details are not available, there seems to have been no evidence that Sun was any more culpable than millions of other businesspeople who routinely get away with massive tax evasion.

Perhaps the most notable Chinese victim of selective enforcement in recent years has been Yang Bin, a brilliant young entrepreneur who in 2001 unwisely tried his hand at some freelance international diplomacy. Without consulting the Beijing authorities, he offered to partner the North Korean dictator Kim Jong Il in setting up a Hong Kong–style special enterprise zone on North Korean soil. Emboldened by the prospect of a vital new source of foreign exchange, Kim was inspired to adopt a more independent-minded attitude in ongoing negotiations with the Chinese government. Furious Chinese officials hit back by arraigning Yang on trumped-up charges of tax-evasion and sentenced him to eighteen years in prison—quite a comedown for someone who had just the previous year been named China's second-richest person by *Forbes* magazine.

If China's wealthiest people can easily be wrong-footed on tax charges, selective enforcement of anticorruption laws casts a long shadow over just about everyone else. Bribes and kickbacks seem pervasive in China and are really regarded by even the most honest citizens as a mere cost of doing business. As the China-watching journalist Richard Hornik has pointed out, China's periodic anticorruption campaigns invariably target even legitimate private entrepreneurs. In *One Billion Customers,* James McGregor has argued that the legal vagueness surrounding corporate law leaves even China's new breed of investment bankers highly vulnerable to selective enforcement. He commented: "They constantly worry that if the political winds change in Beijing, they could be targeted in a political campaign that would characterize them as making billions of dollars from what is essentially privatizing state assets."

Anticorruption crackdowns often go close to the very top. Take the case of Chen Xitong, who in the mid-1990s headed the Communist Party organization in the Beijing region. This positioned him as a formidable rival to Jiang Zemin as Deng Xiaoping's successor. Chen was arraigned by Jiang on corruption charges and sentenced to sixteen years in prison. As June Teufel Dreyer has suggested, there was little doubt about Jiang's agenda. In her book *China's Political System,* she commented: "Jiang had numerous other associates who were equally corrupt but nonetheless had not been investigated." She added that the anticorruption campaign of the mid-1990s was also used as a pretext to intimidate key members of ethnic minorities in Xinjiang and other western provinces who were unhappy with rule from Beijing.

Another striking illustration of how an anticorruption campaign can be used as a tool of unaccountable power came in 2004, when Chinese officials cracked down on two outspoken newspaper editors. The editors, at the Guangdong-based *Southern Metropolis Daily,* had criticized incompetent government efforts to control a major outbreak of SARS (severe acute respiratory syndrome). They were promptly arraigned on charges of breaking China's anticorruption laws and given lengthy jail terms. The charges related to their participation in their newspaper's executive profit-sharing plan. Together with seven senior colleagues, they had recently shared about $70,000 in profits. As the *Boston Globe* Beijing correspondent Jehangir Pocha has reported, the charges were "flimsy." Certainly other Chinese journalists have testified that the profit-sharing benefits involved would normally be considered unexceptional in view of the pair's seniority and their newspaper's commercial success.

Selective enforcement is an almost infinitely versatile tool, and penalties can be flexibly calibrated to suit the situation. Where selective enforcement against a first offender is concerned, the punishment may be no more than a slap on the wrist. But for anyone brought up in Chinese society, a slap on the wrist may be enough. What registers is not just the immediate punishment but rather the possibility that the next time the punishment might not be so lenient. After all, the Chinese justice system leaves plenty of discretion to judges to strike hard, and they are especially likely to do so in the case of repeat offenses. Moreover, as we will now see, "hard" can mean very hard indeed.

A Land Where Minds Are Concentrated

"Depend upon it, sir," said Samuel Johnson. "When a man knows he is to be hanged in a fortnight, it concentrates his mind wonderfully."

In few places are so many minds so wonderfully concentrated as in today's China. Certainly selective use of the death penalty is one of the Beijing authorities' most effective tools for maintaining control.

According to Amnesty International, not only is the death penalty extensively used in modern China, but its use often seems arbitrary. Moreover, in many cases it is applied at the explicit instigation of top officials, who evidently enjoy considerable power to interfere in judicial decision making.

One unnamed member of the National People's Congress quoted in Amnesty's 2004 report disclosed that China executes about ten thousand people a year. If this is correct, it means that in proportion to population, China's execution rate is nearly forty times that of the United States (and the United States is almost alone among developed nations in using the death penalty at all).

Capital punishment is often applied in the case of crimes that are punishable by death in few if any other jurisdictions in the world. As reported by Jane Macartney of the London *Times* in 2006, people have been executed for stealing pigs and cattle. Even white-collar crimes sometimes attract a death sentence. In the case of fraud, for instance, the rule apparently is that where the amount evaded is more than $60,000, the penalty should be either life imprisonment or death.

Smuggling is another activity that routinely invites a strike-hard response (it has to be admitted, however, that in this case the severity of the penalty may reflect no selective-enforcement agenda but rather the centrality of mercantilism in Chinese economic policy). In *Corruption and Market in Contemporary China,* Sun Yan writes that eighteen people received death sentences in a smuggling case in the 1980s.

Then there is the matter of freedom of speech. Anyone who pushes his luck too far risks a strike-hard—*yanda* in Chinese—response. Sentences for sending secret or "reactionary" material over the Internet typically range from a "mere" two to four years' imprisonment. But the death penalty is on the books as a possible remedy for Internet-related offenses. Jasper Becker says that even theft of intellectual property is sometimes treated as a capital offense. Most important for our purposes, although corruption is an unavoidable reality of Chinese life, it is sometimes punished with death.

The result is that in the matter of ruffling the feathers of high officials, almost everyone in China errs on the side of caution.

Corruption's Wider Consequences

Let's now consider more closely the role of corruption in China. As we have suggested, part of the reason that it is widely tolerated is that it provides high officials with a handy pretext for bringing selection enforcement actions. As a tool of power, however, it does not come without costs. If Western theorists are to be believed, corruption is a crippling problem, and one that urgently needs to be rooted out as a first step on the road to economic development.

Evidence from within China seems to confirm this assessment. According to a survey cited by the *South China Morning Post,* corruption cost the Chinese economy between 14 and 15 percent of gross domestic product each year between 1995 and 2001.

Yet if corruption were really so costly to China's development, we have to wonder why Chinese leaders have not been more determined in rooting it out. Several explanations have been put forward. It is often suggested, for instance, that Chinese leaders tolerate corruption because they are hopelessly corrupt themselves.

Yet this does not go the core of the matter. Although Chinese leaders certainly seem corrupt by the standards of, say, Norway or Singapore, they nonetheless keep both their corruption and their resulting conspicuous consumption within clearly defined limits. As we have already noted, oceangoing yachts, for instance, are specifically prohibited. Personal jets are also notable by their absence in China. It is not considered socially acceptable for the wealthy or powerful to employ large staffs of personal servants. A few such servants perhaps, but not the dozens or hundreds that the plutocratically wealthy in Latin America and indeed increasingly even in the United States take for granted.

The more closely you look at Chinese-style corruption, the more obvious it is that it differs fundamentally from the destructively dysfunctional form usually associated with Third World poverty. The difference can be summed up in this way: in terms of its implications for the wider economy, corruption in China functions much more like legitimate payment for services than highway robbery. The distinction here is that payment for services facilitates a market economy's natural tendency to maximize output. Highway robbery by contrast distorts the economy in ways that waste productive resources (most obviously by limiting trade, as in Europe in medieval times and in many parts of Africa even today).

This is not to suggest that Chinese-style corruption is not on balance a drag on output. Rather, there are countervailing forces at work that greatly moderate the net detrimental effect.

This is suggested by the amazing openness with which corruption is conducted in China. Westerners are shocked by this and tend to assume that such openness signifies an enormous drag on output. The true significance, however, is that the corruption concerned is generally of the payment-for-services kind rather than highway robbery. Indeed, bribe taking is often governed by a more or less public "schedule of charges."

Moreover, bribes are in many cases widely and relatively equitably shared within an organization. Consonant with a principle of "performance-based pay" that Adam Smith—not to mention Goldman Sachs, say—would approve of, the higher-ups receive a larger share of the take and those lower down receive a smaller one. But, in the best Confucian tradition, nobody is left out. In many cases bribes evidently function as an unofficial addition to the pay packets of otherwise inadequately paid petty functionaries.

Consider how all this works in practice in a typical governmental function such as issuing passports. If Chinese officials require a bribe of say $20 to issue each passport, the economic effect may be little different from how things work in a less corrupt nation. In the United States, for instance, it typically costs a citizen about $150 in issuing fees to receive a passport. In the American case, the fees are levied officially and accrue to the public purse. The money therefore goes ultimately to pay salaries in the State Department and other public organizations involved in administering the passport system. In the Chinese case, they go directly to officials in the immediate department concerned and are seen as supplements to otherwise inadequate salaries.

The practice of regarding bribes as a legitimate supplement to inadequate salaries is particularly institutionalized in the Chinese health care industry. The point has been highlighted by Patrick Norton, a Shanghai-based partner in the American law firm of O'Melveny & Myers. Suggesting that much corruption in the Chinese health-care industry is in effect "government policy," Norton has explained that public-sector doctors and nurses are openly permitted to boost their pay through kickbacks from suppliers. Writing in 2004 in the journal *China Law & Practice*, he added: "They also accept 'consulting fees' from supplier companies, or resell medical supplies purchased for their institution.... These practices are all illegal. They are also widely known and often tolerated by a government that cannot or will not increase salaries in the health-care industry to the levels necessary to retain leading professionals."

Clearly not all Chinese corruption works in this relatively harmless way, and certainly not all bribes go toward supplementing the incomes of poorly paid ordinary workers. Often indeed high officials receive bribes running into millions of dollars—serious money anywhere, not least in China.

But again the negative economic consequences may be less than they appear. Where large bribes are involved, the ultimate economic effect may be broadly analogous to the huge stock-option packages and other bloated forms of compensation that business executives in the United States routinely award themselves. In each case the money goes to highly talented people who feel a sense of entitlement. Obviously others may take a different view. But in both cases what is happening is that top people are exploiting positions of power for their private benefit. The difference is merely that in the American case what is done is technically legal, whereas in the Chinese one it is technically illegal.

A countervailing factor in the Chinese case is that selective enforcement exists both as a curb on the worst abuses of power and as a tool of the top leaders in holding society together in pursuit of agreed national goals.

What is clear is that those in the West who regard corruption as an insuperable barrier to China's superpower ambitions are overlooking much contrary evidence.

A comment from the veteran Australian China watcher Reg Little may help clarify the matter. Little, who formerly served as a diplomat in East Asia, has put it like this: "The Western media . . . often highlight accounts of Chinese and East Asian corruption. While it is true that extensive records of corrupt practice exist throughout Chinese history, no culture offers a more extensive range of education in the follies and consequences of moral weakness. No culture has shown a comparable capacity to reform and regenerate after periods of self-destructive excess and indulgence. No culture has a more sophisticated understanding of ways to turn to advantage corrupt instincts in both its own and others' cultures."

Today's Chinese society is much more carefully and efficaciously structured than is generally assumed in the West. Predictions in the West that China may suddenly self-destruct seem overdrawn. Provided top leaders remain cognizant of the national interest as they deploy the fruits of the forced-savings system, we can expect China's rapid ascent in the world geopolitical hierarchy to continue. In the next chapter we will consider the implications for the United States.

SIX

In a Confucian America

In the nearly three decades since China embraced the East Asian economic system, Sino-American relations have developed an unmistakable pattern: virtually every time the Chinese and American economic systems rub up against each other, the United States gives way. The pattern has already become so marked that America's continued independence as a sovereign nation is increasingly in question. It is not an exaggeration to suggest that we are witnessing the early stages of a process best described as the Confucianization of America.

To the extent that Americans have any sense of this trend, they tend to discount it. They imagine that Sino-American relations are in a delicate temporary phase in which a farsighted America is wisely cutting Beijing some slack while the Chinese complete a difficult transition to Western capitalism.

In reality there is nothing delicate about China's situation. Not only is China's Confucian power system probably inherently stronger than any Western one, but in Beijing, unlike in Washington, there is no confusion about the stakes. Quite simply, Chinese leaders have long recognized that in a world where everyone is everyone else's neighbor, Confucianism and Western individualism are mutually incompatible. It is a situation that recalls one of Mao Zedong's most famous maxims: Either kill the tiger or be eaten by him.

Every time someone in the United States talks about exporting democracy, Chinese leaders are reminded of the mutual incompatibility of the two systems. In their terms any American attempt to encourage democracy in China constitutes "imperialism" on the part of the United States. The point is often emphasized in the Chinese press. Here, for instance, is how the *People's Daily* put it in 1996: "After the end of the Cold War ... the strategic objective of the United States is to dominate the world. The United States will not allow the emergence of a great country ... [on the] Asian continent that threatens its power to dominate."

From the point of view of the Beijing leadership, China's interests are assuredly not served by a powerful America preaching Western values. Nor are they served by a thriving American democratic system, a free American press, or an independent American intellectual community. It is hardly an exaggeration to suggest that American democracy's very existence constitutes a threat, implicit if not explicit, to the Beijing leadership. As Chinese leaders have no plans to come off second best, they see little alternative but to go on the offensive: in their eyes, it is time to Confucianize the United States.

A key reason why the Chinese challenge is not better understood is that the media in the two nations do not report it. On the American side, the media are naive and Pollyanna-ish; on the Chinese side, manipulative and disingenuous. Although their mind-sets are polar opposites, the media on each side make common cause in presenting a generally upbeat account of how, under American influence, the Beijing regime is making steady progress in Westernizing Chinese society.

In reality Beijing has been making good progress on an entirely different project: the Confucianization of American society. The process, as we will now see, has probably gone further in business than in any other aspect of American life.

Confucius Rents a Jeep

American corporations have increasingly been engaged in China since the late 1970s. They have therefore been among the first American organizations to bump up hard against China's inexorable Confucianism.

It has been a chastening experience. The key to getting along anywhere is, of course, to go along. Unfortunately, going along in China means venturing further and further into a legal and ethical quagmire. Under relentless stock market pressure to generate profits, top American corporations have found themselves increasingly condoning activities in their Chinese operations that just a few years they would have considered unthinkable. They have had to collaborate, and the more shameless their collaboration, the more profits they have made.

A revealing early account of this new American collaborationism has been provided by James Mann. In his book *Beijing Jeep,* Mann tells of the Chinese experiences of American Motors Corporation (AMC), a Detroit-based company that is most famous for its iconic Jeep. As one of the first American companies to set up a factory in China, AMC was also one of the first to experience the contradictions between Chinese and American business methods. Floundering in a highly regulated—and highly manipulated—society, AMC discovered that insisting on doing things the American way was a recipe for endless frustration. So in 1986 it turned around and embraced the Chinese way. It entered a Faustian bargain: in return for cutting itself adrift from Western values, it secured the right to achieve an acceptable investment return in China.

A striking indication of the new attitude was that the company undertook to become an agent for the regime's controversial one-child policy. Not only did it set a salary scale that penalized workers who had more than one child, but it provided financial incentives to women to have abortions.

Of greater commercial significance was the fact that AMC went some way toward embracing the Confucian truth ethic. Following a path previously trodden by American corporations in Japan and South Korea, AMC consented to help the regime's public relations program in the United States. In return for securing a unique, rather artificial, foreign-exchange arrangement that promised to transform its Chinese joint venture's profit prospects, AMC acted as a principal actor in a program to encourage other American corporations to set up in China. In particular AMC consented to have its Chinese factory presented as a model joint venture, an object lesson in how American capitalism could supposedly prosper by cooperating with Chinese socialism.

This is how Mann described the arrangement: "China's primary motivation in making the AMC deal had been to demonstrate to foreigners that American Motors could survive and that business conditions in China were improving. Now China wanted to reap the benefits of that deal. This understanding on publicity was never expressed in such blunt terms. It was more indirect. Chinese officials would say, 'Let's tell everybody how well things are going.' But AMC officials certainly grasped the point and they were happy to oblige."

The public relations campaign was led by AMC's Beijing Jeep joint venture president, Don St. Pierre, who consented to give maximum publicity to various announcements of progress. Mann continued: "St. Pierre persuaded himself that his help in these publicity efforts was, to some extent, merely a matter of fairness. When things weren't going well for American Motors, he had been rough on China in the international press. Now things were going well for AMC, and he was willing to give China a little good publicity. He wasn't really telling the press anything inaccurate. It was certainly true that things for American Motors had improved."

The only problem, of course, was that St. Pierre was holding back. "Although St. Pierre was telling the truth, he was not telling the whole truth," explained Mann. "In his press conferences and interviews he wasn't revealing the details of how or why AMC's China venture had improved. The written agreement signed the previous May barred him from doing that."

It is important to remember that this was a time of widespread skepticism in corporate America about investment in China. The American tariff reductions that were later to pave the way for corporate America's outsourcing from China were still a long way in the future. Meanwhile, early joint ventures aimed at tapping the Chinese consumer market had generally failed, and American business executives were beginning to sense the truth: that in all too many cases, the reason China had opened to American companies was merely to strip them of their most advanced production technologies.

AMC's cooperation provided vital support for a message the Beijing regime then desperately wanted to project: that if a Western company remained patient with China, all problems would eventually be solved. Although AMC's Beijing-based American executives knew better, they nonetheless enthusiastically talked up the business prospects in China. Among various influential American visitors who were treated to AMC's upbeat take on China were Katharine Graham, publisher of the *Washington Post,* and Jane Pauley, cohost of NBC's *Today* program. Like other visitors, they were never told that the terms that made AMC's joint venture profitable were not available to other American companies.

As Mann pointed out, in misrepresenting the AMC story, the Beijing regime was following a well-established Chinese tradition. In fact the "model joint venture" story closely paralleled a "model village" story from the Maoist era. A village called Dazhai became famous throughout China for having dramatically increased its agricultural output on the strength of applying Maoist thought. After Mao died, it was revealed that Dazhai's numbers had been shamelessly faked.

In their parsimony with the truth, AMC's executives had been reduced to the level of the humble villagers of Dazhai: they had become the Chinese Communist Party's willing stooges.

Red Star over Washington

American Motors Corporation probably did not know it, but in its willingness to pander to the Beijing authorities, it was pioneering an epochal new trend in American capitalism. As the years have gone by, more and more American chief executives have deemed it part of their job specifications to function as spokesmen for the Chinese economic system. "Lobbying" is the preferred term for this, but given the nature of Beijing's agenda, a more accurate one might be "deception."

Already by 1997, as recorded by Robert Dreyfuss, the trend for corporate America to represent Beijing's interests in Washington had become a decisive force in American politics. "America's corporate elite have done a fine job unofficially representing the Chinese government in Washington," he wrote in the *American Prospect*. "In effect, the Fortune 500 have become China's public relations machine."

Commenting in 2003, James Sasser, a former American ambassador to Beijing who had previously served as a U.S. senator, put it even more provocatively. "The Chinese really don't do any lobbying," he told the Bloomberg news agency. "The heavy lifting is done by the American business community."

In the last decade there has been plenty of heavy lifting. As the Washington-based China watcher William Hawkins has pointed out, Beijing's surrogates in corporate America have assiduously helped China not only economically but militarily. Repeatedly in recent years American corporations have persuaded Washington to relax once strict limits on the sale of sensitive military technologies to the People's Liberation Army.

"The computer, aerospace, and machinery industries have all lobbied the Commerce Department for less restrictive rules and a shorter list of controlled products," Hawkins wrote in 2006. "Among the items that were taken off the export control list were aircraft engines, ball bearings, machine tools and virtual-reality systems. . . . it seems that the original concerns for national security have been lost."

Of perhaps even greater significance in the long run is American corporations' support for Beijing's economic agenda. Although as recently as 1979 China did not rank even in the top thirty nations as a source of America's manufactured imports, it now ranks first in the world. The dollar value of America's purchases from China rocketed more than 480 times in the twenty-seven years to 2006. This represented a growth rate of more than 25 percent a year.

Not only has this growth been probably unprecedented in world economic history, but it is fair to suggest that the scale of the lobbying needed to make it possible has also been unprecedented.

Corporate America's support for China's trade agenda first became apparent in the 1980s, when major American corporations, led by Coca-Cola and American International Group, successfully lobbied the U.S. Congress for so-called most favored nation treatment for Chinese exports in the American market. This treatment was originally granted for just one year but it was then renewed again and again over the next two decades. With each renewal, wavering members of Congress once again had to be strenuously wooed. Even in the early years when China's impact on the American economy was negligible and the grassroots political consequences in the American heartland had not yet become significant, the lobbying effort was massive. The scale of the task was greatly compounded after the Tiananmen massacre of 1989. In several subsequent years an almost inconscionable amount of arm-twisting was needed to deliver the necessary congressional majorities.

The effort could not have succeeded without massive support from America's most respected corporations. A standout in this regard has been Boeing. Just how far Boeing has been prepared to go on China's behalf became clear in the mid-1990s, when then chairman Philip Condit publicly sought to whitewash China's human rights record. In an interview with the *New York Times* magazine, Condit seemed to imply that China's human rights record was little worse than that of the United States. He said his feelings about China's human rights violations were "the same ones I have about human rights violations in the United States." Speaking long before America's human rights reputation was tarnished by the excesses of George W. Bush's war on terrorism, Condit added: "Some of the struggles we have had with civil rights don't look all that shiny. People have been shot. People have been beaten. I happened to be in China during the Rodney King beating."

Double-talk of this sort played a large part in securing the renewal of China's trading privileges all through the 1990s. But the China lobby's most important contributions were still ahead of it. In particular there was its success in 2000 in securing permanent access to the American market (known to policymakers as PNTR, for permanent normal trade relations). This represented a true historical turning point. Remember that up to the early 1990s, the entire American establishment was united in believing that unconditional access to the American market should be reserved only for nations deemed to be democracies. This policy, of course, increased the pressure on authoritarian regimes to reform themselves. It also helped to shield American corporations and workers from the highly artificial, often overtly predatory, trade tactics resorted to by authoritarian nations.

Why did so many top American corporations back away from their earlier instinct to give China a wide berth? In all but a few special cases, we can eliminate the idea that they were lured by the prospect of exporting to China. As of the late 1990s, corporate America already knew the score: the Chinese market was heavily protected and Chinese leaders evidently intended to keep it that way. Just how well they succeeded was underlined by Patrick Buchanan in *Where the Right Went Wrong* in 2004. According to his figures, American exports to China then accounted for just one-fifth of 1 percent of American gross domestic product! By comparison, Chinese exports to the United States accounted for 10 percent of China's gross domestic product. This meant that getting a deal was vastly more important to China than to the United States. The Americans started out with an almost infinitely stronger negotiating position—but nonetheless proceeded to give away the store. In return for granting China virtually tariff-free access to the American market in perpetuity, all they brought home was a couple of promises—promises that all too predictably turned out to be almost worthless.

Given the scale of this asymmetry, it is, to say the least, obvious that something more than conventional commercial logic was at work for China. Of course, as the story is presented for public consumption, everybody has been behaving entirely honorably. Thus, many American executives have justified their pro-China position by reference to a commitment to the abstract principle of global free trade. They go on to portray the entire outsourcing trend—which increasingly in the last decade has involved American corporations

transferring ever more advanced technology and production functions to factories in China—as America's latest heartening success in Americanizing the
world economy. As pro-China trade lobbyists never tire of pointing out, the
reason American corporations move jobs to China is to boost profits. And
what, they ask, could be more American than the pursuit of profits?

Some of the trend's most enthusiastic media boosters have even gone so far
as to suggest that outsourcing represents a resounding triumph in exporting
American-style freedom. But, to paraphrase Mae West's remark about good-
ness, freedom had nothing to do with it.

Remember that in a free market, participants are supposed to be, well, free.
Yet on the Chinese side of the Sino-American economic "partnership," shackles
have always been the order of the day. Even if we overlook all the mercantilist
devices by which Beijing limits the Chinese people's consumption, the Chinese
economy still ranks as one of the least free in modern economic history.

Consider the exchange rate for China's currency, the yuan. This is subject to
some of the most comprehensive rigging in world economic history. Working
closely with other East Asian governments, the Beijing regime has massively intervened in world currency markets to keep not only the yuan but the entire region's currencies grossly undervalued compared to the American dollar. The
most obvious instance of this rigging came in 1994, when the yuan's dollar value
was reduced overnight by one-third.

Moreover, in an even more controversial departure from American free-
market principles, China's labor market is so rigged that to call it a market at all
is to do violence to the English language. Basically Chinese workers are deprived
of all power to bargain collectively, and their trade unions are government-
controlled facades that are dedicated to oppressing rather than liberating Chinese labor.

The net effect is to force Chinese workers to acquiesce in wages that are
only a fraction of what a free market would pay. Moreover, millions of Chinese
workers work in Dickensian conditions of the sort that were long ago outlawed
in the West. As recorded by the U.S. National Labor Committee, in one factory
that made handbags for Wal-Mart, the workweek was as long as ninety-eight
hours and workers were paid as little as ten cents an hour. In a report on Chinese working conditions, the committee commented: "At the end of the day, the
workers return 'home' to a cramped dorm room sharing metal bunk beds with
16 other people. At most, workers are allowed outside the factory for just one
and a half hours a day. Otherwise they are locked in."

Consider how differently things might look if the Chinese economy were really a free market. In pressing for higher wages and better working conditions, Chinese labor union leaders might start off rather cautiously, but they would soon discover they were pushing on an open door. Thanks to scale economies and improvements in infrastructure, worker productivity has soared. Now massively profitable, many Chinese factory owners could well afford to double or even triple their workers' wages and still earn an adequate return. And once one employer in a district conceded higher wages, others would have to follow.

The important thing is how such an adjustment would affect the United States. With Chinese factories now generating merely a broadly reasonable return rather than a spectacular one, corporate America's outsourcing would slow to a trickle. Suddenly the negative aspects of transferring major production operations to China would loom large. While American boardrooms hungry for huge short-term profits have hitherto been prepared to ignore long-term negatives such as weakened control over valuable production engineering secrets and a damaged public relations image in the American heartland, in the absence of the excess profits currently generated by their Chinese factories, a much more sober view would prevail.

The dynamic that has so powerfully propelled the outsourcing trend is not American freedom but its polar opposite, Chinese authoritarianism. Put another way, American corporations are promoting Confucian values, not those of Adam Smith. It is hardly an exaggeration to suggest that executives of America's greatest corporations are increasingly acquiescing in a role as mere cogs in the wheels of the East Asian economic system.

Perhaps the most remarkable thing about corporate America's pandering is its unrelieved pervasiveness. Anytime the China lobby has needed arms twisted in Washington, literally hundreds of American corporations have appeared from nowhere to lend a hand. The lobby has been staging impressive shows of force since the early 1990s. In 1993 as Bill Clinton, in his first year as president of the United States, contemplated whether to renew China's so-called most favored access to the American market, thirty-seven business groups and no fewer than 298 American corporations came out for China. In a joint statement they urged Clinton not only to renew China's access but to do so without attaching any human rights or other conditions. They went on to suggest that the simple presence of American corporations on Chinese soil was serving to propel China toward democracy.

It is not just the number of corporations that rally to China's cause that is so significant but the speed of their responses. The point has been well made by Robert Dreyfuss. Writing in the *American Prospect* in 1997, he told of how Howard Coble, a Republican congressman from North Carolina, had indicated at a breakfast meeting in 1996 that he was leaning against renewing China's most favored nation status. By lunchtime, Coble's office had received more than forty phone calls urging him to rethink his vote. For lobbyists to react so fast requires a remarkable degree of organization and commitment. It is a reasonable inference that China's agenda is being supported at very high levels almost right across the board in corporate America.

All this is more surprising because lobbying on the sort of broad-brush issues concerned in American China policy is a classic instance of what economic theoreticians call the "free rider problem." The term refers to situations in which people who benefit from a particular resource or action have little incentive to pay for it. Remember that as of the mid-1990s, remarkably few American corporations had yet invested so much in China that Congress's decision mattered greatly. One might have expected therefore that as they grappled with the problem of "making" their quarterly profit numbers, many of them might have been tempted to rein in their spending on pro-China lobbying activities. In doing so each corporation would have felt sure that its individual decision would make almost no difference to the outcome in Congress. And the case for doing so was enhanced by the fact that support for China's trade agenda was generally unpopular among American workers and voters.

Yet top American corporations came out in droves for China. To anyone who understands the workings of Confucian power, none of this is surprising. As Anne Marie Brady has argued in *Making the Foreign Serve China,* China has long displayed a "highly evolved ability to make panderers out of foreigners."

A Telling Comparison: China Versus Russia

Challenged on their support for China's agenda, American executives deny, of course, that they have been Confucianized. They argue instead that they have merely been intent on promoting free trade—and what, they seem to ask, could be more high-minded than that?

This argument can readily be disposed of. Such executives have not been similarly interested in promoting free trade with other nations currently outside the World Trade Organization. Of the several examples that could be cited, the most important and relevant is Russia. It is interesting to note that though in many respects Russia seems to have a better case for joining the WTO than China, corporate America has, to say the least, shown little interest in opening any doors for it.

Yet, in striking contrast to China, not only has Russia become at least semidemocratic, but it seems committed to the idea of developing a capitalist system broadly compatible with that of the United States. All this notwithstanding, as of 2007 Russia not only remained excluded from the WTO but had failed in every effort to secure permanent normal trade relations with the United States.

Why has Russia been marginalized? The stated reason is that the Russian economy is not yet ready to trade on equal terms with the West. While this may be true, it simply deepens the mystery about the highly preferential treatment accorded to China. After all, on any impartial examination, China is even less qualified.

Just the most glaring of China's several disqualifications is that it lacks First World standards in product safety. By all accounts its standards are lower than Russia's. Indeed for years importing nations have had to employ armies of inspectors to check Chinese imports for product safety. Every year countless Chinese products fail such tests in the United States alone.

The seriousness of the problem was frighteningly underlined in 2007 when it was disclosed that a poison ultimately traced to China was the source of an epidemic of deaths among American pets. Then came even more devastating news. Rogue suppliers in China were revealed as the source of diethylene glycol, a highly toxic poison that was being used as a cheap substitute for glycerine in many types of pharmaceuticals and toiletries. As reported in the *New York Times,* the scam had cost the lives of thousands of people around the world, and in particular was being blamed in the deaths in 2006 of 365 people in Panama.

Another clear indication of China's lack of readiness to join the WTO is its inability and/or refusal to control product piracy. Of counterfeit goods intercepted at ports of entry into the United States, four times as high a proportion originates in China as in Russia.

Then there is the matter of economic structure. Here again China seems less well qualified than Russia. While the Russian corporate sector has largely been privatized, virtually all major corporations in China are government-controlled.

The degree of government ownership in the Chinese economy creates a crucial impediment to realizing America's vision of a global trading system in which competition is always fair and the most efficient producers always win. Just the most obvious problem is that government-owned corporations are much more likely than private-sector ones to receive market-disrupting government subsidies.

The two nations' legal systems are also a key issue and in particular these systems' ability to promote efficient business dealings. As the extent of the piracy problem in China suggests, the Chinese legal system is even more incompatible with Western ideas of justice than that of Russia. Then there is China's selective-enforcement system which not only makes a mockery of Western ideas of justice but is highly compromising for Western corporations. By contrast the Russian legal system, though erratic in practice, is in principle at least consonant with that of the West.

Perhaps the most devastating evidence that China has not been ready to trade on equal terms with the United States is that, as the Beijing-based author Jasper Becker has pointed out, even *within China* trade barriers are a major obstacle to trade. In 2002 one Shanghai-based executive reported that his European sporting-goods company had to pay an amount double the then national import tariff to ship his sneakers from Shanghai to the central city of Chongqing. The problem was protectionist fees imposed by provincial governments. Similarly, as reported by Hannah Beech in *Time,* an American automaker discovered that sending a sedan from Shanghai to Ningxia Province was more expensive than shipping it from Detroit to Shanghai, because truckers had to pay bribes every time they crossed a provincial border.

Even China's own corporations are badly disadvantaged by such internal barriers to trade. Here the experience of the Geely automobile company is particularly instructive. As one of China's most successful indigenous carmakers, Zhejiang-based Geely has worked hard to expand its sales throughout China. But in many parts of the country its products are discriminated against by provincial and city authorities anxious to support locally based rivals.

The point was underlined by an episode a few years ago in the eastern Chinese metropolis of Tianjin. The city is home to Xiali, one of Geely's principal rivals. When a local taxi company passed over Xiali's products to buy Geely's instead, city officials were so angry that they ordered an investigation into who had approved the purchase and barred taxi companies in the city from buying any more Geelys.

As Keith Bradsher of the *New York Times* reported in 2006, internal barriers to free trade in China are so significant that Geely has had to resort to setting up three satellite assembly plants in various parts of China to overcome them.

The question that has to be asked is how can China be considered ready for free trade with the West if its internal markets are so seriously distorted.

It is not as if knowledgeable experts did not realize all along that China was not ready to join the World Trade Organization. The absurdity of corporate America's effort to rush China into the WTO was vociferously criticized at the time by the noted China watcher Chalmers Johnson. "Structurally, China is still a Leninist economy and not ready for admittance as a regular member," he commented. "China cannot politically face the unemployment that ending subsidies would cause and regards foreign demands that it do so as attempts to subvert its political system."

He went on to suggest that even after joining the WTO, China not only would remain largely closed to American exports but would routinely flout Western intellectual property rights. All this, he argued, would result in even higher trade surpluses with the United States. Johnson's comments were made in 1997, when America's trade imbalance with China was a mere $50 billion. As of 2006 it had risen more than fourfold to $232 billion.

Despite all Johnson's well-founded reservations, China's WTO application sailed through, while Russia's was contemptuously ignored. What made the difference was the China lobby's superior influence in the United States, not least its ability to play corporate America like a proverbial violin.

Detroit, Silicon Valley, Bow to the Dragon

Just the most obvious of the Confucian tools now working to transform American corporate life is intimidation. Beijing's commercial regulators have no compunction about resorting to disproportionate measures against corporations regarded as not sufficiently well disposed to China. As Beijing enjoys enormous power to micromanage the circumstances faced by any corporation in China, it is hardly an exaggeration to suggest that American corporations that have not adequately Confucianized themselves may have to contemplate writing off their entire Chinese investment.

Adding to the sense of intimidation is Beijing's long memory. Beijing makes clear that Western corporations are judged on their performance over the long run in building a relationship of "mutual trust" with China. This means that even corporations with little immediately at stake in China have had to hedge for the possibility that in future years they might want to increase their commitment. At that point, their failure to be supportive enough of, for instance, China's WTO lobbying agenda in the 1990s would come back to haunt them.

Even many of America's most successful software corporations have been intimidated. The problem was highlighted in 2006 by *Business Week* correspondents Pete Engardio and Catherine Yang. He wrote: "Many U.S. software companies have been unwilling to gather and supply the hard data needed to mount a successful case [on Chinese software piracy]. 'Our bigger challenge isn't the law,' says one official. 'It's getting the evidence you need from companies who don't want to be seen as cooperating with the U.S. government.' "

A similarly ominous Confucian shadow has been cast over America's largest manufacturing companies. The point was startlingly exemplified when the United States–China Economic and Security Review Commission in 2006 invited the Big Three Detroit auto corporations to testify about their problems doing business in China. Not only was none of the three prepared to come forward, *but even their industry organization, the American Automobile Manufacturers Association, refused to testify.*

A key factor is the very different nature of regulation in China. Unacclimated Americans tend to assume that Chinese regulators, like their American counterparts, see their function primarily as ensuring that certain clearly stated and objectively written regulations are observed. This, of course, is decidedly not what Chinese regulation is about. Chinese regulators arrogate to themselves enormous arbitrary power to favor some clients over others. In doing so, they are merely reflecting a pattern already long familiar in other Confucian nations, most notably Japan and South Korea. The term of art is "case-by-case" regulation.

Reminiscing about his time in China, the author James Mann has captured the Chinese regulatory environment with rare clarity. "Western corporations never knew when officials from some Chinese ministry, department, province, municipality, or state enterprise would show up with some new tax or fee, some new regulation," he wrote. "Doing business was utterly unpredictable, and they felt that Chinese officials were constantly testing how much they could pay, how hard they were willing to fight."

An American executive quoted by *Time* has put it even more memorably: "Doing business in China is like being staked to an anthill. They nibble away all the time."

For those American corporations that do not relish being eaten alive, salvation is at hand—but, as we will now see, it comes at a high price.

America's Panderers Without Borders

For decades the goal of almost every major American corporation has been to become one of Beijing's "partners." To the unsuspecting, such a designation seems to betoken an innocuous, if not flattering, status. The term, after all, is conventionally assumed to mean merely that a foreign corporation is acknowledged by the Chinese to be reliable. In reality, however, it is an Orwellian euphemism. China's partners in this sense are proven stooges who have slipped their moorings in Western ethics and are prepared to undertake all sorts of questionable activities on Beijing's behalf.

As a quid pro quo, Beijing offers partners a plethora of privileges and incentives. Some corporations are granted sui generis perks such as the foreign-exchange deal, referred to earlier, that American Motors Corporation arranged. Usually, though, incentives this blatant are not necessary. In a society subject to as much arbitary bureaucratic power as China, the authorities have almost infinite flexibility in calibrating their favors. To take just the most obvious case, the processing of routine applications can be speeded up for favored clients and delayed—often by years—for others.

For foreign corporations that are not doing enough for China, bureaucratic delays are only the most obvious punishment they risk. A much more robust one, Washington-based China scholar Harry Harding has argued, is the "selective targeting of foreign firms for violations of China's laws and regulations." Foreign corporations are increasingly being drawn into the Beijing bureaucracy's selective-enforcement net.

Most American corporations aspire to be as law-abiding in China as anywhere else. But as any corporate executive who has worked in China will testify (at least in private), American corporations in China spend much of their time on the wrong side of the law.

Take, for instance, their policy on something as apparently straightforward as wages. We noted in chapter 5 that Chinese employers are rarely in compliance with minimum-wage laws. Since many of these employers are key suppliers to American corporations, the implication is that corporate America is complicit in the often brutally illegal exploitation of Chinese workers. As reported by Dexter

Roberts and Pete Engardio in *Business Week* in 2006, one compliance officer at an American corporation estimated that only 20 percent of corporate America's Chinese suppliers complied with Chinese minimum-wage regulations and only 5 percent complied with limitations on hours worked.

Another issue is tax. In a nation where almost no one pays his full taxes, American-owned corporations face an acute dilemma: Should they cheat or not?

Then there is the matter of bribery. Virtually nothing gets done in China without money changing hands. Should American corporations pay bribes or not?

And what about the more controversial aspects of the Chinese business entertaining tradition? As Dean Calbreath of the San Diego *Union-Tribune* has reported, foreign companies in China are often expected, for instance, to procure prostitutes for Chinese government officials. Writing in 2000, Calbreath quoted one middle-level executive in an American corporation as saying: "Some people hire two or three hookers just for one guy. Pretty soon, these guys are gonna start asking for a shot of Viagra as well!"

A related controversy concerns the frequent trips that executives at the U.S. headquarters seem to make to China these days. Some of the males among them are reputedly less interested in examining the accounting numbers than in studying some rather more exotic figures—the countless female forms available nightly for inspection in China's ubiquitous girlie bars. Typically the Americans expect hospitable—and deep-pocketed—Chinese business partners to pick up the tab. As recounted by one well-informed American observer I met in Shanghai in 2007, the trend has become so marked that even normally unshockable Shanghai businessmen have been heard to demur.

Of course, the use of sex in business is hardly unique to China. What is new, however, is the pervasiveness of the phenomenon in China and the fact that, at least in their role as hosts entertaining key Chinese decision-makers, even the most ethically minded Americans find it hard to put sufficient distance between themselves and local ethical norms. Ethics apart, there is the simple risk of blackmail. Selective enforcement of Chinese law is only the most obvious risk (on paper, of course, virtually everything that goes on in China's red-light districts is illegal). For major corporations based in the United States, a major additional concern is the potential blowback at home if the truth ever came out.

Persuaded by the Western media that good business these days universally

consists merely in generating quick profits from—hopefully—mutually beneficial transactions, Westerners fail to notice that for top Chinese leaders power
generally matters far more than mere money. Thus when an American corporation starts talking to officials or prospective business partners about entering
the Chinese market, Job One for the Chinese side is to find ways to control the
Americans.

This helps explain something that has long baffled American business: reflecting a general pattern throughout East Asia, the Chinese expect Westerners
to conduct a long courtship before being permitted serious market access. The
Westerners are told that they must "show sincerity" and "build trust"—and this
may mean having to cool their heels in China Inc.'s ante room for years or even
decades on end. In the meantime the Westerners may be permitted token access, typically in some narrowly defined niche where they can be expected to do
little "damage."

Seen from the Chinese side, a relationship is being formed, in which China
fully expects to remain the dominant partner. It helps that in striving to show
their "sincerity" the Americans are almost invariably induced to compromise
themselves, and typically not just under Chinese law but American law as
well. As the Chinese subsidiary's sales are puny to start with, its activities are
typically subjected to little serious oversight at home. By the time a groggy
American Gulliver wakes up, he finds himself comprehensively restrained by
the silky—and sometimes not so silky—threads of Chinese societal control.

Even compared to other foreign corporations in China, the Americans are
working at an exceptional disadvantage. Not only are they answerable to a
particularly unforgiving press and public at home but they have to contend
with the fact that much American corporate law—particularly on crucial issues
like tax evasion and corrupt practices—is global in scope. To say the least, such
law was not written with current conditions in China in mind.

American corporations moreover are peculiarly handicapped in trying to
develop loyal and capable management in China. Only the most obvious problem is that the rise of the two-career family has meant that far fewer capable
American corporate executives than formerly are prepared to accept any foreign assignment, let alone one in a place like China where suitable spousal employment opportunities hardly exist.

This is not a problem for the Americans' formidable Japanese and Korean
rivals, of course. The Japanese and Koreans, as lifetime employers, enjoy a further advantage in that they can spend years or even decades ahead of time

grooming suitable home-office executives for eventual high responsibility in China. With no similar depth of home-grown managerial talent to deploy, American employers often end up by default delegating control in China to local hires, whose incentive system strongly biases them towards serving Chinese rather than American interests.

The Americans are further handicapped by an almost total lack of practical day-to-day support from their government. The contrast with their Japanese counterparts is particularly telling and goes part of the way to explaining why the Americans have been far less successful than the Japanese in penetrating the Chinese market.

If a Japanese corporation encounters unfair or unreasonable treatment in China, it knows that its complaint not only will be heard in Tokyo but will be acted upon. Moreover, the action will be effective: because top Japanese officials are entrusted with enormous discretionary power, they have an almost infinite choice of penalties to deploy in pressuring their opposite numbers in Beijing. This is called horse trading, and every government bureaucracy throughout the Confucian world plays by the same rules. It can be summed up in one phrase: "We give you one, you give us one."

Thus if, say, Toyota runs into problems with an obstreperous or overly greedy government official in Shanghai or Shenzhen, a phone call will promptly be made by a top government official in Tokyo to his opposite number in Beijing. The chances are the matter will be resolved there and then, but if it is not, the Japanese system has plenty of tools at its disposal. At any one time the Beijing authorities have a whole laundry list of favors to ask of Tokyo. Perhaps they want increased landing rights for Chinese airlines at Japanese airports. Perhaps they are pressing to secure the latest Japanese nuclear technology for a new Chinese electricity-generating plant. They may want to increase the number of places for Chinese students at Japanese universities. Not only does Tokyo have the ability to calibrate its favors precisely but it can also impose precisely calibrated penalties. It can make trouble for particular Chinese exports or play China off against Thailand or Malaysia in its quota allocations for agricultural imports.

Seen in this light it is hardly a surprise that whereas the United States runs huge trade deficits with China, Sino-Japanese trade is in broad balance. As a Confucian nation, Japan is organized to support its corporations in China. The United States, with an entirely different tradition, is utterly at sea. It is hardly an exaggeration to say that American corporations in China long ago came to think of themselves as geopolitical orphans—orphans who these days increasingly yearn to be adopted into China Inc.'s extended family. In pandering to the powers that be in Beijing, they have become more Chinese than the Chinese themselves.

America's Cyberspace Supermen Kowtow

A decade ago it would have been unthinkable for America's fabulously successful cyberspace industry to kowtow to Beijing. The unthinkable has now happened, however, and it provides a particularly sobering insight into America's vulnerability to creeping Confucianism.

The fact is that leaders of the American cyberspace community have kowtowed not once but three times:

Kowtow 1. In the late 1990s American cyberspace companies maintained a complicit silence as Americans were deceived into believing the Internet would sweep away China's draconian system of censorship. Most top executives at these companies knew—or at least had good reason to suspect—that the story was false and was intended merely as a propaganda ploy to facilitate China's entry into the World Trade Organization. Keeping quiet while falsehoods on this scale are being propagated is not very American. It is, however, distinctly Confucian.

Kowtow 2. Top American technology companies contracted with Beijing to develop the so-called firewalls that have subsequently enabled Chinese censors comprehensively to block Chinese citizens' access to "dangerous" information. The firewalls are designed to block access not only to unapproved Chinese Web sites but to important Western ones.

Kowtow 3. Major American Internet e-mail and portal companies began cooperating with Beijing's efforts to find and apprehend cyberspace-based Chinese dissidents. They thereby reneged on countless previous promises to protect the privacy of their customers. Yahoo! alone is alleged to have provided the evidence that led to the conviction, on political offenses, of two Chinese citizens; one was sentenced to eight years in jail, and the other to ten.

All this is more surprising because the American cyberspace industry had originally presented itself as militantly fighting to keep the World Wide Web a free-speech zone. Many leading spokesmen for the industry argued for an extreme libertarian position in which portal companies should not do anything to limit access even to pornography or Nazi hate sites. Given this attitude and the Internet's ingenious architecture, it seemed for a while—at least to the technically unsophisticated—that all governmental attempts at control would be rendered futile. At the click of a mouse, anyone anywhere would soon enjoy uncensored access to information from anywhere in the world. The information genie was out of the bottle, and not even the Chinese Communist Party could force it back in again—or so we were told.

However, there was always another side to this story, a side that remained well hidden from the American public until after China's entry into the World Trade Organization was a done deal: all along, the Beijing authorities were working on systems to censor the Internet. A few commentators noted this at the time. In his 1998 book *The Crisis of Global Capitalism,* George Soros pointed out that already then China had developed Internet controls. But it was not until the first years of the new century that the full story came out. Thanks in large measure to the enterprise of the author Ethan Gutmann, it belatedly became clear that for years several American high-technology companies had been working secretly on a vast cyberspace program to enable Beijing to maintain its stranglehold on the Chinese people's sources of information.

The program's planning appears to have been initiated as far back as the mid-1990s. But its launch was delayed until 2001—after China had negotiated all vital approvals to join the World Trade Organization. Known variously as Golden Shield or the Great Firewall of China, it has provided China's feared Ministry of Public Security and other agencies not only with Orwellian tools of Internet surveillance but with the means to shut off Chinese citizens' access to much of the World Wide Web.

For those who believed the propaganda of the late 1990s, perhaps the most disappointing aspect of this whole affair has been the role played by Cisco Systems. Widely regarded as one of the Olympians of the Internet boom, Cisco was all the while a key participant in the Golden Shield program. It has allegedly supplied nearly three-quarters of the router computers that provide the backbone for China's censorship system. Not only did Cisco make big profits helping with Golden Shield, but its chief executive, John Chambers, allowed himself to be widely publicized in China's government-controlled media as a "friend of China."

The other shoe dropped when, under massive pressure from Beijing, the American Internet search engine companies caved in and agreed to censor their Chinese-language services. The move was led by Yahoo!, under its Taiwanese-born cofounder Jerry Chih-Yuan Yang, but was eventually followed by many other companies, most notably Google, AOL, and Microsoft. As of 2007 almost every American Internet search engine company had thoroughly Confucianized its Chinese-language services—expunging, for instance, all references to such banned topics as the Tiananmen Square massacre and Taiwanese independence.

Once again, American China watchers discovered a little late that they had been blindsided. As the Middlebury College–based China watcher Ashley Esarey has pointed out, Internet information in China is now generally as thoroughly censored as that published in the traditional media. With the exception of chat rooms, all online media in China are required to use content provided by mainstream media. Speaking to the *Asia Times* in 2004, Esarey added: "This content is subject to strict party monitoring. There is almost no content widely accessible in China that is not monitored by the Propaganda Department [of the Chinese Communist Party]. . . . Chat rooms routinely erase controversial postings to avoid trouble. Personnel at news media organizations that incur the wrath of the party are dismissed and media organizations themselves that do so are shut down."

According to Hongju Koh, a Yale law professor, foreign content providers such as Yahoo!, AOL, Google, and Skype have employed "internal content monitors" to comply with the Beijing authorities' wishes. In 2005 the Beijing regime followed up with a draconian system for licensing Internet blogs. According to the Paris-based organization Reporters Without Borders, the effect has been to force an unpalatable choice on bloggers: either avoid political subjects entirely or else tamely recite China's official propaganda.

What is so significant about all this is the time line. Up to May 2000, when the House of Representatives passed enabling legislation to facilitate China's WTO entry, little of China's Internet censorship activities had been reported in the mainstream American media. On the contrary, the good news, proclaimed in countless American editorials and on numerous talk shows, was that in the supposed new age of uncensorable information China was rapidly converging toward Western values.

Reporting for the *New Republic* in 1998, William J. Dobson suggested the firewall project was doomed. This take was even supported by Human Rights in China, a controversial New York–based advocacy group. In 1999 executive director Xiao Qiang told the *New York Times*: "The Internet has created a public space for discussion, which China has never had. The whole foundation of Chinese government control is being chipped away at a very fast speed, and over the next five years, there's no way they can stop it."

He added: "Give it some time, and you'll see hundreds of independent voices emerging. China will have independent thinking for the first time. Then there will be no way to turn these people back to the way things were three years ago."

As late as October 2000, *Newsweek* poured scorn on Beijing's Internet censorship program. Writing with Kevin Platt, the magazine's Beijing correspondent, Melinda Liu, commented: "The clampdown is futile. As fast as Beijing can erect barriers, the country's Net users keep finding ways around them. They know the government has access to any e-mail sent to or from mainland-based Internet service providers. No problem. Chinese privacy lovers can hook up to Yahoo or Hotmail for free e-mail accounts outside their government's jurisdiction."

While the congressional vote remained in the balance, Beijing carefully avoided undermining the American editorial writers' parable that a new age of free speech was dawning in China. Beijing did make one or two sallies against alleged abusers of the Internet—most notably in 1998, when it jailed someone for leaking a list of Chinese e-mail addresses to a Western recipient—but it showed consistent restraint in minimizing the publicity surrounding such actions.

In any case, elaborate censorship was not yet necessary because, as the University of Virginia–based Internet expert Bryan Pfaffenberger pointed out, only a tiny trusted elite then had access to the Internet. As of the end of 1999, there were only 9 million Internet subscribers in China, fewer than one per one hundred of population. It subsequently became clear that Beijing had deliberately held back the Internet's growth, dragging its feet on establishing the necessary external bandwidth needed to surf the non-Chinese Web.

Writing in 2000, Pfaffenberger explained: "By carefully controlling the Internet's growth and weaving it deeply into the fabric of the Party's complex network of business and regulatory relationships, the regime is building an Internet user base that has little incentive to use the network for seditious purposes; on the contrary, most Internet users in China have everything to gain by supporting the government line."

Of course the Chinese Internet was growing extremely rapidly and it was obvious that soon tens of millions of ordinary Chinese citizens would be wired. But, as Pfaffenberger realized even then, the regime was well prepared. Presciently anticipating the November 2001 crackdown, he wrote: "The state plans to implement a massive and repressive security infrastructure . . . that will enable precise content monitoring when the network grows too large for manual supervision."

If all this was obvious to Pfaffenberger, countless other so-called Internet experts chose to turn a blind eye. A notable case was Lyn Edinger, a former American diplomat and erstwhile chairman of the American Chamber of Commerce in Hong Kong. In congressional testimony in 1994, Edinger commented: "The people of China increasingly enjoy access to the nemesis of authoritarianism—the flow of information."

The striking thing is that Edinger was then employed by Nortel, a Canadian company that was one of the earliest Western companies to work with Beijing in shackling the Chinese Internet. Nortel went on to make big profits from Golden Shield.

For pro-Beijing propagandists in the trade debate, comments such as Edinger's were all grist for the mill, and their suspect provenance was not even noticed, let alone mentioned. Nor did their provenance seem to matter to President Bill Clinton. Although he had been elected in part on the strength of attacking President George H. W. Bush for "coddling tyrants," he had quickly become Beijing's chief supporter in its bid to join the WTO. In that capacity in March 2000—just two months before the crucial House of Representatives vote—he told a meeting that censoring the Internet was "like trying to nail Jell-O to the wall."

This message was soon amplified by Clinton's chief trade negotiator, Charlene Barshefsky. She suggested that it was a "no-brainer" that the Internet would lead to China's liberalization. Referring to the Beijing regime, she said: "The government is not going to be able to control content. It is not going to be able to control access, keeping in mind as well, access can be provided cross-border. One does not have to locate in China to provide access. And I think that the Net and the availability of information flow on the Net is going to have perhaps the single most profound change on China, engendering tremendous pressure on the Chinese leadership."

Had Clinton or Barshefsky checked the facts before sounding so confident? Probably not. It was a Confucian moment—but with a twist. This sort of mindless repetition of mendacious propaganda is the essence of how top officials operate in a Confucian society. What was different, however, was that Clinton and Barshefsky gave every impression that they believed what they said. In a more mature Confucian society, by contrast, all but the lowest functionaries realize that the official line is generally false.

In any case, as the former *Los Angeles Times* Beijing correspondent James Mann has pointed out, Beijing was gearing up all along to control the Internet. It was just that in the few years immediately ahead of the crucial WTO approvals this intention had to be kept temporarily hidden from Western view. Earlier Chinese officials had been quite explicit in admitting they intended to extend China's media censorship system into cyberspace. In 1995 Telecommunications Minister Wu Jichuan said in a news briefing: "By linking with the Internet we do not mean absolute freedom of information. I think there is general understanding about this. If you go through customs you have to show your passport. It's the same with the management of information." Wu added that the regime was planning unspecified "management measures" to control inflows of data into China's telecommunications system. He went on: "There is no contradiction at all between the development of telecoms infrastructure and the exercise of state sovereignty. The International Telecommunications Union states that every country has sovereignty over its own telecoms."

The question Americans must contemplate now is this: If Beijing can buy the services of Cisco, Nortel, Microsoft, Yahoo!, and Google, whose services can't it buy?

Confucius to Mick Jagger: Get Off of My Cloud

One of the most impressive things about Confucianism is its relentlessness. Nothing and nobody, it seems, escapes a Confucian bureaucrat's will to control. Sometimes the control comes in forms that baffle Westerners. Indeed the compromises demanded may seem so trivial that they do not seem like compromises at all—at least not at the time. But almost every Westerner who does business in modern China comes away diminished, however subtly, by the experience.

An illustration of the point is the superficially amusing predicament the Rolling Stones rock stars found themselves in when they wanted to play in China in 2003. Their visit was duly approved by the Beijing Ministry of Culture but only on condition that they omit several "controversial" songs from their performance.

As the banned songs—the most famous of them was "Let's Spend the Night Together"—were tame by twenty-first-century standards, the ministry's intervention seemed to make no sense. The mystery of the ministry's attitude was deepened by the fact that the banned songs were all in English, a language that the vast majority of the Chinese do not speak. Besides, pirated CD versions had for decades been sold in the streets of major Chinese cities, yet no moral policeman—let alone intellectual-property-rights policeman—seemed in the slightest bit concerned.

It was hardly as if modern Chinese citizens were easily shocked. Commercial sex is more openly available in China today than almost anywhere else in the world. Prostitutes trawl for business in the lobbies of expensive hotels. Sexual services are often used to bribe the dissolute or to ensnare the unwary. Hardcore pornography is routinely sold in the vicinity of famous Chinese landmarks.

The Stones' predicament made for fun headlines in the West. Referring to the numerous Westerners who had bought tickets for the concerts, the group's leader, Mick Jagger, quipped that he was "pleased the Ministry of Culture is doing so much to protect the morals of expatriate bankers and their girlfriends."

Countless columnists in the West mocked what they saw as no more than absurd bureaucratic prudishness. Even ostensibly experienced observers of the Confucian world missed the point. Thus the Tokyo-based conservative commentator William Pesek, writing for the Bloomberg news service, opined that the episode signified "weakness" in Beijing. Other commentators ascribed the episode to the allegedly "mysterious East."

For anyone who understood the Confucian mind, however, there was nothing mysterious, let alone weak, about the Ministry of Culture's position. The ministry was making a none too subtle anti-Western point: its coded message, widely understood throughout the Confucian world, was that Westerners always have their price. Although they loudly proclaim the principle of free speech, they rarely let this get in the way of making money.

It is fair to suggest that the ministry was probably motivated also by an even more disturbing agenda. It was establishing who was boss. Rather in the manner of a dog trainer training a particularly slow-witted puppy, Beijing has been breaking the West in gently. In a series of easy baby steps constantly repeated, Westerners are being trained to bow to arbitrary Confucian authority.

What the Stones confronted was the thin end of a thick political wedge.

While the political principle at issue in the Rolling Stones affair may seem trivial, Beijing's censorship agenda is likely to become ever more assertive in the
years ahead. It is not an exaggeration to suggest that even the editors of America's most prestigious media organizations will—probably in the not too distant
future—find themselves under rapidly increasing pressure to censor themselves. (Only the most obvious conduit for such pressure would be the advertising department.) At that point, the fact that Beijing has already invested so
much effort in inducing other Westerners, however subtly, to renege on the
Western principle of free speech will yield a bountiful return. The point is that
this is a numbers game. As more and more Westerners prove pliable, the remaining few who hold out become increasingly isolated. Thus, if it ever became
necessary to organize a public petition in support of the free-speech rights of,
for instance, the editor of the *New York Times,* those who had already kowtowed
would hardly be in a strong position to rally to his or her cause.

   In the larger scheme of things, what the Rolling Stones did seems so insignificant that no principle was at stake. The trouble is that one compromise
leads to another. Because some artists allow themselves to be censored very
slightly, others may be induced to make somewhat larger compromises. What is
clear is that there is no trip wire that once activated would spur Westerners to
rally en masse in defense of Western free speech. In the fullness of time, this
will come to be seen as the intellectual equivalent of a death of a thousand cuts.

   In postulating such an agenda in Beijing, are we being overly sensitive? Perhaps. But, as we will now see, wider concerns about what China's rise is doing to
the American intellect are by no means without substance.

Confucianizing the American Mind

In a well-ordered Confucian nation, all intellectual life should be safely controlled by the powers that be. It will be a while before American minds are
locked down as securely as those of the Chinese or the Japanese. Nonetheless,
in the last three decades an impressive start has been made in getting American
intellectual processes under Confucian control.

   The degree to which Confucianism has already taken root is particularly obvious in the American think-tank industry. At virtually every major American
think tank, the issue of trade policy is now looked after by analysts who faith-
fully present China's case to Congress and to the American media.

It is fair to say that in promoting China's application to join the World Trade Organization, for instance, American think-tank analysts could hardly have been outdone in spreading false information by the Ministry of Propaganda in Beijing. And to this day they have shown little or no remorse about how blatantly they misled the American public. Virtually the only think tanks in Washington to question the consensus have been a few perennially under-funded organizations such as the United States Business and Industry Council, the Economic Policy Institute, and Ralph Nader's Global Trade Watch—organizations that all along opposed most favored nation status for China. Their firepower has been overwhelmed by the massed ranks on the other side—lavishly funded organizations such as the American Enterprise Institute, the Peterson Institute for International Economics, the Cato Institute, the Brookings Institution, and the Council on Foreign Relations.

Of course, the think-tank industry claims that far from reflecting sordid pecuniary pressures, its support for Beijing constitutes part of a highly intellectually respectable wider agenda to make the entire world safe for free trade. All the circumstantial evidence, however, indicates that this is humbug. For a start, in common with American corporate executives, think-tank analysts have been remarkably less enthusiastic about promoting Russia's case than China's.

Of course, not every think-tank analyst is a fake. The Confucian way does not require such abject intellectual slavery. The principle rather is one that is best described as "elevation." Analysts whose views happen to serve the Confucian authorities' interests find themselves catapulted to prominence. Those whose views are not so acceptable find themselves adroitly marginalized. In such an environment, people of flexible principles quickly emerge to fill more and more key positions. It is called collaborationism, and, as became clear everywhere from France to Lithuania during World War II, it is a force that any well-organized authoritarian regime, no matter how evil, can count on in furthering its aims.

One of the minor scandals here is that though the think tanks have exercised untold influence on American policy in the last three decades, they remain to this day under no statutory obligation to disclose their funding sources. A few institutions such as the Brookings Institution provide a list of names of their benefactors, but by grouping donations in wide bands, they comprehensively obscure their largest sources of funds. Even such sketchy disclosure, however, is the exception rather than the rule. Such a prestigious and influential organization as the Peterson Institute for International Economics, which has

been perhaps the most effective single American nonprofit institution in promoting China's economic agenda in the United States, has provided virtually no
information in recent years on the identity of its benefactors.

To be sure, in response to direct questions, many think tanks state that their
money comes mainly from American sources. It would be interesting, however,
to know which sources in particular, as certain American corporations have become notorious in recent years as outright stooges for Beijing's interests. In any
case, for those with an eye for ambiguous legalisms, "American sources" covers a
multitude. American subsidiaries of East Asian and European corporations
might be included. So might the East Asian subsidiaries of American corporations, many of which are run by Chinese nationals.

We will take a closer look at two of the think-tank industry's key protagonists in chapter 8. In the meantime let's press on with a consideration of other
ways in which the American mind is coming under Confucian influence.

A key factor is that East Asian programs at American and European universities are now largely under East Asian control. Although direct Chinese influence is still the exception rather than the rule, most universities place their
Chinese studies programs within East Asian departments that also focus on the
wealthier Confucian nations, most notably Japan, South Korea, and Singapore.
Such nations collectively control the purse strings, and although their objectives
are not identical with those of China, on many key issues they make common
cause. (Just the most obvious manifestation of this trend is that in the 1990s
both Japan and South Korea invested massively in assembly plants in China.
They thus had a strong interest in opening the American market to Chinese
goods.)

What is a matter of public record is that many of the same East Asia studies
experts who have long been noted partisans of, for instance, Japan's economic
interests have also been prominent in promoting China's. Three in particular
might be mentioned here: Gary Saxonhouse of the University of Michigan,
Jagdish Bhagwati of Columbia, and Ezra Vogel of Harvard.

China seems intent on establishing direct influence over American scholarship. Certainly that seems to be the implication of a recent boomlet in direct
institutional ties between American and Chinese intellectual organizations.
Such partnerships have proliferated in the last ten years and are typically described on the American side as "strategic relationships." Many of the American partners are either think tanks or universities, but even some of America's
federally funded research and development institutions have joined in.

On the Chinese side the "strategic partners" include the Chinese Academy of Social Sciences, which is run and controlled by the Chinese government; the China Foundation for International Strategic Studies, run by the military intelligence department of the People's Liberation Army (PLA); and the Foundation for International Studies, which boasts links to the Ministry of State Security, the PLA intelligence department, and the Foreign Ministry.

What is wrong with such ties? In theory nothing, but in practice often quite a bit. Reflecting a standard problem whenever individualistic Americans interact with Confucian institutions, the likelihood is that such relationships are much more carefully supervised on the Chinese side—because the Chinese are answerable to a highly authoritarian government—than on the American one. Certainly to the extent that these relationships are described as strategic, the "strategizing" is being done in Beijing not Washington.

One key China watcher who has warned of the dangers is Larry Wortzel, a former chairman of the U.S.-China Economic and Security Review Commission. "When one enters into a formal relationship with one of these Chinese government-controlled organizations, they expect the [American] partner to be 'sympathetic' to China," says Wortzel, a fluent Chinese speaker with a background in counterespionage. "The [Chinese] organization will retaliate for published works it does not like by limiting access to Chinese contacts. Thus the organization or scholar who enters into such a partnership must either censor his or her work to comply with the desires of the Chinese partner or lose the opportunities for contacts or relationships."

That is putting it diplomatically. In reality such relationships provide an ideal environment in which a Machiavellian partner can penetrate, compromise, or otherwise weaken the American side.

What is beyond question is that Beijing leaves no stone unturned in trying to influence America's top China-watching intellectuals. By all accounts Beijing in recent years has invented various pretexts to channel lots of money directly into American intellectuals' pockets.

A standard procedure is to engage such intellectuals as "consultants" or "visiting professors." Such assignments often seem to be no more than thinly veiled sinecures.

The point is illustrated at Shanghai-based Fudan University's American Studies Center, which as of 2006 numbered four Americans on its ten-person blue-ribbon panel of distinguished "consultants." Of these, three were well-known American experts on China: Harry Harding of George Washington

University, Ezra Vogel of Harvard, and Robert Scalapino of the University of California (the fourth, Nelson Kiang of the Massachusetts Institute of Technology, was a medical professor). Given that the American Studies Center's stated purpose is to study the *United States,* why seek out American experts on *China?* Why not American experts on *America*—say, Samuel Huntington or William Greider? And if the Fudan authorities are somehow short of experts on China (how many coals do they need in Newcastle, anyway?), would they not do better talking to a few of the more articulate local taxi drivers, whose ability to read the local language could at least be taken for granted?

Key here is how Fudan compensates its panel. No public information is available, of course, but the "hourly rate" may be attractive. Such an inference seems reasonable given that the other half of the panel consists of six superhigh Chinese apparatchiks who would routinely command some of the highest consulting fees in modern China. Of the six, five are former Chinese ambassadors to the United States, and one of them even went on to become China's minister of foreign affairs.

The point is not that the Americans are necessarily being bought or that they are likely to make any conscious adjustments to their thinking. The point merely is that the phenomenon of U.S.-China academic links is a subtly Confucianizing one that provides cover for all sorts of other "partnerships" that do not pass even minimal reality checks.

A similarly troubling illustration of how the American intellectual establishment is Confucianizing itself is the Hopkins Nanjing Center. This Nanjing-based institute is ostensibly a joint venture between Johns Hopkins University of Baltimore and Nanjing University. Evidently, however, Johns Hopkins has little managerial control. Rather, the institute is run by Chinese educational bureaucrats answerable ultimately to China's Ministry of Education. Johns Hopkins is providing "educational branding"—taking a fat fee for sanctifying a product over whose manufacture it has minimal control.

What is clear is that the institute's educational values seem more Confucian than American. Take, for instance, the institute's chairs in journalism and political studies. These are both named in honor of Fei Yi-ming, a Hong Kong–based publisher who for decades functioned as one of Beijing's most important propaganda stooges. He combined his publishing duties running a pro-Beijing newspaper in Hong Kong with service as a member of the National People's Congress in Beijing.

All this notwithstanding, Johns Hopkins seems to be going ever deeper into

China. In 2006 the institute launched a new master's degree in international studies that will be conferred "collaboratively" by Johns Hopkins and Nanjing University and will be recognized in both the United States and China.

Officially, of course, the Hopkins Nanjing Center will get the benefit of at least some American oversight. But the quality of this oversight is questionable given that the chairman of the board, J. Stapleton Roy, is one of Beijing's most prominent American lobbyists (in his capacity as a managing director of Kissinger Associates). Another board member is ex-president George H. W. Bush. His presence may seem more reassuring, but he is known in East Asia for flexible standards in the sort of money he accepts. (He once spoke at a salespersons' rally in Tokyo for Amway, a direct-marketing organization noted in Japan as much as in the United States for controversial selling practices. As recorded by Mike Rogers at LewRockwell.com, Bush was presented as a supporting act for the principal draw, the singer Diana Ross.)

The idea that American scholars work in ivory towers has, of course, always been something of a fiction. Money has often helped shape the American mind. This was explicitly acknowledged long ago in a famous comment by William Rainey Harper, the first president of the University of Chicago. Commenting on the underrepresentation of labor's interests at the university, he remarked: "It's all very well to sympathize with the working man. But we get our money from the other side, and we can't afford to offend them."

That said, there is a difference between the rising Confucian influence we see today and the sorts of pressures exerted by the Rockefellers, Fords, and Carnegies of old. Confucian influence is not only monolithic and all-seeing, but has an elephant's memory.

American Science: Confucius in a Lab Coat

One of the least remarked upon but most important aspects of China's increasing intellectual influence abroad is in American laboratories. American science is going Confucian.

As a rule, the more prestigious the university and the more intellectually challenging—and geopolitically important—the discipline, the more heavily represented are the Chinese among the student body. The trend has been particularly noticeable in engineering schools such as Caltech and the Massachusetts Institute of Technology.

Already as of the mid-1990s Ronald A. Morse, director of international projects at the University of Maryland, suggested that Chinese-born students outnumbered American ones in the university's engineering classes. According to Thomas Friedman, at one point in recent years all the graduate students in mathematics at Johns Hopkins were from mainland China.

Commenting on the rising numbers of foreign students in American universities in his book *War by Other Means: Economic Espionage in America,* John Fialka of the *Wall Street Journal* commented: "The Chinese students tend to be superbright, an elite skimmed from a nation of over 1.2 billion people. They have come to dominate the lower levels of faculties in many universities and they regularly win highly prized research and teaching assistantships, which means that their education is subsidized by the schools and U.S. taxpayers. The situation has reached a point where American undergraduates frequently complain that they can't understand their teacher's English."

The Chinese have followed a path previously trodden by students from other parts of the Confucian world. Already by 1991 students from Pacific Rim nations accounted for more than half of all science and engineering doctorates at American universities, up from 21 percent a decade earlier. Whereas as recently as 1981, there was not a single doctoral candidate from mainland China at an American university, by 1991 there were nearly 1,600.

Of course, foreigners on American campuses are nothing new. But there is worrying evidence that the Chinese influx is different from, for instance, the Europeans who fled Nazism in the 1930s. Invoking the Confucian diktat of loyalty, the Beijing regime expects the overseas Chinese diaspora to remain loyal to China. By contrast, the Europeans who arrived in the 1930s suffered no such conflict of loyalties. Moreover, unlike many top Chinese scientists in the United States today, they harbored not the slightest intention to return to the nation of their birth, let alone to bring back American scientific secrets with them.

Chinese students already in the United States are often recruited by the Ministry of State Security, China's main intelligence agency. As recounted by Nicholas Eftimiades in his book *Chinese Intelligence Operations,* those who refuse to cooperate may face Orwellian forms of coercion, not least threats to wives and children left behind in China.

It is, moreover, common knowledge in American espionage circles that many of China's spy agencies use American universities as "finishing schools" for training young spies. The possible extent of this phenomenon was brought memorably to the attention of General James Williams, a former head of the

U.S. Defense Intelligence Agency, when he visited Beijing. He met many high officers of the People's Liberation Army who, speaking excellent American-accented English, recalled their days on American campuses. Williams made a note of their names and ordered a check of U.S. immigration records. There were no records. "All I can figure is they must have come in under different names," he told John Fialka.

It is hard to exaggerate how vulnerable are American universities. By and large, Chinese students who aspire to study at top American institutions can be assumed to be prevetted by the Chinese authorities. In a nation where people are not allowed to move beyond their home districts without special permits, the right of students to travel abroad is carefully circumscribed. Moreover, any prospective student considered politically unreliable would have to worry that his application to get into Harvard or Yale would be sabotaged (it is, of course, standard procedure throughout the Confucian world to make up stories out of whole cloth to blacken the names of those considered—in however small a way—problematic for the powers that be). In any case, because of language and other difficulties, many American universities delegate the function of assessing East Asian applicants largely to East Asian–born colleagues. Although there is no evidence that any of these latter are under Beijing's control, it is a fair bet that an effort to influence the admissions procedures of prestigious American universities has long ranked high among Beijing's diplomatic priorities in the United States.

All this, as we have already indicated, is of special significance in the sciences. In the long run, as foreign students crowd out native-born Americans in key technological disciplines, American weapons manufacturers and defense laboratories will become increasingly dependent on foreign technicians for pathbreaking expertise. This opens up the possibility that American defense technologies will increasingly be penetrated by Chinese agents (albeit posing as freedom-loving naturalized Americans). Because of its openness, the United States has always run this risk. The difference today is the scale of the problem.

America, Land of the Fearful?

The Beijing regime has long been notorious for its severity in cracking down on its critics at home. Critics abroad, by contrast, have hitherto had little to fear. This may now be changing.

While Beijing hid its claws in the years before it gained entry to the World Trade Organization, it has become increasingly aggressive in disciplining Chinese dissidents abroad in the last few years. The new attitude reflects a rapid strengthening of Beijing's negotiating position in dealing with Western capitals, particularly Washington. Not only is China's position in the world trading system now more or less unchallengably secure, but with every year that passes more and more Americans—in business, the media, the universities, and politics—become dependent on Chinese favors.

Among the first to sense Beijing's steely new confidence have been Chinese-born naturalized Americans. Those with ties to the Falun Gong sect have had particular reason to worry. Their concerns were highlighted in a resolution passed by the United States Congress in 2004. The resolution had been prompted by allegations that Chinese consular officials had intimidated Falun Gong supporters on American soil.

In 2006, a prominent Chinese American Falun Gong activist needed fifteen stitches in his face after intruders attacked him in his home in Atlanta. Two of the intruders spoke Korean and a third Mandarin Chinese. The victim had played an important role in an Internet campaign by the Falun Gong to discredit the Beijing regime. The intruders' brief was evidently to sabotage that campaign (as reported by *Forbes* magazine, they were concerned in particular to find sophisticated software programs designed to get around China's Internet firewalls).

Meanwhile another prominent Chinese-born Falun Gong supporter, this time a Chinese American doctor at Harvard, disclosed not only that he had been threatened in Boston, but that his parents in China had been subjected to regular visits from China's secret police. His parents were told that their son was under superclose Chinese government surveillance—news that they took as a coded threat to his life.

In targeting Chinese-born American citizens, Beijing is evidently banking on the fact that their complaints rarely make waves in mainstream America. Trouble in the ethnic Chinese community can often be passed off as stemming merely from turf wars between the triads, as ethnic Chinese gangs are known.

It seems reasonable to assume that, as with its previous pattern of pushing American corporations ever harder on Chinese soil, Beijing is testing American resolve. Thus, if the Chinese authorities can get away with intimidating United States–based Falun Gong supporters, this may prove the thin end of a thick wedge. Absent a firm response from the United States, we have to wonder how

long it will be before Beijing feels free to resort to similar tactics against mainstream Americans.

Already many American intellectuals have become uncomfortably aware
that they are in Beijing's crosshairs. Several have reported evidence that their
phone conversations and e-mail messages are monitored by Chinese spies. Any
China watcher who is deemed to be going too far in upholding the Western
truth ethic has to look over his shoulder.

The Chinese embassy in Washington has emerged in recent years as an overt
force in intimidating knowledgeable Americans. On several occasions, for instance, embassy officials have pressed American conference organizers to black-
list China critics who have testified before the U.S.-China Economic and Security
Commission. Law firms that have been overtly critical of Chinese trade practices
soon discover that their activities have been noted with displeasure. Sometimes
their American clients have pressured to complain to the partners.

Denunciation campaigns somewhat similar in spirit to those carried out by
Red Guards against "class enemies" in Maoist China have been initiated against
certain key observers. The attacks come mainly in the form of whisper campaigns emanating not only from the China lobby but from its congressional
allies.

Among mainstream American intellectuals, one of the earliest victims was
Richard Fisher, a pro-Taiwan military hawk who in 1999 was forced out of his
job as head of the Asian Studies Center at the Heritage Foundation. His ouster
attracted little attention at the time, partly because he refused to talk about it.
It is believed that a key condition of his severance package was that he remain
silent. The move against him was said to have been initiated by key donors with
lucrative commercial links to Beijing. Fisher went on to become vice president
of the International Assessment and Strategy Center in Washington, but the
episode has cast a permanent shadow over Washington's China-watching community.

Sometimes Beijing has successfully invoked misplaced political correctness
to get even with its American critics. The leading China watcher Steven
Mosher, for instance, was refused a doctorate by Stanford University in circumstances that suggested he was being penalized on political rather than scholarly
grounds. His "offense" had been to document some of the Orwellian consequences of China's efforts to enforce its one-child policy. Mosher, a convert to
Catholicism who now runs the Virginia-based Population Research Institute,
has publicly accused Stanford of bowing to Chinese government pressure.

Another victim whose targeting by the China lobby is public knowledge is Paul Berkowitz, a foreign policy aide to the conservative Congressman Dana Rohrabacher. Both Berkowitz and Rohrabacher strongly opposed the granting of so-called most favored nation status to China. Berkowitz moreover is a noted critic of Chinese military expansionism. He has also offended the Beijing regime by supporting the Dalai Lama and publicizing China's theft of Tibetan cultural treasures. In the late 1990s Doug Bereuter, a pro-Beijing Congressman wrote an innuendo-laden letter asking for Berkowitz to be removed from his then post as an aide to the House International Relations Committee. A whisper campaign against Berkowitz continued into the new decade and persisted even after sixteen Congresspeople, including Nancy Pelosi, Chris Cox, and Rohrabacher, signed a letter outspokenly supporting him. In 2003, a widely read Washington trade newsletter aired allegations that Berkowitz had psychological problems.

The allegations were unsourced and unsubstantiated. Berkowitz lost his position at the committee but landed on his feet when he was hired by Rohrabacher. Bereuter resigned from Congress in 2004 and is now president of the Asia Foundation, a thinly disguised lobbying organization.

The worst of it is that the sort of independent-minded elected officials who came to Berkowitz's aid are an endangered species. To say the least, America's Founding Fathers never envisaged the dominant role that funding by transnational corporations has now come to play in American politics; still less did they anticipate that such corporations would become increasingly dependent on the favors of a despotic foreign regime. In an earlier chapter we suggested that Korean trade officials play a giant game of Whac-a-Mole in repelling imports. The metaphor is even more apt in describing how Beijing and its corporate American stooges crack down on prominent Americans who go too "too far" in upholding the American national interest.

The great irony is that the U.S. Constitution was designed to discourage concentrations of power at home. Oblivious to the risk that the nation could ever fall prey to foreign manipulation, the Founding Fathers structured American society on highly atomistic lines. Precisely for that reason, in today's "global" conditions, the United States is exceptionally easy for foreign powers to penetrate. Worse, concerned Americans find it extraordinarily difficult to make common cause against the alien forces now undermining the values and freedoms the Constitution was designed to uphold.

Legal Eagles Morph into Cocker Spaniels

Few areas of American life seem at first sight more immune to creeping Confucianism than the legal profession. But that may be changing. In their thirst for business, many top American law firms these days are pandering to the Beijing authorities.

The pattern had its genesis in the early 1980s, when American firms fell head over heels in love with the New China. Unfortunately, their affections were not reciprocated.

Betting that China would converge to Western values and thus become a major new market for legal services, almost every major American law firm raced to set up in Beijing or Shanghai. They overlooked the Beijing authorities' continuing commitment to the age-old concept of arbitrary Confucian power. Enjoying the right to override any laws that get in the way, Chinese officials tolerate lawyers only on distinctly Confucian terms: a lawyer's allotted function in the Chinese order is mainly to explain the regime's often high-handed rulings to his or her perennially oppressed clients.

Successive Chinese administrations since the earliest days of Chinese civilization have always contrived to keep the Chinese legal profession carefully marginalized. So when the Americans came calling, the Beijing regime embarked on a relentless campaign to break their will to bring American-style justice to China. A key to the strategy was foot-dragging in granting professional licenses.

This is how *American Lawyer* magazine summed up the story: "For most of the 1980s, Western lawyers [in China] operated in limbo. Their presence was tolerated, perhaps even welcomed, but they weren't officially licensed by the government to practice inside China. Working conditions were often unorthodox. Since they weren't officially sanctioned, many lawyers ran their practices from clients' offices or hotel rooms. Although the atmosphere was highly irregular, the number of Western practitioners grew steadily through the 1980s."

Even after the Beijing Ministry of Justice agreed in principle to issue official licenses to the foreigners, this did not end the waiting. As recounted by *American Lawyer*, the criteria for approval were unstated and the ministry was tight-lipped about each firm's chances for success.

Although the licensing process should have taken no more than a month, it generally took at least a year. One unfortunate American firm, White &

Case, was kept waiting fully five years. While White & Case has declined to explain why, it is a fair inference that the Beijing Ministry of Justice had its reasons.

What is undeniable is that Beijing has systematically rigged the Chinese legal-services market to keep the American firms securely under its thumb.

In a classic example of the selective-enforcement gambit, Beijing has written the rules on foreign lawyers overly strictly but generally enforces them laxly. All through the 1990s, for instance, it was technically illegal for American law firms to maintain more than one office in China, yet many firms maintained at least two—typically in Shanghai and Beijing. The second office was designated a "consulting office," a fiction that fooled no one, least of all the Chinese Ministry of Justice.

Although under the terms of China's World Trade Organization entry, the one-office restriction has now been lifted, American law firms still labor under a host of other restrictions. For example, American firms are forbidden from practicing Chinese law—so in theory it is illegal for them to offer opinions on Chinese legal issues. Consonant with this restriction, Chinese lawyers who join American firms are deemed to have left the Chinese legal profession.

One of the most consequential rules is that before an American lawyer is permitted to work in China, he or she must first have acquired at least three years' experience in the United States. The only purpose seems to be to exacerbate an already acute shortage of good lawyers in China. After all, once young lawyers have spent three years getting established in New York or Chicago, they are understandably loath to move to a completely different jurisdiction. To do so surely involves writing off extensive contacts and experience. In any case, many young lawyers get married soon after qualifying, or at least meet a life partner. For a settled couple to move to China generally involves far more logistical and emotional complications than for a young single person just out of college.

In practice the Chinese offices of top American firms are extensively staffed with American-educated Chinese citizens. The Beijing regime evidently would not have it any other way. Even with law degrees from Harvard or Yale, Chinese citizens are still Chinese and thus, by virtue of their childhood immersion course in Confucian values, can be assumed to approach their work in the "right" frame of mind. If they step out of line, they can readily be pressured through their families. And, of course, simply because they intend to live long-term in the country, they naturally make long-term calculations whenever they find themselves at odds with the authorities.

Given that qualified legal professionals are in such short supply, much legal work emanating from the Chinese offices of top American firms is distinctly sub-par. To a Westerner this might seem like a problem, but for the Beijing authorities it is an opportunity. After all, it opens up all sorts of manipulative possibilities, as American firms are forced regularly to go cap in hand to the Chinese Ministry of Justice to seek absolution for errors and irregularities.

In short, a pattern of Confucian dependency is created. Whether this has had much influence so far on how top partners in Washington and New York conduct themselves is a moot point.

What is undeniable is that American law firms have long been Beijing's most trusted allies in the American establishment. Not only have they often acted directly for Beijing in lobbying top government officials, but more generally they have, by virtue of their position as trusted advisers to American business, helped recruit American corporations to China's cause. It is fair to say, moreover, that they have functioned as the coordination centers of the China lobby's efforts when major votes are taken.

All this follows more or less automatically from the fact that the principal work of most top law firms in Washington is "representation"—in plain language, lobbying. And for the most part these days their most lucrative clients are foreign and transnational corporations pressing trade issues. Among other things, these firms provide testimony before Congress and draft legislation behind the scenes. As pointed out by Pat Choate, a leading authority on Chinese influence in Washington, Chinese embassy officials closely monitor such work as well as all congressional hearings that concern China in any way. It helps that the embassy has plenty of staff: its delegation has long been one of Washington's largest.

Choate adds: "Invariably, witnesses are contacted by the embassy's staff immediately after they testify and comments are made about what they said. The substance of the comments is less important than the fact that the witness knows that the Chinese are watching."

The result is that where Sino-American disputes are concerned, the American legal profession seems a lot less active in promoting American interests than Chinese ones. In Choate's description, top American lawyers are "stateless." This has long been implicit in how they have conducted themselves, but it became quite explicit in 2004 when the Baker & McKenzie firm quietly reincorporated itself as a Swiss *verein* (*verein* is German for "association"). Ranking as by far the largest law firm in the world and formerly Chicago-based, Baker & McKenzie boasts 3,400 lawyers.

Says Choate: "Under the rubric of 'everyone is entitled to representation' the corporate legal profession in the United States can and does justify virtually any activity for which a foreign client will pay large fees."

Sic transit gloria mundi.

A Trade Litmus Test for the American Press

In all the major East Asian societies, self-control is the hallmark of the local media. As the China lobby has grown in influence in the last two decades, this tradition has now made the jump to the United States.

Starting with China's late-1990s campaign for permanent normal trade relations, virtually all the key editorial personnel who have shaped American media coverage of China-related economic issues have been openly in Beijing's camp—either that or, in classic Confucian fashion, they have kept their reservations very private indeed. The pattern has been apparent not only among top newspaper editors, particularly those who look after the editorial and business pages, but among columnists. It has also been apparent in a biased choice of "experts" interviewed on television.

The effect has been that key issues such as human rights, layoffs in the American heartland, and China's previous record of reneging on trade commitments have been swept under the carpet. The press thus played a decisive part in winning the permanent normal trading relations (PNTR) vote for China. In so doing it not only broke decisively with its vaunted tradition of fairness and balance but abdicated its venerable role in "comforting the afflicted and afflicting the comfortable."

What is so surprising about the press's insistent support for the China lobby is that it contrasted so sharply with the views of ordinary Americans (in the face of a gale-force wind of pro-Beijing propaganda, 79 percent of Americans in the spring of 2000 opposed the terms on which China was granted entry into the WTO). Of course, there is no reason why any particular press commentator should slavishly reflect his or her readers' views. But it is strange that so many media organizations that pride themselves on their balance on other issues are so one-sided on an issue that puts them directly at odds with their readers.

The media's pro-Beijing position was out of character in another highly significant sense: although many media commentators are reliably Democratic on other issues, in their support for the China trade lobby they sided with the Democratic Party's arch-bugbears in big business and the K Street lobbying community.

To be sure, some Democratic politicians came out for China, not least the Clinton administration. But the true voice of the Democratic Party was heard not in the administration but in the U.S. Congress, where Democrats, turning their backs on vast favors offered by the China lobby, voted two to one against PNTR.

Many anti-PNTR Democratic congresspeople were outraged by President Clinton's reneging on his strong election commitment to press Beijing on human rights. Most of the rest were concerned—and rightly so, as subsequent developments have indicated—with the impact on ordinary Americans.

The Democratic Party's concerns were echoed by countless left-leaning grassroots organizations such as Friends of the Earth, Global Trade Watch (an organization principally associated with Lori Wallach and Ralph Nader), the Economic Policy Institute, the Institute for Policy Studies, and the AFL-CIO.

Concerns for human rights in China and for the economic welfare of ordinary Americans are normally emphasized in the American media. Of course pro-Beijing press commentators can point out that their views consistently reflected those of almost the entire top tier of the American policy-making establishment. In the spring of 2000 President Clinton could boast that virtually every former Secretary of State, Secretary of Defense, Trade Secretary, and Transportation Secretary not to mention almost every former National Security Advisor had come out for PNTR. But the reason so many former top policymakers backed the China lobby was because they were the China lobby! Only the most notable of the former policymakers who were paid to push PNTR were Henry Kissinger, Alexander Haig, George Shultz, and Lawrence Eagleburger.

From the point of view of a vigilant press, the story was not that these erstwhile respected public servants should be listened to, but that they had been bought.

In truth, as Eric Alterman, author of *What Liberal Media? The Truth About Bias and the News,* has pointed out, an openly elitist American press has sold out on the trade issue. In an impassioned commentary in the *Nation* in 2007, he wrote: "Why does the opinion of the majority of the country get nothing but contempt in public discourse? . . . Why are the arguments of economists like Frank Taussig, Dani Rodrik, Dean Baker and the folks over at the Economic Policy Institute considered beyond the bounds of rational debate? . . . Wealthy people and their corporations own newspapers and fund think tanks, public affairs television, university chairs, advertising campaigns, lecture series and the like. Ordinary people do not. With few exceptions, these same organizations and institutions represent the views of the wealthy and well connected."

A closed-shop mentality has prevailed in the major American media, in which experts and commentators on the other side of the trade issue have systematically been shut out. This has applied even though in many cases their credentials are far more impressive than those of the establishmentarian commentators, and what they have had to say is often fresh, interesting, and extremely well informed (in contrast with the tired platitudes and doctrinal blathering of the establishmentarians).

Perhaps the most telling aspect of the debate has been the discourtesy of the establishmentarians. In championing the "one-way free trade" cause, Thomas Friedman, for instance, has denounced "knaves like Pat Buchanan" who are allegedly duping the American public on the issue. In reality, as Friedman surely knows, few participants in the trade debate are more disinterested than Buchanan. Certainly history will credit Buchanan as one of the most prescient.

The way the American press conducted itself on the PNTR debate was a disgrace to its own traditions. Certainly it was something new for the United States. That said, it was hardly new in the larger context of world journalism. It was, in fact, exactly how the press functions in the Confucian world.

The American press is Confucianizing itself. A key factor is that increasingly in the last twenty years, media professionals have been subjected to a litmus test on trade. Those who embrace laissez-faire ideology have seen their careers flourish. Those who don't haven't.

The litmus test is applied by various players with considerable power to influence a journalist's career. Take, for instance, high-placed news sources in government, in business, in the think tanks, and on Wall Street. For top journalists, easy access to such sources is often critical. It is fair to say that many of the most important sources have long been aggressively in Beijing's camp. In the classic Confucian fashion known throughout East Asia, such sources seek to marginalize and indeed ostracize any reporter who tries to uphold the freedom of the press on China-related issues. The better placed the source, the more likely he or she has been to take a consciously and systematically punitive line against independent-minded reporters.

Even before reporters get the chance to talk to sources, they are already subjected to a litmus test by media proprietors. As a general rule, reporters and editors who indiscriminately support free trade enjoy an inside track in the promotion rat race (or should we say mouse race, given the lack of courage that characterizes so many of the successful contestants?). Proprietors who apply the litmus test include not only Rupert Murdoch's News Corporation (we will consider Murdoch's role in the China debate in more detail in chapter 8) but General Electric (the ultimate owner of NBC) and Viacom. It is no coincidence that these companies have assiduously cultivated business links with China over the years.

The litmus test has also clearly been applied by the China lobby in its little-noticed but crucial networking activities. Like its allies in other branches of the trade lobby, the China lobby has for years had a policy of systematically elevating pro-Beijing media professionals. Suitable candidates have had their reputations expertly burnished through deft socialization. They find themselves invited to all the most exclusive dinner parties, so that they dine nightly with the likes of Henry Kissinger, Zbigniew Brzezinski, George H. W. Bush, and Bill Clinton, not to mention a host of lesser pro-China luminaries such as Brent Scowcroft, Lawrence Eagleburger, and Alexander Haig.

Invitations to give keynote addresses at prestigious gatherings follow. Some corporate sponsors are prepared to pay $50,000 or even $100,000 to a famous columnist or television reporter to open an executive retreat. This creates a system of income apartheid in which some journalists outearn their immediate colleagues by a factor of three or more. The winners in this game come to live at an entirely different level. Soon it becomes second nature to identify with the moneyed elite—a moneyed elite that even by past American standards has had a particularly corrosive effect on the American polity.

Although in the early days most media professionals who were attracted to Beijing's cause were probably sincere in their views, the fact that so much money has for so long been showered on those who say the "right" things has undoubtedly not gone unnoticed among the less scrupulous of the journalistic profession's aspiring superstars. Every profession has its scoundrels and the journalistic profession is no exception. It is a fair inference therefore that in recent years those who have succeeded in the media include a rapidly increasing proportion of unscrupulous stooges.

While not all corporate America's socialization of media people is necessarily so Machiavellian, the fact is that literally trillions of dollars are at stake in the free-trade debate. The debate is of historic concern not only to China and its corporate friends but also to all the Confucian nations—nations that, by no coincidence, have traditions going back millennia of the sort of politically motivated personnel management we have seen in the American media in recent decades.

In the long run the outlook is not just for elevation of Beijing-friendly media commentators but increasingly for direct Chinese control of the American media. For the moment the most obvious evidence of such control is among Chinese-language periodicals published in the United States. As recorded by Richard Bernstein and Ross Munro, China puts money into several Chinese-language publications in the United States and into Chinese-language cable-television stations. In their book *The Coming Conflict with China,* Bernstein and Munro added: "These media organizations are run almost in the same way as their counterparts inside China itself." (It should be noted that Beijing does not reciprocate by allowing any American influence over the countless English-language newspapers and magazines now published in China. Although such publications serve mainly American and European expatriates, they are almost invariably controlled by front organizations for various arms of the Chinese government and are run and edited by Chinese nationals.)

The tactics used by Beijing to control America's Chinese-language publications will undoubtedly be extended to the English-language media.

The experience of the Hong Kong publisher Jimmy Lai represents a frightening preview. When Lai's *Next* magazine offended Beijing in 1994, he found that the Beijing branch of his Giordano fashion chain was closed down on a selection enforcement pretext. Although *Next* was not a major publication and the incident thus received little attention in the West, the action was a classic example of the Chinese bureaucrat's precept "Kill the chicken to scare the monkey." In other words, it was intended not only to deal with Lai but to "encourage" others in the Hong Kong publishing industry. By all accounts the warning was heeded, and it is an open secret that virtually the entire press in Hong Kong these days, including the once staunchly independent-minded and pro-Western English-language daily the *South China Morning Post,* now takes editorial "guidance" from Beijing. Meanwhile *Next* was subjected to an advertising boycott by both mainland advertisers and by many Hong Kong companies intent on currying favor with the Chinese leadership.

Of course, it will be a while before Beijing resorts to similar tactics to silence the *New York Times* or the *Christian Science Monitor.* That said, the net will gradually close on American press freedom. Business, after all, is business, and the suits who answer to shareholders are perennially intent on squeezing the last cent of profits out of the media "properties" they manage. If pandering to Beijing in editorial policies helps the bottom line, so be it. The more heavily American media conglomerates invest in China, the more dependent they will become on Beijing for regulatory favors. The concept of regulation in China gives the Beijing authorities almost infinite power to lean on those under their purview.

In former times when American trade diplomacy with China was done on a bilateral Washington-Beijing basis, American officials enjoyed some power to talk back. But with the coming of the World Trade Organization, that power is now gone. Instead, all trade complaints must be presented to the WTO's "independent" adjudication panels. Any redress the United States might hope for will at best prove symbolic rather than real. WTO adjudication panels are composed largely of representatives of Second and Third World nations (many of which are notorious not only for their corruption but for their hostility to the United States).

Although so far American media corporations' exposure to Chinese commercial blackmail has been relatively limited, this will probably not remain so for long. Already several American media organizations have eagerly made a start on the China market. Viacom, for instance, has partnerships with China Central Television, which is better known as CCTV and is the official conduit of Chinese Communist Party propaganda, and has extended both its MTV and Nickelodeon operations into China. Questioned in 2004 by *Time* magazine, Viacom chief executive Sumner Redstone blandly sidestepped the extent to which Viacom's Chinese operations kowtow to Beijing's censors. He explained: "The programming on our channels in China is co-produced with a Chinese company. We are very conscious of the taste of the Chinese people and the Chinese government. And therefore we don't produce material that invites criticism from China."

Another American media group that is becoming dangerously dependent on Chinese regulatory favors is Disney, which in 2006 committed itself to investing heavily in a new Disneyland theme park in Shanghai. Disney's media interests include everything from the ABC broadcasting network to the Hyperion book-publishing company.

Though Disney executives would undoubtedly deny it, the company is offering the Chinese Communist regime a valuable hostage. An operation as large as Shanghai Disneyland, which will cover more than five square miles, will depend heavily on the continuing support of government officials at every level. The highly political nature of the project should be obvious from the fact that final approval rested with China's State Council (which is effectively the Chinese cabinet). So far Chinese officials have aggressively supported the project. In 2006 they began summarily moving residents out of the area designated for the theme park. They have also been pushing ahead with building vital new transportation links. Clearly the Chinese authorities are doing their best to please. But once Disney's money has been invested, the Chinese will have taken custody of a significant financial "hostage." The onus from then on will be on Disney to do the pleasing. After all, relatively minor regulatory changes—in, for instance, public transit services—could make the difference between profits and losses.

In this chapter we have documented Beijing's success in Confucianizing the United States. How could all of this have happened so suddenly and so unobtrusively? A major part of the reason, as we will see in the next chapter, is the highly controversial role played by America's ostensibly most loyal ally in East Asia.

SEVEN

The Dragon's Fey Friend

Of all the forces propelling China's rise, one of the most important is one of the least obtrusive: Japan. As conventionally viewed in the West, Japan is China's most suspicious rival. The point has become so universally accepted that to question it is to invite derision. Yet the conventional wisdom is utterly wrong. It comes from the same sort of sources—*indeed often precisely the same sources*—who have absurdly misled the American public about other aspects of America's global strategy for decades.

The truth about the Sino-Japanese relationship has been overlooked in part because American scholars and policymakers alike tend to romanticize America's relationship with Japan. They espouse a naively anthropomorphic view in which the United States and Japan are bound together in a veritable deathless union. Nothing and nobody, it seems, can come between them. The mood is epitomized in the way that many Washington-based policy analysts quaintly refer to Japan as "she," a usage virtually never encountered these days with any other nation. Implicit in it is a view of Japan as Uncle Sam's "loyal wife," and subject to 1950s-style limitations on "her" freedom of action.

Yet the idea of an apron-clad Japan baking cakes at home while a muscly Uncle Sam heads out each morning to chop down trees, lasso mustangs, and (importantly for our story) slay dragons is belied by the facts. While in its public behavior Tokyo makes a show of "cuddling up" to Washington, it has not only pursued trade policies deeply damaging to American interests but has consistently lied about these policies.

As for Japan's relationship with China, Americans can be forgiven for being confused. The surface impression is certainly that the Japanese and Chinese are far from friends. But, as we will see, there is a lot less to this ostensible antipathy than meets the eye. For a start, the Japanese deeply respect Chinese culture and recognize it as having played a vastly larger role in shaping their society than the mainly superficial cultural influences they have absorbed from the West.

As for the Chinese people, while it is true that they generally express deep enmity toward Japan, most of them know little about the country. In the case of those admittedly still rare Chinese citizens who do business directly with the Japanese, however, all the evidence is that they have far fewer communication problems than they have with Americans. Certainly as James Fallows has pointed out, Americans place too much emphasis on the bromide that other Asians hate the Japanese. In *Looking at the Sun,* he commented: "This is a classic half truth: true enough to explain some things, but not as true as outsiders, above all the nervous Americans, would like to believe."

In any case, because democracy has so little to do with how policy is determined in either Japan or China, the views of ordinary people count for little. The substance of Sino-Japanese relations is shaped in considerable secrecy by a tiny group of top policymakers in Tokyo and Beijing. All the circumstantial evidence is that behind a pretence of mutual antipathy, officials on both sides have long worked closely together.

In promoting the conventional view that Tokyo and Beijing are seriously at odds, American commentators have produced remarkably little evidence beyond constantly citing a few symbolic issues that are trivial compared to the vast scale of the overall relationship. Two issues in particular—the Senkaku Islands dispute and the Yasukuni shrine controversy—have strongly shaped the conventional view. Yet both these issues are obviously contrived affairs whose only purpose seems to be to deflect Western attention from the highly satisfactory fundamentals of Sino-Japanese relations.

What are those fundamentals? As we will see, in everything from trade flows to technology cooperation, the two nations are working closely together. Of course, both sides know very well that if Americans were to sense this, Washington's commitment to globalism would be fatally undermined. Only the first casualty would be America's acquiescence in the Confucian world's concept of one-way free trade.

Leaders in both China and Japan are heirs to a matchless tradition of political pantomime. Those who take Japan's "We hate China" stance seriously should consider how often in the past they have been blindsided by Japanese officials' geopolitical posturing.

It is worth recalling in particular Japan's "We must import more" campaign of the late 1980s. This was a cast-of-thousands production that began with the setting-up of a blue-ribbon panel, the so-called Maekawa Commission, to consider—or rather to pretend to consider—how Japan might embrace American-style free markets. The major objective was supposed to be to lower Japan's surpluses with the United States. Entering into the spirit of things, the government-controlled English-language newspapers in Tokyo suddenly reversed a previous pattern and started sounding glum about rising surpluses and happy about any occasional decrease. So that foreign visitors might not miss the point, signs were affixed to every luggage cart at Tokyo's international airport saying—in English—"IMPORT NOW!"

Meanwhile the Ministry of International Trade and Industry announced an annual competition for the foreign carmaker that was most successful in increasing its sales in Japan. (This was broadly the equivalent of prison guards organizing a hurdling competition for members of a chain gang. More about the Japanese car market in a moment.)

All this was taken at face value by many English-language reporters, most notably the *Economist*'s former Tokyo correspondent (and soon-to-be editor in chief) Bill Emmott, who in 1989 published a book predicting that Japan's current surpluses would disappear by 2000. As other Japan watchers pointed out at the time, he was merely recycling propaganda—and so even Emmott has now had to admit, given that, far from falling, Japan's surpluses went on to triple in the next seventeen years.

Commentators like Emmott notwithstanding, it was always clear that the "We must import more" campaign was theater. The most telling evidence at the time was in the so-called FS-X affair. This concerned a plan by Japan to equip its air self-defense force with a state-of-the-art fighter jet. Japanese officials could have bought a customized version of America's superadvanced F-16, which was made by General Dynamics and Lockheed Martin and was being marketed with great success to air forces around the world. Or they could rein-vent the wheel by building their own plane. In 1986, they chose the made-in-Japan route and engaged the Mitsubishi group to build a plane that was to become known as the FS-X. In doing so, they deprived the American arma-ments industry of an export order worth billions of dollars. Yet by building their own plane, they ended up paying perhaps three times as much per unit as they would have done had they bought off the rack from the United States. For top officials in Tokyo, none of this mattered. Their key concern was to build Japan's aerospace industry—a fundamentally mercantilist objective that made a mockery of the "We must import more" campaign.

The ultimate comment on this campaign is that none of the major trade is-sues that American negotiators complained about so bitterly in the 1980s was ever satisfactorily resolved—not rice, not semiconductors, not cars, and not even beef (for many years American beef was banned in Japan as "unhealthy," and when Japanese finally agreed to lift the ban in 2007, American producers faced an uphill battle trying to win consumer confidence). In reality, as some of us said all along, the "We must import more" program was intended merely to pull the wool over American eyes. Similarly today, the "We hate China" pro-gram is another staged production. Not for the first time, Uncle Sam is being played for a fool.

How Could Japan Abandon Uncle Sam?

Given all the history the United States has shared with Japan in the last sixty-odd years, Americans are entitled to be bewildered by the suggestion of a spe-cial Sino-Japanese understanding. What could possibly motivate Japan to abandon the United States? they ask.

The question is inappropriate because it is based on the "loyal wife" view of Japan. In reality, nations entering into strategic alliances base their actions on something more than romantic sentiment. They don't have to like, let alone love, one another. There are risk/reward ratios to be calculated. How useful can the partner be economically, for instance, and what are its prospects? For the Japanese the latter is crucial: after all, with less than 2 percent of the world's population, they have always felt the need to ally with the strongest power of the day or at least with the ostensible rising power.

Although Japanese leaders would be the last to admit it, they have understood earlier and more clearly than probably anyone else how badly misguided has been America's economic strategy in recent decades. They have
been equally well informed on China's strategy—and thus have long sensed that
China has been the one to cultivate.

American misunderstanding of Japan's true priorities derives from the false
assumption that Japan sincerely embraced American values after World War
II. Nothing could be further from the truth. In chapter 3, we offered some insights into what really happened during the American occupation. Let's now
consider some significant further evidence concerning Japan's so-called war
legacy. As conventionally presented in the West, this is seen as an insuperable
barrier to better Sino-Japanese relations. But this gets the story backward. The
real issue is what the war legacy says about the evident duplicity with which
Tokyo has treated Washington all these years.

Remember that in contrast with West Germany, a "democratic" Japan not
only never prosecuted its war criminals but did nothing to penalize them. Far
worse, in many cases it went out of its way to honor them. Only the best-known
case was that of Nobusuke Kishi. Imprisoned as a Class A war criminal in the
late 1940s, he became prime minister in 1957.

Another significant indicator is that Japan never paid compensation for the
imperial army's wartime atrocities. Again this represents a stunning contrast
with Germany. Whereas Germany paid more than $70 billion to Nazi victims
and their heirs, Japan's total compensation payments came to just $1 billion.
Perhaps the most startling aspect of the compensation issue is that even the
claims of American victims have been swept under the carpet. Thus tens of
thousands of American prisoners of war who worked as slave laborers in appalling conditions have consistently been rebuffed by their former employers
(who include some of the most famous corporations of postwar Japan).

Not only have Japanese bureaucrats suppressed discussion of the compensation issue at home, but they have succeeded in extending "self-control" even to
the American and, to a lesser extent, British media. We will have more to say
about this in chapter 8. Let's here simply note that the issue of Japan's obligation to compensate wartime victims remains to this day largely taboo among
American Japan watchers. Indeed, up to August 1995, the fiftieth anniversary
of the end of World War II, the subject was the Japan-watching equivalent of
the New York subway's third rail—touch it and you're dead.

(As seen by top officials in Tokyo, the fiftieth anniversary was the last date when the issue might have reached critical mass in the American media. I happen to be one of the few English-language writers to have broken the taboo: I included a short account in a book I published on the Japanese economy in the spring of 1995. Then in *The Rape of Nanking*, a 1997 best seller on the Nanking massacre, the late Chinese American author Iris Chang published an extended account that finally smashed the taboo.)

For anyone who has any remaining illusions about the extent of Japan's commitment to American values, the career of one Takeo Tamiya should prove revelatory. Tamiya was a top doctor and medical educator who played a key part in creating Unit 731, a notorious medical offshoot of Japan's Manchuria-based Kwantung Army. In the words of Kevin Sullivan of the *Washington Post,* the activities of Unit 731 "stand among the most despicable war atrocities in history." The unit's team of doctors used live subjects to conduct extensive research into chemical and biological weapons, as well as the limits of the human body's endurance. According to Sullivan, at least three thousand Chinese and Soviet citizens died in the camp, including many children. Victims were dissected alive or killed after being used for "practice surgery." Some were injected with horse blood; others were placed in pressure chambers to see how much pressure change they could take before their eyeballs exploded.

After the war Douglas MacArthur was apparently persuaded that Unit 731's research findings might be of value to the United States. A plea bargain was therefore entered into in which Unit 731's former researchers and executives were given immunity from prosecution in return for sharing their findings with the U.S. Defense Department.

This cleared the way for a remarkable subsequent career for Tamiya—as the international face of Japanese medicine. His rehabilitation was already well under way before the occupation ended. Evidently unaware of his previous record, top American officials appointed him an adviser to MacArthur on Japanese medical education. Then in 1948, while readers of the American press were reading daily of fresh miracles of Westernization in occupied Japan, Tamiya was named president of the Japanese Association of Medical Sciences. In 1950 he was appointed president of the Japan Medical Association, which in effect made him the grand old man of Japanese medicine. As Tamiya had been educated partly in the United States and spoke fluent English, he went on to represent Japanese medicine at many international gatherings.

Tamiya's appointment could have been derailed at any time by Japanese bureaucrats—if nothing else, through the simple expedient of a leak to the

American press. But his past seems to have remained entirely overlooked until it was finally brought to light—long after his death—by Peter McGill of the London *Observer* in 1983. Two other British journalists, Peter Williams and David Wallace, expanded on McGill's findings in *Unit 731: Japan's Secret Biological Warfare in World War II*, a book published in 1989.

Nor was Tamiya alone among the Unit 731 doctors in finding a place of honor in postwar Japanese medicine. Several others went on to top research jobs at the Japanese government's prestigious National Institute of Health, most notably Akira Shishido, who headed the institute at the time McGill published his account.

Not the least of the controversy surrounding the Unit 731 affair's postwar sequel is what it says about the status of the Hippocratic oath in Japan. Yet the irony is that Japan is full of decent people who would be as appalled as anyone by all this—if only they knew. They have consistently been kept in the dark by Japan's comprehensive system of press censorship. All talk of Japan as a model democracy to the contrary, it is hardly an exaggeration to suggest that the Japanese media are as censored today as they were in the 1930s.

For our purposes the key point is not so much that Japanese leaders do not seem particularly contrite about the past but rather that they want to have it both ways: while in their public statements for Western consumption they loudly proclaim their commitment to Western values, in reality they treat those values as little more than a joke.

How is all this viewed in China? Although common sense would suggest that the war legacy has, to put it mildly, not helped Sino-Japanese relations, the truth is more complicated. For some years after the war, the Chinese people in common with citizens of other victim nations tried to alert the United States to the true facts of Japan's "overnight conversion" to American values. In particular, in China in 1948 (just before the Communist revolution), students organized a nationwide movement of protest at American gullibility about "New Japan." As recorded by the former occupation official Robert Textor, the students' sentiments were endorsed by more than four hundred university teachers in Beijing in a letter to the American ambassador to China.

In subsequent years, however, Chinese leaders, like their counterparts elsewhere in East Asia, came to terms with Japan—terms dictated by the Japanese. As a condition for restoring diplomatic relations, Tokyo quietly pressured the victim nations one by one into renouncing all claims arising out of the war. China resisted for many years but when it began opening up in the 1970s,

Tokyo persuaded Mao Zedong and Zhou Enlai to agree to similar terms. Since then leaders in Beijing have been as zealous as their counterparts in Tokyo in suppressing all but a few token efforts by the Chinese people to pursue the Japanese in Western courts.

Of course, Chinese leaders often denounce Japan's war legacy—but they do so in ways that (1) do not cost Tokyo any money and (2) do not create serious embarrassment for Tokyo's diplomacy in the West. Chinese leaders keep their comments within thoughtful limits. Although they sound fiercely hostile about symbolic issues such as the Yasukuni shrine affair, they have avoided bringing up any specifics that might drive a wedge between Tokyo and Washington. Thus neither Beijing nor its American surrogates seem ever to have fomented trouble for Japan on the slave-labor issue or Japan's failure to compensate former prisoners of war (many of whom were, of course, American). Then there is Tamiya's rehabilitation. Beijing could well have made serious trouble for Tokyo had it expertly leaked this story to the Western press. But not only has Beijing observed a sort of *omertà* on such specifics, even the overseas Chinese in Hong Kong, Singapore, Taiwan, and elsewhere have followed suit. For that matter the overseas Chinese have also been remarkably quiet on the entire compensation issue (evidently fearing not only Tokyo's wrath but Beijing's).

The war-legacy story reveals Japan for what it is: a highly independent-minded, defiantly un-Western nation that is the very antithesis of the "loyal wife" of Uncle Sam's imagination. Top officials in Tokyo take a Machiavellian view of their responsibilities. So do top officials in Beijing. These latter may privately be distressed by Tokyo's callousness about the past; but no less than their Japanese counterparts, they see their principal concern as the future. Viewed in this way, it makes sense for both sides to cooperate—and to do so all too often at Uncle Sam's expense.

Before examining the win-win substance of Japan's relationship with China, let's first consider the diplomatic background.

East Asian Feud? Some Diplomatic History

As conventionally presented in the United States, Sino-Japanese relations have never recovered from imperial Japan's atrocities of the 1930s and 1940s.

The reality is more complicated. All American impressions to the contrary, the Chinese did not sever relations with Japan at the end of World War II. Far from it, they retained extensive links, not least in trade. Only after the Communists came to power in Beijing were relations severed. And the initiative then came not from Beijing or even Tokyo but rather from Washington. A militantly anti-Communist Truman administration leaned on a reluctant Tokyo to support America's boycott of Communist China.

The estrangement continued until President Richard Nixon's historic visit to China in 1972. This provided Tokyo with an evidently eagerly awaited pretext to resume direct contact with Beijing. Almost immediately, a special Sino-Japanese understanding began to develop. What started out as a simple economic partnership had already by the mid-1990s evidently blossomed into a full-scale, if undeclared, alliance.

Hints of a special Sino-Japanese understanding first emerged in September 1972, just seven months after the Nixon visit, when the Japanese announced they would recognize the Beijing regime as the rightful government of China. This amounted to a direct challenge to the United States, which was doggedly to persist in treating the Nationalist regime in Taipei as the Chinese government for another six years.

Given their previous pattern of meekly following Uncle Sam's diplomatic initiatives, Japanese leaders clearly would not have taken such an independent-minded initiative if it had not been an extraordinarily high priority. They were concerned, of course, to curry favor with Beijing, for whom diplomatic recognition was a top foreign-policy objective of the 1970s. By acting so quickly, moreover, Japanese leaders consciously provided other nations with cover in switching to a pro-Beijing stance. Indeed, West Germany followed within two weeks and other nations soon thereafter. When Washington finally recognized Beijing, it did so with the hangdog look of having been upstaged and outmaneuvered.

Tokyo had turned the tables. From now on, a meek Uncle Sam would increasingly follow Tokyo's lead in China policy. Thus, Tokyo set the pace in such crucial subsequent developments as the rehabilitation of the Beijing regime after the Tiananmen massacre and the so-called delinking of trade and human rights policies.

But even earlier—in February 1978—Tokyo had agreed to a $20 billion trade deal with Beijing. Tokyo undertook to build whole state-of-the-art factories for the Chinese and to accept Chinese oil exports in return. The Sino-Japanese rapprochement was further strengthened in August 1978 when officials in Beijing and Tokyo concluded a treaty of friendship.

Then, in an even more significant move—albeit one that has had virtually no attention in the West—Deng Xiaoping chose Tokyo as the first foreign capital to visit after proving victorious in the post-Mao power struggle. This trip, in October 1978, is believed to have been his first outside the Communist world since his student days in France in the 1920s. It preceded by fully three months his much more widely publicized visit to the United States in early 1979. It is probably significant also that on returning from the United States, he stopped over in Tokyo for further talks with Japanese leaders before returning to Beijing. Later the same year, Japanese prime minister Masayoshi Ohira reciprocated by visiting China.

These visits elevated the Sino-Japanese relationship to a new level of mutual trust. In a vital move to help China make the transition to a market economy, Tokyo agreed to provide huge loans to tide Deng's regime over its shaky first months. The significance of all this was well put by the economic commentator John Naisbitt. In his 1994 book *Global Paradox,* he wrote: "No foreign government endorsed Deng Xiaoping's reforms more enthusiastically than Japan."

"Same Script, Same Race"

While many in the West ask why Tokyo would reach an accommodation with Beijing, a better question is what could possibly motivate Tokyo to *oppose* Beijing.

Although it is widely suggested in the West that the Japanese somehow hate the Chinese, this idea seems absurd to anyone familiar with the facts. This is not to suggest that the Japanese are not capable of making cutting remarks about the Chinese. What is less well known in the West but equally relevant is that the Japanese are capable of making similar or indeed even sharper remarks about other nationalities (provided no one of that nationality happens to be in the room).

The truth is that the Japanese are famously practical people who rarely let past history or festering grudges get in the way of good business. On the contrary their natural instinct is to act with anyone, as surely became obvious when, within weeks of suffering two atomic bomb attacks in 1945, they found it within themselves to deal in a reasonable, even hospitable, way with the American occupation. To say the least, compared to the Japanese people's massive if well-hidden resentment toward Americans in the immediate aftermath of Hiroshima and Nagasaki, their antipathy toward the Chinese is mild indeed.

In reality the Japanese are highly cognizant of the fact that they share much culture with the Chinese. The cultures are not identical, of course, and anyone with only a glancing familiarity with the two nations can recite dozens of cultural contrasts. Though the differences often seem sharp, however, they are almost entirely superficial—different tastes in food, for instance, that in turn reflect different environmental influences. Many differences stem from the fact that Japan industrialized much earlier than China and thus the Japanese people are generally richer and better educated than the Chinese (China after all is only beginning to acquire the worldly sophistication that was already much in evidence in Japan as early as the 1920s). As Steven Mosher points out, such divergences notwithstanding, the two nations are little further apart in fundamental philosophy than the United States and France.

In particular the fact that the two nations share both Confucianism and Buddhism creates a fundamental understanding. This point is not new—nor, among those who have lived long term in the Confucian region, is it controversial. As Katherine G. Burns has pointed out, the Japanese themselves often acknowledge their cultural debt to China in the aphorism *Dobun doshu*—"Same script, same race." The two nations' tacit sense of a shared destiny is nicely hinted at in the fact that visas are not required for citizens of either nation visiting the other. By contrast, China places an inevitable sense of distance between itself and both the United States and Europe by insisting that American and European visitors have visas (which are a particularly annoying inconvenience for frequent travelers).

Many notably well-informed foreign observers over the years have testified to the Japanese people's deep sense of fellow feeling for the Chinese. Take, for instance, Pearl Buck, America's most prominent China watcher of the 1930s and 1940s. The first American woman to win the Nobel Prize for Literature, she was born in China to American missionary parents. She spoke Chinese as a native and was revered for her uplifting novel of the Chinese countryside, *The Good Earth*. In the immediate wake of the Japanese attack on Pearl Harbor in December 1941 (and just four years after the Japanese had laid waste to her hometown of Nanjing), she suggested that the Japanese, Chinese, and other East Asian peoples might proceed after the war to form a grand anti-Western alliance. In a letter to Eleanor Roosevelt, she maintained that there was "in all the Oriental peoples a very deep sense that the white man generally is or may be their common enemy, and in the final analysis it remains always a possibility that the point may come when these peoples, even such present enemies as the

Chinese and the Japanese, may unite as colored against white." (It should be pointed out that in those days the use of "colored" in this context was a standard form freighted with no slighting implications.)

The testimony of the French correspondent Robert Guillain is also telling. Guillain, a quintessential professional who spent thirty years reporting from the Confucian world for *Le Monde* in Paris, was one of those rare foreign correspondents who truly understood both Japan and China. In the 1930s he had reported from China on the Japanese military invasion. In December 1941 he was in Tokyo to cover Japan's entry into World War II.

His considered opinion, expressed in a book published in 1970, was that the Japanese were already then psychologically much closer to the Chinese than to the Americans. This despite the fact that Japan was constantly the butt of extravagant denunciations by Mao Zedong. Such abuse did not deceive Guillain. After all, Mao's description of Japanese officials as "capitalist running dogs" and "American stooges" served only, as Mao surely knew, to boost Japan's stock in Washington. The net effect of Mao's rather arch insults was undoubtedly to encourage American policymakers to shower "new Japan" with yet more economic and technological favors.

In *The Japanese Challenge*, Guillain wrote: "Japan stands aloof from the American policy of containment, and most particularly from the policy of surrounding Mao's China with a ring of military power. On the contrary, Tokyo's rule is to handle China very gently. . . . If other nations had to live in the shadow of China, they would no doubt live in dread. Not the Japanese, however. We have seen, for example, how calmly they received the news of their neighbour's atomic experiments. . . . Since its beginnings in 1949 communist China has never threatened Japan and even though China now possesses the bomb Japan does not look upon it as a present menace. 'It will never be China,' they think, 'that will commit the error or the crime of dropping the bomb on us, thus blackening its history and its good name.'"

Guillain continued: "In addition to the cultural likeness between the two countries . . . there is the fact of likeness of race—a fact that makes the Chinese close kin to the Japanese, giving them a feeling of nearness that they can never experience to the same degree with other Asians, still less with men of another color."

As for communication between the Japanese and Westerners, Guillain suggested that this was hindered by a yawning East-West culture gap. Warning that Westerners are particularly likely to underestimate top Japanese officials, he commented: "The [Western] visitor who comes into contact with an important Japanese is often disappointed at finding him hard to talk to—'a man you can't reach.' Indeed, it sometimes happens that the foreigner makes serious mistakes about the importance of the man he is meeting. . . . The foreigner . . . is unaware that even a highly placed Japanese does not care to shine in conversation." He singled out top bureaucrats—the most powerful and feared members of Japan's distinctly Confucian hierarchy—as exemplifying to an extreme degree "the drearier features of Japanese behavior . . . awkward self-expression, heavy going conversation (particularly in a foreign language), unwillingness to answer questions or express ideas, and a liking for secrecy."

The extent to which Japan differs from the West in mind-set is less obvious than it should be because Japanese citizens abroad tend to be atypical. As a matter of policy the Japanese seem to depute their more Westernized compatriots to represent them abroad. The genre is exemplified by the sort of Japanese who looks good in a cowboy hat—someone like former prime minister Junichiro Koizumi, whose witty, backslapping style and Elvis impersonations did so much to endear him to President George W. Bush.

The Koizumi type, however, is rarely truly American. Rather, he is often a consummate thespian—a Japanese acting the part of an American—and as such is even more difficult for Americans to read than his more run-to-type compatriots. The point was well made by Guillain. "One has but to remove a thin veneer to discover a man who is profoundly unlike anyone produced in the United States," he said.

The important point for our analysis is that the sort of communication difficulties that plague Japan's relations with Washington are not present to nearly the same extent with Beijing. Indeed, it is fair to say that a top Japanese official can readily establish greater rapport with a Chinese peer than either is ever likely to enjoy with a Westerner. They know how to frame the right questions and how to read the answers—how much to believe and how much not.

It is important to note that cultural compatibility works for the Japanese and Chinese not only at a personal level but in nation-to-nation dealings. Specifically the two nations' fundamentally isolationist instincts have the ironic but very powerful effect of smoothing relations.

Take the two nations' tight immigration policies. Following a policy generally adopted in the Confucian world, both Japan and China shut out almost all immigrants except for a few special workers. As estimated by the Central Intelligence Agency, Japan had a net immigration rate of exactly zero in

2006, and China's rate was actually negative, meaning that emigration exceeded immigration. A key practical consequence is that neither nation suffers any gnawing sense of insecurity about being penetrated by the other, or indeed by any nation. The Japanese do not have to worry, for instance, about the Chinese stealing their economic secrets or getting inside their defense system. By contrast, in the United States many highly sensitive positions are held by naturalized Americans whose loyalty cannot always be taken for granted. This often results in a degree of ungraciousness in supervision that can actually create the problem it is trying to guard against. The ironic result of the no-immigration policies in both Japan and China is that the two nations tend to treat the other's nationals more as guests than as potential fifth columnists.

The point is also clearly seen in the matter of human rights. True to their isolationist philosophy, the Japanese generally do not try to influence other nations' human rights policies. The contrast with the American view could hardly be more marked. Constant efforts by the United States to influence China's human rights policy are massively resented in Beijing as a neocolonial effort to meddle in China's internal affairs. In essence both Japan and China believe that good fences make good neighbors. Since World War II this has inclined them to a keen respect for the other's sovereignty. By the same token, they make common cause in resenting the universalist nature of America's agenda on political, economic, and social issues.

All that said, cultural compatibility is less important in any geopolitical partnership than a cool calculation of each side's self-interest. The point is no less obvious to today's Japanese leaders than it was to Lord Palmerston, who in a timeless observation noted that "nations have no permanent friends and no permanent enemies—only permanent interests." The ultimate question therefore is where do Japan's interests lie?

As Samuel Huntington has suggested, an unsentimental Japan will choose as its partner the nation considered most likely to lead the world in the years ahead. Although Americans tend to assume that American power will go on forever, the Japanese are not similarly sanguine. They know from experience that Western empires tend to be ephemeral. After all, in the nearly five centuries since Westerners first preached the advantages of the Western way in East Asia, Japan has seen no less than six Western empires come and go—Portugal, Spain, the Netherlands, France, Britain, and the Soviet Union. Will the American empire be different? The odds do not look promising—and, even

had American economic management been a lot wiser in the last twenty years
than it actually has, they probably would not.

The question therefore for the Japanese reduces to this: Should they ally
with the coming power or with the fading one?

I will leave the last word to the American author Mike Rogers, who has lived
in Tokyo since 1984. In a column published at LewRockwell.com in 2005, he
dismissed a then much publicized Sino-Japanese spat over history textbooks as
a "tempest in a teacup" and pointed out that economics was the key to Tokyo's
true relationship with Beijing. He added: "When push comes to shove, I believe
Japan will side with China. At the moment, Japan needs to appease the United
States. But Japan is not so foolish as to risk its future on a sinking America. One
day, soon, Japan and China will pull the plug on financing the United States' red
ink. Of course they will. Only a fool couldn't see that America's future is decidedly dim."

Tokyo to Washington: Bow to the Dragon

To any diplomat who is paying attention, one of the most telling indications of
the true state of Sino-Japanese relations is the way Tokyo has helped open the
door to Beijing at key international organizations.

The pattern goes back to November 1979, when, just weeks after Deng
Xiaoping's Tokyo visit, the Japanese successfully persuaded the development
assistance committee of the Organisation for Economic Co-operation and Development to admit China as a developing-country member. The Japanese also
worked hard to help China join the World Bank and the International Monetary Fund.

Then came the Tiananmen massacre of 1989. If Tokyo's true attitude was
ever in doubt, its response to that devastating glimpse of traditional Chinese
authoritarianism resolved the matter. At a time when Chinese leaders were
covered in obloquy, Tokyo rallied to their side. Even as indignant Western
diplomats pressed for a boycott of China's exports, the Japanese worked with
great skill to marginalize the idea. The Japanese also discreetly pressed the so-
called Group of Seven nations to renew World Bank lending to China.

Tokyo went on in the early 1990s to deploy its enormous Washington lobbying machine to secure ever wider and more secure access for Chinese exports
in the American market. A key stumbling block was a traditional insistence by

successive American administrations that America's trading partners observe certain minimum standards in human rights. Not only did Tokyo openly challenge this policy, but it threw its full lobbying muscle into the fight to "delink" American policies on trade and human rights. Irrespective of how brutally the Beijing regime might crack down on the Chinese people in the future, Tokyo was determined that China be treated in perpetuity as one of America's "most favored" partners.

The point was made explicit by Prime Minister Morihiro Hosokawa. As recounted by the then American ambassador to Tokyo, Michael Armacost, Hosokawa delighted his hosts in Beijing in 1994 by heaping scorn on American efforts to impose Western concepts of human rights on other nations. This came just days after United States secretary of state Warren Christopher had been humiliated in Beijing when he pressed for improvements in China's treatment of dissidents. Hosokawa forthrightly came down on the Chinese side. "Western or European-type democracy should not be forced on others," he said. All this was more impressive because Hosokawa had earlier been presented in almost delirious terms by the American press as a Clinton-like liberal who was working closely with Washington in planting American values in East Asia.

With Japanese help, Beijing's post-Tiananmen rehabilitation proceeded apace in the second half of the 1990s. This opened the way for Tokyo to support China's most ambitious diplomatic objective so far: entry into the World Trade Organization. Japan had earlier signaled its support by facilitating China's participation as an observer in the 1987–1993 Uruguay Round of world trade talks. As the 1990s wore on, Tokyo could hardly have been more helpful. Writing in 1996, the Japanologist Christopher B. Johnstone reported that Tokyo "earned Beijing's goodwill with its consistent support" for China's WTO bid. To the open disgust of American trade negotiators, the Japanese left it to other nations, principally the United States, to talk tough in trying to get China to meet certain standards before it was admitted.

In July 1999 Tokyo did Beijing another historic favor by being conspicuously early in granting final approval to China's WTO entry. The Clinton administration took a further four months to reach merely an outline agreement. And final American approval had to await crucial enabling legislation that was not passed by the U.S. Congress and U.S. Senate until the summer and autumn of 2000.

Tokyo's promptness contrasted remarkably with its normal pattern. As

Western trade negotiators know to their cost, Tokyo generally adopts a ruthlessly manipulative approach in which it stonewalls down to the end. The strategy has repeatedly proved highly successful in squeezing last-minute concessions from the other side.

That Tokyo would make such an exception in this case spoke volumes about its true diplomatic priorities. The point of acting so early was clearly to pressure Washington and Brussels on Beijing's behalf.

It is important to realize that the WTO negotiations took place at a time when almost everyone in Washington believed—utterly wrongly, of course—that Japan was much more vulnerable to the Chinese economic challenge than the United States. As generally presented, the story was that a "hapless" Japan was trapped in the despised "old economy" and thus represented a sitting duck for the rising Chinese. Meanwhile the United States had scored an enormous "success" by moving so fast to exit manufacturing in favor of postindustrial services and thus had cleverly positioned itself beyond the reach of Chinese competition. Worse, in a strange process that no one seemed able to explain, the entire Japanese economy had somehow been rendered a veritable basket case in the wake of the Tokyo financial crash of the early 1990s.

Japanese spokesmen did nothing to counter all this. Quite the contrary, they often encouraged talk in the American media that Japanese industry would be dangerously hollowed out by cheap Chinese labor.

As presented by Tokyo's stooges and dupes in Washington, the story was that, in supporting Beijing, stoic Japanese policymakers were outdoing even the Americans in their support for unfettered, devil-take-the-hindmost free-trade dogma. Given a Washington consensus that it was Japan not the United States that had most to lose from China's rise, Clinton administration officials now looked like pedants, if not sissies, in pressing for better terms from Beijing.

As it turned out, these officials gave away the store—America's store, that is, not Japan's.

Importing: The Sincerest Form of Diplomacy

As we have noted, the most obvious evidence that there is something more to Sino-Japanese relations than constant bickering is in the two nations' recent trade patterns. While China has pursued a notoriously one-sided trade policy with the United States, its trade relations with Japan could hardly be more balanced or mutually beneficial. Thus, almost completely unbeknownst to even sophisticated American observers, *China now buys more than twice as much from Japan as from the United States. Japan meanwhile buys nearly 60 percent more from China than from the United States.*

This relationship, moreover, owes remarkably little to physical propinquity. After all, with the development of superefficient global transport services, it is often now almost as inexpensive to send goods around the world as to ship them next door. This applies in spades in the case of high-tech components, which the Chinese import on a vast scale from Japan (rather than, of course, from the United States). The real reason China and Japan do so much business together is political. To put it in plain terms, the principle is, "If you scratch my back, I'll scratch yours."

None of this is to suggest that Sino-Japanese trade relations are always harmonious. Precisely because both the Chinese and the Japanese are such tough negotiators, tensions are always present. But they are always manageable. The result is a carefully calibrated trade relationship that sometimes yields a small surplus for Japan, sometimes a small deficit. The important point is that the imbalances are small in the context of one of the largest bilateral trade relationships in the world. For the record, Sino-Japanese trade totaled nearly $230 billion in 2006, and the result was a surplus of $8 billion for Japan. Full disclosure: a strict accounting would require various minor adjustments, most notably for Sino-Japanese trade conducted through Hong Kong. But the fact that Sino-Japanese trade is broadly in balance is not in dispute. This is, of course, in marked contrast with U.S.-China trade, which totaled more than $320 billion in 2006 and produced a surplus of $232 billion for China. (The latest numbers on bilateral trade relationships can be checked in the CIA *World Factbook,* which is available on the Internet. Each nation's major import partners are given, as well as the extent of their trade.)

The term of art for the Sino-Japanese economic relationship is "managed trade." It refers to a system in which government officials constantly override or at least second-guess market forces in guiding a nation's trade flows. Managed trade works best where, as in both China and Japan, government officials enjoy huge arbitrary powers to shape their nation's economic workings.

In such circumstances a formal rules-based international trading system of the type the World Trade Organization is trying to establish is largely irrelevant. When trade disputes arise between China and Japan, officials on both sides tend to eschew international trade courts in favor of face-to-face horse trading. Precisely because such officials are so powerful (they can if they wish make trouble for one another across a whole range of product categories), they can generally work flexibly and quickly to find win-win solutions to most problems. For Westerners, the best way of putting this is that officials on both sides negotiate like tycoons rather than lawyers.

All this helps explain why Tokyo could afford to take such a preternaturally relaxed attitude to negotiations for China's entry to the WTO. For nations like the United States that are committed to Western-style rule by law, it was important to get the terms right. For East Asian nations run on the principle of government by men, the formal terms were largely irrelevant.

As the Japanese and Chinese had known all along, efforts by aggrieved American interests to use quasi-Western legal procedures to induce the Chinese to trade in an American free-market way would always be doomed. For a start, the workings of the Chinese economy are just too far removed from Western laissez-faire. In any case, with the best will in the world, such an approach is inherently cumbersome. Worse, the practical reality is that the WTO's formal dispute-resolution procedures are fatally vulnerable to manipulation. Apart from anything else, many of the judges deputed to adjudicate in WTO disputes come from corrupt Third World countries (this reflects the fact that such countries form a large proportion of the WTO's 150-plus members).

The conclusion is inescapable: in the crucial matter of international trade, the Chinese and Japanese are making sweet music together. Meanwhile a forlorn Uncle Sam sits by the phone waiting for Chinese and Japanese orders that never come.

Japan as China's Santa Claus

If Japan's contributions to China's rise were limited merely to diplomacy and trade, they would be substantial enough. But in almost every area of policy, Japan has consistently helped China.

As we have already mentioned, Japan's help in technology has been particularly significant. Although Tokyo strictly controls transfers of Japanese production secrets abroad, it has often made an exception for China. It has not given away the store, of course. As a matter of the highest national policy Japanese officials insist that the most advanced production techniques be reserved for home use only (thus ensuring that Japanese workers have a consistent productivity edge over foreign counterparts). That said, Japan has plenty of older technologies to pass along to less developed nations—and in recent decades it has given pride of place to China in its hand-me-down policy. Many of these technologies are considerably more advanced than the indigenous Chinese technologies they replace, and they thus contribute appreciably to Chinese growth. Japan strengthens the effect by bringing in thousands of Chinese engineers every month for on-the-spot training in Japanese factories. Moreover, as we will see, Chinese students are now a major force at Japanese universities. A large proportion of them study engineering and science and thus make vital early contacts with future leaders of Japanese industry.

That China is specially favored under Japanese technology policy is obvious by comparison with, say, India, Russia, or Brazil, which are broadly at the same level of development but have been conspicuously shortchanged by Tokyo.

Japan's technological generosity to China has been apparent in everything from steel and shipbuilding to copiers and plasma displays. Tokyo's help in promoting the rise of the Chinese semiconductor industry has been particularly impressive. The pattern goes back as far as the late 1970s, when Tokyo-based Toshiba agreed to teach the Chinese how to make memory chips. During the 1980s, the Chinese received further important transfers of chip technology from such Japanese high-tech leaders as Matsushita and Fujitsu. Then in 1996, NEC partnered with the Beijing government in Project 909, an ambitious effort to propel China to the leading edge in semiconductors. The result, according to the American Sinologist Michael Klaus, was that in six years the Chinese shot from three generations behind the industry leaders to less than one generation behind.

Japan's indulgence of China's superpower ambitions has even extended to helping China's defense buildup. As the Council on Foreign Relations scholar Adam Segal has pointed out, Japan has consistently ignored efforts by the United States to deny key "dual-use" technologies to China. Dual-use technologies are ones that can be employed in both civilian and defense applications. Virtually all the key components needed in advanced missiles these days are considered dual-use and are readily sourced by the Chinese either directly from Japan or, in sensitive cases, through intermediaries. Equipped with state-of-the-art Japanese components, China's missile program is already one of the world's most advanced. Chinese missiles are now believed capable of reaching the West Coast of the United States. Moreover, China in 2005 became only the third nation after the Soviet Union and the United States to put humans into space.

Japan has even transferred key nuclear power technologies to China. It played an enabling role in particular in the construction of China's path-breaking first nuclear power station, which opened at Qinshan near Shanghai in 1991. Tokyo-based Mitsubishi Heavy Industries built the reactor pressure vessel, the crucial core of the power plant and the one major element the Chinese could not make for themselves. This was at a time when the United States still maintained an embargo on the transfer of such geopolitically sensitive technology.

Mitsubishi acted, of course, with the full approval of the Japanese government and the immediate effect was to provide the French, Germans, and Canadians with vital political cover to follow suit in breaking the American embargo. The American nuclear equipment industry remained constrained by the embargo into the latter half of the 1990s, by which time it was more or less dead.

It is interesting to note that, like so many other key aspects of Sino-Japanese cooperation, Japan's contribution to creating China's now thriving nuclear power industry has received virtually no publicity in the West. As of 2007, Wikipedia's Qinshan Nuclear Power Plant entry did not even mention Mitsubishi or Japan. And even though it did refer to recent contributions by Westinghouse, it failed to note that this company's nuclear division is now part of Toshiba of Tokyo. This is "atoms-for-peace," of course, but it is hard to see Tokyo being similarly generous in furthering the nuclear ambitions of, say, Pakistan, let alone North Korea. Indeed, whereas Tokyo has zealously punished both India and Pakistan for testing nuclear weapons, its response to similar testing by China has been, as Katherine G. Burns has pointed out, remarkably more indulgent. While in a nod to American sensibilities the Japanese uttered pro-forma condemnations, they did essentially nothing tangible to punish China. In Beijing, as in Tokyo, it is tangible responses that count.

Another aspect of the Sino-Japanese relationship that deserves closer attention in the West is aid flows. Japan is now the world's largest aid giver, and its aid policy has long overwhelmingly favored China. According to the political scientist David Arase, Japan accounted for two-thirds of all China's receipts of bilateral aid in the 1980s and 1990s. By contrast, for all the talk of a U.S.-China "strategic partnership," China's aid receipts from the United States were zero. In the wake of the Tiananmen massacre, Japanese officials resisted American and European pressure to cut back its aid to China. In the end, under great pressure from Washington, Tokyo temporarily suspended payments—but only for about a year, after which it rapidly made up the backlog with a surge in subventions.

Perhaps the most telling aspect of Tokyo's aid policy is how the money has been spent. Given Japan's previous history in China, it might be assumed that Tokyo would want to spend its money on humanitarian projects such as, say, providing decent housing and health care for people orphaned by the Nanking massacre. In fact, Tokyo has done nothing of the sort. Rather, it has concentrated on supporting Beijing's massive regional construction programs, which are, of course, aimed at speeding China's emergence as an export superpower. In particular it worked closely with top Chinese officials on improving China's antiquated transportation infrastructure, thereby providing Chinese industries with the modern roads, railroads, and ports needed to serve world markets. In addition, Tokyo has supported Chinese investments in telecommunications equipment, air control systems, and other high-tech infrastructural improvements. Again the evident purpose is to speed the growth in China's exports.

Although Japan's help is virtually invisible not only to ordinary Chinese citizens but even to most Western observers, it has powerfully served the agenda of top Chinese leaders—which is the whole point.

Aid apart, a pro-Beijing bias is apparent in many other aspects of Japanese government policy. Take Tokyo's regulation of its citizens' foreign travel options. Tokyo tightly controls airline landing rights with the intention of channeling Japanese tourists to favored foreign nations. In the last two decades, China has been the major beneficiary of such regulation. Throughout the 1980s and 1990s China was one of the fastest-growing destinations for Japanese tourists. Thus, on figures published by the Japan Tourism Marketing Company, between 1995 and 2005, the number of Japanese visitors to China rose from 1,305,000 to 3,390,000, an increase of nearly 160 percent. By comparison travel to Taiwan, formerly a favorite Japanese destination, grew a mere 24 percent. And the United States, once the Japanese people's biggest destination by far, actually saw a decline of more than 15 percent. Japanese visitors to the U.S. mainland in 2005 totalled a mere 1,364,000—little more than 40 percent of the China figure. One factor that clearly contributed to America's loss of position was the war on terror. Another factor was Japanese regulation: as a key geopolitical initiative, Japanese officials have encouraged travel to China at the expense of most other destinations. They have done so in particular by manipulating landing rights at Japanese airports to favor the Chinese tourism industry. The point is that there is a permanent, regulator-induced shortage of airline capacity into and out of Japan. Although countless nations would love to establish direct airline links to Japan (because this would greatly increase their foreign exchange receipts from big-spending Japanese tourists), for the most part Tokyo blocks them. By permitting plenty of airline capacity between Japanese airports and both Shanghai and Beijing, Japanese regulators direct the flow of Japanese tourist traffic disproportionately to China. By contrast, by heavily restricting direct flights to Russia, for instance, it deprives the Russians of a lucrative source of tourist earnings. From an individual Japanese tourist's point of view, it is still possible to vacation in Russia, but the exigencies of Japanese regulation make air travel there both inconvenient and expensive.

Even more important than tourist travel is the evidence of educational travel. Not only do many Japanese students these days study in China, but, even more significantly, countless Chinese students study in Japan. This latter trend has been a notable factor in Sino-Japanese relations since the early 1990s. Up to that time, most of China's brightest students had gone to the United States. Since then they have increasingly preferred Japan—so much so that, utterly overlooked by the American press, Japan in 2003 passed the United States to become the world's top overseas destination for Chinese students. The total of Chinese students studying at Japanese universities came to nearly 71,000—well ahead of a total of 65,000 at American universities. The Japanese total had more than tripled since 1993, whereas the American total had risen by a mere 44 percent. All this is more remarkable because the United States has had a longer tradition than Japan of providing quality education to foreign students. It also enjoys a strong linguistic advantage in that the Chinese find it easier to speak English than Japanese (sentences are structured much the same in Chinese and English, whereas Japanese sentence structure is radically different).

Why have so many Chinese students suddenly started flocking to Japan? One factor often mentioned is a more restrictive American immigration policy in the wake of the September 11 atrocities. But this hardly explains very much. The Chinese do not lack for choice. Countless universities throughout the advanced world now compete to attract top Chinese students, not least some of the finest in Britain, France, Germany, and Australia.

Many Chinese students choose Japan because they see it as having passed the United States as the world's technological leader. Another factor driving the trend is money. As far back as the mid-1980s, Tokyo launched a well-funded program to attract foreign students to Japanese universities. All the evidence is that Chinese students have been the main beneficiaries.

This fact clearly runs counter to all stereotypical Western views of Japanese attitudes to the Chinese. It is a far more telling guide to the reality of modern Sino-Japanese relations than all the negatives stressed in accounts in the Western media.

Significant Silences: Listening to the Unsaid

By definition the news media spend more time reporting what is said than what is not said. Unfortunately, in the Confucian world, the real message is all too often in what is not said.

Nowhere is the unsaid more significant than in Sino-Japanese relations. Anyone who looks closely notices that, for all their thespian professions of mutual antagonism, Japanese and Chinese officials seem remarkably reluctant to say anything that might make *real* trouble for one another. In particular, neither side has done anything to damage the other's diplomatic ties with the West.

Thus, as we have already noted, for all their bitter rhetoric about Japan's war legacy, the Chinese thoughtfully steer clear of the one aspect of the issue that Tokyo *really* wants left unmentioned—Japan's absolute refusal to compensate war victims. Meanwhile the Japanese have kept quiet about the more controversial aspects of, for instance, China's trade policies.

More generally, the unsaid is a key factor in almost every aspect of Sino-Japanese relations. The Japanese have been quite discreet in, for instance, not alluding to the extent to which the United States is now being penetrated by Chinese agents. Moreover, they have never tried to make any diplomatic capital out of the sometimes extremely coercive measures resorted to by Beijing in intimidating Chinese-born naturalized Americans in the United States.

The Japanese have also kept their counsel even on occasions when Washington, finding itself in a shouting match with Beijing, has desperately craved verbal support from American allies. Indeed, often on such occasions, the Japanese have seemed by their silence tacitly to be in China's corner.

As the Washington-based China watcher Ted Galen Carpenter has observed, Japan was notably quiet when the Chinese conducted missile tests in the Taiwan Strait in 1996. Interpreting the tests as an attempt to intimidate

Taiwan, the Clinton administration felt it necessary to mobilize two aircraft carrier battle groups. The move drew little support in East Asia, not even in Japan. The best the Japanese could do was chillily to express "understanding" of the American initiative.

The pattern was repeated in 2001 when, after a midair collision with a Chinese military plane, an American spy plane had to make an emergency landing on the Chinese island of Hainan. Although all the evidence indicated that it was the Chinese pilot who had caused the incident, the Chinese insisted on an apology. In the meantime, they detained the American crew. As the standoff continued, Washington vainly hoped for support from Tokyo. A spokesman for the Japanese prime minister merely said, "We hope this case will be settled in an appropriate and acceptable manner." As Carpenter tartly pointed out, Beijing could draw as much comfort from such a comment as Washington. In the end the Bush administration swallowed its pride and said it was "very sorry."

Carpenter commented: "One expects firm, public support of the U.S. position from loyal allies. Such support was not forthcoming from the East Asian allies in the spy plane incident any more than it had been in the 1996 crisis in the Taiwan Strait."

Tokyo's pattern of tacitly pro-Chinese silence has been so noticeable that it has even been remarked on by such a Japan-friendly observer as Thomas Friedman. In *The Lexus and the Olive Tree,* Friedman noted that Japanese executives have conspicuously refrained from complaining about China's theft of foreign intellectual property. He added: "Japan holds America's coat and goes on doing as much business with China as it can—even taking advantage of whatever markets the United States loses in its confrontation with Beijing."

A similar point has been made by Robert O'Quinn of the Heritage Foundation. Not only is Tokyo reluctant to support American efforts to talk tough to Beijing on trade, but Japanese corporations often undermine America's negotiating position by taking advantage of China's tactic of boycotting American exporters whenever Washington complains.

American trade negotiators were particularly aggrieved when in 2007 the Japanese offered no support for an official American complaint about China's vast program of export subsidies. In a jab directed principally at the Japanese, John Engler, president of the National Association of Manufacturers, commented: "We hope that other countries will reconsider joining the case, recognizing that it is not fair to have the United States do all the heavy lifting."

If the Japanese rarely side with Washington on contentious aspects of Sino-American relations, the Chinese have been even more restrained in what they say about Japan. Even when they are ostensibly being hostile, they almost invariably contrive to speak in meaningless clichés that do little or nothing to undermine Tokyo. Indeed, many of their insults, as we have already pointed out, actually boost Japanese interests, not least their traditional portrayal of Japan as "America's lackey." For Japanese officials perennially anxious to deflect American criticism over Japanese trade policies, such "insults" are manna from heaven.

The Chinese have also observed a discreet silence on the extent to which Japanese influence now pervades the upper reaches of both Washington society and the American media. Still less have they publicized the extraordinary extent to which the Japanese have hollowed out top American corporations (as is well known to Chinese leaders, if not to the American public, such ostensibly world-beating American corporations as IBM, Hewlett-Packard, Caterpillar, and Boeing now depend on Japan for some of their most advanced manufacturing technologies).

Another issue on which Beijing's silence has been remarkable (at least up to the time of this writing in 2007) is Tokyo's defense policy. Beijing has rarely if ever discussed the more sensitive aspects of this policy. That Beijing's silence has been helpful to Tokyo is an understatement. Yet Japan's defense policy is full of highly embarrassing "contradictions." Just the most obvious is the fact that Japan's entire defense establishment is unconstitutional! After all, Japan's peace constitution rules out the keeping of any military force. Calling an army a "self-defense force" fools no one, least of all the Chinese. Japan's "self-defense force" testifies to the fact that Japan's ostensibly Western legal system is a Potemkin village. By extension Japan is not a Western-style rule-of-law democracy—a point that, had it been publicized long ago by China's lobbyists in Washington, could have set the cat among the pigeons for Japan's entire effort to present itself as America's most sincere political pupil. Not the least of the consequences might have been that American policymakers would have taken a tougher line on Japanese trade policies.

Of course, in justifying its military might, Japanese officials claim that they have found a convenient "loophole" in the constitution. But, as the noted French Japan watcher Robert Guillain argued as far back as 1970, this is an "unconvincing sophism" and would be laughed out of any Western court. The intent of the framers of the Japanese constitution was unambiguous, and they made sure that there would be no loophole to exploit. It would have been extraordinary if they had done otherwise. After all, the constitution was written by skilled American lawyers who were explicitly concerned, as a top priority, to avoid any ambiguity on military matters.

Even if the Japanese constitution were changed and the Self-Defense Forces were legalized, embarrassing questions would still remain. First, there is the impressive scale of Japan's military activities. Why do they need to be so large? It is a question that is rarely asked. Although Japanese officials have long pretended that Japan depends on the United States for its defense, few nations are actually more militarily independent. As measured by the London-based International Institute for Strategic Studies, by the early 1990s Japan ranked third in the world after only the United States and Russia in military spending. Yes, Japan's troop numbers are relatively small but this is more than made up for by the ultra-sophistication of its weaponry. In this sense Japan is rather like Israel—a nation whose wealth enables it to punch way above its weight. Indeed Japan's military budget exceeds Israel's by a factor of four and it boosts 40 percent more troops. Put like this, Japan is clearly no milquetoast. And this says nothing of Japan's unique industrial hegemony as the world's main and, in many cases, even sole source of the most sophisticated components and materials needed to make advanced weapons.

The question that might be asked is this: If Tokyo is content to live under an American defense umbrella, why does it need its own umbrella too? For some reason Japan's Chinese critics consistently stop short of asking this question. Yet no question would do more to make mischief for Japanese diplomacy in the United States.

If Tokyo were forced to answer frankly, it would have to admit that it has long recognized that American power is in rapid decline.

This brings us to another interesting instance of Chinese silence. Although Tokyo has a long record of pulling the wool over Washington's eyes on Japanese economic policies, Chinese officials have done nothing to alert the American public to the reality of what has been going on. Not only has Japan systematically targeted one American industry after another (and thus speeded the destruction of the once unchallengeable industrial base on which America's victory in World War II was based), but it has often supplied dual-use military technologies to nations regarded by the United States as problematic or even hostile. The most notorious publicly disclosed instance came in the mid-1980s, when it was revealed that superadvanced Japanese machining technologies had helped render Soviet submarines almost undetectable to American surveillance.

This provoked a dangerous crisis in Japanese-American relations and provided a major inspiration for Washington's "Japan-bashing" phase of the late 1980s. There is no record of Beijing ever having tried to use this crisis to drive a wedge between Washington and Tokyo.

Then there is the anomaly of Japan's nuclear status. Defense analysts privately agree that Japan, like Israel, is undoubtedly an undeclared member of the nuclear weapons club. The point was made explicitly in an article by Nick Rufford in the London *Sunday Times* in 1994. The British Defense Ministry, Rufford reported, had informed Prime Minister John Major that "Japan has acquired all the parts necessary for a nuclear weapon and may even have built a bomb which requires only enriched plutonium for completion." Moreover, Japan has long held enormous stockpiles of plutonium for its nuclear power program, and its H-2 rocket, which has launched huge satellites into orbit, is regarded as capable of delivering a nuclear strike. Writing in the *Washington Quarterly*, Marc Dean Millot commented: "This is the stuff of virtual nuclear power. Only a political decision is needed to make it real."

True, Japan has never conducted test detonations—but then neither has Israel. The fact is that Japan has long been the world's most advanced nation in nuclear power, a status that was enhanced in 2006 when Tokyo-based Toshiba took over the old Westinghouse Electric nuclear division. One powerful piece of symbolism overlooked in most press accounts was that Westinghouse had played a historic role in the development of nuclear engineering. In the early 1940s it had pioneered the manufacture of the vital centrifuge equipment needed for separating uranium isotopes; its laboratory head, Edward Condon, went on to become Robert Oppenheimer's deputy in developing the first American atomic bombs.

All this is the more significant for how Japan compares with other nations. After all, the Bush administration is determined as one of its highest objectives to deprive Iran of key nuclear power technologies that the Eisenhower administration transferred to Japan half a century ago.

In truth, nuclear power has been one of Japan's most intensively targeted industries over the last fifty years. The question Beijing could raise—but significantly has not—is why? As of this writing in 2007, Beijing had still done almost nothing to question Japan's intense interest in nuclear technologies. Nor had its stooges and surrogates in the America policymaking community. All this seems more understandable when you realize that, as we will see, Japan transferred key nuclear technologies to China in the 1980s.

The plot thickens when you realize that, having invested in in-flight refueling for its air force, Japan has developed the capacity to deliver long-range military strikes. Such capabilities would not be necessary if Japan believed that the only defense threats it faced were those on its doorstep in Asia. Again, Chinese leaders have conspicuously avoided drawing attention to the obvious conclusion—that Japan is no longer Uncle Sam's helpless little ward.

Of course, Japanese leaders maintain that Japan has not only not developed nuclear weapons but never will. The reasons they offer, however, make no sense.

Japanese leaders claim that they have been restrained by a special "nuclear allergy" resulting from the atomic bomb attacks on Hiroshima and Nagasaki in 1945. Such an allergy defies common sense. Consider how things would look if the positions were reversed. Suppose it was the United States, not Japan, that had first suffered nuclear attack. Having seen, say, Boston and Chicago obliterated in an instant, would Americans regard this as a reason *not* to build a nuclear arsenal in the postwar era? To ask the question is to answer it. Precisely because Japan was the world's first nuclear victim, it more earnestly hankers to make itself safe from nuclear attack than almost any other nation. (Ordinary Japanese citizens may or may not share this aspiration—but they have no power to influence the policy.)

Another reason the Japanese often give for disavowing any nuclear ambitions is that Japan's extremely high population density makes it uniquely vulnerable to nuclear attack. Again, the test is to reverse the positions. If the United States were uniquely densely populated, would anyone in Washington cite this as a reason not to establish a nuclear deterrent?

All the real-world evidence is that a nuclear deterrent is the best military insurance policy money can buy. The point was demonstrated rather clearly in the early years of the new century in the differing ways Iraq and North Korea were treated. Lacking an effective nuclear deterrent, Saddam Hussein ended up on the gallows. By contrast, a potentially nuclear-armed Kim Jong Il was wooed with flattering words and promises of lavish economic aid.

It can be assumed that Japanese leaders are no less farsighted than Kim Jong-il—and no less capable of taking out suitable insurance.

It can also be assumed that Chinese leaders know this. Yet for some reason they have chosen not to make an issue of it.

Many more examples could be cited of a pattern of remarkable discretion in the "bitter" rhetoric on both sides. But already it should be clear that, all conventional wisdom to the contrary, both Tokyo and Beijing are especially careful not to embarrass each other in the West in their public rhetoric. Why therefore do American policymakers persist in viewing the two nations as fated forever to try to do one another down? It is time to consider the much-publicized "impediments" to good relations between Tokyo and Beijing.

Three Rocky Square Miles as Deal Breaker?

As Japan and China grew closer in the late 1970s, various issues suddenly popped up that—at least as reported in the Western press—seemed to threaten the entire relationship. We will consider the most famous of these, the Yasukuni affair, in the next section. But first let's look at the Senkaku Islands dispute, which emerged even earlier as a supposed flash point. Although less well known to the Western public, it continues regularly to be cited by scholars and Washington lobbyists alike as evidence that the Chinese and Japanese can never be friends.

Administered by Japan but claimed by both Taiwan and China, the Senkaku Islands (known to the Chinese as the Diaoyu Islands) have repeatedly been not only a source of angry words between Tokyo and Beijing, but the scene of many colorful—and, at least in East Asia, widely publicized—demonstrations by Japanese and Chinese political activists.

But how seriously should we take this controversy? One hint is that the islands have never been inhabited by anyone, let alone by either the Japanese or the Chinese. There is, moreover, the matter of their size—or lack of it. They are a few tiny godforsaken rocks, *with a total area of less than three square miles.* About equidistant from the nearest Japanese and Taiwanese territory (a distance of about 100 miles in each case), they are utterly remote from mainland China. Indeed they are so insignificant that they did not merit a single mention in the 1970 edition of the *Encyclopaedia Britannica.* Taiwan did not stake a claim to them until 1972 and it was only in the wake of Taiwan's action that the mainland Chinese felt obligated to follow suit.

The mystery of the Senkakus' supposed significance is increased when you realize that the world is full of similar territorial disputes. Such disputes are so common that, in the absence of special factors, they languish for generations unnoticed by the world's media. The United States alone is party to at least eight such disputes: one each with the Bahamas, Haiti, the Marshall Islands, and Tokelau, plus at least four with Canada. The Senkakus apart, China is engaged in countless territorial disputes with, among other nations, India, Bhutan, Malaysia, the Philippines, Vietnam, North Korea, Russia, and Tajikistan, not to mention Taiwan. Many of these disputes involve large territories and significant populations.

Similarly for the Japanese, the Senkaku dispute pales into insignificance compared to a vastly more serious—if less well known—territorial dispute with Russia. This concerns several Russian-occupied islands in the Kuril chain that boast a combined area of nearly two thousand square miles (making them about the size of Delaware). Before they were seized by the Soviet Union at the end of World War II, the islands had long been ruled by Tokyo and were home to tens of thousands of Japanese citizens.

Those who take the Senkaku dispute seriously point out that there is talk of oil in the vicinity. They omit to mention, however, that exaggerated notions of hidden natural resources are more or less par for the course in territorial disputes around the world. Certainly it is clear that even if the supposed oil deposits prove recoverable, the cost would be nearly prohibitive (the Senkakus are surrounded by deep, hostile seas).

Reviewing the time line from the vantage point of the twenty-first century, it is clear that the dispute has been greatly exaggerated for propaganda purposes. It is a smoke screen intended to conceal from the West the reality of an increasingly close—and indeed increasingly friendly—Sino-Japanese economic relationship.

This time line starts in the early months of 1978, when it was already becoming obvious to the Japanese—if not yet to the Americans—that China had decisively put Maoism behind it and was about to embark on a historic, intelligently thought-out program of economic development. Determined to get in on the ground floor, Tokyo quickly negotiated a $20 billion agreement, noted earlier, to help China's development. Then Japanese and Chinese officials sat down to negotiate the Sino-Japanese Treaty of Peace and Friendship. The talks soon raised alarm bells in Moscow, where China was regarded as a sworn enemy. Soviet leaders went public in April 1978 with a blunt warning to Japan not to get too close to China. The warning was evidently intended to alert Washington and thereby enlist American help in keeping Sino-Japanese relations from becoming too close.

Embarrassed by the Soviet intervention, the Japanese and the Chinese evidently cast around for some way of quelling Washington's suspicions. They found it in the Senkaku dispute. Reacting with remarkable speed, top Chinese officials authorized the dispatch of a bizarre flotilla of more than thirty fishing boats, some armed with machine guns, to converge on the Senkakus and claim them for Beijing. Thus just five days after the Soviet Union's concerns had made headlines, the story was that Beijing and Tokyo were close to a diplomatic rupture over a few uninhabited rocks. The *New York Times's* said it all: "Isle Fight Imperils Japan-China Treaty."

Thus was born the Senkakus' career as a stumbling block to closer Sino-Japanese relations. Since then the story has constantly been embroidered upon. In particular so-called "rightists" from Japan, traveling from Tokyo nearly a thousand miles away and dropping in for just a few hours, have repeatedly set up anti-Chinese structures topped with Japanese flags. Days later the Chinese (traveling several hundred miles from the nearest inhabited Chinese territory) then come by and laboriously undo the Japanese efforts. All this is recorded for posterity by swarms of helicopter-mounted Japanese and Chinese television crews. And the result is massive media coverage that drowns out all questions about how close Sino-Japanese economic relations have been becoming.

To say that the Senkaku dispute is contrived is an understatement. Who pays the very considerable cost of mounting so many demonstrations so far from home is just the most obvious of many questions that the Western press never asks.

The presence of Japanese rightists alone is a dead giveaway. Although the Japanese right's antics are invariably taken at face value by the American press, the fact is that there is no serious China-hating right wing in Japan. Indeed, this should be obvious from the fact that Japan's markedly pro-China economic policy over the years has never been challenged in Japanese electoral politics, let alone on Japanese streets. If there really are a lot of hatemongers out there, why did they not emerge in force to challenge Tokyo's ardent support for China's WTO bid? And why above all have they remained silent for decades as untold billions of dollars of Japanese tax money have gone toward speeding China's emergence as an economic superpower? And where, for heaven's sake, is the rightists' organizational structure—their John Birch Society or National Rifle Association? They don't have one. They don't even have a single identifiable leader, let alone someone of the fame of Barry Goldwater or Jean-Marie Le Pen.

The fact is that after more than two decades in Tokyo I have yet to meet a single Japanese citizen who conforms to the China-baiting profile of the Western press's imagination. A typical right-wing demonstration in central Tokyo runs to perhaps twenty or twenty-five people, often far fewer. This is implicitly obvious in the fact that news photographs of right-wing demonstrations are al- most invariably close-ups. Landscape shots are not published for the simple reason that they would reveal a laughably low turnout. Moreover, most of the "demonstrators," as the Dutch author Karel van Wolferen has pointed out, are not interested in the issues but are merely rent-a-mob types with day jobs in organized crime. A full explanation of the Japanese right wing is beyond our re- mit, but as in other aspects of Japanese public life, much of what passes for right-wing activism is merely theater.

At the end of the day we come back to the fact that the Senkakus are so in- significant. To put the issue in perspective, it is worth comparing it with a *real* territorial dispute. Take, for instance, the North-South problem in Ireland. Representing one-sixth of the total area of the island of Ireland and nearly one-third of the total population, Northern Ireland has provided the locale for countless ancient Irish legends. To this day the Northern Irish town of Ar- magh, where Saint Patrick reputedly ministered, remains the ecclesiastical cap- ital of the entire island. Yet in a spirit of common sense and goodwill in 1999, the people of the Irish Republic rejected two thousand years of tradition and formally renounced their claim to Northern Ireland.

By comparison, any suggestion that the Senkakus could be the occasion of serious bad blood between Beijing and Tokyo is laughable. Warren Buffett and Bill Gates are more likely to fall out over the tab for a couple of Cherry Cokes.

Dance of the Shadow Boxers

As we have noted, nothing has done more to foster the illusion of perennial tension between Tokyo and Beijing than the controversy over the Yasukuni shrine in Tokyo. Japanese leaders have repeatedly chosen to pay their respects at the shrine and in so doing have implicitly honored Japanese war criminals.

The first thing to note is that the visits are not new. Nor do they betoken any sudden new twist in Sino-Japanese relations. The controversy has bubbled along for nearly three decades, and at no point has it proved a stumbling block to more substantive aspects of an extremely extensive and mutually beneficial Sino-Japanese relationship.

Like Halley's comet, the controversy comes and goes. Yet every time it reap- pears, American correspondents, with an eye to page 1, play it as if it were new news. In reality, as we will see, it is an even more obviously theatrical production than the Senkaku dispute.

Of course, on a superficial view the Yasukuni issue *seems* serious. The shrine commemorates by name each of 2.5 million men and women who died in the service of Japan's military forces. Among them are many war criminals who in-flicted terrible atrocities on China in the 1930s and 1940s. Not the least con-troversial is General Iwane Matsui, who was hanged by the Americans in 1948 for his part in the so-called Rape of Nanking. The term refers to a massacre that proceeded for several weeks in 1937 in present-day Nanjing, a city then known as Nanking. On James Fallows's carefully conservative estimates, Matsui's forces massacred at least 140,000 civilians and raped 20,000 women. Others put the numbers much higher.

Matsui was among fourteen "Class A" war criminals whose names were en-shrined at Yasukuni in 1978. (The Class A designation refers to top military and civilian leaders who held the highest administrative positions in Japan's war effort.) Matsui's enshrinement notwithstanding, many Japanese prime minis-ters have paid their respects at Yasukuni in subsequent years—and in so doing have made the previously obscure shrine well known to television viewers around the world.

But why would any decent person go out of his way to honor someone like Matsui? And why in particular would a succession of "pro-American" Japanese prime ministers? And how come, for heaven's sake, the Japanese have insisted on maintaining as their principal war memorial a shrine that for nearly thirty years has been so notorious? Why can't it do like other nations and build a na-tional war memorial that honors an unknown soldier or otherwise avoids creat-ing unnecessary controversy?

These are important questions. Yet they have never been carefully consid-ered, let alone satisfactorily answered, by the American press.

One problem in discussing all this is that there is no general agreement on key facts. The Yasukuni "facts" are indeed sufficiently flexible that in at least one version, Japan is portrayed as the wronged party, and its sincere efforts to conduct ceremonies of "forgiveness" at the shrine are supposedly being misrep-resented by malign propagandists in Beijing! This version has been presented in particular by the Japan-based political commentator Sean Curtin.

Let's here consider merely the most accepted version as presented in the American press. To the extent that American commentators try to rationalize the Yasukuni story, they see it as a bizarrely dysfunctional exercise in Japanese

"democracy." In paying their respects at the shrine, Japanese politicians are supposedly pandering to a large group of rabidly anti-Chinese voters who regard
the Rape of Nanking as a hoax. Yet, as we have already pointed out, the fact that
no party espousing such extreme views has ever won electoral support stands as
mute testimony to the derisory nature of the Japanese right-wing.

Any attempt to get to the bottom of the Yasukuni affair must start with
some history. The shrine dates from the nineteenth century and was officially
government-controlled up to the end of World War II. It was then "privatized"
by the Americans and disappeared from view for many years. As the author
William Holstein has pointed out, Americans who lived in Tokyo in the 1960s
remember it as "abandoned and dilapidated." At some point it underwent ren-
ovations, but before 1979 it had received virtually no attention abroad. The
Nexis English-language newspaper clippings database records only a handful of
pre-1979 press mentions, none of them controversial.

Yasukuni's debut as a geopolitical controversy dates to April 1979, when the
New York Times, the *Washington Post,* and the Associated Press, among other English-speaking news organizations, belatedly reported an event that had taken
place secretly the previous October: the enshrinement of the fourteen war
criminals' names. Japanese government officials seemed apologetic, explaining
that the long-privatized shrine had come under far-right control and there was
nothing the government could do about it. And the worst part of it was that a
previously planned visit to the shrine by Prime Minister Masayoshi Ohira was
imminent.

Common sense suggests that Ohira, described as a devout Christian, might
simply have changed his plans and given the now tainted national monument a
wide berth. He was under no obligation to go through with the visit. Indeed, his
predecessors had omitted to visit the shrine in several previous years, and, as we
will see, his successors were to steer clear of it entirely during the peak years of
U.S.-Japan trade tensions in the latter half of the 1980s and in the 1990s.

Instead, Ohira pressed ahead regardless. Perhaps even more significant is
what he did not do. Given that Yasukuni's original purpose—to honor those
who had fallen in battle—had now been compromised, he surely should have
initiated a national quest to find a different way to honor Japan's war dead. He
did not do so, and none of his successors has made any serious effort either.

Perhaps an even more remarkable aspect of this affair is that often over the
years Japanese officials have seemed to go out of their way to fan the flames of
controversy. Repeatedly as the Western press's interest has seemed to flag,

inflammatory—and clearly contrived—new twists have been added. In August 1985, for instance, it was announced that Prime Minister Yasuhiro Nakasone's visit was made in an "official" capacity. This represented "new news" because previous prime ministerial visits were declared—after the fact—to have been merely private. Another of the many rather "manufactured" aspects of the controversy concerns who pays for the flowers laid at the shrine. Sometimes prime ministers pay out of their own pocket; sometimes they bill the hapless Japanese taxpayer.

Also, the controversy's impact has often been greatly magnified by rather extensive—and evidently carefully planned—advance publicity. In much the way a deft Hollywood publicist might whip up excitement ahead of the world premier of, say, *Ben-Hur* or *Titanic,* Japanese officials often get everyone talking well ahead of an impending Yasukuni visit.

These visits often take place on or about August 15, which is the anniversary of Japan's World War II surrender. Sometimes the prime minister kicks things off by making a statement well ahead of time about his intentions for the anniversary. In 1985, for instance, Nakasone indicated in advance that his visit would be "official." This more or less guaranteed the presence of the world's television cameras.

On other occasions prime ministers have made deliberately ambiguous remarks about their intentions, thereby opening the floodgates to a torrent of anxious speculation abroad. Top Japan scholars, interviewed on CNN, the BBC, and National Public Radio, earnestly try to guess the prime minister's intentions. Much significance is attached to the exact date of his visit. A visit on August 15 is considered more offensive than one on August 13 or 14. This twist alone does much to heighten the drama. (Although Prime Minister Junichiro Koizumi visited the shrine six times between 2001 and 2006, on all but the last occasion he avoided August 15.)

What is so striking about all this unpredictability is that it is so un-Japanese. Japan is rightly noted for the absolute predictability of its rituals (most of which receive little attention abroad precisely because they are so predictable). If Japanese officials were sincere in wanting to minimize the Yasukuni controversy's notoriety, they could start by simply eliminating the "permutations and combinations" aspect that keeps the story on the front burner. And, of course, if they were really thinking straight they could obviate all trauma by building a new, less controversial memorial.

There is a term for all this: press management. But what earthly purpose does it serve? As we have already noted, there is no electoral justification for the visits.

That said, the strange goings-on at Yasukuni are not without a certain rationale. As with the Senkaku controversy, the key to the affair is the time line. Take, for instance, the date when the fourteen Class A war criminals' names were "secretly" registered at the shrine—mid-October 1978. This is highly significant given that it came just a week before Deng Xiaoping's historic first trip to Tokyo.

It seems clear in retrospect that the Yasukuni enshrinement was an exercise in careful Japanese-style contingency planning. The news was "warehoused" for release anytime a diversionary action might be required to calm American suspicions. As it happened, the significance of Deng's 1978 visit went almost entirely unnoticed in the West (partly because Deng's new role as China's top leader had not yet become widely obvious). In the end, news of the enshrinement was not released until six months later when Washington finally began taking the New China seriously. A United States Senate Foreign Relations Committee delegation had been in Beijing days before the news was released, and just one month previously the Chinese had hosted an important visit by United States treasury secretary Michael Blumenthal.

It is also probably significant that the next major twist in the story—the "shock" of Nakasone's announcement that he was planning an official visit to Yasukuni in August 1985—coincided with the conclusion of a particularly significant agreement for Japan to transfer advanced nuclear power technology to China. It was this agreement, concluded at a time when transfers of American nuclear technology to China were banned under U.S. law, that paved the way for Japanese corporations to play a vital role in founding the Chinese nuclear power industry. Only the first fruit of the agreement was a deal—referred to earlier—for Mitsubishi to supply the enabling technology for China's first nuclear reactor. Adding insult to injury, Japan owed its expertise in nuclear power in the first place to receipts of American technology in the 1950s.

In reacting to Nakasone's visit, Beijing used such extravagant language that the American press for years thereafter took it as given that the Japanese and Chinese were engaged in a mini–cold war.

Then an interesting thing happened: the prime ministerial visits stopped. Apart from one isolated occasion in 1996, the controversy would remain dormant until 2001, when the visits were suddenly resumed on the full schedule of the first half of the 1980s. Again there is a significant coincidence here in that 2001 marked the beginning of a new mood of strident China bashing in the United States. Americans had suddenly gone from euphoria to despond as the great late-1990s Internet stock bubble collapsed. Millions of investors had been impoverished and the American economy entered its first recession in nine years. As the media began to focus on the impact of the outsourcing trend on American jobs, China became widely identified as an economic threat not only to the United States but (highly erroneously, of course) to Japan. It was predictable therefore that the American media would play the renewed round of Yasukuni visits as an expression of Japanese solidarity with America's anti-China mood.

Why do Chinese leaders tolerate the implied insult of the Yasukuni visits? For the same reason they have always done. Because the pattern started in Deng Xiaoping's time, let's consider his position. Like his Japanese counterparts, he realized that some powerful contrivance was needed to deflect American attention from the reality of a fast-burgeoning, mutually advantageous Sino-Japanese partnership. The story also served Deng's domestic agenda by allowing him to react suitably ferociously in condemning the Yasukuni visits, even as he quietly blocked Chinese citizens from pursuing war claims against Japan in American courts. (As a crucial concession to Tokyo, Deng had quietly endorsed Mao's renunciation of Chinese individuals' compensation claims arising out of Japan's imperial aggression.)

What is clear is that Deng must have been as pleased as his Japanese counterparts at the way the Yasukuni controversy deflected attention from the strengthening fundamentals of Sino-Japanese relations. Thus in the *Washington Post*'s first account in 1979, a Japanese commentator was quoted suggesting that the enshrinement was "part of a movement that would deny the responsibility of all Japanese people and particularly war leaders for Japan's aggression in the 1930s and 1940s." This same point, with its strong hint that the visits were an exercise in China baiting, has been repeated in English-language reports ever since.

Yet to the Chinese, the Yasukuni affair has always seemed almost as much an insult to the United States as to China. Not to put too fine a point on it, it makes Uncle Sam look ridiculous. After all, it was the United States, not China, that undertook to reform Japan after World War II. The new values that Japanese leaders supposedly espoused with such alacrity and enthusiasm were American values. And postwar Japan has ever since been presented as Exhibit A in Washington's case for believing that American values are universally applicable. The story of Japan's supposed conversion to American values is the main premise of

America's post–World War II ideology; yet the Yasukuni visits, if they mean anything, mean that that premise is false.

Japanese prime ministers are clearly not unaware of the risk that the Yasukuni visits pose to Japan's pro-American image. How else are we to be interpret the remarkable halt in Yasukuni visits after 1985? This coincided with a sudden, and very dangerous, rise in anti-Japanese feeling in Washington in the wake of the Plaza Accord of September 1985. Although the American dollar subsequently fell by almost half against the Japanese yen, the anticipated improvement in America's trade deficit never materialized. Quite the contrary, the deficit actually tripled between 1983 and 1986. The episode was widely and correctly seen as highly humiliating for the United States. Hence the fact that hostility about Japanese trade practices soon became so intense that Americans began questioning the entire story of Japan's embrace of American values.

In the circumstances any further Yasukuni visits in the 1980s might well have thrown gasoline on the flames of American anger. After all, there was the not inconsiderable point—generally overlooked at times when Tokyo-Washington relations are going smoothly—that several of the Yasukuni honorees bore ultimate responsibility for the deaths, in appalling conditions, of many tens of thousands of American prisoners of war. As documented by Linda Goetz Holmes in *Unjust Enrichment: How Japan's Companies Built Postwar Fortunes Using American POWs,* four in every ten Americans captured by the Japanese died in custody. This meant the death rate in Japanese POW camps was more than thirty times that in German ones. Of special significance is the fact that a principal cause of death was starvation. Yet Tokyo could well afford to feed the Americans. This was because the United States had sent large amounts of money to the Japanese regime via the Red Cross to pay for the prisoners' proper care. The money was however, diverted by top Japanese leaders to pay for Japan's war effort—while the intended beneficiaries died by the thousand from malnutrition, lack of medicines, and grossly unhealthy living surroundings. The conditions in which American prisoners were kept throughout Japan's then huge empire were very similar, which, as Holmes suggests, evidently reflected policies set at the highest levels in Tokyo.

Although little of this history came out at the time of America's Japan-bashing mood in the late 1980s and early 1990s, it is clear that top Japanese officials feared that further Yasukuni visits could easily provoke bitter American recriminations.

Perhaps the most significant thing about the Yasukuni "vacation" was that there was no prime ministerial visit even in the immediate wake of the Tiananmen massacre in 1989. This made no sense if the point of the visits is "to send a message" to Beijing. It was more understandable, however, to anyone who knew that Japanese diplomats were then strenuously trying to get the West to move on from the Tiananmen massacre and focus on rebuilding good relations with Beijing.

When the Yasukuni-visiting schedule was resumed in 2001, the political circumstances had changed utterly. By then the urban myth of Japan's economic collapse had become indelibly lodged in the American mind. Not only were the Japanese no longer seen as economic rivals by the United States, but they were regarded as the firmest of allies in countering Chinese economic expansionism. With China's admission to the World Trade Organization a done deal and anti-Chinese feeling rising in the United States, Yasukuni was reinstated as a potent—but to both the Japanese and the Chinese absurdly fatuous—token of supposed Japanese solidarity with the United States.

Who Blocked Japan's United Nations Bid?

For believers in the conventional view of Sino-Japanese relations, Beijing's true feelings were pointedly made clear in 2004 after Japan tried to join the United Nations Security Council. Japan seemed to many UN members to have a good case: after all, it had long contributed close to one-fifth of the United Nations' total budget—about as much as the United States and more than the *combined* contributions of the other permanent members (China, France, Britain, and Russia). Nonetheless, the bid was opposed by Beijing and duly collapsed. Tokyo was left to lick its wounds. So was Washington, which had strongly encouraged the Japanese bid in the first place.

How can this episode be seen as anything other than evidence of a seriously strained Sino-Japanese relationship? How indeed.

In reality the entire episode was utterly misunderstood in the West. The commentators made the elementary mistake of assuming that Japan was sincere in its bid. This reckoned without the counterintuitive character of Japanese diplomacy. Japan did *not* want a United Nations seat—and still does not, at least not yet. The reason is that Tokyo's true sympathies in Middle East policy are so dangerously at odds with Washington's that the differences can be successfully papered over only so long as the Japanese stay out of the diplomatic limelight.

The reason all this is not obvious to American Japan watchers is that they consistently fail to read the cultural tea leaves in Tokyo. They have long misconstrued the impeccable hospitality, large speaking fees, and flattering comments they receive from the Japanese as an indication of unconditional Japanese support for American foreign policy.

In a word, American policymakers view Japan as America's doormat. This overlooks the commonsense notion that few nations have ever aspired to be anyone's doormat. Although Tokyo quietly fumes at being taken for granted in Washington, the practical reality of power politics in the post-1945 era has inhibited it from directly challenging the American-led world order.

Thus when, in the wake of the September 11 atrocities, American officials pressed Japan to seek a Security Council seat, Japanese diplomats felt they could not say no. Caught between a rock and a hard place, they resorted—not for the first time—to political theater. On the one hand, in a nod to American wishes, they went through the motions of seeking a seat; on the other hand, they found an ingenious way of sabotaging their own bid. This was a classic case of the Japanese tactic of *menju fukuhai:* to cooperate with the face but disobey in the belly.

Tokyo's solution was to position its bid as part of the so-called Group of Four application undertaken with three other candidates for Security Council seats. None of the other Group of Four candidates—Germany, India, and Brazil—was viewed favorably by the United States. Moreover, these nations' candidacies were strongly opposed by regional rivals: Italy in the case of Germany; Pakistan in the case of India; and both Mexico and Argentina in the case of Brazil. That China reportedly opposed Japan's bid was really beside the point.

To put the Group of Four bid in personal terms, it was as if the Japanese ambassador to the United States had put his name up for Washington's posh Cosmos Club but insisted that the entire cast of Monty Python's Flying Circus be let in at the same time! The Group of Four bid was dead on arrival, as the Japanese had planned all along.

This was not the first time Japan had to wriggle out of an American effort to put it on the Security Council. On an earlier occasion in the 1990s, it also went through the motions but combined its application with a demand for a drastic overhaul of the Security Council, which would have eviscerated the existing permanent members' veto powers. Presented with such a poisoned chalice, Washington quietly allowed the matter to fizzle. On another occasion, Japan agreed to put its name forward in a joint application with Germany. Again highly predictably, this proved a nonstarter. It was opposed by many Third World nations who have long complained about the Security Council's already pronounced Eurocentricity. And, of course, Germany's bid was also unpopular with many European nations (which were already suspicious of Germany's enormous behind-the-scenes influence in the European Union).

As for the failure of the Group of Four bid, Bush administration officials took it all in good heart as one more instance of "clueless" Japanese diplomacy. But common sense says that the Japanese got exactly what they wanted—to be kept out of America's quarrels. Certainly to anyone who has followed Japanese diplomatic history, it is obvious that Israel is the elephant in the room. While the Japanese work hard not to offend Israel and are adept at finding suitably vague or ambiguous words to finesse their differences with Washington's Middle East policy, they are actually resolutely in the Arabs' camp. Not only do they take a non-Western view of the rights and wrongs of the Israel-Palestine issue, but, as a matter of practical diplomacy, they want to do nothing to alienate their 1.3 billion customers in the Muslim world (many of whom indeed live in nations like Indonesia and Malaysia that are close, if generally unobtrusive, Japanese allies—and are strongly anti-American to boot).

It does not take much imagination to see how large the problems could become if Tokyo had a United Nations veto. Suppose, for instance, that the Bush administration tacitly encouraged an Israeli nuclear strike against Iran. Tokyo would be expected to support Israel in the Security Council; but if it did, Japanese citizens and corporations for generations to come would be targets of all sorts of official and unofficial anger in the Muslim world. This would not be so much a no-win for Japanese diplomacy as a total catastrophe.

Tokyo's record of dissembling on the Middle East goes back to the 1960s, when it succeeded for a while in presenting itself, at least in American eyes, as a quiet partisan of the Israeli cause. Then in the early 1970s came the Arab boycott. Forced to make a clear-cut choice, Tokyo left an astounded Uncle Sam in the lurch and came out for the Arabs.

Given all this, it is clear that in opposing Japan's candidacy in 2004, China secretly helped extract Japan from a tight corner. Had China really wanted to make trouble, it would have done the opposite and smilingly taken the lead in sponsoring a special VIP-style application for Japan alone. It would then have sat back and cackled as hapless Japanese diplomats maneuvered between the Scylla of Washington's pro-Israel policy and the Charybdis of Muslim rage.

Those who accept the conventional version point out that Tokyo seemed to work hard to buy the support of several small nations for the G4 initiative. Surely it would not have done so had it not been sincere in its bid? In reality the amounts involved were trivial for a Japanese foreign aid budget that in 2004 totaled nearly $9 billion. In any case, the money hardly went to waste. After all, when Tokyo makes an aid grant, its principal motivation is not to benefit the recipient nation but rather to generate business for corporate Japan (which gets to provide the recipient with a power station, a new railroad system, or whatever).

As far as Japan's position on the United Nations is concerned, the key is timing. Someday—probably quite soon—Tokyo will genuinely aspire to a Security Council seat. But it will do so only after Washington has lost its power to call the shots in the Middle East (and to make trouble for Japanese trade policies).

Japan's 2004 Security Council bid should be seen as the joke it was—a joke at the Bush administration's expense. Japan played its part to perfection. So did China.

A Japanese Wrench in America's Works

We have already seen that Japan's trade relationship with China is well balanced and mutually satisfactory. The contrast with Japan's trade relationship with the United States could hardly be sharper. Indeed, Japan ranks second only to China as the nation with the largest bilateral surplus with the United States. Although various factors help create this surplus (and they do not all testify to bad faith in Tokyo), a key factor is clearly Japanese mercantilism. This should give the lie to the idea of Japan as a loyal American ally.

A major reason why this is not better understood is that most Western commentators not only know little about international trade but are dismissive of its importance. True to their globalist sensibilities, they regard mercantilism as self-defeating, even idiotic, and thus are indulgent, to say the least, about the way Japanese trade policies have damaged the United States over the years.

Yet it is in trade that Tokyo's true geopolitical priorities are most clearly visible. It is hardly an exaggeration to suggest that the effect of Japanese trade policies has been broadly the economic equivalent of dropping several A-bombs on America's erstwhile unchallengeable industrial leadership. Certainly judged by its cumulative effect, Japanese mercantilism has hitherto at least done more to undermine American economic power than the Chinese variety. This is not only because Japan has been a player for a lot longer but also because its impact has been disproportionately felt at the most sophisticated levels of American manufacturing.

Why do Japan's trade policies represent such an important insight into the true state of the Tokyo-Washington relationship? At the core of the argument is the fact that scale economies are crucial in many industries. The point matters particularly in the most advanced, capital-intensive industries that formerly were the mainstay of American prosperity. In such industries, by definition, sunk costs are a major proportion of total costs. Producers that can maximize their sales by selling in the largest number of markets around the world enjoy an enormous advantage. The greater their production run, the lower their sunk costs per unit, and thus the more competitively they can price.

For the sake of simplicity let's assume there are just two nations in the world, Japan and the United States. By indulging in "one-way free trade," Japan gives its companies a huge advantage in scale economies. Whereas the Americans merely have the American home market, the Japanese have this plus their own home market (which in consumer products is typically about 50 percent the size of the American market and can be a much greater proportion for many types of advanced manufactured products).

A second consequence of Japan's trade policy is that it creates a sanctuary at home where its corporations can—if they are sufficiently cartelized (which they are)—price extremely high. This creates huge home-market profits that are then invested in ever more advanced production technologies that have rapidly improved their productivity. These corporations are free to price superaggressively abroad, often selling below cost in an effort to weaken foreign competitors.

We do not here have space for a full discussion, but it is useful to exemplify the point by reference to the automobile industry. In few industries has Japan's pattern of deception been so egregious.

To many of the Washington elite, of course, the American car industry is merely an embarrassment—a dying industry whose wounds have been largely self-inflicted. The best solution, it seems, might simply be to put it out of its misery or at least, as Thomas Friedman has openly argued, have it taken over by the Japanese.

There is, however, another side to the Detroit story—a long history of bad faith and bare knuckles in Tokyo that utterly belies the standard presentation of a fair Japanese victory. Of course, Detroit's Washington detractors are probably right that the American car industry now generally trails in productivity and quality; but they are utterly wrong to imply, as they often do, that the outcome was always a foregone conclusion or that Detroit's problems today are all its own fault.

Up to the early 1970s, Detroit clearly led the world and did so while paying wages at least twice Japanese levels. In those days it was the Americans, not the Japanese, who were feared in Europe, and rightly so. The Americans' technical leadership was abundantly apparent in large market shares in Britain, France, and Germany, among many other European nations.

Since then a pattern of unfair trade by Japan has increasingly shaped the outcome of global competition. In particular the Japanese market has remained closed to all but token foreign competition.

Of course, the allegation that the Japanese market is closed has long been hotly disputed by the Japanese industry's many dupes and stooges in Washington. But this is merely the triumph of lobbying power over truth.

In trying to deny that the Japanese market is closed, many American commentators have taken a blame-the-victim approach. The problem, they say, is that the American companies have "not tried hard enough" in Japan. Prominent advocates of this position have included David Sanger, former Tokyo bureau chief of the *New York Times,* and the *Washington Post*'s well-known commentator George Will (who propounded his views at a time when, unbeknownst to his readers, his wife worked for the Japanese car industry's Washington lobbying organization).

To anyone who knows Japan, the apologists' line is disgracefully at odds with reality. The fact is that it is not just the Americans who are shut out of the market. It is virtually every carmaker in the world.

The Japanese establishment deploys a host of techniques to limit foreigners' access. The result is that the combined market share of all foreign carmakers has remained remarkably constant at a mere 4 to 5 percent for more than twenty years. The foreign share has not increased even on those rare occasions when the yen has risen sharply on foreign-exchange markets (the yen rocketed nearly 80 percent against the American dollar between 1990 and 1995, for instance).

It is particularly significant that there are no Korean cars on Japanese roads. Japan's American apologists sometimes suggest this reflects some special Japanese antipathy to all things Korean. But how, therefore, do they explain the fact that Korean is Japan's favorite foreign cuisine? In any case, there is the matter that other Korean products have somehow not been subject to this alleged discrimination. The Korean-owned chewing-gum-to-heavy-chemicals giant Lotte, for instance, is a major presence in many aspects of Japanese life. Then there is the Samsung group. Though formerly locked out of the Japanese electronics market, it has now become a fully accredited, highly visible player there.

The fact is that the Korean carmakers are shut out as a matter of Japanese industrial policy. So too—very visibly—are such European giants as Volkswagen, Peugeot, and Fiat. As for the American makers, they have long been accused of failing to make suitable cars for Japan. This gets the story backward. Why after all should they design cars for Japan if they know they are locked out of the market?

Besides, the Detroit companies *do* make plenty of cars suitable for Japan. Almost all their European cars qualify. Designed with high gasoline prices in mind, they come in both right-hand- and left-hand-drive versions (the Japanese drive on the left). Moreover, many of these cars are made in Germany to the highest German engineering standards. Take, for instance, General Motors' Adam Opel subsidiary. The Opel line sells strongly throughout Europe and does so in the face of the full weight of Japanese competition. Where is Opel in Japan? After years of battling trade barriers there, it finally shut down in Japan in 2006.

Then there is the story of Renault, the French car company that bought an ostensibly controlling interest in Nissan in 1999. Although the Nissan group's distribution system is Japan's second largest, Renaults are shut out of Nissan showrooms—with the result that there are virtually no Renaults on Japanese roads. (In the late 1980s Washington asked Tokyo to break the Japanese car industry's control of Japanese car distribution so that distributors could sell foreign and Japanese makes side by side. Tokyo said no.)

The wider point here for our consideration of Japan's place in the China-America-Japan triangle is not so much that Japan's policies have long been mercantilist (though they have), nor is it even that the United States has been the largest victim of Japanese mercantilism (though it certainly has). Rather, the point is that Japan has gone to such extraordinary lengths to misrepresent its true agenda. Not only have Japanese officials lied about their policies but they have systematically interfered in America's internal affairs to promote an elite consensus favorable to those policies.

The most obvious way this has been done has been by marginalizing the careers of key decision makers—typically journalists, academics, or public servants—who believe that trade policy matters. People have been defamed and their livelihoods have been sabotaged.

By the same token the careers of those whose trade views are considered helpful to Tokyo have flourished. Has Tokyo intervened actively to promote the careers of such people? By definition, as so much of the action takes place behind closed doors, there are few smoking guns. What is clear is that Japan possesses both the motive and the means. And if it is prepared to defame those it regards as problematic, it surely is prepared to resort to the less controversial— and less humanly reprehensible—tactic of advancing the careers of those it considers helpful.

Having satisfied ourselves that, in contending with the dragon, the United States can hope for little help from its "closest ally," let's take a hard look at why America's intellectual elite has been so slow to speak out about America's problems with the Confucian world. It is time to look at some good American Confucians.

EIGHT

A Few Good Confucians

We have seen how the United States is increasingly becoming Confucian-ized. The trend is driven in large measure by the defection one by one of key Americans to the Confucian cause. Let's now take a closer look at some ex-amples of the trend.

We will call them the good Confucians—good that is in the sense that they win approval in Beijing. In their efforts to promote China's interests in the United States, they often resort to Confucian tools for manipulating the public information process. They are increasingly represented everywhere that politi-cal ideas are discussed or acted upon—from the media and the universities to big business and politics.

Why would any American consciously espouse a cause so obviously at odds with the Western tradition? As legal scholars point out, establishing a witness's motive is often beyond the resources of even the most capable lawyer. It is a fair guess, however, that various motives are at work.

Some good Confucians are no doubt intellectually committed to the cause, in much the way that in the mid-twentieth century some left-wing activists in the United States and Europe genuinely saw Soviet Communism as the future. Some American Confucians probably accept the bleak Confucian view of the human condition: the human race en masse is, they believe, incorrigibly stupid and fractious and therefore cannot be held in check except by a ruthless, tightly knit elite, unashamed to stoop to deception, coercion, and worse.

The catch-22 nature of the Confucian truth ethic precludes them from ever talking frankly about their mission. But if they were to do so, they might invoke Jeremy Bentham's motto, "The greatest happiness of the greatest number is the foundation of morals and legislation." Certainly it is clear that China's own leaders regard authoritarianism as essential to maintaining order in a complex world.

The great bulk of America's good Confucians, however, are not selfless adherents to a higher cause. Rather, they believe in something a lot less elevated—their own personal interests. For whatever reason, they have come to accept that they can most effectively feather their own nests by throwing in their lot with the emerging Confucian establishment. They are Confucians only by default. Some have certainly been coerced into breaking with Western individualism. Others are merely opportunists jumping on a fast-moving bandwagon.

For the most part such Confucians are united by a secret Confucian credo—the same credo that guides the life of virtually every Chinese citizen. Though it has never been written down, if it were it would read something like this: "I am not at all sure that what my Confucian superiors ask me to do is right. But nothing I can do—and nothing any other individual can do—to oppose Confucianism will alter the outcome. In the meantime I can best advance my own interests by going with the flow."

This is the nihilistic creed of collaborators everywhere—the true spirit of Vichy France. More to the point, it is the spirit of 1930s East Asia. Almost forgotten in the West now, top British and American residents of East Asia in those days openly rooted for the Japanese fascists against Chinese nationalists—and continued to do so even after they knew the truth about the Nanking massacre. Their motive was money. In those days of chaos in China, Japan was the country that mattered in East Asia—at least it was the country that mattered to any Briton or American interested in furthering his own private interests. It was the Japanese who hosted East Asia's best diplomatic parties and showered their friends with the most tasteful and expensive gifts. It was the Japanese who made a policy of paying overly fat fees to Western experts and speakers. It was the Japanese who could adroitly rig a questionable deal—either financial or commercial—to line any venal Western pocket.

A particularly egregious example of Western collaborationism from that era was the story of the British diplomat/historian/intelligence officer Malcolm Kennedy. Kennedy not only mercilessly defamed a Western contemporary who had issued a prescient early warning about Japanese militarism, but dedicated a book in the late 1930s to the top Japanese militarist Koki Hirota. Hirota was foreign minister at the time of the Nanking massacre and was hanged afterward as a Class A war criminal. None of this harmed Kennedy's post–World War II career. His friends in Tokyo adroitly helped him escape responsibility for his "youthful indiscretions," and he went on to become the grand old man of post-war British Japan studies. He was eventually decorated with the Order of the British Empire by Queen Elizabeth, and his papers form the centerpiece of a major collection in Sheffield University's Japan-funded East Asian studies department.

Among East Asia watchers, the rancid ethics of 1930s-style collaborationism are now again the order of the day. The difference these days is merely that the collaborators are working to serve China's interests even more than Japan's (in any case, as we have seen, China's interests and Japan's are far more often closely aligned than is generally understood in the West).

Many of China's American collaborators operate openly as trade lobbyists. Indeed, the list of good Confucians in the Washington trade lobby would fill a Who's Who. Starting with George H. W. Bush, Henry Kissinger, Alexander Haig, and Brent Scowcroft, virtually every retired top American official who has helped shape American foreign or trade policy in the last four decades now works openly to further China's economic interests—and does so even when these interests quite obviously conflict with those of the United States.

Such people are easily seen through, and increasingly, if very belatedly, the American press is coming to view their activities with appropriate skepticism, if not contempt. What we will focus on here are some good Confucians whose pro-China agenda is not so explicit. We look first at publisher Rupert Murdoch and then at insurance tycoon Maurice Greenberg, the economist Nicholas Lardy, and finally the journalist Ian Buruma. Think of this as an *Upstairs, Downstairs* sort of drama, perhaps set on a grand ocean liner, in which people of all ranks have speaking parts. Up in the stateroom, Murdoch and Greenberg are sipping sherry with the captain (played by a quietly-in-control Hu Jintao). The waiters are half-familiar faces from presidential administrations past. Meanwhile down in the engine room, younger and more hirsute versions of Lardy and Buruma, stripped to the waist, are shoveling coal into the giant furnace.

Collaborationists or idealists alike, good Confucians know one thing the rest of us are only beginning to sense: they are changing the world.

Citizen Kane Enters a Confucian Twilight

Of all the conversions to China's cause, few seem more unlikely than that of Rupert Murdoch.

Long before he first pandered to China in the 1990s, Murdoch ranked as one of the world's richest entrepreneurs. So money alone explains little of Murdoch's conversion to the Confucian way.

Indeed, the pre-Confucian Murdoch, in his independence of spirit and ebullient individualism, seemed to epitomize everything Confucian society is not. Starting with one daily newspaper in Australia in the 1950s, he had already by the mid-1990s built up the largest media empire in history. With increasing help from Beijing, his News Corporation's holdings have continued to grow apace in the new century: the company now publishes more than 170 newspapers, operates a worldwide satellite television network, and publishes, through HarperCollins, a significant share of all books read by Americans. In the words of the *Washington Post* columnist Richard Cohen, Murdoch's record makes previous iconic American media tycoons such as Joseph Pulitzer and William Randolph Hearst (the latter the inspiration for the classic Orson Welles movie *Citizen Kane*) seem like "pikers."

Even with all this behind him, however, Murdoch seems no more capable of standing up to Beijing than the general run of frail, easily compromised American mediocrities who are so well represented in Beijing's web of influence and obfuscation.

It is all such a contrast with the "let's change China" mood in which Murdoch entered into his relationship with Beijing. Like so many unacclimated Westerners before him, he seems to have held originally that exposure to the Western media would change China. He made the point publicly in 1993, declaring that modern communications technology was "an unambiguous threat to totalitarian regimes everywhere."

His words did not go unnoticed in Beijing. As his newly acquired Hong

Kong–based satellite television company was already then trying to build an audience in China, top Chinese leaders did not lack for a suitable rejoinder. They immediately reacted by tightening their ban on privately owned satellite dishes. In response, a checkmated Murdoch set out on a deeply humiliating goodwill mission to Beijing. As recounted by author James McGregor, Murdoch was so eager for absolution that he humbly endured many studied slights and put-downs at the hands of the Chinese bureaucracy. A lower-level Chinese official even opened one meeting by saying, "I understand you are an Australian company. Tell me what you do."

Murdoch ended up undertaking to follow China's strict media rules to the letter. As summarized by McGregor, Murdoch's pitch went like this: "We are very influential and want to be the Chinese government's friend. We want to make money in China, not trouble."

If remarks by Chinese president Jiang Zemin in 1998 are anything to go by, the pitch succeeded. As reported in the Chinese press, Jiang "expressed appreciation for the efforts made by world media mogul Rupert Murdoch in presenting China objectively and cooperating with the Chinese press."

Other observers have been less complimentary. When Murdoch launched a takeover bid for the *Wall Street Journal* in 2007, seven of the paper's China-based reporters openly lambasted him. In a letter to controlling shareholders in Dow Jones & Company, which owned the paper, they wrote: "Rupert Murdoch has a well-documented history of making editorial decisions in order to advance his business interests in China and, indeed, of sacrificing journalistic integrity to satisfy personal or political aims."

In so doing they echoed a comment made years previously by the Hong Kong–based commentator Philip Bowring, who accused Murdoch of "buying commercial favors through media bias," and itemized several questionable efforts by Murdoch to win favor in Beijing. These notably included a decision to drop BBC World News from his East Asian satellite broadcast service (after the BBC's coverage of Chinese human rights issues raised hackles in Beijing). The Murdoch organization also kowtowed when its HarperCollins book-publishing business backed out of publishing the memoirs of Chris Patten, a leading critic of China's human rights policies who served as Britain's last governor of Hong Kong.

What is clear is that the "totalitarian regime" he referred to in 1993 is an increasingly important source of Murdoch's profits. According to statutory financial disclosures, News Corporation's wholly owned Star television subsidiary is beholden to the Beijing authorities for access to the vast Chinese market. This is because Hong Kong–based Star's broadcasts are distributed in China by government-licensed (and generally government-owned) Chinese distributors. Courtesy of these arrangements, Star enjoys a particularly large audience in Guangdong, one of China's richest provinces. Star also depends on approval from Beijing to pipe its content into thousands of hotels throughout China and actively cooperates with Beijing's superstrict censorship requirements.

In view of the scale of Murdoch's interests, his conversion to the Chinese cause is a devastating development in itself. What makes it even more so is that he has given cover to the rest of the American media establishment to behave in a similar fashion. Thus when top media moguls like Viacom chief executive Sumner Redstone and Time Warner chairman Gerald Levin gathered in Shanghai in 1999 to celebrate fifty years of Communist rule, the conference turned into what the journalist Tina Rosenberg described as "one great big icky fawning session." The Americans, of course, were the ones doing the fawning. Among other things, Redstone told the meeting that Western media groups "should avoid being unnecessarily offensive to the Chinese government."

Undoubtedly Murdoch's most important service to Beijing came in 1999, when he threw his worldwide media empire behind China's bid to enter the World Trade Organization. Even by the standards of other Western media organizations, the Murdoch media were highly economical with the truth about the downside of China's WTO ambitions.

Murdoch's *New York Post*, for instance, presented the issue as if there were only two choices: either throw American markets more or less unconditionally open to Chinese exports or else risk dangerously "isolating" China. This conveniently overlooked the fact that the United States had never previously felt it necessary to provide vast trade privileges to other nations as a precondition for establishing civilized diplomatic relations. Indeed even today Russia has not been granted so-called "most-favored-nation" status in the American market, yet no one suggests that this ipso facto isolates Moscow. The *New York Post* also suggested that approving the WTO trade deal would provide the United States with "far greater opportunities to lobby China on human rights." This was positively Orwellian in its mendacity. The truth was the direct opposite. Trade sanctions were the only effective tools the United States had in trying to moderate China's human rights policies and once China joined the WTO their use was explicitly prohibited.

Meanwhile Murdoch's social links with China have grown apace. A key development has been his third marriage, in 1999, to the Hong Kong–based television presenter Wendi Deng. Born in the Xuzhou area of China in 1969 and the daughter of a politically orthodox Mao-era factory manager, Deng is nearly forty years Murdoch's junior. She has already given him two children who are expected to inherit large stakes in his media empire.

What does the future hold for Murdoch's brand of journalism? Already its Confucian cast seems assured. Certainly remarks in March 2001 by James Murdoch, one of the News Corporation titan's heirs from a previous marriage, are suggestive. In a conference speech, James sided with Beijing in alleging that the Falun Gong "clearly does not have the success of China at heart." He went on to characterize the foreign media as "destabilizing forces" that were "very, very dangerous for China." As recorded by Joshua Kurlantzick, the younger Murdoch even criticized Hong Kong democracy supporters, and suggested that they should accept the reality of life under a strong-willed "absolutist" government.

Even the most cynical Beijing "princeling" could hardly have put it better.

"All I Want in Life Is an Unfair Advantage"

Of all the China-friendly American opinion leaders who have influenced the American trade debate in recent decades, few have worked harder than the controversial insurance magnate Maurice "Hank" Greenberg. For thirty-seven years—from 1968 to 2005—he headed American International Group (AIG) and built it into America's tenth-largest corporation. He also built it into probably the biggest single pillar of Confucian power in the United States.

Known to subordinates as a "screamer" and notorious for a take-no-prisoners business style, Greenberg embarrassed himself in the 1990s when he commissioned an authorized history of the company and then was forced to suppress it in circumstances that suggested the author had stumbled—perhaps unbeknownst to himself—on skeletons in the Greenberg closet. In the end Greenberg was driven from office in 2005 after an investigation by New York attorney general Eliot Spitzer, who entered charges of deceptive accounting. Even in ostensible retirement, however, Greenberg continues to cast a long shadow over AIG via a foundation that controls a large block of shares.

To his admirers, it was Greenberg's hard-charging style that built AIG. In reality, however, the decisive aspect of his leadership was different: his geopolitical strategy. More than anyone else, Greenberg has functioned as East Asia's advocate in the American policy establishment. AIG has been rewarded with sweetheart deals throughout the Confucian world as regulators have rigged East Asian markets to provide AIG with exceptionally high returns.

Greenberg's role in the Chinese trade debate dates back to 1975, when—with Mao Zedong and Zhou Enlai still hanging on—he became one of the earliest American business leaders to visit Communist China. Even earlier he had established himself as a major factor in American relations with Japan. He had discovered that to fend off charges of mercantilism, Japanese officials desperately needed a few token American corporate success stories to cite in Washington. Although Japanese officials were not prepared to open up to, say, American cars or rice, offering a small piece of the insurance action to a house-trained American partner like AIG was different. This followed from the mercantilist logic of Japanese trade policy: remember that most of the jobs involved in providing a service like insurance in Japan are necessarily Japanese jobs, irrespective of who owns the companies involved.

By all accounts AIG has been laughing all the way to the bank ever since. In 1992, the *Economist* reported that Japan was AIG's "most profitable market anywhere." This reflected the fact that Japan's regulated premium scales generally provided underwriters with guaranteed high profit margins. The Japanese market has been a slam dunk for any insurer lucky enough to be permitted a piece of it.

Rarely has AIG's sweetheart status in Japan been more clearly acknowledged than in 1997, when the company was given a unique regulatory approval: in a remarkable example of cross-ministry cooperation, Japanese regulatory agencies permitted AIG to pioneer the sale of travel insurance via vending machines at Japanese airports. Such insurance is highly controversial, being regarded by most experts as an ethically questionable effort to exploit irrational fears. After all, if people need insurance, they need it all the time, not just on a plane. Airport insurance is also questionable because premiums are exorbitant for the extremely low risk involved. In securing the right to do business at Japan's airports AIG was effectively granted a license to print money.

Despite much talk in recent years that the Japanese market has opened up to other American companies, as of 2005 AIG still accounted for fully 65 percent of all property and casualty premiums received by foreign insurers in Japan. Meanwhile AIG has remained the most visible American corporate supporter of Japanese public relations activities in the United States.

AIG has gone on to provide similar services on similar terms to several other mercantilist East Asian nations. In his lighter moments, Greenberg has even been known to allude to the ease of AIG's success. As recorded by Devin Leonard and Peter Elkind of *Fortune* magazine, Greenberg has more than once been heard to say: "All I want in life is an unfair advantage." (The line is not original: it comes from the famous nineteenth-century financier Daniel Drew.)

A measure of Greenberg's personal standing in China is that he was among the first foreigners to be made an honorary citizen of Shanghai. In 1992 AIG achieved a highly significant first when it was permitted to establish a wholly foreign-owned life insurance company in China. It went on to become the only wholly foreign-owned company to be permitted to sell insurance in eight of China's largest cities. Greenberg had prepared the ground well. Two years beforehand he had partnered with Zhu Rongji, then mayor of Shanghai and a future premier of China, in setting up an international business advisory council in Shanghai.

AIG is unique in that it is a "reverse multinational" that started out not in the West but in China. Founded in Shanghai in 1919, the company was ejected from China after the Communist revolution, only to return in the era of Dengist reform. One might assume that AIG owes its special treatment in the modern Chinese market to its origins. But this would be naive: after all, hundreds of other companies established by Westerners in China before the revolution have not been welcomed back. AIG owes its favored status largely to an impeccable record of collaborating with the mercantilist agendas in Beijing and other East Asian capitals.

Up to the 1970s it was still largely an East Asian business, albeit one owned by Americans. As the years have gone by, it has invested its growing East Asian profits in making ever larger acquisitions in the United States and Europe. As of 2005 East Asia's share of its total revenues had fallen to a mere 29 percent—but this was still a bigger proportion than at almost any other American insurance company. More important, it was a vast figure in absolute terms given the immense scale of the company's worldwide business. Although the company does not clearly identify the geographical source of its profits, it is a fair inference that it is disproportionately profitable in East Asian markets. In playing the token American success in such markets, AIG implies that its profits are attributable to superior management. This, of course, allows East Asian trade propagandists to cite AIG as "proof" that any American company that "tries hard enough" can succeed in the region.

Greenberg has served on the boards of countless key nonprofit institutions.

At the Council on Foreign Relations, the Maurice R. Greenberg Center for Geoeconomic Studies stands as a monument to his role in American policymaking. The center is a prominent arbiter on China-related issues and has rapidly established itself as a leading source of "Don't worry, be happy" propaganda. Its director, Sebastian Mallaby, a former *Economist* magazine Tokyo correspondent and arch proponent of the Japan-hits-the-wall story of the 1990s, has a long record of exaggerating about the American economy's supposed relative strength.

Even as recently as 2006, when the United States' dependency on foreign borrowing already rivaled that of the late-era Ottoman Empire, Mallaby persisted with his feel-good message. Writing in the *Washington Post,* he commented: "American business is in a golden phase right now because its imaginative culture fits the challenges of the post-industrial age."

One of Greenberg's most controversial interventions in the American policymaking process came in the 1990s, when he more or less single-handedly broke the Washington-based Heritage Foundation's previously strong anti-Beijing stance. By the late 1990s Heritage had become a key supporter of China's entry into the WTO.

Heritage's change of heart began in the early 1990s, just as AIG mounted an intensive, and ultimately successful, effort to become the first major Western insurance company into New China. The controversy was compounded when in 1996 Heritage hired Taiwan-born Elaine Chao, a future labor secretary in the administration of George W. Bush, as a distinguished fellow. As described by John Judis in the *New Republic,* this appointment seems to have helped precipitate the departures—in apparently contentious, if still largely secret, circumstances— of Richard Fisher and Richard Allen, two of Heritage's most prominent critics of the Beijing regime. Adding gasoline to the flames was the fact that Chao's father, a wealthy Shanghai-born businessman, was believed to have owed his fortune in large measure to business ties to the Beijing leadership.

Shortly afterward a pro-Beijing line became apparent even in the activities of Edwin Feulner, Heritage's president since 1977 and a former stalwart of the Taiwan lobby. According to Judis, Feulner pointedly ignored prodemocracy advocates on a visit to Hong Kong and instead spent his time with Hong Kong's pro-Beijing chief executive, C. H. Tung. Heritage also feted Tung on visits to Washington in 1997 and 1999. In deference to Tung's sensibilities, Heritage even excluded the Hong Kong press from a banquet in Tung's honor.

The controversy bubbled up again in the run-up to the congressional votes to admit China to the WTO. In March 2000, the top Heritage China watcher, Stephen Yates, called on conservatives to stall China's application. As reported by the *Washington Post,* Greenberg protested vociferously to Feulner. Shortly afterward Yates, a Mandarin-speaking former Defense Department official, coauthored a new memorandum titled "How Trade with China Benefits Americans." (This was an impressive early instance of reverse convergence: forcing an offender to recant publicly in the most humiliating way is, of course, a key technique of people control throughout the Confucian world.)

A leading voice at the U.S.-China Business Council and in several other pro-China business organizations, Greenberg had led corporate America's entire effort to get China into the World Trade Organization. In that capacity he had by 1997 become so partisan on China's behalf that the author Robert Dreyfuss dubbed him "the unofficial Chinese ambassador to the United States."

What is clear is that no Chinese ambassador could have been more articulate in glossing over the more troubling aspects of Chinese economic expansionism. At a time when China's belligerent military posture and its human rights violations were causing deep misgivings at all levels in American society, Greenberg presented China's case at a congressional hearing in 1996 in these terms: "Patience is essential. We should step back, take a deep breath and examine carefully the ties that bind us together. . . . An increasing number of Chinese genuinely wonder if the U.S. has embarked on an orchestrated campaign to obstruct their progress."

How much patience is necessary? Quite a lot, it seems, given that more than a decade later, in 2007, Greenberg implicitly admitted that China's acceptance of Western values seemed as far away as ever. This is how he put it in a Council on Foreign Relations report: "Democracy cannot be obtained by outside pressure on a nation but only adopted from within. In the case of China, I doubt that the incredible progress they have made since the end of the Cultural Revolution could have occurred if there were political turmoil in China. We should stop pressing China to adopt a democratic system—that is up to them."

Perhaps the ultimate insight into Greenberg's role in the rise of Confucian economics is that in the 1980s he was reportedly offered the job of deputy director of the Central Intelligence Agency. He had the good taste to turn it down. But it says much about the process by which American foreign policy is made—a process that Greenberg has so assiduously helped shape—that he was offered the job in the first place.

A Confucian Quote Machine

One of the Washington China lobby's greatest achievements has been to establish near-total control over the media's sources of information on sensitive aspects of China policy. In this endeavor it has been crucial to ensure that key Washington think tanks are seeded with the "right" sort of China experts—that is, experts who can be relied on to further Beijing's interests.

The East Asian studies departments at major Washington think tanks are now heavily populated with good Confucians. Undoubtedly the most prominent is the economist Nicholas Lardy, whose record of good Confucianism is outstanding even by Washington standards.

When the American media get hot under the collar about China, Lardy is always there to offer a soothing word. His aim constantly has been to persuade the American media to underestimate both what is happening in China and how fast China's rise is undermining the existing American-led world order.

His temporizing style has been obvious for two decades. After he visited China in the mid-1980s, for instance, he came away outspokenly skeptical. While Chinese leaders were visibly gearing up for a massive export drive, Lardy predicted "a marked slowing in China's trade expansion in the years ahead." In particular he questioned a leaked report that Beijing planned to boost total Chinese trade (imports plus exports) to more than $200 billion by 2000. In a monograph published by the Asia Society in 1987, *China's Entry into the World Economy,* Lardy overlooked the obvious parallels between China's strategy and those of the earlier East Asian miracle economies and called the target implausibly high.

All this was, of course, just what the China trade lobby wanted to hear. The lobby's modus operandi has been to use any means available to calm fears that rising Chinese exports might kill American jobs.

In the event, Chinese policymakers far exceeded their goal. China's exports alone in 2000 came to $249 billion and its imports came to $225 billion, making a grand total of $474 billion, more than double the ambitious target.

Economists' predictions are often wrong, of course, not least about East Asia. But Lardy's errors are systematic. For two decades he has almost invariably undershot in predicting China's economic trajectory. Yet, despite some truly egregious mistakes, Lardy remains Washington's preeminent expert on Sino-American economic relations.

Lardy is an iconic example of a Washington type: a designated expert who owes his prominence not to any record of superior authority but rather to the fact that his insights serve the agenda of powerful lobbying interests. He is a determined apologist both for the Beijing regime and for an American trade policy that subordinates the long-term national interest to corporations' short-term profits. He is prominent in the field not because he is so often right but rather because he is so often wrong—in the approved direction.

Formerly head of a university international studies department in Seattle, he joined the Brookings Institution in Washington in 1995 and quickly became one of Bill Clinton's China advisers. Then in 2003 he became a senior fellow at the Institute for International Economics, and as of 2005 he was the institute's second-highest-paid employee, with a $230,000-a-year package, not counting the lucrative speakers' fees the China lobby showers on its favorites.

In an impressive measure of his visibility, he has long been one of the most frequently quoted China watchers. Meanwhile, he ranked alongside two former American ambassadors to China as a vice chairman of the National Committee on United States–China Relations. This committee initiated the so-called ping-pong diplomacy of the early 1970s and has acted as principal host to Chinese leaders in the United States ever since.

Sometimes Lardy's pro-China spin is so blatant that even the Washington press corps, comatose though it is on China policy, should long ago have spotted it. In 1996, for instance, he helpfully downplayed an announced plan by Beijing to acquire managerial control of Western news agencies in China. Although the principal agencies involved—Reuters and Dow Jones—denounced the plan as an evident effort to censor the news, Lardy offered a more innocent explanation: Beijing was attracted to the media business by the prospect of making large profits! (For the record, investment returns at Dow Jones in particular have been notably mediocre for decades. In any case, the whole thrust of Beijing industrial strategy is directed toward manufacturing and is concerned primarily with jobs, not profits.)

In the immediate aftermath of the Tiananmen massacre, Lardy crusaded against the West's imposing economic sanctions. He was the principal source for a *New York Times* article in which the Chinese economy was presented as a basket case. The article talked of a terrible Chinese balance-of-payments crisis, capital flight, corruption, a tottering banking system, out-of-control subsidies, runaway inflation, and the threat of an uprising by the poor; implying that top Chinese officials were economic ignoramuses, Lardy said China's attempted switch to a market economy had stalled and added: "It is hard to see what the sources of growth will be in the next few years." In fact, in 1989 China's exports rose 10.5 percent—slow growth by Chinese standards but actually three times Japan's performance in that boom year for Japanese industry. China went on in 1990 to boost its exports by another 18.1 percent.

In giving evidence before a Senate subcommittee in 1991, he argued that China's then-incipient trade surplus was a temporary aberration and would soon be followed by deficits. His testimony helped keep American markets open to China's one-way trade policy at a time when memories of the Tiananmen Square massacre were still fresh. Yet it was already clear to most China experts that China was closely following the mercantilist approach to trade of the East Asian economic model. China's trade numbers were headed in the same direction as Japan's, Taiwan's, and South Korea's—up. China's subsequent trade performance resoundingly confounded Lardy's prediction: from a mere $10.4 billion in 1990, China's bilateral surplus with the United States rose to $12.7 billion in 1991, and to $18.3 billion in 1992. As of 2005, it had hit $202 billion—the largest trade imbalance between any two nations in history.

He has consistently served as one of Beijing's most trusted allies in the fight against "China bashing." In 1994, he declared that China was already "one of the most liberal economies in the developing world," citing its increasing openness to foreign direct investment. Yet more than a decade later, this investment still occurred only on the Beijing government's terms.

Those terms included, as we have seen, a ban on acquiring majority control of corporations in key industries, the transfer of vital technologies to China, and the turning of a blind eye to the theft of much of this technology by Chinese rivals.

Perhaps Lardy's greatest service came in helping China's negotiations to join the World Trade Organization. In a fit of apparent naïveté in 1998, he enthusiastically welcomed an ambiguous commitment by the Chinese to respect Western intellectual-property rights. As all subsequent experience has indicated, the commitment was just one more lie in a consistent pattern by Beijing to treat Washington as a rube with a short attention span.

When in 1999 the Chinese made some minimal concessions on agriculture and foreign direct investment, Lardy rushed to welcome the moves as a "dramatic change." In 2000 he warned that if Congress failed to approve permanent normal trade relations for China this would undermine the reformers in Beijing. His reasoning defied common sense. Certainly, as Jim Mann pointed out in the *American Prospect* at the time, it ran directly counter to the tough-talking show-me attitude the United States has taken to Russia. Lardy to the contrary, a similar attitude was surely appropriate with China. After all, if the United States were to hang tougher, this would surely pressure China to make further concessions. It was China that was the supplicant, not the United States. The reformers would be vindicated in saying that without genuine reform China risked being frustrated in its fervid effort to gain full entry to the world trading system.

Even after China's WTO entry had been accomplished, Lardy's wildly erroneous predictions continued. In July 2005, for instance, he predicted an overall Chinese trade surplus of $75 billion to $80 billion for 2005. This proved to be less than half of the actual figure of $161 billion. In commenting to Business Week Online in January 2006, he contrived to sound as if China's trade performance in 2005 somehow reflected weakness rather than strength. Explaining why China's global surplus had risen in 2005, he said: "The big driver isn't on the export side but on the import side. Export growth fell a bit, but import growth was barely half what it was in 2004, so there has been this ballooning of the trade surplus."

Poor China, you might think. Yes, the growth in imports at 17.6 percent was a little lower than the average for China in recent years. But a mercantilist East Asian nation hardly worries about subpar import growth. The real story was China's exports, which grew by 28.4 percent.

Lardy is hardly alone as a China apologist. However, he has more to answer for than most. As a Chinese-speaking East Asia specialist, he has long had a front-row seat in witnessing China's successful emulation of the East Asian trade model. Although he has undoubtedly understood better than almost anyone the mercantilism at the heart of the model, he somehow has failed to alert the American public. In reviewing China's early growth in the 1980s, he never let on how closely China's industrialization resembled that of Japan, Taiwan, and South Korea in earlier decades. Just as between 1961 and 1973 Japan increased its dollar-denominated export revenues more than eightfold, it was clear that the Chinese were hoping to achieve a similarly powerful export expansion in the 1980s and 1990s.

Nor has Lardy ever joined the dots between China's trade policy and its savings performance. As we have seen, all the East Asian economic miracles have been driven by savings. The region's savings rates in turn are based on suppressed consumption. And the cornerstone of the region's suppressed-consumption policy is mercantilist trade.

It should be noted that in 2005, as his long-term record first came under scrutiny in Washington, Lardy began sounding considerably more critical of Chinese economic policies. He even began to win approval among some China realists by arguing that the Chinese yuan was undervalued. This, however, was hardly much of an exercise in dragon baiting. As Robert Samuelson pointed out, China's key policy was not a low yuan but rather its mercantilist agenda of pushing exports ever higher. In any case, it was a reasonable bet that the Beijing regime secretly wanted a stronger yuan but for good negotiating reasons did not say so (better the Americans come as supplicants). After all, with a current account surplus of 7 percent of gross domestic product in 2005, China enjoyed the strongest trade position, in proportionate terms, of any major nation in the last half century.

Behind the Mask: A Writer Censors Himself

Unlike Rupert Murdoch or Maurice Greenberg, the Anglo-Dutch journalist Ian Buruma is hardly known outside the East Asian studies field. For all that, he exemplifies the growing influence of good Confucianism in American life.

Based in recent years in upstate New York and a prolific author on Chinese and Japanese themes, Buruma is principally known as a reviewer of other people's books. It is hardly an exaggeration to say that he functions as the Confucian studies field's literary gatekeeper, at least where books of interest to American policymakers are concerned. His reviews have been published in some of the most prestigious publications in the English language, including the *New York Times,* the *New York Review of Books,* the *New Republic,* the *Spectator,* and the *Financial Times.*

Buruma is important in part because some of the books he reviews are important. Moreover, some of the books he does *not* review are also important. If Westerners are ever to understand the Confucian challenge, it will take books to persuade them. Even the longest magazine article or scholarly paper is too short to sketch in much of the necessary background. To see deeply into the Confucian world, you must first correct myriad Western assumptions concerning supposedly universal aspects of the human condition. It is a classic Confucian catch-22: You cannot know anything until you know everything.

In the circumstances, Buruma's role as reviewer in chief of Confucian-interest books is a pivotal one. Yet, he has not approached his responsibilities impartially. On the contrary, both in public and, even more, in private he has launched unfounded attacks on the characters of key intellectual opponents. In particular he has sought to paint as racist any commentator who posits the existence of a distinctively different East Asian system of economics.

He is noted in the field particularly for his leading role in sabotaging the prospects of a key book published in 1994. This book, a powerfully written, exhaustively researched analysis by one of America's most influential liberal thinkers, packed the potential to induce a veritable sea change in American attitudes to the Confucian economic phenomenon. As such it was—with reason—viewed by top government officials in East Asia as a major geopolitical challenge, and, as is the tradition in the field, the author was subjected to a highly coordinated series of ad hominem attacks. The flavor of this campaign can be gleaned from the fact that the author's children were told by teachers at their Washington school that their father was a racist. One of the ultimate sources of this charge was a five-thousand-word review in the *New Republic* in which Buruma, in sneeringly contemptuous terms, portrayed the author as a "Neo-Orientalist"—a charge that in the context carried an unmistakable implication of racism. Yet Buruma offered no evidence in support of the proposition—because no evidence existed. The charge was a fabrication. The entire campaign was a classic demonstration of the principle that if enough people make an accusation, no matter how obviously false, it will stick. (So as not to contribute unwittingly to Buruma's defamatory agenda, I have withheld this writer's name. This is necessary because the evidence is that once people start alleging racism, no matter how groundless the charge may be, some doubt always lingers in the minds of those not directly familiar with the facts.)

Buruma is important too because he exemplifies a pattern in which influential positions in the American media are occupied by people who implicitly or explicitly censor themselves.

Take, for instance, his book *Bad Elements: Chinese Rebels from Los Angeles to Beijing.* This was a study of political activism in the Chinese diaspora. As such it represented a golden opportunity for a capable writer to tackle major controversies. Not the least of these was a long-standing suspicion that the Chinese diaspora had been penetrated by undercover agents of the Chinese Communist Party. A careful look at this question would have provided not only compelling reading for the general public but crucial guidance for Western policymakers.

Given that Buruma had earned a degree in Chinese literature from the

University of Leyden and had lived much of his life in the Confucian world, he was better qualified than most to investigate the infiltration allegation and to help identify the fakes. Instead, he consistently looked the other way. The closest he came to addressing the infiltration charge was this comment in his first chapter: "In the course of talking to Chinese exiles and activists, I found almost no one with anything good to say about anyone else. Mention a name, and I would be told that person was a liar, a government agent, a spy, an opportunist, a gangster, an extremist, or corrupted by sex and power."

Buruma treated each of the purported dissidents he interviewed as equally legitimate, thereby boosting the credibility of some undoubted fakes. Even when Harry Wu, an internationally famous dissident whose credentials as a genuine thorn in Beijing's side are beyond doubt, questioned the bona fides of other dissidents, Buruma changed the subject. Unlike many other self-described Chinese dissidents, Wu has suffered deeply for his beliefs, having spent nineteen years in some of the grimmest prisons imaginable. Buruma's published account of his breakfast interview with Wu focused bizarrely on Wu's table manners. Describing Wu as "fiercely spearing his ham and scrambled eggs," Buruma added: "He gobbled his breakfast up in big mouthfuls. The sound of his mouth working on his ham and eggs was all that broke, for a few seconds at a time, his tirade against his fellow Chinese."

Other than the reference to Wu's "tirade against his fellow Chinese," nothing of Wu's insights into the infiltration issue was mentioned. It was as if a Chinese journalist had interviewed Simon Wiesenthal but in the resulting article had chosen to focus on the Holocaust survivor's chopstick technique rather than his Nazi-hunting work.

Buruma's coverage of Japan's war legacy has been even more troublingly incomplete. As we saw in chapter 7, this is a subject on which both Beijing and Tokyo have much to hide. Beijing after all has cooperated with Tokyo in covering up the fact that imperial Japan's victims have never been compensated. In 1994 Buruma was presented with a unique opportunity to expose this cover-up in *The Wages of Guilt: Memories of War in Germany and Japan,* a book contrasting German and Japanese approaches to war guilt. Nonetheless he remained silent on the compensation controversy.

Defending his approach at a public meeting in Tokyo some years ago, Buruma said that the word "compensation" did appear in the book. He then pointed to a single sentence referring to the fact that some victims of one little-known Japanese atrocity had never been compensated. The passage was couched in such a way that the uninitiated might assume this was exceptional and that Japan had otherwise pursued a compensation policy broadly similar to that of Germany. Such an assumption would have been encouraged by Buruma's tone of contempt for Tokyo's various war apologies—a tone implying that he would be the last person to cover for Tokyo on an issue like compensation.

Perhaps the most Confucian aspect of this affair was how *The Wages of Guilt* was received in the West. The book was widely commended, often by top literary figures or prominent experts on East Asia. In the *Christian Science Monitor,* the Harvard-based Japan watcher Herbert Bix praised the book's "unusual reach." In *Foreign Affairs,* the famed Japanese American neoconservative Francis Fukuyama talked of "an absorbing and important book." In the London *Times,* the top British academic Brendan Simms described it as "highly informative." In the *Financial Times,* A. C. Grayling found it "salutary reading." And in Canada, it was short-listed for the Lionel Gerber Prize, one of the world's most important nonfiction awards.

Conspicuously absent was any mention of the book's lacunas. It is clear that most of the celebrity reviewers had no idea the book was wanting. Unfamiliar with the finer points of East Asia watching, they simply assumed from Buruma's tone that Japan's compensation policy had been as unstinting as Germany's. This assumption was clearly implied in a review by the British writer Paul Johnson.

Of course, Buruma's economy with the truth could hardly have gone unnoticed by professional East Asia watchers. But even they failed to raise the matter. They knew only too well that a frank discussion would have infuriated their friends and sponsors in East Asia—and cut them off from a huge flow of speaking opportunities, consulting fees, research subventions, and much more. It would also have infuriated Buruma, who could be depended upon to seek revenge via his book-reviewing activities.

Why would someone of Buruma's standing—he is a journalist of some significance—put his name to such an incomplete account? Let's leave that to posterity. Let's also pass over the question of why Buruma has devoted so much of his career to book reviewing (an occupation whose "hourly rate," as any reviewer can tell you, makes the wages at Wal-Mart look princely).

One point, however, needs emphasizing: the idea that Buruma was unaware of the book's incompleteness is not tenable. He worked in his youth for the *Japan Times,* a semi-official Foreign Ministry mouthpiece noted among its staff for its "self-control" on the compensation issue.

Furthermore, as someone who was born and brought up in Holland, Buruma was undoubtedly aware of his home country's pathbreaking role in the compensation controversy. As far back as the 1980s Dutch feminists had begun pressing Tokyo to compensate the so-called comfort women (many of whom were Dutch citizens captured in the then Dutch East Indies). Although little of the Dutch controversy has ever been published in English, it has repeatedly made headlines in the Netherlands. Almost the first person Dutch editors would have turned to for expert commentary was an internationally known Dutch writer with high-level access in Tokyo. His name: Ian Buruma.

In this chapter, we have seen how deeply Confucian influence has already penetrated at every level in the American intellectual establishment. If the American mind is increasingly at risk, what remains of the traditional America we were all brought up to respect? It is time for a reckoning.

NINE

Globalism *or* Democracy?

A few months after the United States invaded Iraq in 2003, President George W. Bush received a worried Senator Joseph Biden in the Oval Office. Suggesting that the post-Saddam era was not proceeding as planned, Biden, a prowar Democrat who was then the ranking minority member on the Senate Foreign Relations Committee, pressed Bush on the problem of Iraq's Shiite-Sunni factionalism and the power vacuum that had been created by the disbandment of the Iraqi army. As recounted in a recent book by Lee Iacocca and Catherine Whitney, Biden recalled that Bush seemed preternaturally serene. America was on the right course and all would be fine, said Bush. "Mr. President," Biden finally asked, "how can you be so sure when you don't yet know all the facts?" Bush reached over and put a steadying hand on Biden's shoulder. "My instincts," he said. "My instincts."

In those two words, Bush unwittingly defined what was wrong with his Iraq policy. By extension the fact that he could affect such casualness on a matter of such geopolitical significance spoke volumes about the general context in which American foreign policy has been created in recent years. Particularly in East

Asia, American policymakers have far too often allowed their instincts to trump the facts.

As we consider how China's rise will change the world order, this is assuredly no time to rely on instincts. Rather, we must focus on facts and let them lead us where they may. We must consider not just some of the facts but all of them, *especially those facts that seem at odds with our instincts.*

Whatever Westerners' instincts may suggest, the facts presented in this book show that the world is changing in a way that is clearly at odds with Western expectations. In reviewing our analysis, let's start with a consideration of how misguided has been the general intellectual climate in American policymaking in recent decades.

The Times Are Out of Joint

If the suddenness of China's rise were the only issue here, it would be clear that we were sailing into uncharted waters. Add the rapidity of America's relative decline and we have more than a hint of epochal new forces at work.

Even before these developments became widely evident, there were already several premonitions that the Western-defined world economic system was in trouble. Consider some of the surprises American policymakers and economic commentators have encountered in the last sixty years:

The rise of Japan. In the early years after World War II, virtually every American economic expert took a remarkably unflattering view of Japan's prospects. American occupation officials, for instance, assumed Japan's post–World War II role would be merely to make "knickknacks" for richer nations. Speaking in 1951, Earl H. Pritchard, a founder of the Association for Asian Studies and a noted authority on both Japan and China, summed up the scholarly consensus in these terms: "Japan is going to have a very serious difficulty of making a go of it economically." To say the least, the economics profession's subsequent embarrassment was intense. "Not only did American economists not predict the Japanese miracle but they have never been able to explain it," says Chalmers Johnson.

The triumph of mercantilism. The case for free trade constitutes one of the principal load-bearing pillars on which the entire edifice of Western economic thought is supported. Yet that pillar is now visibly crumbling. In the early days when Western theorists first noticed Japan's startling combination of fast growth and rigid mercantilism, they dismissed it as an aberration and argued that Japan would have done even better if it had pursued orthodox Western policies. Now that half a dozen East Asian nations have emulated both Japan's mercantilism and its growth, all bets are off.

An ever shifting definition of the benefits of trade. Just as the Bush administration has experienced "negative mission creep" in its constantly revised definitions of success in Iraq, economists have faced similar difficulties with America's free trade policy. In the 1970s they confidently presented trade liberalization as a formula for increasing America's then still healthy trade surpluses. Later they promised merely that liberalization would help restore American trade balances to breakeven. By the 1990s, the spiralling deficits forced a radical rethink. This time, in a tacit admission that liberalization had weakened America's trade performance, the economists argued that trade deficits did not matter anymore. The main benefit now was that by "showing a good example," America could help win authoritarian nations like China for democracy.

Second coming of the strong state. Westerners have long held that the more personal freedom a nation's citizens are given, the more productive they will be. It is a view that was propounded with exceptional ideological fervor in the last thirty years, with the result that the United States and to a lesser extent many other Western nations have dismantled much of the regulation that had previously provided some structural backbone to their economies (and in particular had shielded them somewhat from the industrial policies of other nations). Yet even as the state has become ever weaker in the West, there has been no similar development in the Confucian region. Quite the contrary, a strongly interventionist state has clearly played a major role in the rise not only of Japan, but also of both South Korea and Taiwan. Interventionism has been manifest not only in highly detailed industrial policies but in a strong role by the state in channeling bank lending.

The humbling of the Western press. The most respected organs of the Western press have constantly blindsided themselves—and their

readers—in their coverage of the entire Confucian region. In particular
they have repeatedly predicted "Westernizing" developments—such as
the breakup of Japan's keiretsus and Korea's chaebols and a meltdown in
permanent employment—that have never materialized. A future editor-
in-chief of the *Economist* wrote a book in 1989 predicting that by 2000
Japan would be running trade deficits. In reality Japan's trade *surpluses*
continued to soar. The worst offenders in misstating the facts of East
Asian economics have been publications such as the *Economist*, the *Wall
Street Journal*, and the *New York Times*, which are otherwise generally respected for the accuracy and honesty of their coverage.

In view of facts like these, it has been clear for a long time that there is
something wrong with how Western observers view the the non-Western
world. That said, all the above surprises pale in comparison with the one we will
now consider: the rise of China.

China: Fastest Export Growth in History

In the 1950s and 1960s Mao Zedong often called the United States a "paper
tiger." It was an epithet that drew only laughter from Americans. Half a century
later, no one is laughing—at least no one who knows the facts. On many key
economic measures China has already turned the tables. Only the most obvious
is trade. Whereas the United States in the 1950s and 1960s generally enjoyed
the world's largest trade surpluses, today that distinction has passed, of course,
to China.

Behind this performance is a truly phenomenal rise in China's exports.
As of 2006, these totaled $974 billion—just $50 billion less than America's
figure of $1.024 trillion. As I complete this book in 2007, all the evidence is
that China will pass the United States *this year* in total exports. By comparison, in 1956—the year Mao first used the paper tiger epithet—America outexported China more than ten to one. As recently as 1997 America's
advantage was still nearly four to one. Since 1979, China's dollar-denominated export revenues have increased by more than 16 percent a year on
average—probably the highest sustained rate of export growth of any nation
in history.

To Americans and Europeans, the most obvious aspect of this export-or-die strategy has been that Beijing has persuaded thousands of Western corporations to set up export-oriented subsidiaries on Chinese soil. Less obviously but almost equally important, Beijing has invested massively in providing exporters with a first-class infrastructure. Much investment has gone into telecommunications networks, for instance; even more has gone into roads, railways, ports, and airports. Meanwhile Beijing has fostered the development of countless indigenous manufacturing companies to supply parts and materials to China's Western-owned export platforms. The result is that the China-sourced content in Chinese exports has increased dramatically in the last decade—and with it the size of China's current account surpluses.

For the United States the most significant part of this story is that, compared to the earlier East Asian industrializers, China has only just started. If China were ever to match Japan's per capita income, it would be twenty times larger than it is today. Put another way, the Chinese economy would be more than four times America's.

Rubbing salt in the wounds of Western free-market theory is that China's government is one of the world's most repressive. The authorities often use the death penalty for nonviolent crimes such as fraud, forgery, tax evasion, and political offenses. Although they now try to hide from Westerners their notorious practice of staging executions in packed public stadiums, such events reportedly continue even today in the more remote parts of the country.

Having seen what oppression can do, now let's consider how the United States—the world's greatest exemplar of democracy and individual freedom—has been doing.

American Power: Implosion at Lightning Speed

Just sixty years ago the United States was not only by far the strongest power of that time but of any time. Neither the Roman nor the Chinese empires ever came close to the global influence America held then. But the speed of America's relative decline in subsequent years must count as a record in world history.

It is chastening to recall that it was precisely because its economy was so strong that the United States had won World War II. American troops may have been no less brave than those of Germany and Japan, but what made the difference was that, thanks to the then seemingly unchallengeable American lead in advanced manufacturing, they enjoyed a wide edge in matériel.

Even though the war had been the most destructive in history, the United States seemed to have little difficulty financing a tremendous worldwide postwar industrial recovery. These days, by contrast, the burden of financing recovery merely in Iraq—a Third World nation with fewer than 30 million people—is adding visibly to the strains on the United States budget. Just how weak the United States had become was already evident even earlier in the fact that, as Paul Craig Roberts has noted, the United States could never have gone to war in the first place without the implicit say-so of its main creditors, the governments of China and Japan (which could have brought financial markets up short had they signalled their disapproval as the United States moved its troops into position for the coming hostilities).

True, not every aspect of America's economic predicament looks equally disastrous. America's share of world output, for instance, still seems respectable. Measured at market exchange rates, America's output recently represented fully 28 percent of the world total. Although this is a mere one-half of the proportion in 1945, it nonetheless seems to represent incontrovertible evidence that the United States remains—as the globalists love to assert—by far the world's greatest economic superpower.

The trouble is that this calculation, based as it is on an unrealistically inflated value of the dollar, is a statistical illusion. For well over a decade the dollar has been on the economic equivalent of a heart-lung machine. With each year that passes, the scale of the necessary East Asian support has increased. Absent such support, no floor would be in sight for the erstwhile "mighty" dollar. As William Holstein, author of *The Japanese Power Game* and a former top editor at *Business Week,* observed on a visit to Japan in 2007, it is a fair bet that, if allowed to float freely, the dollar would fall by at least half against the Japanese yen. And an even greater fall would appear to be necessary against several other currencies, not least the Chinese yuan. This, of course, would bring a commensurate plunge in America's stated share of world output and would further curtail America's ability to project economic power abroad.

Any analysis of America's economic weakness must start with trade. *America's imports now exceed its exports by nearly two to one.* This is a truly extraordinary position for any nation, let alone for one that thinks of itself as the world's sole superpower. Each dollar by which imports exceed exports represents an extra dollar the United States must somehow borrow abroad. America's current account deficit, at 6.5 percent of gross domestic product in 2006, represented the largest percentage deficit incurred by any major nation in peacetime since Italy in 1924. Moreover, whereas Italy's 1924 performance—a deficit of 7.7 percent—was temporary and was cut in half the following year, there is no solution in sight to the American trade problem. Quite the contrary, absent a wrenching policy reversal that would be disruptive not only for the United States but for the entire world economy, the problem is set to get progressively worse. Even with such a policy reversal it would take at least ten years, and more like fifteen, of economic restraint by the American nation to restore America's trade position to the black.

At the root of America's trade problem is an implosion in America's once world-dominating manufacturing base. If America is ever to dig itself out of its hole, it must stage a massive renaissance in manufacturing and thereby win back lost markets around the world. Manufacturing industries are crucial because in general their products are much more exportable than those of service industries. As I pointed out in my 1999 book *In Praise of Hard Industries: Why Manufacturing, Not the Information Economy, Is the Key to Future Prosperity,* American manufacturers have historically exported about eleven times as much per unit of overall output as service companies.

Advanced manufacturing in particular is key because it not only is highly capital-intensive, but also offers great potential for a sophisticated nation to accumulate large amounts of secret production know-how. Capital-intensive, know-how-intensive manufacturing powerfully leverages each worker's productivity and thus makes possible disproportionately high wages—wages that are invulnerable to undercutting by the less-well-equipped workers of poorer nations.

The United States used to dominate almost right across the board in advanced manufacturing. Now leadership has passed to Japan and to a lesser extent to Germany—and the results are stunningly apparent in the ability of these nations to maintain and enhance their position in world trade even in the teeth of a rapidly rising Chinese challenge. Indeed, manufacturing industries in both Japan and Germany have continued strongly to boost their exports *despite the fact that they now pay factory-floor wages above American levels.* Between 1999 and 2006, Germany's trade went from a current account deficit of $21 billion to a surplus of $135 billion, while Japan's current account surplus jumped from $107 billion to $174 billion.

Although the United States should long ago have acted decisively to shore up its manufacturing base, the sad fact is that in the last twenty years total American manufacturing jobs have fallen by about one-third. No revival is even remotely in prospect. On the contrary, given the prevailing combination of an overvalued dollar and a totally open domestic market, American manufacturing companies are rapidly shutting down what little remains of their domestic production capacity and shifting it abroad. Just since George W. Bush took office in 2001, 3 million manufacturing jobs have been lost.

The aerospace industry provides a particularly compelling example. This used to be one of America's greatest net exporters and as such represented one of four main manufacturing pillars underpinning America's seemingly effortless economic superiority (the other pillars were electronics, automobiles, and production equipment). Even with wages twice to five times those in Germany and Japan in the first decades after World War II, American aerospace companies were dominant virtually right across the board, and they remained a major contributor to the balance of payments into the 1980s. Today, however, more and more of the advanced components and materials on which the industry depends are being outsourced from other advanced nations, particularly Japan, but also Germany, Italy, South Korea, and Britain. This has resulted in major layoffs of American workers. Between 1990 and 2004 alone, the industry's total workforce fell from 1,120,000 to a mere 593,000.

The most spectacular manifestation of the trend has been in the new Boeing 787, which will be largely foreign-made. Outside experts calculate that only about 30 percent of the plane's manufacturing will be conducted in the United States. By comparison the 777, which was launched in 1994, was about 70 percent built in the United States, and the 727, launched in 1963, was 98 percent.

The same pattern of rapidly falling employment is apparent in almost all the formerly strong exporting industries. Electronics, for instance, is another disaster zone. So is the automobile industry.

America's trade problem is being exacerbated by the increased outsourcing of advanced services. The trend has been driven in part by a plunge in the cost of international telecommunications. Another factor has been that, with ever-cheaper computing, advanced services have become ever more labor-intensive. Formerly, many advanced services—the writing of computer software, for instance—were extremely capital-intensive and thus there was little incentive to move jobs abroad.

As low-wage countries have become rapidly more proficient in tackling more and more complicated service tasks, their exports to the United States have soared. The trend has been led by India, which started in the 1980s by doing humble data-entry work. This involved mainly keying handwritten and printed materials into computerized form. Then the Indians got into software and call centers. Now they are moving into medical testing, accounting, and legal work.

All this is more disconcerting considering that many commentators in the 1990s raised false hopes that the New Economy would prove America's economic salvation. As I pointed out in *In Praise of Hard Industries,* however, such hopes were unrealistic, as already then the United States had lost whatever comparative advantage it may once have enjoyed in the more important areas of advanced services.

With outsourcing now undermining the American job base from both the manufacturing and services ends, the picture that emerges is reminiscent of Barry McGuire's rollicking hit song from the mid-1960s—the one that went "Three wheels on my wagon and I am still rolling along . . ."

In the song, all the wheels eventually came off. The American economy is headed the same way.

Biggest Change Agent Since the Caravel?

The contrasting economic fortunes of the United States and China in recent decades are closely related. In large measure they reflect the fact that the Confucian economic system is engaged in a zero-sum game with Western capitalism.

The key to the entire Confucian economic phenomenon is a revolutionary new savings regime in which consumption is systematically suppressed. This creates enormous savings surpluses that are then, by virtue of detailed industrial policies, deployed in boosting productivity in key industries—in the jargon, targeted industries. Not the least such industries are ones that were previously mainstays of the American economy.

Manifestations of China's version of the suppressed-consumption policy run the gamut. Consumer credit is tightly curtailed. A wall of trade barriers and an undervalued yuan block the Chinese people's access to foreign consumer goods. Much consumption potential is choked off by the simple expedient of allowing government-controlled companies to fleece the consumer. By charging exorbitant prices, such companies suppress the sales volume of key consumer goods. Their high profit margins are then channeled into investments in the latest production technologies. Meanwhile zoning restrictions keep housing both extremely cramped and extremely expensive. This enables government-owned land development companies to skim off huge profits from China's booming housing market; and in one way or another this money too generally goes into improving industrial productivity.

Following in the footsteps of the earlier Confucian industrializers, Beijing uses the banking system as its main instrument in directing savings flows into favored industries. To this end it maintains majority stakes in most of China's significant banks. The banks favor industries where, because of the ready availability of new, more advanced production technologies, investment promises to yield disproportionately large productivity increases. Suitable cartelization enables manufacturers to maintain strong pricing in consumer markets while moving in lockstep to ever more advanced production methods. A key point is that the cartels ensure that older, less efficient production capacity is shut down, thus minimizing the risk of dangerously destabilizing capacity gluts and bouts of below-cost selling.

China's epic version of suppressed consumption has generated savings rates of typically more than 40 percent of gross domestic product in recent years. Saving on this scale has hitherto been virtually unheard of not only in the West but even in other parts of the Confucian region. In the short run the suppressed-consumption policy's effect has been to condemn the Chinese people to much lower living standards than they would otherwise enjoy. The upside is that the resulting boost to investment means that the rate of increase in productivity—and by extension in living standards—has probably been the fastest in world history. In the long run therefore the Chinese people can aspire to an excellent return on their involuntary sacrifices (at least those of them who survive to collect the social dividends).

Because the suppressed-consumption concept blatantly violates China's WTO commitments, it has had to be hidden from Western view. One key consequence is that the Chinese authorities—and their spokesmen in the Western economics community—have invented an entirely misleading explanation for the high savings rates: the Chinese people, it is said, are exceptionally concerned about the future and thus salt away an exceptionally large amount of their incomes in savings. The truth is, of course, that if insecurity were all that was needed to boost a nation's savings rate, the whole Third World would long ago have saved its way into the First.

In the early decades after World War II, it was perhaps understandable that there was little curiosity in the West about the unnaturally high savings rates that were beginning to emerge in East Asia. Given that China boasts more than six times the population of all the earlier Confucian industrializers combined, however, the emergence of the Confucian savings regimen now clearly represents one of the great turning points in history. Economic leadership of the world is passing from nations that have long championed individual freedom to others that often pursue diametrically opposite policies. In the fullness of time the rise of the Confucian savings phenomenon may well induce the biggest transformation of the world power map since the first Portuguese and Spanish voyages of discovery more than five hundred years ago. Yet, far from comprehending the scale of the Confucian challenge, the American establishment persists with policies that assume it away.

America's Road to Ruin

If madness is doing the same thing over and over again and expecting different results, future historians are going to ask sharp questions about the American nation's psychological state in recent decades.

Up to the early 1980s it was perhaps reasonable for experts and nonexperts alike to defer to David Ricardo's wisdom on trade. Certainly most professional observers, this writer included, took it on faith that Ricardo's early-nineteenth-century trade model would work in the end for the United States. But with every trade agreement that was signed, the evidence that, in modern conditions, there was something wrong with Ricardo's theory became ever clearer.

The pattern has been depressingly predictable. Each trade agreement was first presented to the American public as a marvelous opportunity for American manufacturers to win new markets and generally advance their position against foreign competitors. Then, with negligible exceptions, the big export opportunities never materialized, and America's trade position just ratcheted into an ever weaker position.

By the mid-1980s the writing was unmistakably on the wall. It was at this time that, in a desperate measure to try to turn around the trade trend, the Reagan administration acquiesced in a massive devaluation of the American dollar. In the subsequent two years, the dollar fell by nearly half against the Japanese yen, and almost as much against other key currencies. Yet the U.S. trade deficits not only did not disappear but actually worsened.

Nevertheless, the Washington establishment continued to ignore the warnings and instead in the mid-1990s pressed ahead with the most ill-advised one-way free-trade deal yet: the creation of the World Trade Organization. The WTO was established as the successor to the General Agreement on Tariffs and Trade (GATT), which had previously governed America's trade relations. As Chalmers Johnson has pointed out, the shift from GATT to the WTO constituted a historic, if well-hidden, shift in American trade policy. GATT had promoted a quite limited and pragmatic agenda in which the United States opened its markets to a select group of allies and in return received their support in the cold war. By contrast, the WTO was founded on an ideological commitment to universal free trade. It was dogma for the sake of dogma and thus constituted a far larger, less focused, and less manageable economic experiment—and from the point of view of the American national interest, one that was much more gratuitously risky. Moreover, it was being undertaken despite obvious evidence that the original GATT arrangement had, contrary to all expectations at the time of GATT's founding in the late 1940s, proved costly to America's economic prospects. (The assumption behind the GATT quid pro quo had been that the United States was so superior in its fundamental culture and institutions that it could afford to indulge the allies without risking any serious diminution in its lead. By the mid-1990s most of the allies had broadly caught up, and both Japan and Germany clearly had leapfrogged ahead in key areas of advanced manufacturing.)

In espousing the WTO, Washington was giving away the store. In a devastating article in the *American Prospect* in 1997, Chalmers Johnson showed how clearly the WTO would work to America's disadvantage. On the one hand, the WTO did not outlaw the nontariff barriers that East Asian nations use to protect their markets; on the other, it did outlaw direct attempts by the United States to retaliate against such protectionism.

Johnson explained:

Tariffs are no longer important in international trade, but so-called non-tariff barriers such as national industrial development policies, regulations with differential effects on foreign and domestic firms, unique standards, collusion among a country's firms to keep out foreigners (China's state-owned sector, Japan's *keiretsu*, South Korea's *chaebol*), governmental administrative guidance of privately owned enterprises, and the failure to enforce antimonopoly laws are all beyond the scope of the WTO. On the other hand,

Section 301 of the American Trade Act, which allows the U.S. government to assist American firms facing access barriers in foreign markets, is explicitly barred. Unless and until the WTO faces up to the Catch 22 in its charter, it remains a menace to the livelihoods of all working Americans.

Of course, the WTO has ostensible mechanisms for punishing nations that break the rules. The operative word is ostensible.

The founding of the WTO led directly to America's next major trade fiasco: the opening of the American market to China, a nation that both economically and politically stood for values utterly at odds with those of the United States.

The decision to throw the American market completely open to China was wrong on several counts. The first of the problems was on the American side. The United States had not yet even begun to digest previous trade liberalization measures vis-a-vis other nations. With the Commerce Department and the United States Trade Representative's Office already grossly overextended trying to make earlier trade agreements work, a new one with China was the last straw.

In any case, as Chalmers Johnson pointed out in 1997, China's economic arrangements were so incompatible with America's that the whole concept of a balanced, fair Sino-American trade relationship was out of the question. Referring to the Ricardo case for free trade, he commented: "It sounds great but to work in practice, free trade requires tolerable symmetry—a mutual commitment among participating nations to disavow promotion of domestic industry at the expense of trading partners."

He added: "In a sense, the China trade problem is not a trade problem at all but one of 'systems friction.' . . . One of the secrets of China's development strategy, which borrows heavily from the experience of Japan and other successful Asian nations, is to bend the rules and norms of capitalism in order to achieve national wealth and power. In this view, economics is inevitably a zero-sum game, in which some nations win and others lose. China has never aimed at becoming a 'market economy' but rather at engaging and exploiting other economies to become a great power."

Even setting aside the fact that the Chinese system is fundamentally mercantilist, a key problem is that there are many internal barriers to trade within the country—with the farcical result that it is often easier for a manufacturer in, say, Shanghai to ship his output to the United States than to Guangdong or Chongqing. Moreover, as became clear in a spate of tainted-food scandals in

2007, China is scandalously lacking in the sort of First World controls necessary to protect the world's consumers from fraud and criminal negligence.

China's unreadiness was, however, considered beside the point as Washington negotiated with Beijing in the late 1990s. The outcome had been predetermined by corporate America. China would be admitted as a full member of the world trading system, even though Russia, which in many ways was better qualified for membership, was to be kept out. Almost without exception, American executives were motivated not by any export prospects in China—which even with the best will in the world would for the most part remain negligible for years to come—but with outsourcing. In other words, this was just another opportunity to shut down capacity at home and move jobs overseas. All the while, however, the American press generally presented closer trade relations with China as a vast new opportunity for American exporters.

The root of the problem is in American corporate chieftains' quarterly efforts to "make their numbers." It is easy for Beijing to arrange business conditions so that huge profits are virtually guaranteed for any compliant American corporation. It is a process that makes shooting fish in a barrel seem like a fair challenge. In return for the license to print money in China (at least for the duration of the next few quarters), American corporations merely have to transfer crucial technologies to Chinese soil.

For just a few years of profits, America is giving away a technological inheritance that took generations to accumulate. Depleted of its reserves of proprietary production know-how, the United States loses most of its comparative advantage in world markets. Now that virtually all restrictions on the movement of American capital have been abolished, there is generally no reason anymore why corporate America should invest at home. Better to invest abroad, particularly in China, where the government makes it so easy for the collaborationist-minded to turn a profit.

Neither the American nation nor the American workforce has had any influence over the process. Even American shareholders are not consulted—and if the truth were frankly disclosed to them, they would in many cases oppose the deals as undermining their long-term interests.

The big gainers are in the first instance just a few thousand top corporate executives who reap huge returns via bonuses and stock options. Meanwhile, bloated short-term corporate profits make possible an orgy of influence buying not only in Washington but in the American media and in the universities. The silence of designated whistle-blowers must be bought, thus obviating any risk that a suddenly aroused American people might intervene to stop the looting of the nation's industrial patrimony.

Incompatibility of the Two Systems

Globalism is clearly not delivering the promised economic dividends for the American nation. But an even bigger problem in many ways is hidden just below the surface: the tectonic tensions radical globalism is engendering between the West and the Confucian region. The least controversial way of putting this is that Confucian societies are stronger than our Western societies. Although this judgment is likely to be hotly contested by those who, like George W. Bush on Iraq, trust to their "instincts," observers who know the East Asian region have noticed a consistent pattern—a pattern that, to say the least, is not encouraging.

One public indication that all is not well has been Rupert Murdoch's about-face in his relations with Beijing. As we saw in chapter 8, he was suddenly persuaded in the mid-1990s to switch from principled opposition to the Beijing regime to blatant collaboration with it.

It is, of course, possible that a Machiavellian Murdoch intended his initial hostile stance merely as an opening gambit in securing the best terms. The balance of probability, however, is against this. After all, he did not need to go public with his original challenge to Beijing. Nor did he have to use such provocative language. If he was merely jockeying for bargaining position, he did not have to do so much damage to his reputation in the West.

To people familiar with the Confucian region, the Murdoch about-face was par for the course—merely a public version of something they have witnessed privately dozens of times among friends and associates. One day a prominent Westerner—be he a journalist, a scholar, a business executive, or a diplomat—is an uncensored font of truth. The next he has gone silent (actually catatonic is often a better description). The day after that he is spreading falsehoods about his erstwhile close friends and colleagues fighting the good fight against the implications of Confucian economics.

So far, foreigners in China seem to have had more success in upholding Western ethics than their colleagues elsewhere in the region. But the signs are not encouraging. There is, for instance, the fact that virtually every Western employer in China seems to be complicit in enforcing the one-child policy— often to the point of pressuring women to have abortions. It seems clear that in future years things can only get worse. So far, with the cold war not yet forgotten, both Westerners in China and their superiors back home have been alert to potential problems and thus have had their guard up. Meanwhile, at least up to the time of China's entry into the World Trade Organization, their Chinese hosts have had a strong incentive to avoid the more controversial techniques they might otherwise resort to.

But the evidence from other parts of the Confucian region is that powerful pressures are brought to bear on any Western resident who insists on upholding the Western truth ethic. Such people rarely thrive in East Asia. Just the most obvious of the risks they run is character assassination.

The authorities make extensive use of the military concept of "mass" in countering whistleblowers. Thus if one person utters an unwelcome truth, ten ostensibly impeccable authorities will instantly be mobilized to discredit him, and a complicit audience of a hundred collaborators will nod in unison as he is denounced as either psychologically unbalanced or evilly intentioned. Meanwhile his few friends and allies will be pressured into silence. In the eyes of uninformed bystanders, he cannot win. They will ask, "If what you say is true, why are you the only one saying it?" Irrespective of how well informed he is or how ethically motivated, he will not prevail. Generally the first thing that happens is that he loses his job. Faced with apparently overwhelming evidence against him, his company simply lets him go.

The most memorable manifestations of the denunciation weapon at work came during the Cultural Revolution in Maoist China. For the most part, however, as Ivan Hall has pointed out, denunciation campaigns in modern East Asia are conducted discreetly and thus are difficult or impossible to document.

The story of E. Herbert Norman is an exception. Born in Japan in 1909 to Canadian Methodist missionary parents, Norman was not only one of the most linguistically proficient scholars in the history of Japanology but one of the most ethical and intellectually acute. He went on to become a Canadian diplomat and in that capacity was continually dogged by allegations that he was a crypto-Communist (as well as a homosexual). The ostensible source of these allegations originally was General Douglas MacArthur's chief of intelligence operations in occupied Japan, the controversial American general Charles Willoughby. It seems clear, however, that Willoughby was a surrogate for cronies in the Japanese establishment, who had good reason to fear what Norman might otherwise have done in opposing their secret agenda to sabotage American reform efforts.

The last straw for Norman came in 1957, when his close friend from Cambridge University in the 1930s, the Japanese economist Shigeto Tsuru, testified against him before a subcommittee of the United States Senate. This reopened a case that had been closed after Norman had been cleared in 1952. Norman committed suicide the following week. Tsuru meanwhile went on to become a major figure in postwar Japanese economics.

All the evidence is that Tsuru had been coerced into destroying his friend. According to Norman's biographer Roger Bowen, Tsuru was under no compulsion to testify and did so voluntarily. Moreover, not only had Norman and Tsuru been friends for more than twenty years, but Norman had gone out of his way to help Tsuru at great personal risk in wartime England in 1942. It is probably not a coincidence that the convicted war criminal Nobusuke Kishi had become prime minister of Japan just a month before Tsuru dropped his bombshell. Kishi, widely regarded as the principal architect not only of the East Asian economic system but of modern Japan's antidemocratic political system, would not have relished having someone as capable and potentially well positioned as Norman who otherwise seemed destined to go to the top in Canadian diplomacy as an interlocutor in the critical first years of the Japanese economic miracle.

Defamation apart, coercion in various forms is a major problem for Westerners in East Asia. The most obvious manifestation is the mechanism of selective enforcement. Westerners who do business in China—or in any of the other major Confucian nations—have to put themselves on the wrong side not only of local law but also often of Western law.

The problem is exceptionally acute for Americans because American laws, much more than those of other Western nations, apply extraterritorially. Though American laws often extend to China, they were not written with modern Chinese conditions in mind.

A particular problem is the need to bribe officials. This constitutes a blatant breach of America's Foreign Corrupt Practices Act. Thus any American who hands over a bribe is potentially subject to severe penalties—up to five years in prison—under American law. Once he gives his first bribe, he is forever afterward a hostage to the vagaries of selective enforcement. The Chinese recipient may be an agent provocateur—but even if he is a bona fide bribee, higher authorities within the Chinese establishment undoubtedly have ways of making him talk.

There is also the problem that many Western residents of East Asia quickly seem to lose their moral compass where sex is concerned. It is no secret that for those who take a relaxed view of these things, sexual opportunities abound in the region. For married Westerners an obvious risk is entrapment. Unlike their local colleagues, they are bound not only by a very different view of marital responsibilities but by unforgiving divorce laws. All this suggests yet another Confucian catch-22: people are entrapped in ways they are reluctant to discuss even with close friends.

Another issue is money. Prominent or influential Western residents who are prepared to play the game with the local establishment can do very well. Some residents have been known to reap huge profits from the region's rigged stock markets. Certain stocks, typically very thinly traded ones, are readied for takeoff. A privileged few are invited aboard.

For those of delicate sensibilities, even more discreet arrangements can be made. In at least one major East Asian nation (not China), prominent foreigners in, for instance, the financial services industry have been encouraged to import a rare or extremely luxurious foreign car as the ostensible "family car." Arrangements are then made to ensure that the car is sold for a "good" price in the local used car market. Most foreign residents would not dare resort to such a gambit, because they would—understandably—fear that red tape would block them from getting the car through customs. Moreover, they know very well that finding a bona fide buyer would be like looking for a needle in a haystack. And even in the unlikely event of finding such a buyer, the seller would still be in a weak bargaining position.

None of this restrained one prominent East Asia–based correspondent some years ago from importing a superexpensive foreign sports car. He later sold it for a profit that, if the rumors were correct, paid for an apartment in one of the American West Coast's most expensive cities. This man was the bureau chief of one of the West's most prestigious publications and in that capacity played a crucial, overtly propagandistic role in misrepresenting the facts of the local economy to his influential readership. He could never look the more knowledgeable of his peers in the eye again—but he still had that apartment.

In the same nation the story of another foreign correspondent is also revealing. A courageous man of exceptionally strong character, he had for decades distinguished himself as the ultimate straight arrow in a city otherwise known for its highly collaborationist long-term foreign community. Soon after he suffered head injuries in a traffic accident, he was discovered to have gone over to the other side. He had become the local establishment's behind-the-scenes gauleiter at the foreign correspondents' club and in that capacity has been a major propaganda asset ever since.

Another story of the "Confucian twilight" concerns a journalist who stumbled on some geopolitically damaging intelligence about the government of one of the major Confucian nations (again not China). He refused the usual blandishments and stuck by the Western truth ethic. His health suddenly deteriorated and he sought help from local doctors. After an invasive examination (done unusually for this procedure under general anesthetic), his symptoms—a dysfunctional gut accompanied by depression—got very much worse. The local doctors gave him some advice on coping with his physical symptoms. They also prescribed certain country-specific drugs. These turned out, after an alert New York physician instigated an investigation, to be depressants. A videotape was somehow secretly taken on his property that caught him in the depths of a deep depression. It was then distributed to discredit him.

Then there is the story of a gifted journalist who wrote a book that angered more than one East Asian nation. Her book sold well and became significantly influential. It was systematically targeted for denunciation as supposedly wildly inaccurate. Meanwhile her personal life became an issue. Somehow word leaked out that she was having an affair. Although this was seriously compromising for her family life, it soon became so widely known that she no longer hid it. In the end she entered a deep depression and took her own life.

Much more could be said, but to anyone who is paying attention there is a pattern here: At least where sensitive geopolitical issues are concerned, little truthful information ever emerges from the East Asian region. And few capable, truthful observers last long in the region. The effect is a bit like the Bates Motel: the Western truth ethic checks in—but it does not check out.

Let's sum up. Even if Westerners were better equipped to stand up to the pressures in East Asia, the ethical divide is so wide that, absent careful controls on the Western side, it is utopian to believe the Western and East Asian systems can coexist for long as equals. One system or the other inevitably will prevail—and the record suggests it will not be the Western one.

It is, to say the least, unseemly for Americans to be exposed to such an ethical and legal twilight zone.

"The Dragon Will Go Away"

Ever since concerns about the rise of the New China were first voiced in the 1980s, various highly publicized commentators have argued that, one way or another, the dragon will go away. Either China will collapse of its own weight, or, more happily for all concerned, it will, by embracing Western values, find a comfortable place within the Western-defined world order.

One story is that the Chinese nation will fly apart. This version has been promoted in particular by Kenichi Ohmae, a controversial former partner of McKinsey & Company who in recent years has been a prominent adviser to the Chinese. All the serious evidence is against this proposition. For a start there is the matter of ethnic homogeneity. According to the CIA's numbers, 92 percent of China's 1.3 billion people are Han Chinese. Han Chinese dominance is diluted only in a few of China's most remote—and poorest—westerly provinces. Even if these provinces were somehow to break away, the diminution in China's standing in the world order would be minimal.

Those who are persuaded by the breakup argument are victims of "recentism"—they are unduly influenced by the recent past and not sufficiently cognizant of previous history. Whereas China was rent apart by regional warlords in the first half of the twentieth century, this was an aberration in an empire that had otherwise held together for most of its two-thousand-year history. The forces that caused the civil wars have now disappeared, while those forces that have traditionally held China together have staged a strong renaissance.

Another version of the dragon-will-go-away story is that China is destined to converge to Western values and norms. By implication, those of its economic and political peculiarities that now seem so awkward or destabilizing for the world order will also gradually fade away. This version appeals powerfully to many prominent Western intellectuals, but it is fair to say that the less they know about China, the more enthusiastically they espouse it.

Advocates of the view that China will somehow become Westernized often premise their argument on the assumption that the Chinese savings rate will quickly decline to the more natural levels of the West. They also believe that authoritarianism and corruption will come to be recognized by Beijing as fundamental roadblocks to China's ever becoming an advanced nation. Thus, willy-nilly, Beijing will come to accept that reform along Western lines is the only way forward.

One flaw in this argument is, of course, that it overlooks the fact that it is precisely China's authoritarianism that is driving the savings rate. There is also the point, as we discussed in chapter 5, that China's pervasive corruption provides top officials with a useful, if highly counterintuitive, tool to control society, via the principle of selective enforcement.

Finally, there is the industrial-strength version of the dragon-will-go-away story: the Chinese economy will simply implode. This case was strongly argued in 2000 by the Shanghai-based lawyer Gordon Chang in his book *The Coming Collapse of China.* The least offensive thing to say about this analysis is that China's trade surplus multiplied sevenfold in the following six years.

Looking to the future, we can expect Western policymakers to continue to be confused by all such stories and others yet to be invented. Such stories pander to a strong streak of wishful thinking in the West. Certainly the evidence from the earlier Confucian industrializers is that tales of this sort are quietly promoted by the authorities as a way of diverting attention from the fundamental incompatibility of the East Asian and Western economic systems.

It is even possible that, in an effort to perpetuate its trade policies in the face of rapidly rising Western disquiet, China might stage an economic funk of the sort that we saw in Japan in the 1990s. Major economic sectors may be presented as on the brink of collapse. Certainly this is an "Armageddon option" the authorities might invoke if protectionist feeling really seemed about to tip the United States and Europe into a full-scale retreat from globalism.

What is certain is that so far the Beijing authorities have managed the Chinese economy's rise extremely well. The betting is that they will continue to do so. While observers like Chang may have a point in suggesting that many of the Chinese banking system's loans are nonperforming, this in itself is not indicative of an economy headed off a cliff. The Chinese economy is not a capitalist one, and top economic planners have plenty of noncapitalist tools available to minimize the effects on the larger economy. Certainly that proved to be the case with Japan's financial implosion of the 1990s.

All in all, China is likely to remain a going concern.

The Dragon Moves to Hegemony

As we have noted, the extraordinary size of China's savings rate is no accident. It has been generated by countless antidemocratic measures imposed by highly determined—indeed ruthless—leaders in Beijing. The result in the short term has been great austerity, even deprivation, for the hapless Chinese populace.

While we have noted that in the long run the suppressed-consumption strategy pays off in a fast rise in consumers' living standards, it is clear that as far as Chinese leaders are concerned this is entirely secondary. For them, the main concern has been to build China's power. Economic success has funded not only growing Chinese economic influence around the world but a rapid buildup in military strength.

That power is the key goal is strongly suggested by the unprecedented rigor of China's brand of suppressed consumption. Even compared to the experiences of other East Asian nations at a similar stage of development, China's economic austerity regimen seems exceptionally harsh. Certainly the result has been savings rates extraordinarily higher than even nations like Japan and South Korea have managed.

What is undeniable is that China has been boosting its economic clout at an extraordinary rate. The impact has been felt particularly in foreign-currency markets. Twenty years ago, China's currency reserves were less than those of, for instance, the Netherlands. As of 2006 they passed Japan's to become the world's largest. While the consequences are not apparent to ordinary citizens or even to press commentators in the West, they have been profound for the world banking industry. The Chinese are already a powerful voice—perhaps the single most powerful one—in setting world exchange rates. Going forward, Chinese leaders will increasingly be courted by top financial people around the world, not least in the United States.

Then there is the military dimension. It is not an accident that the recent rate of growth in China's military spending—at an average of more than 10 percent a year since the mid-1990s—has been one of the world's fastest.

While a detailed discussion of likely future U.S.-China military rivalry is beyond the scope of this book, a few points can be made. First, analysts at the U.S. Naval War College calculate that China will draw broadly level with the United States as a military power in the Asia-Pacific region by 2020.

Moreover, China is now poised to become an increasingly formidable competitor in military technology. China has always been blessed with the first essential in this endeavor—plenty of people to throw into the fray. In the past, however, it has fallen down not only in the educational level of its scientists and engineers but in the quality of the equipment it can provide them with. Economic success is helping to remedy these shortcomings.

Also, it seems likely that an intensive effort to develop new military technologies could pay large dividends. After all, military technology remains what it has always been: a work in progress. As the nuclear technology at the core of the American defense system dates back more than half a century, we seem overdue for a shift to even more efficient forms of destruction that will render present American defenses hopelessly obsolete.

What the twenty-first century will bring is anyone's guess. Just as few experts a century ago would have predicted that within four decades atom bombs would have wiped out whole cities, it is fair to suggest that there may be some military technology surprises ahead of us in the new century.

Certainly China is unlikely to want to acquiesce forever in a subordinate military role. With more than four times America's population and boasting one of the world's oldest cultures, it clearly sees itself as the natural leader of the world order. Moreover, whether one likes it or not, America's individualistic ideology constitutes a potent provocation. Mao Zedong's comment on Western imperialism half a century ago comes to mind: from a Beijing point of view, the choice is still between killing the tiger or being eaten by it.

No one knows where future developments in military technology will lead. But it is clear that China's chances of getting there first have been improved immeasurably thanks to its embrace of the East Asian economic system.

America's Choice: Globalism *or* Democracy

Having satisfied ourselves that China is destined in coming decades to become an increasingly powerful force in world affairs, let us now consider the implications for American policy.

Americans have an epochal choice to make: either globalism *or* democracy. They cannot have both.

Quite simply, in a globalist world, democracies are increasingly vulnerable to manipulation by more authoritarian nations. The problem is particularly serious in the case of the United States because the machinery of American democracy depends so heavily on campaign contributions. It would be nice if it were otherwise; but over the years repeated efforts at political reform in the United States have failed. For those who live in the real world, therefore, money politics must be considered a given as Chinese money casts a lengthening shadow over the world polity.

In a related point, we also have to accept that money greatly influences how the American media cover the issues. Editors whose views serve advertisers rise to the top. Money also works at a different level by creating a parallel universe of pseudo sources for the press. The most obvious are think-tank analysts. Increasingly too, money has shaped key academic disciplines, particularly those related to politics and international policy.

Of course, money has almost always been a force in shaping American politics, but up to the early decades after World War II, it was generally wielded by identifiable wealthy individuals who owed their ultimate loyalty to the American nation. Their behavior was not only shaped (if sometimes rather loosely) by American ethics but subject to the sanction of American laws. More subtly but perhaps more importantly, wealthy political donors had a stake in the outcome. Not only did they personally have to live with the societal consequences of their favored policies, but, perhaps more important, their children and grandchildren had to do so too. Few people aspire to be remembered as cads by their grandchildren.

While this simpler world was hardly Eden (certainly not for American blacks, whose rights had only just been discovered as a political cause), it was informed by a sense of accountability that is lacking today. With the rise of globalism, more and more of the money flooding into the American political process either comes from abroad or is ultimately controlled by foreign corporations or even foreign governments. By definition such money is not meant to serve the American national interest. Worse, many of the foreign nations whose interests the money serves are, to say the least, not sympathetic to American democracy.

Moreover, on issues like trade policy virtually all foreign money is lined up on the same side—and against the American national interest. The record shows that this renders prudent policymaking almost impossible. By contrast, in days gone by, when domestic American interest groups dominated the influence-buying process, the money often lined up on opposing sides of important issues, thus leaving room for those who championed the general public good to make a difference.

What explains the rise of foreign money in American politics? First, foreign producers have become a major factor in the American domestic market. This reflects the fact that the tariff barriers that once gave American producers—and their American workforces—an inside track in serving the American market are gone. Also, the United States has fallen in relative global economic influence. Many foreign corporations that were still only a negligible force a few decades ago have now come to dominate key industries. Moreover, cheap international travel and virtually cost-free global communications have also played a part in that they have greatly simplified the problems for top executives in

Frankfurt, or Zurich, or Tokyo in keeping tabs on operations in the United States. Obviously it is not the job of such executives to look out for the American national interest. The problems of the American inner cities, for instance, are hardly more of a concern for them than those of the slums of Calcutta or Rio de Janeiro. Further, although their rhetoric sometimes suggests otherwise, they have never taken any effective action to discourage the headlong rush to increasing foreign indebtedness by the American nation.

Even American corporations these days are hardly more cognizant of the American national interest. Now that American tariffs are gone, American executives no longer automatically make common cause with their home workforces on trade issues. Worse, executives have been conditioned by a globalist-minded press to believe that it is now quixotic if not softheaded to worry about the impact of one's decisions on one's employees at home, let alone on the wider American national interest. Moreover, the rise of China as a vast low-wage manufacturing platform for American corporations has meant that they are now increasingly concerned to curry favor with the top leadership of the Chinese Communist Party.

This has brought out to an extreme extent a streak of collaborationism for which American corporations have long been noted. In the 1980s and even in some cases into the 1990s, American corporations collaborated with apartheid in South Africa. As the conservative Washington policy analyst William Hawkins has pointed out, the record of American business in Nazi Germany was even more shocking. Such industrial leaders as IBM, Standard Oil, ITT, and Ford worked hand-in-glove with Adolf Hitler all through the 1930s and even into the 1940s.

A basic problem is a lack of symmetry. While American corporations increasingly renounce their loyalty to their home country (and often do so pridefully, as if they were displaying commendable moral courage), the same is not true of their foreign counterparts. Quite the contrary. Foreign corporations typically function quite consciously as agents of their home governments' foreign policy. This applies in spades to corporations based in East Asia, and to a lesser extent to those of continental Europe (particularly Germany); but even in a nation as ostensibly globalized as Britain, corporations are much more willing to cooperate with government in serving the national interest than are American corporations.

The issue that brings all this into sharp focus is America's now scandalously heavy dependence on foreign borrowing. No major nation in modern times has become remotely so indebted. The closest historical parallel is with the Ottoman Empire a century ago. American presidents these days, like the Ottoman sultans a century ago, are surrounded by flatterers whispering assurances that all is well. Today, as a century ago, many of these flatterers are bankers who profit from extending ever more credit to the gullible and self-satisfied.

The problem is compounded by the fact that so much of the credit is coming from one highly controversial source: China. To say the least, China's political agenda is utterly incompatible with that of the United States. For the moment Beijing's influence has been confined mainly to discouraging any action in the United States that might put American trade policy on a sounder footing. But as the United States becomes ever weaker and more dependent on Chinese credit, Beijing's influence is likely to extend widely into other areas of American policy. Indeed the pattern for the United States to depend on Beijing for credit is already beginning to resemble the relationship between a colony and the imperial capital.

In the long run, assuming unchanged policies, the contest between China and the United States reduces to the age-old battle between the group and the individual. To understand the extent of the threat that the Chinese Communist Party poses to an individualistic America, think of a bulldozer setting out to level a sand dune. The bulldozer may be dwarfed at the outset, but, given time and patience, it will level the dune. The Chinese Communist Party sees itself as the bulldozer and America as the dune. The bulldozer is a carefully designed machine that has the advantage of concentrated strength. The dune is made up of countless unique grains of sand but lacks any ability to mobilize its weight to resist the bulldozer.

How far the bulldozer will choose to go in leveling the sand dune is uncertain. What is clear, however, is that the United States is exceptionally vulnerable by reason of the pronounced individualism of its society.

Think of it this way: the first job of any Confucian bureaucracy is to emasculate all potential institutional rivals. The more atomized a society is, the easier it will be to reshape along Confucian lines. Confucian-style institutions can then be developed that in one way or another facilitate control from the top.

In this sense, American society is ready-made for Confucianizing. As a matter of high policy, all large concentrations of power in the United States have long been systematically dismembered. This is exemplified most obviously in antitrust policy. Not only are American corporations strictly forbidden from organizing cartels, but any corporation that becomes too powerful risks being broken up. (Witness the fate of the old AT&T. More generally, many American corporations—IBM and Microsoft are examples—have had to pull their punches to stay out of antitrust trouble.)

To Confucian power holders, America's system of separation of powers is another manifestation of grave institutional weakness. Then there is the fact that even compared with other Western democracies, the permanent civil service in the United States is notably weak and unable to wield independent institutional power.

The United States is in many ways the world's most individualistic society, and precisely for this reason it is a sitting duck for the manipulative techniques of Confucian power. Indeed there is hardly an institution of any size left in the United States that can truly be said to stand unequivocally for the American national interest. Quite to the contrary: virtually all institutions are now globalist not only in mind-set but in structure and are thus easily divided against themselves.

For the Beijing bulldozer the sand dune of American individualism is therefore a pushover. There may be some rocks in the dune—a few independent-minded politicians like Byron L. Dorgan, Ernest F. Hollings, Marcy Kaptur, Jim Webb, Dennis Kucinich, or Dana Rohrabacher for instance, who refuse to budge. There may be some philanthropists like Roger Milliken or the late Sir James Goldsmith, who throw themselves into the fray. But politicians and philanthropists are individuals, and individuals eventually pass from the scene. There may even be an occasional boulder—a large, strongly led corporation like Microsoft that at least for a time tries to resist the leveling process. But, as we have seen, the boulders too do not resist forever.

This sand dune, however, hardly lacks for potentially effective protection. All it needs is a solid concrete wall around its perimeter. To that subject we now turn.

A Wall Around the Sand Dune

The solution to America's China problem can be summed up in one word: tariffs. Tariffs not only would provide some badly needed space between the American and Chinese economic systems, but would if pursued with resolution restore the more important elements of the status quo ante that existed in the United States of the 1950s.

Initially at least, tariffs should be applied *at a uniform rate across all manufactured imports* (otherwise, major distortions would result as opportunists sought to exploit categorization anomalies). They should be introduced gradually to minimize disruption to the world trading system. The eventual target would be a tariff level of 15 or 20 percent. The effect in reviving American industry would be modest at first but would prove powerfully cumulative. Within one decade American trade might be in balance again, and within two decades the American economy would have taken its place again at the leading edge in many of the most advanced manufacturing industries (industries that are disproportionately important both in creating highly paid blue-collar jobs and in boosting exports).

It would be implicit in any program to introduce tariffs that the United States would *withdraw from the World Trade Organization*. Eventually the United States could go on to negotiate a new trade regime in which nations that are sincerely committed to fair and mutually beneficial trade would be provided with preferential access to the American market. But all of these nations would have to maintain a common wall of tariffs against outsiders, and of course they would have to reciprocate fully any preferential terms they enjoyed in the American market.

Tariffs would minimize the extent to which the American dollar would need to be devalued—though some significant devaluation would probably still be necessary. What is clear is that the time when devaluation alone might have done the trick is long gone. The problem has simply grown too large, and a devaluation alone would take far too long to induce a vigorous renaissance in advanced manufacturing.

It goes without saying that the United States should also work to *improve its savings rate* and to *eliminate its budget deficit*. A tariff regimen would boost at least modestly the savings rate (by dint of suppressing consumption of imported goods) and, by bolstering tax revenues, would serve to narrow the budget deficit.

As part of any new trade regime, the United States would probably want to adopt a *value-added tax* or find some other mechanism to counter the effects of the value-added taxes now standard throughout Europe and East Asia (including China). This is a complicated matter, but the main point is that although value-added taxes are supposedly neutral in their effects on world trade, other nations' value-added taxes work in practice to put the United States at a serious disadvantage.

Put this starkly, this plan may seem extreme. But that in no way reflects on the plan's inherent common sense. Rather, it betokens the undeserved success the globalist lobby has had in persuading American intellectuals—particularly those who lack formal economic training—that free trade dogma is revealed truth.

There is nothing sacred about free trade, and this is obvious to anyone familiar with economic history. In its years of greatest relative success in the nineteenth century, the American economy was heavily protectionist. As the Ohio University economic historian Al Eckes has documented, America's founding fathers strongly believed in tariffs. So did every Republican president before Dwight Eisenhower (not least Abraham Lincoln). Moreover, many other nations have ridden a policy of intelligent protectionism to achieve spectacularly high growth over the years. Beginning in the latter half of the nineteenth century both Germany and Japan based their rises on strongly protectionist trade policies. The same goes, of course, for China today—a nation that is growing faster than almost any other in history.

The globalist lobby has conditioned Americans to believe that any return to tariffs would lead inevitably to a second coming of the Great Depression. Yet the contention that the Smoot-Hawley tariffs of 1930 caused the Great Depression is an urban myth. Indeed, the time line alone shows that trade had little to do with the troubles of the 1930s. In a major study that has been generally accepted by economists of all political persuasions, the Nobel Prize—winning economist Milton Friedman has shown that the true cause of the Great Depression was not Smoot-Hawley but disastrously misguided monetary management.

In taking extreme free-trade ideology at face value, the American elite has forgotten something it once fully understood: that economics is an imprecise, often equivocal, science. In years gone by economists were generally far more frank in admitting their discipline's limitations than they are today. Indeed, their caution was the butt of a famous witticism by Harry S. Truman. Noting that his economic advisers always hedged their bets by saying "on the one hand . . . on the other hand," Truman opined that what he needed was a - one-handed economist. In reality Truman was well served by his economists' two-handedness. Any honest economic discussion should be grounded in a recognition that economic policies invariably create bad as well as good consequences. Whether a policy is appropriate in any particular circumstance therefore depends on a careful, disinterested assessment of whether the identifiable pluses outweigh the identifiable minuses.

As far as free trade is concerned, such a determination has rarely been beyond dispute even in the days when America's trade position was far stronger than it is today. As Sir James Goldsmith argued in *The Trap,* the case for global free trade has always seemed utopian. For it to work in textbook fashion, governments and corporations must hold themselves to a standard of self-control rarely if ever seen in the real world.

An analogy will make the point: Washington is full of liberal politicians who uphold the ideal of educational equality. In practice, however, they rarely entrust their own children's education to the Washington public school system. Irrespective of how much one may wish the real world to be different, to expect American manufacturing industries to sink or swim in today's highly predatory, dysfunctional world trading system is no more responsible than to abandon one's children to a drug-ridden public education system.

Given the record scale of America's trade deficits—not to mention the federal government's dependence on foreign creditors—those who oppose protectionism must answer this question: What is the alternative?

The apologists—and their supporters in America's globalist boardrooms— will portray all this as defeatism. Let them. There is a difference between courage and foolhardiness. No one thinks less of a lion because he refuses to enter a crocodile-infested swamp. Today's world trading system is a swamp where only the crocodiles can win. In the lion's natural habitat, the savannah, his agility and speed make him second to none. The survival instincts that have made him the king of beasts tell him that that is where he should stay.

If this argument seems overdrawn, it is because the East Asian trade lobby and its American surrogates have so dominated the debate for so long. To a previous generation, it seemed obvious that Russian and Chinese authoritarianism represented a potentially fatal threat to the West's way of life—so obvious that in the late 1940s and early 1950s Western governments felt it necessary to institute extraordinary measures to shield their political and economic systems from contact with the Communist world. They did so despite the fact that the West then enjoyed a huge economic lead. In the mid-1950s, after all, the United States alone produced more than four times as much as the Soviet Union and China combined.

If America's policies do not change, the nation's decline will quickly become irreversible. Within twenty years, perhaps much sooner, China will have passed the United States to become the world's largest economy. A decade after that, America's days as the world's most advanced economy will have become a rapidly fading memory. If we felt threatened by Chinese authoritarianism when China was poor, how much more threatened will we feel when China is rich?

Notes

ONE: A Dragon on Steroids

4 **Richard Bernstein and Ross Munro:** Richard Bernstein and Ross Munro, *The Coming Conflict with China* (New York: Knopf, 1997), p. 136.

8 **The Japanese economy has been built largely on foreign technologies:** In the early decades after World War II, Tokyo expertly coopted the United States federal government's help in forcing American corporations to transfer key technologies to Japan in the name of cold war solidarity. According to a study by James Abegglen, this effort saved the Japanese at least $65 billion.

9 **winkling key technologies out of the United States and Europe:** As quoted by *Manufacturing & Technology News* (July 24, 2006), here is how one consultant described the process: "The Chinese government puts down technology transfer as a condition. You can't get in unless you give up your technology. You can't get in unless you get into a joint venture with a local partner. Then these American companies' core competencies get hit—that core competence that they put a lot of money and time and energy into—is gone."

10 **China's savings rate is hard to overlook:** In a scientific study conducted for the World Bank some years ago, the economist Aart Kraay concluded that the excess was equal to nearly 10 percentage points of gross domestic product. Although his analysis was based on data that ended in 1995, it is probable that the excess has remained at least as high since.

17 **Xiaoming Huang:** Xiaoming Huang, *The Rise and Fall of the East Asian Growth System, 1951–2000* (Abingdon, U.K.: RoutledgeCurzon, 2005), p. 99.

20 **sold only about 4,000 vehicles:** Evan Ramstad, *Wall Street Journal,* July 11, 2006.

21 **Laura W. Young:** Wang & Wang Web site, www.wangandwang.com, 2006.

23 **an ephemeral intellectual fashion to scorn manufacturing:** Kenichi Ohmae began arguing that "manufacturing does not matter" in the 1980s. In *The Borderless World* (New York: Harper Business, 1990), Ohmae wrote: "When money, goods, people, information, and even companies crisscross national borders so freely, it makes no sense to talk of 'American industrial competitiveness.' The only thing that matters is that IBM competes with DEC and Fujitsu." This characterization overlooked the not inconsiderable fact that nations derive five to ten times more of their national income from wages than from profits. If you want to have a high-wage nation, industrial competitiveness is vital. Ohmae, the then head of McKinsey & Company office in Tokyo, was alleged to have been an undeclared lobbyist for Japan. What is clear is that the United States took his case for deindustrialization to heart. Japan did not.

26 **the United States outexported China by a factor of four to one:** U.S. exports in 1996 totaled $625.1 billion versus China's exports of just $151.2 billion.

29 **enforcers of Beijing's one-child policy:** Speaking on the PBS program *Newshour* on May 23, 2000, the Chinese dissident Harry Wu said that foreign employers were obliged to fire any woman who gives birth without a government permit.

32 **When was the last time a major American newspaper took a searching look:** Based on an archive search in the fall of 2007, it appears that the the *New York Times,* for instance, has not investigated car market protectionism in Japan in more than a decade. As for South Korea, the most recent critical articles that came up were written by William J. Holstein and Stephanie Strom in March 2002 and September 2000 respectively.

32 **CNN's otherwise refreshingly frank Lou Dobbs program:** Based on an archive search in 2007, it seems that the Lou Dobbs program has never taken a serious look at trade barriers in either the Japanese or South Korean car markets. In 2004, however, it did devote a few minutes of air time to criticisms by Congresswoman Marcy Kaptur and the policy analyst Alan Tonelson.

32 **Robert Kagan and William Kristol:** Steven Mosher, *Hegemon* (San Francisco: Encounter Books, 2000), p. 140.

TWO: "Don't Worry, Be Happy"

35 **"basket case":** Few observers worked harder to promote the myth of the "collapse" of the East Asian economic model than Sebastian Mallaby, erstwhile Tokyo bureau chief of the *Economist.* Writing in the *National Interest* in 1998, he commented: "The argument in Japan is no longer about whether to dismantle unWestern controls on the economy—it is about how quickly to do so. Intellectually Japan's economic model is dead." Contrast that with the reality on the ground in East Asia a decade later. Not only has the Japanese economic model survived fully intact—the keiretsus, the cartels, the trade barriers, and even lifetime employment are still going strong—but Japan's current account surpluses have, of course, continued to soar.

More important for our story is the fact that elsewhere in East Asia the model is being copied more closely and more extensively than ever. This is obvious in the case of China, but it is true also of South Korea and Taiwan. Mallaby's prediction was all the more interesting because, as he surely knew, his predecessors had constantly predicted the collapse of the Japanese model (and particularly lifetime employment) over the previous thirty years. Indeed several of Mallaby's Japan-watching predecessors—most notably Brian Reading, Christopher Wood, and Bill Emmott—had actually written whole books explaining why the Japanese economic model was supposedly finished. All such predictions had proved embarrassingly false. The truth is that they owed their origins to Tokyo-inspired propaganda. All along, Japanese officials have had to pretend that the East Asian model is on the verge of breakdown to deflect attention from the fact that its linchpin is a system of protectionism that runs completely counter to Japan's commitments to its trade partners. (This point is most obvious in the case of the lifetime employment system, which simply could not survive if the Japanese market were open to the world.) Mallaby was speaking Tokyo's propaganda. None of this did his career any harm. The following year he was hired by the *Washington Post* as a top columnist, and in 2007 he became director of the Maurice R. Greenberg Center for Geoeconomic Studies at the Council on Foreign Relations. (See Chapter 8 for a discussion of the propagandistic agenda of the center's chief sponsor, Maurice Greenberg.) Has Mallaby learned anything from his mistakes? It seems not. Writing about Chinese economic competition in 2006, Mallaby argued that "American business is in a golden phase right now."

39 **the problem of institutional mendacity has been exacerbated:** The pattern of prominent foreign residents in East Asia collaborating with local elites in pulling the wool over the West's eyes goes back to well before World War II. But in the early days such residents' comments were widely seen through by diplomats and other intelligent Western observers. Things changed in Japan in the 1950s and 1960s, when several American residents came to be accepted as honest brokers in interpreting the Japanese miracle. A key part was played by the Harvard-educated consultant James Abegglen, who for decades was presented to succeeding generations of American business executives as the ultimate guide to how to succeed in Japan. It is clear, however, that from early on he regarded his principal function as doing public relations on behalf of the Japanese establishment. He is believed to have been the inspiration for many early commentaries in the Western press portraying Japan as supposedly one of the "most open markets in the world." Suggestions of this sort were already a commonplace in the *Economist,* for instance, as far back as the early 1970s. In a commentary written under his own name in 1972 (and published by the Japan Society of New York), Abegglen suggested that the Japanese market was already then broadly as open as that of the United States. He wrote: "The two nations appear to be about equally 'free trading'—but the United States is becoming more protectionist. Japan is committed to a course aimed at eliminating all export incentives and opening most major industries to competition from imports and foreign investment. By the mid-1970s Japan could well be the least protectionist country in the world and the most competitive." As we record elsewhere in these notes, this testimony was resoundingly contradicted by a comment in 2000 by Minoru Makihara admitting that up to the late 1980s the Japanese market remained "closed and tightly protected." See page 327. Abegglen secretly renounced his American citizenship in the late 1990s but continued to advise American clients, including one major American aerospace company, for some years thereafter. He died in 2007.

40 **the Chinese almost immediately reneged:** All this is more understandable when seen from a Chinese point of view. Chinese leaders make no bones about their pattern of reneging on their trade promises. In 2000, China's trade negotiator Long Yongtu commented: "Diplomatic negotiations involve finding new expressions. If you find a new expression, this means you have achieved a diplomatic result. In terms of meat imports, we have not actually made any material concessions." As for a promise to import more American grain, Long said that this was merely a "theoretical opportunity."

40 **lied about its policies on export subsidies:** See Richard Bernstein and Ross Munro in *The Coming Conflict with China* (New York: Knopf, 1997), p. 137.

40 **The United States fell for the same trick again:** See Richard Bernstein and Ross Munro in *The Coming Conflict with China* (New York: Knopf, 1997), p. 140.

41 **Beijing agreed to join the World Intellectual Property Organization:** See Xiaoming Huang, *The Rise and Fall of the East Asian Growth System, 1951–2000* (Abingdon, U.K.: RoutledgeCurzon, 2005), p. 155.

41 **a qualitatively different, much more devastating, threat:** One of the more unexpected side-effects of the prevalence of software piracy in China has been to force the Dell company to withdraw from the Chinese personal computer market. As reported in 2005 by the newsletter *Manufacturing & Technology News*, Dell was stymied by the fact that it was competing with Chinese suppliers who paid no royalties to Microsoft. Dell, by contrast, like most other personal-computer makers around the world, was contractually obliged to pay royalties to Microsoft for every machine it sold worldwide and in return got the right to preinstall Microsoft software in its products. Because Chinese makers could count on customers to install cheap pirated software, they sold their products without software and gave their customers the benefit of a much lower price.

41 **Tim Phillips:** As quoted in *The Coming China Wars* by Peter Navarro (Upper Saddle River, N.J.: FT Press, 2006), p. 38.

41 **Not only has the Chinese government turned a blind eye:** Speaking in 2006, Carolyn Bartholomew, vice chairman of the U.S.–China Economic and Security Review Commission, reported that on a recent trip to China, she and her colleagues were astonished to be told by one top official at the Chinese Ministry of Commerce that piracy was "negligible." Bartholomew tartly added: "Just walk down the street in Beijing and you will be offered pirated CDs. Entire shopping malls are devoted to knock-off goods." As reported by the Office of the U.S. Trade Representative, piracy levels across all lines of copyright business in China were running at between 85 and 98 percent in 2006.

42 **"Chinese promises on intellectual property . . .":** It is hard to exaggerate China's role in the world counterfeit industry. Writing in the *Seattle Times* (February 13, 2006), Kristi Heim quoted the Office of the U.S. Trade Representative as saying that as of 2004, 67 percent of all piracy-related seizures at American borders originated in China.

44 **apologist interpretations of the food shortages:** In a book published in 1976, John Gurley, an economics professor at Stanford, strongly defended China's food-distribution system: "The Chinese—all of them—now have what is in effect an insurance policy against pestilence, famine, and other disasters. In this respect, China has outperformed every underdeveloped country in the world . . . it would not be farfetched to claim that there has been less malnutri-

tion due to maldistribution of food in China over the past twenty years than there has been in the United States."

45 **"Whatever the price of the Chinese revolution. . . .":** Quoted by Steven Mosher in *China Misperceived,* p. 154.

45 **One scholar who seems to have done particularly well:** China has had good reason to look kindly on Lieberthal. After all, as President Bill Clinton's senior director for Asian affairs at the National Security Council, he played a decisive role in 1999 in shaping the terms on which China entered the World Trade Organization. In particular he negotiated a preparatory agreement in which the United States granted permanent normal trade relations to China. He then "spun" this agreement as a major benefit to the United States. Commenting on the outline agreement in November 1999, he predicted that after a "few years," the agreement would reduce America's bilateral trade deficits with China. In the event, the deficits have of course continued to balloon, rising from $69 billion in 1999 to $232 billion in 2006. Speaking on PBS's *Newshour* in November 1999, he commented: "The most fundamental thing we get out of this deal is an enormous increase in our access to the Chinese economy. This is in services, it's in the export of our industrial products, of our agricultural products. Essentially China will now, after a brief phase-in, have to play by the same rules that we and many other countries around the world play by: greater transparency, more rules-based fairness to [foreign] firms that will be treated in most sectors just as Chinese firms are. So, we should see a very substantial increase in our exports to China, a very substantial increase in our economic engagement with China. At the same time this builds in key protections for American labor to protect us from surges of Chinese exports to the United States."

He was resolutely opposed on the same program by Robert Scott of the left-of-center Economic Policy Institute, who commented: "This is a lose-lose agreement for workers in both the U.S. and in China. This agreement failed to obtain progress, in particular, on labor and human rights. No progress was made in those areas at all. The agreement is a commercial failure. The benefits that have been promised by the administration are illusory. They're not going to be there. . . . And finally, the agreement itself is unenforceable. So I'm concerned, I think, that China is not yet ready to join the WTO, and I think this agreement is premature."

All the subsequent evidence has proved Scott right. The agreement that Lieberthal sold in such rosy terms in 1999 has been little more than an outsourcing deal for corporate America. In the subsequent seven years, American exports to China were to rise by a mere $42 billion, just one-fifth of the $206 billion rise in China's exports to the United States. The agreement was probably the China lobby's greatest triumph over the American public interest.

49 **'the eyes, ears and mouthpieces':** Y. Hu in a speech delivered to the Communist Party Central Committee Secretariat, February 8, 1985. It was printed in the *People's Daily* on April 14 the same year.

50 **the Associated Press journalist J. C. Lao:** See Steven Mosher, *China Misperceived* (New York: Basic Books, 1990), p. 77.

50 **Wang Xiangwei:** BBC Worldwide Monitoring, June 6, 2005.

51 **John Pomfret:** Pomfret was allowed back into China a few years later.

66 **"China is going to have a free press":** Thomas Friedman, *The Lexus and the Olive Tree* (New York: Farrar, Straus, 1999), p. 154.

66 **a full-size commercial airliner by 2020:** "China to Develop Large Commercial Aircraft by 2020, Official Says," *International Herald Tribune*, March 12, 2007.

70 **Russell Roberts:** "Protectionists Never Learn," *Wall Street Journal*, March 12, 2007.

71 **grossly exaggerated accounts of Japanese economic difficulties:** Few American commentators did more to exaggerate the problems than Harvard's Michael E. Porter, famed head of Harvard's Institute for Strategy and Competitiveness. In his book *Can Japan Compete?* (New York: Basic Books, 2000), he suggested that Japanese industry faced disastrous competitiveness problems because it had supposedly ceased to innovate in the mid-1980s. Thereafter, wrote Porter, its export drive had supposedly become increasingly dependent on industries so laughably low-tech they might embarrass, say, Afghanistan or Somalia. Among these were yeast, flaked cereal, and, most memorably, "raw bovine and equine hides"! Porter's list overlooked thousands of superadvanced high-technology products that were then—as he was writing—driving not only Japan's export boom but the world technology revolution. Examples included laser diodes, mobile phone components, semiconductor-grade silicon, gallium arsenide, ceramic capacitors, steppers and other semiconductor-making equipment, aerospace-grade titanium, ceramic jet engine parts. . . . Perhaps the most damning comment on Porter's blindness was that, measured as a proportion of gross domestic product, Japan's current account surplus had already as the book went to press in 1999 hit 2.5 percent. By contrast, the American current account *deficit* had reached a record 3.6 percent. The unmistakable implication surely was that it was the United States that was becoming the world's competitiveness basket case. Porter's farcically upside-down view of his field would have been less forgivable but for the fact that he was the victim of one of the most elaborate confidence tricks in Japanese propaganda history. Intent on talking down Japan's competitiveness at every opportunity (to deflect attention from the booming Japanese trade surpluses), Japanese propaganda operatives surrounded him at every stage and "managed" his view of reality. To cap it all, the book was praised as a "masterpiece" by Shinji Fukukawa, a former head of the Japanese Ministry of International Trade and Industry. The *Economist*, which led the effort in the West to portray Japan as a basket case (and which since the 1960s has consistently presented key aspects of the Japanese economic system as "breaking down"), nominated *Can Japan Compete?* as one of the top three nonfiction books of 2000.

71 **I was alone among Tokyo-based financial observers:** The first of my articles anticipating Japan's subsequent banking and financial asset problems was published in *Euromoney* in September 1987 and was headlined "Why the Japanese Banks are Shaky." This focused on the Japanese banks' dangerously excessive lending to real estate speculators. I issued a further warning in the same magazine in February 1989, this time about the unsustainable level of stock prices. The Tokyo stock market crash began in the first days of January 1990.

71 **the book's subtitle:** In predicting that the Japanese economy would pass that of the United States by the year 2000, my bet was that, in a bid to restore American competitiveness and reverse the already rapidly worsening American trade trend, the Clinton administration would have no option but to instigate a timely and massive devaluation. The dollar had already been devalued by more than half against the Japanese yen in 1985–1987, but this had clearly not been enough. Indeed, as I completed *Blindside* in 1994, the American current account deficit had risen back up to $122 billion—just $1 billion shy of the "disastrous" level it had reached in 1985. Meanwhile, Japan's current account surplus more than doubled between 1985 and 1994. Another massive dollar devaluation was necessary if American manufacturing was ever to be-

gin reclaiming ground lost to the Japanese in the previous two decades. Such a devaluation would, of course, have drastically reduced America's standing in the world economic pecking order and boosted Japan's. Hence my subtitle.

In the end President Bill Clinton did not take my advice. Indeed, shortly after *Blindside* was published, he did the opposite and acquiesced in a strong dollar policy. In the short run this improved the American trade deficits (because it greatly reduced the dollar cost of American imports, particularly imports of essential Japanese-made advanced components, materials and machines that the United States could no longer make). In the longer run, however, Clinton's high dollar undercut any chance of a recovery in American industrial competitiveness. Given that in the eleven years after *Blindside* was published America's current account trade deficit ballooned more than sevenfold—rising from $114 billion in 1995 to $862 billion in 2006—all the evidence is that my view of the dollar-yen exchange rate was right. As it happens, in a letter to Senator Ernest Hollings on July 11, 1995, President Bill Clinton described *Blindside* as "a good book." But it is clear that he became aware of my argument only after he had already committed himself to a strong-dollar policy.

74 **Paul Ingrassia and Joseph White:** If *Comeback* seemed full of hype, it was nothing compared to *Making It in America,* a 1994 book by former Commerce Department official Jerry Jasinowski and consultant Robert Hamrin. Boosted by an endorsement from the business guru Tom Peters, Jasinowski and Hamrin told of "a dramatic comeback that has made American manufacturing the industrial powerhouse of the world."

74 **Such wishful thinking:** The further the commentators were from Japan, the more absurdly they indulged in wishful thinking. New York–based Karen Elliott House was a particularly memorable example. Writing in the *Wall Street Journal* in 1992, she compared the Japanese economy to children's toys called Shrinkies, which were advertised to "shrink right before your eyes."

75 **Toyota boosted its sales by 61 percent:** The numbers in this paragraph come from the Value Line Investment Survey.

75 **farcically at odds with reality:** A notable example of how misinformed Western commentators were was the "bridges to nowhere" story. Supposedly Japan's "slump" had become so serious and intractable that by the late 1990s top budgetary officials had taken in desperation to building bridges to nowhere. The point was repeated unchecked by people like Paul Krugman of the *New York Times*, Bethan Hutton of the *Financial Times*, and Martin Woollacott of the *Guardian*. The commentators cited no substantiation and clearly felt that none was needed. Yet, as a moment's reflection would surely have suggested, there was not a shred of truth in it. After all, in a mountainous nation with one of the highest ratios of cars to road space in the world, it would have taken a truly perverse genius to build bridges to nowhere. Everywhere one travels in Japan the problem is a lack of bridges, which results in notably circuitous traffic routing. How did the myth get started? The ultimate source was a headline in the *Economist* in April 1998: "The Bridge to Nowhere in Particular." This described the Akashi Kaikyo Bridge, a 2.4-mile-long bridge that had just been completed. The bridge links Japan's main island—Honshu—to Awaji Island. And because Awaji has a bridge to the island of Shikoku, the Akashi Kaikyo serves Shikoku as well. To the editors of the *Economist,* Awaji may be "nowhere"—but it is hardly so for the 157,000 people who live there. As for Shikoku, its population, at 4.1 million, is one-fifth larger than Connecticut's. The bridge's genesis owed nothing to the supposed depression economics of the 1990s—construction had begun as far back as 1986. In any other country, the Akashi Kaikyo would have

been hailed for what it was: a stunning economic achievement. With a main span of 2,177 yards, it ranked then—and still does—as by far the longest bridge in the world. It is in fact one of the greatest achievements in the history of civil engineering.

76 **And most areas of the non-financial economy did fine:** As UCLA management profes-
sor Sanford Jacoby has pointed out, all through the 1990s Japanese consumer affluence was abundantly apparent on the roads, which were full of late-model cars. Japan's huge electronics stores were constantly packed with free-spending males. Indeed, the Japanese had become so wealthy that the most advanced new products—from the latest games machines to the most spectacular new flat-screen TVs—were often launched in Japan months or even years before they reached the United States.

"Japan is a very affluent country with an income distribution much less unequal than in the States," said Jacoby. "Those in the bottom two-thirds of the income distribution enjoy a higher quality of life than their U.S. counterparts. As for the upper one-third, they, too, benefit from Japan's high level of public services, as well as the security that comes from a stable, cohesive society."

Even in the late 1990s, when commentators abroad were performing daily last rites for the Japanese economy, the palpable prosperity on the ground there stunned visiting Americans. Nathanial Gronewold, a University of Minnesota graduate who studied economics in Hi-
roshima in 1997 and 1998, recalls: "My time in Hiroshima went down in the record books as two of the worst years for Japan's economy. But the affluence I witnessed in and around Hiroshima was a stark contrast to the scores of empty storefronts and offices in downtown Minneapolis, which was supposed to be booming at that time." Although Japan's real estate crash in the early 1990s has received plenty of attention, the construction boom Gronewold witnessed in Hiroshima was no mere local aberration. Throughout the country, not least in Tokyo, building con-
tinued at a rapid rate. As measured by the now defunct architectural Web site skyscrapers.com, 80 skyscrapers were built in Tokyo in the 1990s, versus just 49 in the 1980s (with skyscrapers be-
ing defined as buildings rising at least 115 feet). In Osaka, the total was 56 versus 18; in Yokohama, 19 versus none. London's total, by comparison, was 33 versus 28. New York actually registered a decline: only 103 skyscrapers were built there in the 1990s, versus 257 in the 1980s.

Perhaps the most visible progress of all was in fashion. Up to the late 1980s the Japanese had been avowedly fashion laggards. That changed in the 1990s—so much so that by 2000 the Paris-based fashion guru Suzy Menkes had pronounced Tokyo the world capital of street fashion. Meanwhile the editors of GQ magazine named Tokyo "the coolest city on the planet." By 2007 Japan's lead had become so institutionalized that many of the world's most prestigious fashion houses were trying out their newest ideas first on the superfashionable—and super-affluent—teenage girls of Tokyo. In an article headlined "Testing What's Hot In The Cradle Of Cool," *Business Week* reported that Japan's ascendancy had given rise to a new cot-
tage industry: "cool hunt" tours in which visiting foreign fashion executives paid $800 a day to be shepherded around Tokyo's most fashionable boutiques. The visitors were typically spend-
ing between $20,000 and $100,000 buying up clothes to ship back home for design teams to copy.

Meanwhile Japan's purchases of luxury brand-name goods grew by leaps and bounds in the 1990s. As reported by Craig Simons of the Cox News Service (April 20, 2006), Japan recently accounted for more than two-fifths of all the world's purchases of such goods (the real thing, that is, not cheap fakes). Citing an analysis by Goldman Sachs, he gave the following figures for the share of the world luxury-goods market accounted for by each country and region:

1. Japan: 41 percent
2. United States: 17 percent
3. China: 12 percent
4. Europe: 16 percent

76 **emphasizing Japan's economic negatives:** One of Japan's simplest emphasize-the-negatives gambits was also one of its most effective: the deregulation of a previously strict policy of keeping city centers clear of down-and-outs. All through the 1980s foreigners had marveled at the almost total absence of street people in Japan. They reasoned that this stemmed from supposedly preternatural Japanese economic powers. The real reason was more prosaic. As James Fallows documented in the *Atlantic* in April 1988 ("The Other Japan"), Japan always had its share of street people, but it merely chose to hide them away. Up to the early 1990s, the police had been highly efficient in keeping them confined to a few remote Skid Row–type areas such as the Sanya district of Tokyo. In Japan's new "emphasize the negatives" mode, this policy was reversed. Soon street people were camping out in front of Japan's most famous five-star hotels. They were not nearly as numerous as in New York or London, but their in-your-face positioning could hardly be overlooked by high-level foreign bankers and government officials. There is plenty of evidence that the authorities not only tolerated the high-visibility homeless encampments but actually encouraged them. How else can we interpret an eyewitness account by the Japan historian and former American cultural diplomat Ivan Hall. In a covered passageway leading from the Tokyo subway to the massive five-star Keio Plaza hotel one evening in the mid-1990s, he saw homeless men wait in line as a subway official handed out huge sheets of cardboard and cheap futon mattresses. Already suspicious about the sudden visibility of Japanese homelessness, Hall lingered discreetly to watch as the recipients then proceeded to build little cubicles in which they settled down for the night. He recalls: "I peered into one of the cubicles to find a middle aged *oji-san* (gentleman) curled up in bed reading a book and flicking his cigarette ashes into an ashtray he or somebody had provided!"

THREE: Genesis of a New System

81 **the Japanese bureaucracy's hidden agenda to minimize private ownership:** Statistics cited by Michael Carney of Concordia University dramatically underline the remarkable degree of egalitarianism in modern Japan. As of 1996, the wealthiest fifteen families in Japan controlled just 2.8 percent of corporate assets.

81 **many of the most outspoken skeptics were British or Australian:** MacArthur's story that Japan had undergone an "overnight conversion" to Western values was devastatingly critiqued by the Australian public servant William Macmahon Ball. Ball, who was noted for fearless integrity, served as Australia's chief representative in Japan during the early years of the occupation and was also the British Commonwealth's representative on the Allied Council, an advisory body charged with overseeing the American occupation. On page ix of *Japan: Enemy or Ally?* (New York: Institute of Pacific Relations, 1949), he commented: "There has been no fundamental change in Japan's social structure or in the outlook of her leaders."

82 **"A tendency towards complacent self-dramatization . . .":** Richard Storry, *A History of Modern Japan* (London: Penguin, 1960), p. 240.

85 **a bizarrely expressed concern for his troops' health:** See Robert Textor in *Failure in Japan* (New York: John Day, 1951), p. 101.

87 **they resurrected the same electoral system:** *Encyclopaedia Britannica,* 1970 edition, "Proportional Representation."

89 **have never been able to make their voice heard:** The influence of women voters in Japanese politics may be notable for its absence, but this has not stopped Japanese public relations operatives from constantly suggesting that the country has been making fast progress in women's rights. The message has generally been stated implicitly rather than explicitly. As James Fallows has pointed out, an iconic example of the phenomenon was a *Life* magazine cover story in 1964 which argued that Japan was engaged in "a hectic drive ... to outAmericanize America." The cover photograph was of a young Japanese woman at a bowling alley. Dressed in a kimono and wearing austere *tabi* socks, she was seen grinning broadly as she rolled an American-made bowling ball down the alley. The implication of course was that Japanese women were becoming more assertive. Today, more than forty years later, all the evidence is that Japan's "democratic" institutions have never reflected that assertiveness.

92 **The Singaporean system:** Jon Woronoff in *Asia's Miracle Economies* (Armonk, N.Y.: Sharpe, 1987).

96 **just eight banks controlled 80 percent of Japanese industry:** See Robert Textor in *Failure in Japan* (New York: John Day, 1951), p. 61.

100 **Conrad Brandt:** *Encyclopaedia Britannica,* 1970 edition, "Kuomintang."

100 **headed its propaganda department in 1925–1926:** *Encyclopaedia Britannica,* 1970 edition, "Mao Tse-tung."

100 **Other leading Communists:** *Encyclopaedia Britannica,* 1970 edition, "Chou En-lai."

105 **the beginnings of the Korean miracle:** Ezra Vogel in *The Four Little Dragons* (Cambridge, Mass.: Harvard University Press, 1992).

FOUR: Let There Be Savings!

116 **Nowhere has the policy been more effective than in China:** According to the 2005 edition of the *China Statistical Yearbook,* China had built up a treasure trove of savings totaling 11.9 trillion yuan, or more than $1.4 trillion, as of 2004. This represented nearly four times the total in 1995 and nearly seventeen times the total in 1990.

116 **embryonic form:** Maoist China used a crude version of suppressed consumption to achieve a savings rate of about 30 percent of gross domestic product. See Andrew J. Nathan, *China's Transition* (New York: Columbia University Press, 1997), p. 54.

117 **Moreover, Hutton is mistaken in implying:** Data on the age structures in China, Russia, Lithuania, and Latvia come from the *CIA World Factbook.*

118 **Japan's savings rate rocketed:** Edward Denison and William Chung in Hugh Patrick and Henry Rosovsky, eds., *Asia's New Giant* (Washington: Brookings, 1976), p. 117.

118 **Edwin Reischauer spotlighted:** See Edwin Reischauer, *Wanted: An Asian Policy* (New York: Knopf, 1955), p. 109.

119 **the suppression of consumer credit services:** See Lester Thurow in *The Future of Capitalism* (New York: Morrow, 1996), p. 296.

120 **ranging from expensive watches to boats:** Boating is one of several categories of conspicuous consumption that have been targeted for explicit suppression in China. As recorded by Keith Bradsher in the *New York Times* in 2006, the authorities maintain a ban on yachts except those used solely on lakes. But few wealthy Chinese people go boating even on lakes. In an earlier article in 2004, Bradsher commented: "The economic boom has certainly created plenty of fortunes big enough to afford yachts. But they have never caught on among rich Chinese, who, unlike the boating set in the West, tend to keep their consumption as inconspicuous as possible. And no wonder, considering how widespread tax evasion and dubious dealings are here: few people want their lifestyles to attract official attention." The use of private planes has also been heavily discouraged. Up until 2004 the Chinese were banned from owning private planes, and the use of private planes there remains heavily restricted. Speaking to the *Financial Times* in 2005, Jeff Lowe, vice president of the Gulfstream private jet company, suggested there were more private jets based at the Orange County airport in California than in all of Asia. In a report in 2006, Singapore-based Channel NewsAsia estimated the total number of private jets in China at just twenty. By comparison there were an estimated seven thousand in the United States.

120 **Cars have long been singled out for special levies:** Writing in 2006, Lim Hua Sing, a professor at Tokyo's Waseda University, estimated that prices for Japanese cars in China ran three times Japanese home market levels (*Asahi* English-language edition, February 11–12, 2006).

121 **The problem is particularly acute in older buildings:** For an early account of the privatization of the Chinese housing market, see "For Sale at Last in China: Dream Homes, but No Sink," by Seth Faison, *New York Times*, September 3, 1998. He wrote: "In Shanghai, as in many other Chinese cities, most housing is still in low-rise buildings where tenants have to share a kitchen and a toilet with their neighbors."

122 **$80 a square foot:** Xinhua, March 25, 2006.

122 **Beijing residents typically pay about eleven times their income:** As quoted by Tyler Marshall and Mark Magnier in the *Los Angeles Times* in 2004, Hua Min, head of the Institute of the World Economy at Shanghai's Fudan University, suggested a middle-class Chinese already then was required to spend as much as twenty-five times his annual salary to buy an apartment, compared to two or three times for a typical American.

123 **the urban percentage:** See *South China Morning Post*, March 3, 2007.

123 **China's rate of new building:** Figures in this paragraph are based on statistics supplied by Plunkett Research and published in the financial disclosures of Country Garden Holdings.

129 **"plastic":** This article (in the *Washington Monthly* in May 2003) was by the normally well-informed Joshua Kurlantzick. Describing credit cards as "America's biggest new export," Kurlantzick wrote: "Foreign governments and global lenders have both tried to encourage developing world consumers to open their wallets and global consumers have happily

obliged. Until recently, credit cards were unheard of in China. Today, however, Chinese use plastic for more than $200 billion worth of transactions annually."

129 **they were required to go in person:** Rowan Callick, *Australian,* November 27, 2006.

132 **the average level of tariff had fallen to 23 percent:** Thomas Klitgaard and Karen Schiele as quoted by AFX, May 20, 1997.

FIVE: Power Begets Power

143 **the key word in China's traditional Confucianism:** *Encyclopaedia Britannica,* 1970 edition, "China."

144 **an attempt to reassure the West:** See Daniel A. Bell, "China's Leaders Rediscover Confucianism," *International Herald Tribune,* September 15, 2006.

145 **no discernible embarrassment:** See Hongbin Li, Lingsheng Meng, and Junsen Zhang, "Why Do Entrepreneurs Enter Politics? Evidence from China," *ASAP,* July 2006.

147 **Mark Kitto:** See Richard McGregor, *Financial Times,* May 4, 2005.

147 **Sohu.com:** "The Flies Swarm In," *Economist,* January 24, 2006.

148 **"will stop at almost nothing . . .":** Richard Bernstein and Ross Munro, *The Coming Conflict with China* (New York: Knopf, 1997), p. 14.

149 **In further pioneering moves:** Joseph Pechman and Keimei Kaizuka in Hugh Patrick and Henry Rosovsky, eds., *Asia's New Giant* (Washington: Brookings, 1976), p. 320.

150 **from 40 percent to 60 percent:** Christine Wong, Christopher Heady, and Wing T. Woo, *Fiscal Management and Economic Reform in the People's Republic of China* (Hong Kong: Asian Development Bank/Oxford University Press, 1995), p. 131.

150 **Beijing does not allow local governments:** Andrew Browne, *Wall Street Journal,* September 15, 2006.

155 **permitted to nominate just two of nineteen board members:** See George Chen, "Foreigners Can Profit, but Beijing Decides Executive Lineup," Reuters, August 29, 2006.

158 **a plethora of new opportunities:** Information in this paragraph is drawn from Gordon Chang in *The Coming Collapse of China* (New York: Random House, 2001), p. 78.

164 **treated as a capital offense:** Jasper Becker, *The Chinese* (New York: Oxford, 2000), p. 335.

164 **between 14 and 15 percent of gross domestic product:** Cited by June Teufel Dreyer in *China's Political System* (New York: Pearson Longman, 2004), p. 163.

SIX: In a Confucian America

176 **no fewer than 298 American corporations:** Immanuel C. Y. Hsu, *The Rise of Modern China* (New York: Oxford University Press, 1999), p. 967.

179 **European sporting-goods company:** Hannah Beech, *Time,* September 5, 2006.

180 **"Structurally, China is still a Leninist economy . . .":** Chalmers Johnson, "Breaching the Great Wall," *American Prospect,* January 1997.

181 **the Big Three Detroit auto corporations:** It is hard to exaggerate the degree to which even once powerful American corporations have been forced to bend their values to serve the Beijing regime's agenda. A notable case concerns an employee of Beijing Jeep who was arrested for holding a Christian ceremony commemorating Tiananmen. The company fired him for nonattendance and refused to rehire him when he emerged from prison. As Tina Rosenberg reported in the *New York Times* (September 18, 2005), the matter went all the way to the top of Chrysler Corporation, which by then was the ultimate owner of Beijing Jeep. Only direct lobbying by Chrysler's chairman got the victimized employee his job back.

182 **A much more robust one:** Addendum by Harry Harding to Council on Foreign Relations report, "U.S.-China Relations: An Affirmative Agenda, a Positive Course," 2007.

183 **Should American corporations pay bribes or not?:** Just how relevant this question is can be judged from, for instance, the fact that the Chinese advertising business is completely corrupt. Not to put too fine a point on it, advertisers have to bribe top executives of the state-owned media to get the best advertising rates. As recounted by the China-based advertising executive Tom Doctoroff in *Billions: Selling to the Chinese Consumer* (New York: Palgrave Macmillan, 2005), discounts of up to 70 percent off standard rates are available to advertisers who are prepared to play the game the "Chinese way."

184 **they have become more Chinese than the Chinese themselves:** Countless examples could be cited of how "Chinese" some of America's most esteemed corporations have become. Take AT&T. When in 2001 one of its employees, Li Shaomin, a New Jersey–based American citizen, was charged by Beijing with spying against China, AT&T's top management not only did not support him but actively undermined his attempts to get justice. As recounted by Tina Rosenberg in the *New York Times* in 2002, Li was charged as part of an attempt by Beijing to intimidate ethnic Chinese working for non-Chinese organizations. AT&T blocked Li's boss, Salvatore Cordo, from collecting signatures for a protest petition. Cordo commented: "I wasn't asking for a public statement—I wasn't naive. But there was an absolute terror on the company's part to do a damn thing that could be even remotely interpreted as helpful."

186 **Yahoo! alone:** See *International Herald Tribune,* February 9, 2006 and December 8, 2006.

187 **China had developed Internet controls:** George Soros, *The Crisis of Global Capitalism* (New York: Public Affairs, 1998), p. 110.

189 **William J. Dobson suggested it was doomed:** See William J. Dobson, "Protest.org," *New Republic,* July 6, 1998.

191 **Wu Jichuan:** Quoted by Bill Gates in *The Road Ahead* (New York: Viking, 1995), p. 236.

199 **Chinese-born students outnumbered American ones:** John Fialka in *War by Other Means: Economic Espionage in America* (New York: Norton, 1997), p. 153.

199 **all the graduate students in mathematics:** Thomas Friedman in *The World Is Flat* (London: Penguin, 2005), p. 351.

208 **impassioned commentary:** Eric Alterman, "Dude! Where's My Debate?" *Nation,* February 26, 2007.

SEVEN: The Dragon's Fey Friend

215 **the bromide that other Asians hate the Japanese:** See James Fallows, *Looking at the Sun* (New York: Pantheon, 1994), p. 249.

217 **Their key concern was to build Japan's aerospace industry:** The background to the FS-X affair was explained in an e-mail message to the author in 2007 by Kevin Kearns, a former top State Department official who played a key role in the effort to sell an American plane to Tokyo. Kearns wrote: "FS-X was part of Japan's overall industrial strategy to break into aircraft building, both defense and commercial, to move up the value-added chain, and to leapfrog out of its component parts production relationship with Boeing—even though that was a lucrative and growing business in which it built ever-increasing sections of Boeing's commercial aircraft. FS-X was an important part of Japanese nationalists' strategy to break free from dependence on licensed production of American weapons systems and eventually go it alone militarily—looking to the day that the Constitution would be revised from self-defense only. Finally, FS-X was a technology and systems integration laboratory, to show that the Japanese had or could develop those skills necessary to build and assemble highly complex systems without foreign assistance. FS-X demonstrated convincingly that Japanese thinking was strategic, comprehensive, thorough, integrated, and concentrated completely on furthering Japan's industrial, technological, and eventually military dominance—all the while manipulating foreigners (in particular the Americans) into believing Japan was tinkering aimlessly and expensively in an ill-conceived project."

219 **top American officials appointed him:** "Tamiya," *Nihon Jinmei Daijiten* (Tokyo: Kodansha, 2001).

225 **"In addition to the cultural likeness . . .":** Robert Guillain in *The Japanese Challenge* (London: Hamish Hamilton, 1970), p. 269.

225 **Westerners are particularly likely to underestimate top Japanese officials:** See Robert Guillain in *The Japanese Challenge* (London: Hamish Hamilton, 1970), pp. 68–69.

225 **"Japan stands aloof . . .":** These quotations are from Robert Guillain in *The Japanese Challenge* (London: Hamish Hamilton, 1970), pp. 268–271.

228 **"tempest in a teacup":** "Japan & China—Tempest in a Teacup," Mike (in Tokyo) Rogers, LewRockwell.com, April 25, 2005.

228 **The pattern goes back to November 1979:** Commentary by Katherine G. Burns, Stimson Center.

228 **If Tokyo's true attitude was ever in doubt:** One of the most revealing accounts of how staunchly Tokyo supported Beijing in the aftermath of the Tiananmen massacre has come from Michael Armacost, who served as the American ambassador to Tokyo from 1989 to 1993. In his book *Friends or Rivals? The Insider's Account of U.S.-Japan Relations* (New York: Columbia University Press, 1996), he recounted how Tokyo so vehemently took Beijing's side that "a disconnect between the U.S. and Japan became a serious possibility." He explained: "Japan's foreign policy professionals criticized the West for overreacting to the events at Tiananmen, privately criticized our human rights diplomacy as bordering on meddlesome interference, and expressed sympathy for Chinese concerns about the potential implications

of growing domestic disorder." Armacost pointed out that though forty thousand Chinese exchange students in the United States took a leading part in urging sanctions against Beijing, at least sixty thousand Chinese students in Japan remained "curiously mute." Armacost was too diplomatic to offer an explanation, but to anyone familiar with East Asia, his implication was unmistakable. The right to demonstrate is extremely tightly controlled in Japan as in other parts of the region, and action by Chinese students was simply suppressed. Armacost went on to allege that though Tokyo ostensibly supported Western sanctions, it dragged its feet and contrived to find loopholes in the rules (citing a "humanitarian" exemption clause to provide support for the construction of a major chemical fertilizer plant, for instance). Within three months of the massacre, Japanese technical assistance personnel were already back in China. High-level political contacts between Tokyo and Beijing were resumed shortly afterward.

229 **Hosokawa delighted his hosts in Beijing:** See Hobart Rowen, "Clinton's Myopic Asian Trade Policy," *Washington Post*, April 10, 1994. Rowen, a now dead commentator who was noted for strongly pro-Japanese views, wrote: "The Japanese are making their displeasure known in many ways, some not subtle. [Deutsche Bank analyst Kenneth] Courtis said in a letter to clients, for example, that Hosokawa had a cozy visit with top Chinese officials, discussing new yen loans and closer China-Japan relations. That was on the heels of Secretary of State Warren Christopher's humiliation in Beijing, when his demand for improvement in China's treatment of dissidents was rebuffed. Pointedly, Hosokawa came down on the Chinese side. 'Western or European-type democracy should not be forced on others,' Hosokawa said."

241 **"Japan has acquired all the parts necessary for a nuclear weapon . . .":** Nick Rufford of the *Sunday Times* (January 30, 1994), as quoted by Marc Dean Millot in "Facing the Emerging Reality of Regional Nuclear Adversaries," *Washington Quarterly*, Summer 1994.

241 **its laboratory head, Edward Condon:** In a historical account at its Web site, the Los Alamos National Laboratory states: "Edward Condon, who had directed the Westinghouse Research Laboratory, had agreed to serve as his assistant, supplying industrial expertise (as well as a background in quantum mechanics) to complement Oppenheimer's academic experience."

241 **Beijing had still done almost nothing to question Japan's intense interest in nuclear technologies:** Beijing's behavior was exceptionally significant at the time of Toshiba's takeover of the Westinghouse nuclear business in 2007. After all, this was supposedly a time of especially serious Sino-Japanese tensions. Yet Beijing said nothing to embarrass Tokyo.

248 **"abandoned and dilapidated":** William Holstein in *The Japanese Power Game* (New York: Scribner's, 1990), p. 156.

250 **the date when the fourteen Class A war criminals' names:** Although Japan is a country where "the past keeps changing" (that is, the authorities think nothing of adjusting the official record retrospectively for propaganda purposes), the date of the enshrinement is generally accepted to have been October 17, 1978. See, for instance, "Storm after Koizumi's shrine visit," by Peter Alford and Mark Dodd in the Sydney-based newspaper of record, the *Australian*, August 16, 2006. See also articles by Greg Torode and Julian Ryall in the *South China Morning Post*, August 16, 2006, and by Hiroshi Osedo/Reuters in the Queensland *Courier Mail*, October 18, 2005.

251 **almost as much an insult to the United States as to China:** It is important to realize
that the Rape of Nanking exemplified the East Asian concept of "total war." As such it
represented—on an admittedly appalling scale—an end-justifies-the-means approach that
Chinese leaders had often used against their own people. Thus, the Chinese see the Rape of
Nanking significantly differently than Westerners do. Although the massacre has long been
presented in the West as an utterly inexplicable, motiveless outbreak of mad-dog savagery
(and thus, as Westerners often imply even if they rarely state it ostensibly, signifying a streak
of special brutality in the Japanese people's very DNA), the Chinese have always known that
it was a fully rational, if particularly repulsive, application of the concept of total war. The
Japanese hoped that by making an example of the then Chinese capital, other Chinese cities
would surrender without a shot. This was a highly Machiavellian calculation. As such it was
not dissimilar to the many brutal decisions the Chinese Communists had made during their
long struggle to win control of China. As one of Mao Zedong's top generals in the 1940s and
1950s, Deng was himself implicated in countless Communist atrocities. After all, Mao Zedong had once boasted that he had had forty-six thousand of his enemies buried alive.
Widely considered the greatest mass murderer in history, Mao was certainly as convinced as
any militarist-era Japanese general that the end justifies the means. In the interests of balance, it should be added that Chiang Kai-shek's decision in 1938 to breach the Yellow River's
dikes demonstrated a similarly appalling calculation. As recorded by James Kynge in *China
Shakes the World* (London: Weidenfeld & Nicholson, 2006), the maneuver, which was undertaken to halt a Japanese advance, cost the lives of as many as nine hundred thousand Chinese
civilians. It left millions more homeless.

254 **The Group of Four bid was dead on arrival:** A little-noticed episode reported by Brian
Knowlton in the *International Herald Tribune* shed a revealing light on Tokyo's true intentions.
When the fate of the Group of Four bid became obvious, the United States in June 2005 put
up a counterproposal in which Japan and one other nation (whose identity was never revealed but was probably India) would become Security Council members. This proposal,
which clearly had a far greater chance of success than the Group of Four proposal, was
peremptorily turned down by Tokyo and was even criticized by Japanese foreign minister
Nobutaka Machimura as "a difficult curveball." Prime Minister Junichiro Koizumi softened
the message, describing the proposal as "good for Japan, but not good for other countries in
the Group of Four." He added: "We can't adopt a plan that's only good for Japan. We have to
think about the global community as a whole." Such selflessness—not always apparent in
Tokyo's dealings with the outside world—might have seemed admirable but for the fact that
the Group of Four bid was already a no-hoper. If Tokyo sincerely aspired to become a Security Council member, its attitude to the American proposal made no sense. If, however, it was
not sincere, its attitude made all the sense in the world.

257 **bad faith and bare knuckles in Tokyo:** Only the most public instance of the ruthlessness
with which the Japanese establishment has fought the battle against Detroit has been its
pattern of resorting to character assassination against anyone who tells the truth about
Japan's trade barriers. In the 1980s a notable victim was the then chief executive of Chrysler
Corporation, Lee Iacocca, who vociferously and correctly charged that Japan used trade barriers to keep foreign cars out of the Japanese market. One memorable attack on his character came from Kenichi Ohmae, then a top partner in McKinsey & Company. Writing in
Beyond National Borders (Homewood: Dow Jones–Irwin, 1987), Ohmae strongly suggested
that Iacocca was a racist. Referring to the fact that Iacocca was contemplating running for

president of the United States, Ohmae commented: "This potential presidential candidate is . . . a man who would strengthen the Yellow Peril psychology that is growing in the United States today." Ohmae took exception particularly to Iacocca's charge that the deteriorating trade trend signified that the United States was becoming a colony. As Iacocca pointed out, for decades virtually the only products the United States had been able to sell to Japan were wheat, corn, coal, and other low-grade materials, whereas Japan sold mainly advanced manufactured goods to the United States. Ohmae's position was that Japanese markets were open and that any foreign corporation that failed in Japan was incompetent. This presentation, uttered as standard boilerplate by all Japan's apologists at the time, was later contradicted by Minoru Makihara, vice chairman of Japan's powerful Keidanren business organization. In a devastating gaffe in speaking to foreign journalists in 2000, Makihara admitted that as recently as the late 1980s the Japanese market had been "closed and tightly protected." He was trying to make the point that there had been some subsequent opening of the market—a lot of opening, if he was to be believed. His statement about the late 1980s, however, was no more than the unvarnished truth. He had forgotten how vehemently people like Ohmae had argued in the 1980s that the Japanese market was supposed to be open.

EIGHT: A Few Good Confucians

267 **the younger Murdoch even criticized Hong Kong democracy:** Joshua Kurlantzick, "The Dragon Still Has Teeth: How the West Winks at Chinese Repression," *World Policy Journal,* March 2003.

272 **His temporizing style has been obvious for two decades:** One of the more notable manifestations of this style has been an effort to question the validity of official statistics on United States–China trade imbalances. In an early contribution, he argued that after suitable adjustments, America's 1993 bilateral deficit would have been just $12 billion, not $23 billion as officially reported. He tried again in the late 1990s, arguing that the 1997 deficit was really $36 billion, not $50 billion. In a recent effort he calculated that the 2003 deficit was really "only" $110 billion, not $124 billion. It was as if a man standing on a railroad line speculated about how far away an approaching train was. Much skill and effort might be devoted to calculating the figure. But all that should be of entirely academic interest compared to the key point, which, of course, is the train's direction of travel.

274 **helping China's negotiations to join the World Trade Organization:** One of Lardy's more notable contributions in this respect was a chapter he wrote in *Asia After the "Miracle,"* edited by Selig Harrison and Clyde Prestowitz (Washington: Economic Strategy Institute, 1998). He suggested that China was pursuing a very much more open trade policy than Japan and that American observers were therefore wrong to assume that it would generate an "ever-growing global surplus." He explained: "China does not have a systemic global current account surplus but rather a pattern of trade in which its global current account balance swings from several years of deficit to several years of surplus, and unlike Japan, it has not adopted macroeconomic and exchange-rate policies that would result in growing global current account surpluses. . . . China has dramatically reduced trade barriers in recent years." Viewed from the vantage point of nearly a decade later, we know that the predicted swing back into deficit never happened. Rather, China's surpluses had as of 2006 rocketed more than fourfold. The truth is that it should have been obvious to any intelligent observer in 1998 that China was al-

ready closely copying Japan's mercantilist trade approach—and that all comments to the contrary were merely the usual self-serving rationalizations of the Washington trade lobby.

277 highly coordinated series of ad hominem attacks: I know from both my own experience and that of many friends and allies that misrepresentation is a major occupational hazard for any commentator who has the knowledge—and courage—to challenge the Japanese economic establishment.

Typically defamation comes in highly indirect ways. A notable case in point was a strange book that surfaced in the early 1990s that had ostensibly been co-authored by two of America's best-known economic commentators, one a top Washington policy analyst and the other a famous Detroit chief executive. An ostensible attack on Japanese trade policies, the book was couched in the most egregiously racist terms. Needless to say the ostensible authors had had nothing to do with the book's genesis and would never have dreamt of making their case in such a despicable, not to mention self-defeating, way. The book was a fake cooked up to try to discredit two upstanding people whose effectiveness in making reasoned criticisms of Japanese trade policy had become a major thorn in the Japanese government's side. The book's real authorship was traced back to a company in Tokyo. A law suit followed and remaining copies of the book were pulped by an order of an American court.

In my own case, one of the most memorable efforts to discredit me followed a similar course. This time the medium was not a fake book but rather a fake Web site. Entitled *East of the Rising Sun,* the site was presented in such a way that a casual observer—at least one who did not know me and had never read my work—might assume it was my home page. Such an assumption would have been reinforced by the fact that, as of the late 1990s, the site came up as many four times in the first ten Yahoo responses to searches for my name. The site not only used egregiously racist language to refer to the Japanese people but a satanic image from *Nightmare on Elm Street* to depict them. The site's operator, who gave his name as Martin Normart, claimed to be a major fan of my 1995 book *Blindside: Why Japan Is Still on Track to Overtake the U.S. By the Year 2000.* A sequel to it all is that, although Normart was ostensibly a Web site designer, he has disappeared from the Web and all efforts in recent years to trace him have drawn a blank.

I had a somewhat similar experience when my 1999 book *In Praise of Hard Industries: Why Manufacturing, Not the Information Economy, Is the Key to Future Prosperity* came out. This time the book was "espoused" by a fake site whose ostensible agenda was anti-Semitism. An interview with me was listed among the site's "papers." The implication was the interview had been granted to the site and that in some way it furthered the site's hate agenda (egregiously represented in the titles of the other papers on its menu). In reality the interview had been granted to Amazon.com's business books editor. It had been merely appropriated by the neo-Nazi site and had, of course, nothing to do with Jews, Israel, or any of the other issues discussed in such despicable terms at the site.

This site tends to come up particularly prominently when my work is in the news. In recent years my attempts to get the word out have continued to encounter various troubling impediments. There have been countless problems with Amazon.com alone. Often my books have been "lost" at Amazon.com or have been seriously misrepresented. As of September 2007, searches by title for *In Praise of Hard Industries,* for instance, drew a blank. The book was findable if my name was spelled correctly but even then it was seriously misrepresented because the publication date was given as 2001. This implied that my statement at my Web site that the book had anticipated the bursting of the New Economy bubble was false. In reality the book had been published in September 1999, six months before the bubble burst.

277 **a long-standing suspicion:** Governments throughout East Asia are known for their skill in infiltrating agents into top positions in all sorts of ostensibly independent and even antigovernment groups. Thus, the suspicions of China's overseas dissidents that their ranks have been penetrated by government agents were hardly unfounded. To say the least, Buruma's tone in skipping lightly over the issue did less than justice in that it implied the dissidents were psychotically jealous of one another if not overtly paranoid. In reality, it is hardly an exaggeration to suggest that East Asian governments strive to control everything that is controllable. The pattern is familiar in a nation as ostensibly Westernized as Japan, where even "consumer groups" are actually establishment fronts, typically run by the wives of top government officials. Hence the strange phenomenon, reported by James Fallows in the *Atlantic* in September 1987 ("Playing by Different Rules"), that Japan's "consumer" groups campaign to block imports of cheap foreign rice and thus help to sustain Japan's rice prices at five or six times world market levels.

278 **boosting the credibility of some undoubted fakes:** Buruma lavished particular attention on Dai Qing, an environmentalist and adopted daughter of one of the People's Liberation Army's founding fathers. While it may be going too far to suggest she is a fake, she is probably the Beijing economic establishment's favorite "dissident." In 2000, she strongly urged the United States to grant permanent normal trade relations to China. Dai, a Beijing-based journalist who has studied at Harvard and moves frequently between China and the United States, argued that this would improve China's human rights policies. Other dissidents, most notably Harry Wu and Wei Jingsheng, espoused the commonsense view that once granted unconditional access to the American market, China would no longer have much incentive to respond to American pressure for better treatment of dissidents and democracy advocates. In an editorial page article published in the *Los Angeles Times* just before the Congressional vote on PNTR, Dai wrote: "Permanent normal trade relations would send the Chinese people a powerful and positive message: The most powerful industrialized nation today will work with the Chinese people to build a new world order. This would put enormous pressure on both the government and the general public to meet the international standard not only on trade, but also on other issues, including human rights and environmental protection." These sentences were soon featured prominently at the Web site of the US-China Business Council, a key lobbying organization that played a central role in the PNTR campaign.

279 **Conspicuously absent was any mention of the book's lacunas:** Among those who did not notice how much Buruma left unmentioned were his associates in the literary department of the *New York Times*. The newspaper listed the book among its selection of the "most notable books" of the year and described the book in these terms: "An examination, by an impressively informed and empathetic journalist, of the ways in which the cataclysms of our century have shaped national identity."

NINE: Globalism or Democracy?

373 **John Foster Dulles:** See Chalmers Johnson in *Asia After the "Miracle,"* edited by Selig Harrison and Clyde Prestowitz (Washington: Economic Strategy Institute, 1998). Johnson wrote: "The classic example of American condescension was John Forster Dulles's Cold War remark that the Japanese might succeed in exporting to the United States shirts, pajamas, and perhaps cocktail napkins."

288 **Just since George W. Bush took office in 2001:** "Trade Deficit Shoots Up in March,"
Associated Press, May 10, 2007.

286 **economic equivalent of a heart-lung machine:** Just how hard this machine has had to
work lately is apparent from the fact that, as calculated by the Harvard University economics
professor Kenneth Rogoff, the United States has been soaking up as much as three-quarters
of the world's excess supply of savings. See "Too Much Money," *Business Week,* July 11, 2005.

291 **the Washington establishment continued to ignore the warnings:** One of the most
famous of all the warnings came from Ross Perot, who in 1992 predicted a "giant sucking
sound" if the North American Free Trade Agreement was implemented. His point was that
the agreement would prove devastating for American trade and jobs. He was opposed by
most of the American establishment, including American press commentators, who argued
that the new era of free trade with Canada and Mexico would powerfully improve America's
already serious trade problem. The agreement duly came into force in 1994, and the resulting
economic damage has been even greater than Perot anticipated. As the CNN trade hawk Lou
Dobbs pointed out in 2006, America's trade deficit with Mexico and Canada rocketed from
a mere $9.1 billion in 1993 to $128.2 billion in 2005. Dobbs added: "Instead of opening new
markets to U.S. products and services, the U.S. government over the past ten years has negotiated nothing more than a series of outsourcing agreements."

296 **denunciation campaigns are conducted discreetly:** Sometimes they are not so discreet.
Take the case of a noted American academic expert on East Asia who for a time worked for
an East Asian–funded quasi think tank in Washington. He had joined the organization in
good faith, believing it to be genuinely interested in promoting "mutual understanding" and
in particular conveying a truthful account of East Asian affairs. As time went by he became
increasingly critical of his foreign masters and their motives and eventually resigned in somewhat acrimonious circumstances. When he began discussing his experiences frankly, false rumors about his sex life were propagated to damage him. The episode probably did something
to curb his comments and it certainly "encouraged the others."

297 **someone as capable and potentially well-positioned as Norman:** Not only was Norman the most highly regarded and accomplished Japan watcher of his day but he was on inti-
mate terms with Lester Pearson, the then Canadian Minister for External Affairs. Pearson,
who was one of the most internationally active statesmen of his time and would go on in
1963 to become Prime Minister, repeatedly defended Norman against McCarthyite allegations and, as a tacit rebuke to Washington, appointed him ambassador to Egypt. His confidence was richly rewarded when Norman played a critical role in resolving the Suez crisis of
1956. It was in large measure because of Norman's work that Pearson won the Nobel Peace
Prize in 1957. As Norman's biographer Roger Bowen has suggested, Norman would have almost certainly shared the Peace Prize with Pearson had he not been driven to suicide six
months earlier. Less than a month before Norman died, Pearson had described him as "doing
extremely important work at a very difficult post in a way which commands my whole-
hearted admiration." Precisely because Norman had done such a good job in Egypt, his credibility had been strongly boosted and he thus posed an even greater threat than ever to a
Japanese establishment intent on misleading the West about its economic policies.

298 **Another issue is money:** The temptations in China run the gamut, from the trivial to the
colossal. More or less by definition the trivial is easier to document. Take for instance the

black-market currency transactions that foreign residents in China used in many years to supplement their incomes. The key to the scam was that foreigners were permitted to buy yuan at a preferential exchange rate. A minor racket developed in which foreigners sold yuan to Chinese citizens. The only correct policy, one adopted by, for instance, the prominent Beijing-based foreign correspondent Jane Macartney, was never to sell to the Chinese in any circumstance. Unfortunately, not everyone observed this rule. There were many examples of foreigners being arraigned for breaking the rules. More important for our purposes is that probably far more foreigners were quietly coerced into cooperating with the authorities in return for charges being discreetly dropped.

298 **Prominent or influential Western residents who are prepared to play the game:** Another way that compliant Westerners can be discreetly rewarded is through questionable art-market transactions. In an article in *Forbes* (February 12, 1996), Christie Brown explained: "In a China that is neither wholly capitalist nor wholly socialist, art is a kind of currency of corruption—a way of buying favors without anything so crass as a direct exchange of cash." According to a Shanghai-based expert quoted by Brown, one technique is to channel the bribe through a public art auction. The bribee puts an art object up for sale, and the briber bids the price up to an inflated level. The technique is not only wonderfully discreet but often nontaxable.

301 **"Armageddon option":** It is interesting to speculate how Beijing might react if Washington were to get *really* serious about remedying America's trade deficits. Assuming Washington resorted to tariffs on Chinese-made goods (and it is hard to see how any effort to address the imbalances could succeed without doing so), Beijing would undoubtedly respond with gambits kept in reserve for just such a crisis. One obvious move that might stay Washington's hand would be to initiate a process of political liberalization—or at least pretend to do so. Some of the steps would be quite easy. At little cost to either itself or the nation, the Chinese Communist Party could, for instance, change its name and call itself, say, the Confucian Party. It could also copy earlier East Asian nations in bringing in some token form of democracy. It need look no further than Japan, whose experience with cosmetic forms of democracy (and highly contrived electoral systems) goes back to the 1880s. Another gambit might be to go in the opposite direction, with some stridently aggressive move such as staging some carefully rehearsed military feint against, say, Japan. Given the aptitude for political theater in both Tokyo and Beijing, it is entirely possible that we may see some sensational demonstration of mutual enmity, perhaps with the Japanese and Chinese navies taking shots at each other over the Senkaku Islands. Stranger things have happened. Indeed in 1996 the Japanese navy felt it necessary to fire on some Taiwanese fishermen who came too close to the Senkakus (and this despite the fact that the Japanese constitution outlaws not only the Japanese navy but a fortiori any activity by that navy to threaten unarmed foreigners). The way to judge Sino-Japanese relations will, however, remain the same—not by the headlines in an ever gullible American press, but in the little-discussed but crucial trends in bilateral trade.

303 **Editors whose views serve advertisers rise to the top:** In the American magazine industry, for instance, it is an open secret that East Asian advertisers have increasingly pressured editors to avoid, or at least to downplay, certain "sensitive" issues. Not least of these is East Asian mercantilism. Particularly where the Japanese and South Korean brands of mercantilism are concerned, the American press holds back. It is probably not an accident that Japanese and South Korean corporations are big advertisers.

For the moment the American press remains more forthright about Chinese mercantilism but this may be changing. The point is that though Chinese advertisers are still only a small factor in the American media, their importance is growing very rapidly. It is a fair bet that their spending is likely to become an important influence within a decade. Certainly it is well known that Beijing hopes that by the 2010s, one-fifth of the world's top 500 corporations will be based in China.

Another problem is the increasingly concentrated ownership of the American media. As such observers as Senator Byron Dorgan and Paul Craig Roberts have pointed out, concentration of media power has clearly resulted in a drastic reduction in the diversity of comment. Not to put too fine a point on it, top editors are increasingly cognizant of the business interests of the controlling corporations. In most cases these corporations have already established important businesses in China and thus have offered up "hostages" to the Beijing authorities.

306 **This is exemplified most obviously in antitrust policy:** Because the selective-enforcement mechanism is for the most part highly unobtrusive in its effects, it is difficult to document. In the antitrust field, for instance, it is clear to experienced observers that hundreds, probably thousands, of American companies compromise themselves in East Asia. That few such instances ever come to light does not mean that selective enforcement is not powerfully at work. The mere threat of compromising information being passed on to the U.S. Justice Department is enough to break the will of most corporate boards. The result is that corporate boards tacitly opt to collaborate with East Asian regulators. Such collaboration takes many forms, most obviously the transferring of key production technologies to East Asia—technologies that otherwise the top board would want to keep safely at home. In the case of Japan, the dangers created by differing antitrust regulations were identified by U.S. government officials as far back as the 1980s. As reported by the *Journal of Commerce* in 1988, the U.S. Transportation Department was worried that American companies in Japan were being induced to participate in cartels or other activities that would put them on the wrong side not only of Japanese antitrust law (which is virtually never enforced), but of American antitrust law (which is of course rigorously enforced whenever the evidence justifies prosecution). The newspaper quoted an unnamed Tokyo-based American executive saying: "The United States puts so much emphasis on anti-trust and this puts us at a clear disadvantage. Other countries in the region simply do not inhibit their industries in the same way."

306 **Consider some of the surprises:** Another notable surprise is a phenomenon best described as the Anglophone trade meltdown. Virtually without exception, English-speaking nations have suffered dramatic—and utterly unanticipated—deterioration in their trade positions in the last two decades. Their plight contrasts remarkably with a trend for most advanced non-Anglophone nations to run ever larger trade surpluses. While America's current account deficit of 6.5 percent of gross domestic product in 2006 was the worst in American history, this was exceeded by an 8.1 percent deficit in New Zealand. Meanwhile Australia, Ireland, and Britain recorded deficits of 6.2, 4.6, and 2.5 percent respectively. The Anglophone meltdown extended even to Pakistan (a deficit of 4.4 percent) and India (3.3 percent). Of course, trade deficits have been a commonplace of English-language discourse since Britain's early post–World War II days as "the sick man of Europe." In reality, however, Britain's deficits in the 1950s and 1960s were puny by today's standards. It is chastening to recall that Britain's deficit in 1967—the year Prime Minister Harold Wilson was forced to devalue the pound—was a mere 0.7 percent.

The Anglophone meltdown contrasts particularly sharply with, of course, Confucian East Asia. The current account *surpluses* in South Korea, Taiwan, Japan, China, Hong Kong, and Singapore in 2006 ran respectively 0.2 percent, 2.8 percent, 3.6 percent, 7.1 percent, 11.1 percent, and a truly phenomenal 29.2 percent. (Linguistic note: policymaking in both Hong Kong and Singapore has, of course, long since slipped its former moorings in Anglophone culture.) Other major surpluses in 2006 were earned by Denmark (1.8 percent), Belgium (1.9 percent), Austria (1.9 percent), Germany (4.7 percent), Sweden (7.7 percent), the Netherlands (8.2 percent), Switzerland (13.1 percent), and Russia (14.3 percent). Russia owed its performance in large measure to soaring energy prices. So did Canada, which with a surplus of 1.9 percent was the lone significant Anglophone nation in the positive column. A cynic might conclude that national trade performance correlates closely with how seriously the *Economist* magazine is taken: whereas the New Zealanders believe every word, smirking Singaporeans just recall the old maxim, "Whom the gods would destroy, they first make mad."

Bibliography

Amsden, Alice. *Asia's New Giant*. New York: Oxford University Press, 1989.

Armacost, Michael. *Friends or Rivals: The Insider's Account of U.S.-Japan Relations*. New York: Columbia University Press, 1996.

Austin, Greg, and Stuart Harris. *Japan and Greater China*. Honolulu: University of Hawai'i, Press, 2001.

Baker, Raymond. *Capitalism's Achilles' Heel*. Hoboken, N.J.: Wiley, 2005.

Becker, Jasper. *The Chinese*. New York: Oxford University Press, 2000.

———. *Dragon Rising: An Inside Look at China Today*. Washington: National Geographic, 2006.

Bernstein, Richard, and Ross Munro. *The Coming Conflict with China*. New York: Knopf, 1997.

Black, Eugene. *Alternative in Southeast Asia*. New York: Praeger, 1969.

Blackman, Carolyn. *Negotiating China*. Crows Nest, New South Wales: Allen & Unwin, 1997.

Bowen, Roger, ed. *E. H. Norman: His Life and Scholarship*. Toronto: University of Toronto, Press, 1984.

Brady, Anne-Marie. *Making the Foreign Serve China*. Lanham: Rowman & Littlefield, 2003.

Brahm, Laurence. *Zhu Rongji and the Transformation of Modern China*. Singapore: Wiley, 2002.

Buchanan, Patrick J. *The Death of the West*. New York: Thomas Dunne Books, 2001.

———. *The Great Betrayal*. Boston: Little, Brown, 1998.

———. *State of Emergency*. New York: Thomas Dunne Books, 2006.

———. *Where the Right Went Wrong*. New York: Thomas Dunne Books, 2004.

Burstein, Daniel, and Arne De Keijzer. *Big Dragon.* New York: Simon & Schuster, 1998.

Buruma, Ian. *Bad Elements.* London: Weidenfeld & Nicholson, 2001.

————. *Behind the Mask: On Sexual Demons, Sacred Mothers, Transvestites, Gangsters, and Other Japanese Cultural Heroes.* New York: Meridian, 1984.

————. *The Wages of Guilt: Memories of War in Germany and Japan.* New York: Farrar, Straus & Giroux, 1994.

Cairncross, Frances. *The Death of Distance.* London: Orion Books, 1997.

Chang, Gordon. *The Coming Collapse of China.* New York: Random House, 2001.

Choate, Pat. *Agents of Influence: How Japan's Lobbyists in the United States Manipulate America's Political and Economic System.* New York: Knopf, 1990.

————. *Hot Property: The Stealing of Ideas in an Age of Globalization.* New York: Knopf, 2005.

Chua, Amy. *World on Fire.* London: Heinemann, 2004.

Clissold, Tim. *Mr. China.* New York: HarperBusiness, 2004.

Cohen, Stephen. *Cowboys and Samurai.* New York: Harper, 1991.

Dobbs, Lou. *Exporting America: Why Corporate Greed Is Shipping American Jobs Overseas.* New York: Warner, 2004.

————. *War on the Middle Class: How the Government, Big Business, and Special Interest Groups Are Waging War on the American Dream and How to Fight Back.* New York: Viking, 2006.

Doctoroff, Tom. *Billions: Selling to the Chinese Consumer.* New York: Palgrave Macmillan, 2005.

Dorgan, Byron. *Take This Job and Ship It.* New York: Thomas Dunne Books, 2006.

Dower, John W. *Origins of the Modern Japanese State.* New York: Pantheon, 1975.

Dreyer, June Teufel. *China's Political System.* New York: Pearson Longman, 2004.

Eftimiades, Nicholas. *Chinese Intelligence Operations.* Annapolis, Md.: Naval Institute, 1994.

Fallows, James. *Looking at the Sun: The Rise of the New East Asian Economic and Political System.* New York: Pantheon, 1994.

Fenby, Jonathan. *Generalissimo: Chiang Kai-shek and the China He Lost.* London: Free Press, 2003.

Fialka, John. *War by Other Means: Economic Espionage in America.* New York: W. W. Norton, 1997.

Fingleton, Eamonn. *Blindside: Why Japan Is Still on Track to Overtake the U.S. by the Year 2000.* Boston: Houghton Mifflin, 1995.

————. *In Praise of Hard Industries: Why Manufacturing, Not the Information Economy, Is the Key to Future Prosperity.* Boston: Houghton Mifflin, 1999.

————. *Unsustainable: How Economic Dogma Is Destroying American Prosperity.* New York: Nation Books, 2003.

Fishman, Ted. *China, Inc.* New York: Scribner's, 2005.

Friedman, Thomas. *The Lexus and the Olive Tree.* New York: Farrar, Straus & Giroux, 1999.

————. *The World Is Flat.* London: Penguin, 2005.

Gallagher, Mary Elizabeth. *Contagious Capitalism: Globalization and the Politics of Labor in China.* Princeton, N.J.: Princeton University Press, 2005.

Gates, Bill. *The Road Ahead.* New York: Viking, 1995.

Gertz, Bill. *The China Threat.* Washington: Regnery, 2000.

Gilley, Bruce. *China's Democratic Future.* Chichester: Columbia University Press, 2004.

Goldsmith, Jack, and Tim Wu. *Who Controls the Internet?* New York: Oxford University Press, 2006.

Goldsmith, Sir James. *The Trap.* New York: Carroll & Graf, 1994.

Gomory, Ralph, and William Baumol. *Global Trade and Conflicting National Interests.* Cambridge, Mass.: MIT Press, 2000.

Goodman, David. *Deng Xiaoping and the Chinese Revolution.* London: Routledge, 1994.

Goodstadt, Leo. *Uneasy Partners.* Hong Kong: Hong Kong University Press, 2005.

Grofman, Bernard, Sung-Chull Lee, Edwin A. Winckler, and Brian Woodall (eds). *Elections in Japan, Korea, and Taiwan under the Single Non-Transferable Vote: The Comparative Study of an Embedded Institution.* Ann Arbor, Michigan: The University of Michigan Press, 1999.

Guillain, Robert. *The Japanese Challenge.* London: Hamish Hamilton, 1970.

Gutmann, Ethan. *Losing the New China.* San Francisco: Encounter Books, 2004.

Hagstrom, Linus. *Japan's China Policy.* Abingdon: Routledge, 2005.

Hall, Ivan. *Bamboozled! How America Loses the Intellectual Game with Japan and Its Implications for Our Future in Asia.* Armonk, N.Y.: Eastgate, 2002.

———. *Cartels of the Mind.* New York: W. W. Norton, 1998.

Hilpert, Hanns Gunther, and Rene Haak. *Japan and China.* Basingstoke: Palgrave, 2002.

Hira, Ron. *Outsourcing America.* New York: AMACOM, 2005.

Holmes, Linda Goetz. *Unjust Enrichment.* Mechanicsburg: Stackpole, 2001.

Holstein, William. *The Japanese Power Game.* New York: Scribner's, 1990.

Horsley, William, and Roger Buckley. *Nippon: New Superpower.* London: BBC Enterprises, 1990.

Huang, Xiaoming. *The Rise and Fall of the East Asian Growth System, 1951–2000.* London: RoutledgeCurzon, 2005.

Huang, Yasheng. *Selling China.* Cambridge, U.K.: Cambridge University Press, 2003.

Huntington, Samuel P. *The Clash of Civilizations.* New York: Touchstone, 1997.

Hutchings, Graham. *Modern China.* Cambridge, Mass.: Harvard University Press, 2001.

Hutton, Will. *The Writing on the Wall.* London: Little, Brown, 2007.

Ingrassia, Paul, and Joseph White. *Comeback: The Fall and Rise of the American Automobile Industry.* New York: Touchstone, 1995.

Jansen, Marius. *The Making of Modern Japan.* Cambridge, Mass.: Belknap, 2000.

Jasinowski, Jerry, and Robert Hamrin. *Making It in America.* New York: Fireside, 1995.

Johnson, Chalmers. *Blowback: The Costs and Consequences of American Empire.* New York: Henry Holt, 2000.

———. *MITI and the Japanese Miracle.* Tokyo: Tuttle, 1986.

Jones, F. C. *Manchuria Since 1931.* London: Royal Institute, 1949.

Kennedy, Paul. *The Rise and Fall of the Great Powers.* New York: Random House, 1988.

Kristof, Nicholas, and Sheryl WuDunn. *China Wakes.* New York: Vintage, 1995.

Kuttner, Robert. *Everything for Sale.* New York: Knopf, 1998.

Kynge, James. *China Shakes the World.* London: Weidenfeld & Nicholson, 2006.

Ladany, Laszlo. *Law and Legality in China*. Honolulu: University of Hawai'i Press, 1992.

Lardy, Nicholas. *China's Entry into the World Economy*. New York: Asia Society, 1987.

———. *Integrating China into the Global Economy*. Washington: Brookings, 2002.

Lee, Charles. *Cowboys and Dragons*. Chicago: Dearborn, 2003.

Lee, Ching Kwan. *Gender and the South China Miracle*. London: University of California Press, 1998.

Lieberthal, Kenneth. *Governing China*. New York: W. W. Norton, 1995.

Lind, Michael. *The Next American Nation*. New York: Free Press, 1995.

Lu, Xiaobo. *Cadres and Corruption*. Stanford, Calif.: Stanford University Press, 2000.

MacArthur, John R. *The Selling of "Free Trade."* New York: Hill & Wang, 2000.

Mann, James. *Beijing Jeep*. New York: Simon & Schuster, 1989.

———. *The China Fantasy*. New York: Viking, 2007.

McGregor, James. *One Billion Customers*. New York: Free Press, 2005.

Mohamad, Mahathir, and Shintaro Ishihara. *The Voice of Asia*. Tokyo: Kodansha, 1995.

Mosher, Steven. *China Misperceived*. New York: Basic Books, 1990.

———. *Hegemon: China's Plan to Dominate Asia and the World*. San Francisco: Encounter Books, 2000.

Nader, Ralph (Introduction). *The Case Against Free Trade*. San Francisco: Earth Island, 1993.

Nathan, Andrew J. *China's Transition*. New York: Columbia University Press, 1997.

Oberdorfer, Don. *The Two Koreas*. New York: Basic Books, 2001.

Overholt, Williiam. *The Rise of China*. New York: W. W. Norton, 1993.

Patrick, Hugh, and Henry Rosovsky, eds. *Asia's New Giant*. Washington: Brookings, 1976.

Pekkanen, Saadia, and Kellee Tsai, eds. *Japan and China in the World Political Economy*. Abingdon: Routledge, 2005.

Pomfret, John. *Chinese Lessons*. New York: Henry Holt, 2006.

Porter, Michael. *Can Japan Compete?* New York: Basic Books, 2000.

Prestowitz, Clyde. *Three Billion New Capitalists*. New York: Basic Books, 2005.

Rand, Peter. *China Hands*. New York: Simon & Schuster, 1995.

Reischauer, Edwin. *Wanted: An Asian Policy*. New York: Knopf, 1955.

Rohwer, Jim. *Asia Rising*. London: Brearley, 1995.

Schumpeter, E. B., ed. *The Industrialization of Japan and Manchukuo, 1930–40*. London: Routledge, 2000.

Shelp, Ronald, and Al Ehrbar. *Fallen Giant*. Hoboken, N.J.: Wiley, 2006.

Shenkar, Oded. *The Chinese Century*. Philadelphia: Wharton School, 2004.

Soros, George. *The Crisis of Global Capitalism*. New York: Public Affairs, 1998.

Spence, Jonathan. *The Search for Modern China*. New York: W. W. Norton, 1991.

Steinfeld, Edward. *Forging Reform in China*. Cambridge, U.K.: Cambridge University Press, 1998.

Stiglitz, Joseph. *Globalization and Its Discontents*. New York: W. W. Norton, 2002.

Stuttard, John. *The New Silk Road*. New York: Wiley, 2000.

Sun, Yan. *Corruption and Market in Contemporary China*. Ithaca, N.Y.: Cornell University Press, 2004.

Taylor, Robert. *The Sino-Japanese Axis*. New York: St. Martin's Press, 1985.

Terrill, Ross. *The New Chinese Empire.* New York: Basic Books, 2003.

Terry, Edith. *How Asia Got Rich.* Armonk, N.Y.: M. E. Sharpe, 2002.

Textor, Robert. *Failure in Japan.* New York: John Day, 1951.

Thurow, Lester. *The Future of Capitalism.* New York: Morrow, 1996.

Todd, Emmanuel. *After the Empire.* New York: Columbia University Press, 2003.

Tonelson, Alan. *The Race to the Bottom: Why a Worldwide Worker Surplus and Uncontrolled Free Trade Are Sinking American Living Standards.* Boulder, Colo.: Westview Press, 2002.

Vogel, Ezra. *The Four Little Dragons.* Cambridge, Mass.: Harvard University Press, 1992.

Wade, Robert. *Governing the Market.* Princeton, N.J.: Princeton University Press, 1990.

Wallach, Lori, and Michelle Sforza. *Whose Trade Organization?* Washington: Public Citizen, 1999.

Weidenbaum, Murray, and Samuel Hughes. *The Bamboo Network.* New York: Free Press, 1996.

Wolman, Bill, and Anne Colamasca. *The Judas Economy.* New York: Addison-Wesley, 1997.

Wong, Christine, Christopher Heady, and Wing T. Woo. *Fiscal Management and Economic Reform in the People's Republic of China.* Hong Kong: Asian Development Bank/Oxford University Press, 1995.

Woronoff, Jon. *Asia's Miracle Economies.* Armonk, N.Y.: M. E. Sharpe, 1987.

Wu, Harry, with George Vecsey. *Troublemaker.* New York: Times Books, 1996.

Acknowledgments

I am greatly indebted to my literary agent, Fredi Friedman of Fredrica S. Friedman & Co., for her uncommon wisdom and unstinting support. At Thomas Dunne Books, my gratitude goes to Tom Dunne for his confidence in the project, as well as to his colleagues, Rob Kirkpatrick, Lorrie McCann, John Parsley, Mark LaFlaur, and Sean Desmond, for much hard work in turning the manuscript into a book.

My understanding of key political issues has been greatly sharpened over the years in discussions with James Fallows, Pat Choate, and Robert Kuttner. In the world of practical politics, the intellectual honesty and fearlessness of Ernest F. Hollings, Byron Dorgan, and Marcy Kaptur have been a source of inspiration.

June Teufel Dreyer in Miami, Patrick Mulloy in Washington, and Robert Wade in London read parts of the manuscript and made valuable suggestions. Others who have helped in various capacities include Paul Craig Roberts, Bob Baugh, Kevin Kearns, Alan Tonelson, William Hawkins, Paul Berkowitz, and Ivan Hall. Parts of the argument were first published by David Goodhart, editor of *Prospect* magazine in London, and Michael Tomasky, editor of the *American Prospect* in Washington (an unrelated entity despite the similarity in name).

A special word of gratitude is due to my wife, Yasuko Amako. Many years ago she suggested an understanding: she would refrain from trying to influence the specifics of my writing, while in return I would make sure that nothing I wrote fostered ethnic tensions. The bargain has been an easy one for me, in that it merely obligates me to do what I intended to do anyway. I am very grateful for the fact that, at least within my own household, I have enjoyed complete intellectual freedom to tell the truth about East-West relations.

Eamonn Fingleton
Mita, Tokyo
November 8, 2007

Index

trade deficits of, 23, 26, 61, 63, 185, 272,
    327n272
trade fiasco of, 293
treasury bonds, 24
universities, U. S., Chinese students in,
    199–200

vacation time, 125
value-added tax, 151, 308
values. *See also* Confucianization, U. S.
    East-West convergence of, 3, 5–6, 28, 62,
        188
    groupist, 16–19
venereal disease, inspections for, 85
Viacom, 212

wages, 69, 175
war
    cold, 100
    on terror, 235
    total, 326n251
    WW II, 221–22, 223, 225, 251–52,
        290–91
war crimes/criminals, 218–21, 237, 246–53,
    278–79, 325n250
war on terror, 235
Washington. *See also* Sino-Japanese relations
    Chinese embassy in, 202
    Confucianization of, 263–64, 272–76
    think tanks in, 272–76
    Tokyo and, 228–30, 257
Washington view, 1–3, 6
    denial in, 34–36
    free trade in, 7–8, 290–92
    of Japan, 214–15, 254
    trade deficits in, 63
wealth. *See* economic growth
Weisman, Steven, 153
Wen Jiabao, 2
West
    China savings rate consequence to, 119
    East-Asian economic system kept from, 6–7
West Germany, 222
Western commentators. *See* commentators,
    Western

Western logic, 5, 38–39
Western truth ethic, 51, 202, 299
Westerners
    China resident, 40, 297–98, 331n298
    Confucianism values adopted by, 28–30
    in East Asia, 40, 297–98, 331In1298
    individualism of, 30, 156, 196, 307
    savings view of, blind spot in, 10
    wishful thinking of, 299–301
Westernization, 5–6, 28, 62, 111–12, 169,
    283–84. *See also* liberalization
    Japan's alleged, 80, 81, 219
What Liberal Media? (Alterman), 208–9
women's rights, 320n89
workers
    conditions, 175, 182–83
    income of, 116
    U. S. corporation exploitation of,
        182–83
World Bank, 228
world economy, 5, 64
world order, 303
World Trade Organization (WTO), 52, 103,
    135, 270–71
    breaches/violations against, 153, 290
    China v. Russia in, 177–80
    GATT v., 292
    internet censorship and, 191
    Sino-Japanese relations and, 229–30
    U. S. media on China's application to,
        207–9, 266, 274–75
    withdrawal from, 308
World War II, 221–22, 223, 225, 251–52,
    290–91
Wortzel, Larry, 196
WTO. *See* World Trade Organization

Yahoo!, 186, 188
Yasukuni shrine affair, 221, 246–53

zaibatsus, 94, 95, 109
zero sum game, with capitalism, 289–91
Zhou Enlai, 112
Zhu Rongji, 150
zoning system, housing, 121–24

Eamonn Fingleton, a prescient former editor for *Forbes* and the *Financial Times*, has been monitoring East Asian economics since he met supreme leader Deng Xiaoping in 1986 as a member of a top U.S. financial delegation. The following year he predicted the Tokyo banking crash and went on in *Blindside*, a controversial 1995 analysis that was praised by J. K. Galbraith and Bill Clinton, to show that a heedless America was fast losing its formerly vaunted dominance in advanced manufacturing to Japan. His book *In Praise of Hard Industries: Why Manufacturing, Not the Information Economy, Is the Key to Future Prosperity* brilliantly anticipated the Internet stock crash of 2000. His books have been read into the U.S. Senate record and named among the ten best business books of the year by *Business Week* and Amazon.com.